Transactions of the Royal Historical Society

SIXTH SERIES

II

LONDON 1992

British Library Cataloguing in Publication Data

Transactions of the Royal Historical Society,
   —6th Series, vol. II (1992)
   1. History—Periodicals
   I. Royal Historical Society
   905   D1
ISBN 0–86193–131–9

Made and printed in Great Britain by Butler & Tanner Ltd, Frome and London

CONTENTS

PAGE

Presidential Address: English Landed Society in the Twentieth
    Century: III, Self-help and Outdoor Relief.
    F. M. L. Thompson   I

Charles I, the Privy Council and the Parliament of 1628.
    Richard Cust   25

Improvised Genocide? The emergence of the 'Final Solution'
    in the 'Warthegau'.
    Ian Kershaw   51

Westminster and the Victorian Constitution.
    Roland Quinault   79

Catholic, Anglican or Puritan? Edward Sackville, Fourth Earl
    of Dorset and the Ambiguities of Religion in Early Stuart
    England (*The Alexander Prize Essay*).
    David L. Smith   105

The War of the Scots, 1306–1323 (*The Prothero Lecture*)
    A. A. Duncan   125

MULTIPLE KINGDOMS AND PROVINCES

The Venetian Mainland State in the Fifteenth Century.
    John D. Law   153

The Creation of Britain: Multiple Kingdoms or Core and
    Colonies?
    Jenny Wormald   175

Anglo-Portuguese Trade in the Fifteenth Century.
    Wendy R. Childs   195

Problems of Comparing Rural Societies in Early Medieval
    Western Europe.
    Chris Wickham   221

Report of Council for 1991–1992
Officers and Council 1992   247

TRANSACTIONS OF THE

ROYAL HISTORICAL SOCIETY

PRESIDENTIAL ADDRESS

By F. M. L. Thompson

ENGLISH LANDED SOCIETY IN THE TWENTIETH CENTURY III. SELF-HELP AND OUTDOOR RELIEF

READ 22 NOVEMBER 1991

AN ultra-slow motion serial whose episodes appear at intervals of twelve months needs a recapitulation of the story so far, however excellent the retentive capacity of scholars in comparison with soap opera audiences. The characters in question are the landowners, great and not so great, and the landed families who were already well-established on their estates and in their country houses in late Victorian Britain: and also the newcomers who have continued, throughout the twentieth century, to purchase landed estates and country houses. The main plot concerns the structure and distribution of landownership, and I have suggested that reports of the virtual disappearance of great estates in the last hundred years have been greatly exaggerated. There have been great changes, but while some individuals or entire families have fallen off the boat others have clambered aboard, so that in the 1990s perhaps one-third or more of the land of Britain is held in sizeable estates of 1,000 acres and upwards, compared with rather over one-half in the 1890s. The changing composition of the cast of landowners, and the wildly fluctuating fortunes of particular members of the cast, have fascinated many observers of the social and political scene, and these features provide the sub-plots. The undoubted decline of landed and aristocratic political and social predominance, leading to the virtual elimination of their influence on public life, and the equally undoubted decline, impoverishment, and extinction of some once great and famous landed families, have tended to become confused as cause and effect in some accounts. Leaving on one side the wealthy newcomers and their social significance, the colourful, bizarre, or pitiful stories of members of the old guard who have fallen on hard times have proved irresistible and have furnished apparent proof of a general decline and crisis of the aristocracy, to the neglect of the survivors of the old guard, who are numerous, many of them prosperous, and some extremely wealthy if no longer extremely powerful in a Victorian way. Indeed, given the generally inhospitable or hostile climate of the last hundred years for landed aristocrats and the way of living represented by the Victorian and Edwardian country house and the London season, it is survival which is remarkable and needs explanation, rather than decline.

Survival is, in the first place, a matter of keeping out of trouble and steering clear of danger: in this context and in this century that perhaps means, above all, being lucky enough not to have too many men in the family of fighting age at the time of the two Wars, and fortunate enough to have a bare minimum of deaths of heads of families. The majority of families have had three deaths of heads since 1890, and many, such as the dukes of Bedford, Beaufort, Marlborough, and Roxburghe, and the marquesses of Bute, have had but two deaths since death duties began to become serious after 1909, and the marquess of Bath only one; unlucky families, like the Seymour dukes of Somerset, have suffered six deaths and successions in the same period. The demographic lottery should not be given too much credit: the Grosvenors have had five new dukes of Westminster since 1890, and four since 1909, without this cascade of successions making any noticeable dent in their survival. Death is unavoidable, but it has long been possible to soften its effects on family fortunes through prudent management. Few have been as forthright as the 9th earl of Sandwich who announced publicly in 1943 that he had transferred the Hinchingbrooke estate to his eldest son.[1] Many have quietly turned the traditional family arrangement of the strict settlement on its head, and have vested the family estate in a private company or an offshore trust, or transferred the title to the eldest son or other heir during the father's lifetime. Steps to avoid, or at the least to reduce, death duties have been part of the standard practice of the financial management of estates since the 1920s. They are the basic form of self-preservation, neglected or rejected only in individual instances where the continuation of a family

---

[1] *Burke's Peerage* (1949 edn.), sub Sandwich. The move served its purpose, since the 9th earl survived until 1962, comfortably beyond the reach of the rule subjecting gifts made less than 5 (previously, 7) years before death to estate duty. In another sense the eldest son frustrated his father's intentions by renouncing the peerage in 1964, unavailingly since he, the former viscount Hinchingbrooke, failed to regain a seat in the Commons in the 1964 election. What happened to the Huntingdonshire estate is not clear: *Debrett's Distinguished People of Today* (1990 edn.), sub Montagu, Victor Edward Paulet.

estate was subordinated to higher considerations, such as a total breakdown in relations between owner and heir, or a complete refusal by an owner to contemplate his own mortality. Avoidance of death duties, however, is fundamentally a negative form of self-help, an exercise in damage limitation which may prevent or contain the erosion of capital; in itself it does nothing to increase income, clear off accumulated debts, or add to capital assets, important elements in twentieth-century survival.

More positive, constructive, and creative forms of self-help had always been part of the survival kit of individuals who were down on their luck, harried by their creditors, or simply squeezed by inescapable expenditures that continually exceeded income. Making a good marriage was always a favourite ploy, if not with an heiress then with a wealthy bride, and if not often on the grandiose scale of the Grenvilles who picked off four landed heiresses in less than a hundred years on their way to becoming dukes of Buckingham in 1822, then on the more modest level of the earl of Burford, later 9th duke of St Albans, who sedulously sought an heiress in Regency England, and having failed in his pursuit of the Gascoyne heiress who took her £12,000 a year of Liverpool money to Lord Cranborne, 2nd marquess of Salisbury, contented himself with marrying the fifty-year old widow and heir of the banker, Thomas Coutts, he being aged twenty-four at the time.[2] Marriage is not only a lottery, but it is also a rare event, a once in a lifetime chance, at least until late in the nineteenth century. A more readily and continuously available expedient for financial troubles was to close down the family house, perhaps let it and the shooting to some businessman, and withdraw to live inexpensively abroad in a pleasant Italian villa for a period of financial recuperation. This offered comparatively small, but steady, annual savings rather than the possibly spectacular rewards of a successful marriage: it was still a well-tried device which frequently produced good results, as it did for the 12th earl of Pembroke in the 1820s.[3] A rather more obvious way of helping oneself out of difficulties was to find a job—'get on your horse', as it were—found a business, seek a fortune from work and enterprise. There are few, if any, examples of this before the late nineteenth century, except at the level of landowner acting as capitalist in the development of the resources of his own estate, although a trickle of younger sons did venture forth to make fortunes in East Indian trade or West Indian sugar islands. It excited sympathy as well as comment when the marquess of Chandos had to make a genuine effort to earn

[2] Carola Oman, *The Gascoyne Heiress* (1968), 50–1.
[3] F. M. L. Thompson, 'English Landownership: the Ailesbury Trust, 1832–56,' *Economic History Review*, 2nd ser. XI (1958), 123.

his living, as chairman of the LNWR in the 1850s, while waiting for the 2nd duke of Buckingham, his spendthrift father, to die.[4] Jobs, for eldest sons or for the holders of hereditary titles, traditionally meant sinecures rather than serious work. For impoverished nobles, and indeed for not so impoverished nobles who found it a struggle to make ends meet, relief in aid of inadequate incomes from personal possessions customarily came from their links with the patronage system. Once the days of Old Corruption were over, which had been able to produce more than £23,000 a year for earl Bathurst in the 1820s as a teller of the Exchequer or £14,000 a year for viscount Cathcart as lord vice-admiral of Scotland, the possibility of 'going out to govern New South Wales' still had a long run ahead of it.[5] Power or powerful connections were the levers which procured outdoor relief for the upper classes, without the inconvenience or disgrace of a workhouse test or labour test.[6] The question to face is whether, and to what extent, these well-tried devices of self-help and outdoor relief, which had long proved their worth for needy individuals, have been harnessed to group survival in the twentieth century.

Marriage has continued to prove popular among the landed class. That is not quite so banal a statement as it may appear at first sight; one way for members of a group, which felt itself to be doomed, to respond to their predicament would have been to decline to perpetuate themselves, while in a different mood one way of expressing a possible disappearance of social differences might have been to adopt the habits of the 1980s and cohabit and procreate without paying much attention to marriage. In real life, for what it is worth, the proportion of the old nobility (those holding hereditary titles created before 1885) who never married seems to have increased somewhat in the interwar period, to around 15 per cent of the group born between 1885 and 1914, and then to have declined to about 10 per cent of the group still living in 1990, a percentage destined to decline further as some of the younger ones now alive decide to get married.[7] This is no more than negative

---

[4] F. M. L. Thompson, 'The End of a Great Estate,' *Econ. Hist. Rev.* 2nd ser. VIII (1955), 50.

[5] F. M. L. Thompson, *English Landed Society in the Nineteenth Century* (1963), 72–3. H. Belloc, *Complete Verses* (1970), 207, poem on Lord Lundy written in 1907.

[6] John Bright's original phrase, in a speech at Birmingham in 1858, was: 'This excessive love for the balance of power is neither more nor less than a gigantic system of outdoor relief for the aristocracy of Great Britain': J. Morley, *The Life of John Bright* (1913), 274.

[7] The figures are derived from a sample, amounting to approximately 10 per cent of the 'population', of holders of 'old' hereditary titles (those created before 1885) who died between 1951 and 1960: *Who was Who, 1951–60*, all names under the letters B, D, R, and T; and from a second sample, amounting to approximately 15 per cent of the 'population' of holders of similarly 'old' titles who were living in 1990: *Debrett's Distinguished People of Today* (1990 end.), all names under the letters A, B, and C. These two samples are used

evidence, that the group has not felt threatened by material crisis or insecurity to the point of indefinitely postponing marriage in pursuit of retrenchment, and has not abandoned hope in its future – although the decline in family size, which has been continuous since the early nineteenth century and is currently well below two children per completed family, suggests that faith in the future has tight limits. This global view of aristocratic nuptiality is also consistent with a hypothesis that the confidence of the group in its own survival faltered in the interwar years and then recovered after 1945: but it does not prove it.

For marriage to have the effect of being a means of survival or advancement it is necessary not merely for there to be a union of new blood with old stock, but also for the new blood to have a high money count. Here the evidence of marriage patterns over the last hundred years seems to be inconclusive, ambivalent, and even perverse. On the one hand, the marriages of the holders of old hereditary titles, or their heirs, have become steadily less and less exclusive, so that in 1990 barely 11 per cent of their first marriages were to wives from similarly aristocratic families, and virtually none of their second or third wives, indicating their readiness to embrace non-aristocratic and non-landed women on a large scale.[8] On the other hand, marriages to heiresses or very rich brides seem to have peaked in the 1890s and early 1900s, and to have declined markedly since the First World War. A really good heiress could, indeed, still provide long-lasting sustenance for an ailing family. The Cholmondeleys appear to have been in serious financial difficulties in the 1880s and the 4th marquess, soon after he succeeded to the title and estates in 1884, put Houghton Hall (Sir Robert Walpole's house) and its 17,000 acre Norfolk estate on the market. It failed to find a purchaser, because of the depressed state of the land market, and somehow he managed to hang on to Houghton, until in 1913 his son and heir brought salvation by marrying the only daughter of Sir Albert Edward Sassoon, the millionaire Bombay merchant, banker, and millowner, and Aline Rothschild, daughter of Baron Gustave. Sassoon did also have an only son, so that Sybil was not the sole heiress to the Sassoon fortune at the time of her marriage; but when her brother, the third Sassoon baronet, died unmarried in 1939 one can assume that much of his £2 million estate also came her

---

extensively in this paper and are not subsequently referenced in detail. T. H. Hollingsworth, *The Demography of the British Peerage*, Supplement to *Population Studies*, XVIII (1964), Table 11, 20, found high rates of 'never married' for all cohorts born between 1700 and 1874 (a range of 13% to 21%), a drop to 10% for the 1875-99 cohort and a rise to 13% for the 1900-24 cohort; his figures relate to a much larger universe which includes the younger sons and grandsons of title-holders.

[8] 144 first marriages have been contracted by holders of 'old' titles living in 1990, of which 16 were to wives belonging to equally 'old' landed and titled families.

way. At any rate no other explanation, apart from the Sassoon marriage, has been offered for the dramatic turnround in the Cholmondeley fortunes in this century. Not only does the present marquess, the 7th, still own Houghton Hall, with most of its original estate, and the second large family seat of Malpas with 10,000 acres in Cheshire, but also when he inherited in 1990 his father left the largest will ever proved in Britain, an estate of £118 million. This surpassed the previous record of £92 million, held by Dorothy de Rothschild, and easily exceeded in nominal, although not in real, terms the pre-1950 probated record £36 million left by Sir John Ellerman in 1933, or the £52 million left by Ellerman's son in 1973.[9] The £118 million estate, perhaps 40 per cent of it in land, might be considered a sign of negligent financial management by the 6th marquess for omitting to transfer enough to his eldest son during his lifetime, a particularly puzzling omission since on the 6th marquess's own succession in 1968 most of the death duties had been avoided by putting much of the estate into the Rocksavage Estate Company.[10] If that is the reward of negligence, then many would happily settle for a life of carelessness.

The young lord Rocksavage, transformed into the marquess of Cholmondeley, has become the most eligible bachelor in the upper class, though his tastes for making TV documentaries and secretiveness may not make him into a typical member of the Ascot and Newmarket set. In 1977 the young duke of Roxburghe married Lady Jane Grosvenor, described as 'possibly the most eligible—and certainly the prettiest—heiress in the land.'[11] Lady Jane, however, was an heiress only in the sense of being a very rich girl, as she has a brother, who became 6th duke of Westminster in 1979, and an elder sister, who married the 5th earl of Lichfield in 1975. The heiress who is credited with underpinning the Roxburghe fortunes and enabling the present duke to retain undiminished the 60,000 acre family estate and its lucrative salmon fishing on the Tweed (the charge for a rod for a week is of the order of £4,000), is Mary Goelet who married the 8th duke in 1903 and brought with her the fortune of $50 million that she inherited from her American industrialist father.[12] The Spencer-Churchills are another

[9] Thompson, *Landed Society*, 320. *Burke's Peerage* (1949 edn.), sub Sassoon. *The Sunday Times*, 'Private peer who inherited £118 million and a distaste for public prying,' 16 Dec. 1990, 10. W. D. Rubinstein, 'British Millionaires, 1809–1949,' *Bulletin Institute of Historical Research*, XLVIII (1974), 219. *Dictionary of Business Biography*, II, 255, 264 (Ellerman).

[10] *The Sunday Times Supplement: Britain's Rich, the Top 200*, 2 April 1989, 57, valued the 6th marquess of Cholmondeley at no more than £45 million, and dropped him altogether from the 1990 list.

[11] *The Times, Saturday Review*, 9 Nov. 1991, 16.

[12] *The Times*, 9 Nov. 1991, 18. May Goelet was known as 'America's richest heiress' in 1903: Maureen E. Montgomery, *Gilded Prostitution: Status, money and transatlantic marriages, 1870–1914* (1989), 162.

family in which one marriage to a very wealthy American heiress, that of the 9th duke of Marlborough to Consuelo Vanderbilt in 1895, may have had a long-lasting effect, in the sense that the 11th duke still has Blenheim and an 11,500 acre estate and there have been no more heiress marriages in the interval – unless, that is, some of Aristotle Onassis's money came the duke's way when one of Aristotle's former wives put in a short spell as the duke's second wife.[13]

A tally of three heiress-marriages that were successful in apparently making an important contribution to the preservation of large landed estates over the following hundred years or so is interesting, but little more than that. Many other examples of marriages to heiresses or very wealthy brides can be cited, pointing in different directions as to their efficacy in prolonging the life of landed families. The 5th marquess of Northampton no doubt received a handsome fortune from his marriage in 1884 to Mary Baring, only daughter and sole heiress of the 2nd lord Ashburton; but with Castle Ashby, Compton Wynyates, and a large slice of Islington, the Northamptons have never been in pressing need of outside assistance. When another Baring girl, daughter of the 1st lord Revelstoke, married the 6th earl Spencer in 1887 she may, on the other hand, have brought valuable reinforcement to Althorp, where money had not been plentiful. The 18th viscount Dillon's marriage in 1907 to one of the daughters of Sir John Tomlinson Brunner, one of the founders of the Brunner Mond chemical company, would seem, however, to have been abortive: she had no children, and although the Dillon title survives the former estates in Oxfordshire and Ireland do not. The only daughter of the 6th marquess of Londonderry brought £200,000 to her marriage with the 6th earl of Ilchester in 1902, but this good fortune has not brought lasting benefits to the Fox-Strangways, the present earl being a chartered engineer, managing director of a provincial newspaper company, and retired RAF group captain, living unobtrusively in Westerham far from the west country and the family's vanished 32,000 acres. With contradictory indications such as these of the effects of heiress-marriages a general review and analysis of the marriage market would put the matter into perspective: I am not going to attempt an exhaustive count, and indeed am not capable of conducting one, but some observations with some quantifiable basis can be attempted.[14]

[13] Consuelo was thought to have brought a fortune of $10 million with her in 1895: Montgomery, *Gilded Prostitution*, 167. The 11th duke of Marlborough m(1) 1951 Susan Hornby, divorced 1960, m(2) 1961 Mrs Tina Livanos, former wife of Aristotle Onassis, divorced 1971, and m(3) 1972 Rosita Douglas: *Debrett's Distinguished People*.

[14] I owe information on the £200,000 portion of Lady Helen Vane-Tempest-Stewart (which comes from her father's will, 6th marquess of Londonderry, d. 1915) to Dr Didier Lancien, University of Toulouse.

All the marriages of American women to the holders of peerages, or heirs to the titles, which took place between 1870 and 1914, and between 1915 and 1939, have been studied by Dr Maureen Montgomery.[15] There were sixty in the first group, forty-four in the second: in addition she studied two control groups of peers who did not marry Americans, composed of 147 such marriages made between 1880 and 1889, and 186 marriages from 1900–09. This convenient collection of data on a total of 437 marriages is large enough to inspire some confidence in a broad social and economic analysis of the marriage partners. As a start, it should be recognised that the American brides, by definition, did not come from families of hereditary landowners. Subject to that qualification, the American brides were not outstandingly different in social background to the domestic brides who did not come from landed or titled families, who were around 40 per cent of non-American partners. That is to say, the Americans came as much from the same backgrounds of successful professional, diplomatic, and military families as their British counterparts, and no more than those were they exclusively or predominantly the daughters of super-wealthy industrialists or bankers. The Americans, or at any rate their parents, may well have been rather more wealthy on average than the competition, for they had first to cross the Atlantic and set up an appropriate menage in a strange country before they could integrate into the same marriage market of the London season and the country-house circuit: only a few American women were wooed on home ground by the reverse flow of peers landing in New York in search of an heiress. The notion that all American brides were very rich derived from a couple of marriages at the top of society when Consuelo Yznaga married the 8th duke of Manchester in 1876 and Consuelo Vanderbilt the 9th duke of Marlborough in 1895. The cry was taken up by the sensationalist press on both sides of the Atlantic, which proclaimed that titled bachelors en masse were hunting for American heiresses, and painted a picture of a brisk trade in titles for dollars to prop up a degenerate aristocracy that amounted to 'gilded prostitution'. The truth was more prosaic. Perhaps as much as one-third of the sixty pre-1914 American brides were very rich, a few of them being heiresses or co-heiresses in the strict sense; the proportion among the forty-four interwar marriages may have fallen to as little as one-seventh.[16]

All the same, it is a much higher proportion than among the pre-

[15] Montgomery, *Gilded Prostitution*, on which the following para. rests.

[16] Montgomery, *Gilded Prostitution*, supplies data for 'seriously rich' American brides on 42–3 for 18 who were in the list of New York's 400, and on 123–38 for wealthy individuals from outside New York. It is difficult to pinpoint the very wealthy among interwar marriages: the families of Chase, Guggenheim, Post, Sears, Wendell, and Whitney have been counted.

1914 non-American marriages, in which no more than four or five per cent seem to have brought in any serious money from outside landed circles, from banking, brewing, chemical, and glass families. It can be confirmed that middle-class American women, especially those from the commercial, non-professional, middle class, marrying into the British landed elite were likely to have been significantly more wealthy than middle-class British women marrying into the same elite. The significance of this finding, however, requires elucidation. There is some relationship between marrying serious American money before 1914 and the long-term survival of a landed family into the 1990s, but it is rather weak. The descendants of four of these marriages are currently on the list of substantial landowners who own estates of 10,000 acres or more, and a further eight have descendants who still own some land though on a more modest, often single-farm, scale. That, however, leaves one half of the ultra-rich marriages which have failed to produce any landed successors in the 1990s, although in most cases the hereditary titles are still alive, shorn of land: this is no better than the general survival rate for the landed elite as a whole, where it is reckoned that fifty-two per cent of the landed families who held estates in 1880 of over 3,000 acres still own estates of at least 1,000 acres today.[17] Looking through the other end of the telescope, there are currently some 110 families of old-established landowners who owned large estates in the 1880s and still own large estates of the 10,000 acre variety. Only ten per cent of these families have made a marriage with an heiress or very wealthy bride in the last hundred years, and that includes no more than five of the Americans—Anne Wendell who married the 6th earl of Carnarvon in 1922; Alice Thaw to the 7th marquess of Hertford in 1903; Barbara Chase to the 8th marquess of Lansdowne in 1938; Consuelo Vanderbilt to the 9th duke of Marlborough in 1895; and May Goelet to the 8th duke of Roxburghe in 1903. All the rest of the American bride-prices would seem to have run into the sand, or into the Inland Revenue.[18]

The comparative unimportance of marrying money in securing the long-term survival of the landed elite is confirmed by the indifference shown by the sons of that elite to the daughters of home-grown

[17] F. M. L. Thompson, 'English Landed Society in the Twentieth Century: I,' *ante*, 40 (1990), 14.
[18] The list of 110 surviving large landowners in Britain in 1990 has been compiled from entries in the current *Who's Who* and *Debrett's Distinguished People*, which still in many cases specify an acreage owned; and from R. Perrott, *The Aristocrats* (1968), amended and updated in the light of specific references in *The Sunday Times: Britain's Rich, the Top 200* (1989 and 1990), and J. Paxman, *Friends in High Places* (1990). The Carnarvon fortunes may have been in need of refreshment in 1922 after the 5th earl's Tutankhamen excavations.

millionaires. The families of eighty-six British millionaires who died between 1900 and 1950 leaving probated estates of £1 million or more can be traced through the standard reference works.[19] Between them they produced 176 daughters, most of whom got married. Five of them were only children, heiresses in the full sense. Their marriages were not particularly exciting or significant in landownership terms, except possibly in one case. When the brewer Michael Bass was given a peerage he managed, at the second attempt (first creation 1886, second creation 1897) to obtain a special remainder in default of male heirs to his daughter Nellie and her heirs male. This was shortly after Nellie Bass had married Colonel Bruce Baillie, MP, head of an old Scottish family, laird of Dochfour and 165,000 not very valuable acres around it in Inverness. Lord Burton, who had previously been tenant of some of Baillie's deer forests, thus became his father-in-law; and in course of time the 3rd lord Burton, when he inherited from his grandmother in 1962, figured as one of Scotland's larger landowners. Whether one considers that the beer money bought a large sporting estate, or contributed to preserving an old Scottish family estate, is largely a matter of taste.[20]

The other millionaire heiresses made more of a social than a landed impression. Eleanor Williamson, only child of the 1st and last lord Ashton, the linoleum manufacturer whose giant mausoleum dominates the town of Lancaster, made an elevated rather than landed match in 1899, when she married the eldest son of Arthur Wellesley Peel, 5th son of the Prime Minister, Speaker of the House of Commons, and 1st viscount Peel. Her husband was in his turn a politician and a cabinet minister in the 1920s, and was raised to an earldom in 1929; their eldest son became in due course chairman and managing director of the Williamson firm, and was involved in other Lancashire industries, but neither he nor this branch of the Peel family were ever landowners on any scale. The coal owner, viscount Rhondda, also had an only child: she married one of the local South Wales gentry in 1908, Sir Humphrey Mackworth, who was a 7th baronet and a 3,000 acre man, but she divorced him in 1923 and devoted the rest of her life to editing *Time and Tide* and being a governor of LSE. Grace, only child of Sir John

[19] There are 374 millionaires who died 1900–49 listed in Rubinstein, 'British millionaires', of whom 66 held inherited titles and were established landowners. Of the remaining 208, 110 received hereditary titles, and of those 86 have been traced in *Burke's Peerage*, *Who was Who*, and *Debrett's Distinguished People*. Those who remained commoners probably had a different marital experience, and it is likely to have been one with fewer contacts with high society.

[20] *Burke's Peerage* (1949 edn.), *Debrett's Distinguished People*. W. Orr, *Deer Forests, Landlords, and Crofters* (1982), 193. Bass already had an estate near Burton in 1873. The 1st lord Burton left £1 million in 1908.

Maple the furniture dealer, first tried marriage to the German diplomat baron von Eckhardstein, but then in 1910 took as her second husband a Colonel Weigell, an MP and for a short time in the 1920s a Governor of South Australia, who duly received a baronetcy and did some agricultural things like presiding over the Land Agents Society and the Royal Agricultural Society: he was a member of the lesser gentry and the professional and administrative class, not of the elite. Lastly in this little set, Catherine Buchanan was the only daughter and heiress of the Glasgow distiller James Buchanan, who was created lord Woolavington but failed to secure a remainder to his female heirs. In 1922 she married Captain Narcissus Macdonald of the Scots Guards, whose father had settled in Buenos Aires. The whisky money induced this family to change its name to Macdonald-Buchanan, to set up in a manor house in Northamptonshire, and to take a keen interest in racing. The two sons of this marriage are reasonably gentrified. In 1950 the elder son married a daughter of the 14th earl of Westmorland (though they were divorced in 1969), and in 1960 the younger married a granddaughter of lord Bicester. Both have served as Sheriff of Northamptonshire; the elder has been senior steward of the Jockey Club, the highest, though unpaid, position in the racing hierarchy, and the younger serves family interests as a director of James Buchanan & Co. Both sons live in the country, one near Stow-on-the-Wold and the other at Muir of Ord, as well as having fashionable addresses in Cadogan Place and Cadogan Lane, but there is no evidence that the family has become landed in a serious way.[21]

The remaining 171 daughters of twentieth-century millionaires all had siblings, and all except two had brothers, but many of them would nonetheless have been heiresses in the loose sense of being very wealthy young women. A mere handful of them, barely a dozen, married into old-established landed families from the titled aristocracy or the landed gentry, and even fewer of these matches were of significance to the survival of great landowners. All four of W. H. Smith's daughters married well, as they might have expected when they had a leading politician as well as newsagent for their father. Two married Dyke Acland brothers, from the prominent west country family, one married into a cadet branch of the Seymour dukes of Somerset, and the youngest married the 5th earl of Harrowby: conceivably this last had

[21] Lt-Col. W. E. G. A. Weigell has an entry in *Burke's Landed Gentry* (1937 edn.), of no ancestry, but his father had returned from Australia, where he was born, and in 1866 married Lady Rose, 2nd dau. of the 11th earl of Westmorland, and can be assumed to have had an entrée into society and to have been wealthy. Lord Ashton left £10.5 million in 1930; Lord Rhondda £1.1 million in 1918; Lord Woolavington £7.1 million in 1935; and Sir John Maple, 1st and only bt., £2.1 million in 1903. Earl Peel later succumbed to the temptation of owning a large sporting estate in Wensleydale.

some effect, as her grandson the 7th earl still owns the family seat of Sandon Hall in Staffordshire, although he is substantially a banker, with Coutts and National Westminster, and not one of the surviving large landowners. By the same reasoning Lilian Coats, younger daughter of the 1st lord Glentanar of the sewing thread firm, may have been of assistance in the survival of the Wellesleys through her marriage, in 1909, to the 5th duke of Wellington. There was precious little landed element in the marriage of the eldest daughter of Weetman Pearson, 1st viscount Cowdray, to the 3rd lord Denman in 1903; perhaps a shade more in the marriage of the brewer's daughter Fanny Gretton to Brigadier Sir Henry Robert Kincaird Floyd, 5th baronet, in 1929, as their grandson is a Lincolnshire farmer, former Sheriff of Rutland, and director of the Burghley Estate Farms; and about the same in Phoebe Phillimore's marriage to Sir Charles Rose, 3rd baronet, whose son continues to own and farm the Hardwick estate at Whitchurch, Oxfordshire, the fourth generation in possession. When Sir Charles Cayzer's daughters Gwendoline and Winifred married, respectively, Admiral Jellicoe, 1st earl, and Admiral Charles Madden, 1st baronet, however, it was a symbolic recognition of the source of their father's millions in shipbuilding; while Eva Mond's wedding to the future 2nd marquess of Reading in 1914 signified the role of her father, Lord Melchett the founder of ICI, in public life, since Rufus Isaacs, 1st marquess of Reading, was a successful lawyer, Attorney-General, and later Viceroy of India, not a member of the landed elite. Finally, it is not without interest that Beatrice, third daughter of the millionaire banker Gervase Beckett, in 1923 married the third son of Sir William Eden of Windlestone Hall, Bishops Auckland, 7th baronet. The interest is biographical and political: this was Anthony Eden.[22]

What explanations can be suggested for these patterns of aristocratic and millionaire marriages? It is clear from the figures that marrying into money has played very little part in the recent family histories of those old-established landed dynasties that still have great landowners at their heads in the 1990s. In a few instances such marriages probably have played an important part, but in general they have not been a necessary condition of survival. It could be argued with equal plausibility either that the order of the landed aristocracy in general has not been aware of any crisis in their affairs that required such extreme measures, or that heiresses, monied daughters, or their parents have been only

---

[22] Anthony Eden m(1) 1923 Beatrice Beckett, divorced 1950, and m(2) 1952 Clarissa Spencer Churchill. W. H. Smith left £1.7 million in 1891, and his son, 2nd viscount Hambleden, left £3.5 million in 1928; lord Glentanar £4.3 million in 1918; viscount Cowdray £4 million in 1927; lord Gretton £2.3 million in 1947; the 2nd lord Phillimore, with a legal fortune, £2 million in 1947; Sir Charles Cayzer £2.2 million in 1916; lord Melchett £1 million in 1930; and Sir William Gervase Beckett £1 million in 1937.

too acutely aware of the declining attractions of aristocratic partners. In the absence of direct evidence on the point one may speculate that the second possibility scarcely affected pre-1914 marriages, and many of those continued to have financial as well as matrimonial effects over the next fifty years. In support of the first possibility it may be significant that the landed elite even neglected their traditional activity of taking in each other's washing and building on the misfortunes of other aristocratic families by marrying landed heiresses. Landed heiresses have been few and far between in this century, perhaps oddly in view of widespread family limitation and the prevalence of one- and two-child families, but there have been some. Perhaps the greatest was, and is, Elizabeth Millicent Sutherland-Leveson-Gower, long known to be heir to the earldom of Sutherland and to Dunrobin Castle with much of the, admittedly depleted, Sutherland estates: in 1946 she married a Guards captain called Janson, not the kind of match for a great heiress which an eighteenth- or nineteenth-century family would have expected. Lesser landed heiresses such as the only child of the 10th earl of Scarborough and the only child of the 6th lord Somers, married respectively the third son of the 2nd lord Northbourne and the third son of Sir Frederick Hervey-Bathurst (in 1923, and 1947) although the old Northumbrian family of the Swinburnes of Capheaton did not entirely disappear when the only child of the 8th baronet married Granville Browne, a younger son from nearby Alnmouth, for he became Browne-Swinburne of Capheaton while vanishing from the stud books.[23]

Victorian drawing rooms would have buzzed with gossip and intrigue at the thought of such heiresses throwing themselves away on younger sons of obscure families. That may, indeed, point to the most likely hypothesis: that Victorian drawing rooms had lost their social power, and the Victorian matriarchy had lost its influence. Changing marriage patterns may simply have been the result of changes in the style and ambience of the London season and marriage market, and of virtual devolution of control over the choice of marriage partners to the younger generation itself. This is not the occasion on which to develop this thought, which requires a sequel to Leonore Davidoff's study of the Victorian social scene, *The Best Circles: Society, Etiquette, and the Season* (1973). The suggestion is that the relaxation of the formality and centralised cohesion of the Season meant on the one hand that the sons and daughters of established aristocratic and landed families no longer automatically passed through the mills of a single marriage

[23] Elizabeth Sutherland-Leveson Gower is countess of Sutherland in her own right by the terms of the Scottish earldom of c. 1235, while the dukedom passed to a kinsman on the death of her uncle, the 5th duke, in 1963. She, and Joan Swinburne, inherited estates; in the case of Scarborough and Somers the family seats (the disposition of the land is not known) passed to the kinsmen who inherited the titles.

market, and on the other hand that fewer millionaire businessmen found it necessary, even when aspiring to join the establishment or to obtain titles, to gain entry into high society. The result of declining opportunities for the young of old families and the young of the very rich to meet socially was that most millionaires' daughters, something like two-thirds of them, found marriage partners from within their parents' circle of middle-class businessmen, while the remaining one-third was largely professional and service middle-class with only a gentle squeeze of the aristocratic embrace. The result for the sons of the old families was, indeed, a lowering of the exclusive fences which had formerly restricted the field of choice of partners largely to the landed aristocracy and gentry and their cadet branches (plus a small, but fairly continuous, amount of new blood from the new rich). This lowering meant that perhaps sixty per cent of interwar marriages of eldest sons were outside the old aristocratic-gentry network, and over eighty per cent of such marriages since 1945. In some very broad sense this great and increasing majority of marriage partners came from middle-class families: the middle class in question, however, appears to have been largely professional, military, and agricultural, and insofar as it was also a financial and business middle class it did not include many daughters of exceptionally rich businessmen.[24]

Marriage, it may be concluded, has not been used to any great extent as a means of self-help by a declining aristocracy. Indeed, as hinted earlier, marriage may well have had more impact as a weapon of self-destruction.[25] One in four of the interwar marriages ended in divorce, and one in three of the marriages of those still living in 1990 have already done so; multiple divorces have become not uncommon, for example Sir Simon Codrington, 3rd baronet, is on his fourth wife after three divorces between 1959 and 1988. Unfortunately there are no obvious or accessible sources for studying the economics of divorce, either of the costs of the proceedings themselves, or probably of greater importance, the effects on estates of supporting ex-wives or dividing assets. Codrington, however, still retains the family seat of Dodington, near Chipping Sodbury, and some at least of the 5,000 acres which the family owned in the 1880s; while at the other extreme of wealth, in an earlier generation the 2nd duke of Westminster had four wives and three divorces between 1901 and 1947 without noticeably impairing

[24] Based on analysis of the marriage partners of all daughters of the 86 millionaires, deceased 1900–49, who have been traced; the marriage partners of all holders of hereditary titles in the 1951–60 sample (56 first marriages, 10 in group never married); and the marriage partners of all holders of hereditary titles in the 1990 sample (171 first marriages, 17 in group unmarried).

[25] Thompson, 'English Landed Society in the Twentieth Century: I,' *supra*, 5th ser., XL (1990), 23–4.

the Grosvenor millions. It must be left an open question whether, on balance, the break-up of marriages has made a significant contribution to the break-up of estates.[26]

Perhaps surprisingly, the harder grind of earning a living has not been used by a declining aristocracy to the extent that might have been anticipated if the whole order had been in grave economic decline and financial difficulties. It is certainly true that members of landed families began to find income-yielding occupations during the interwar period on a scale unheard of in the nineteenth century, and that this trend has become more pronounced since 1945. The distribution of these jobs between those who still retain landed estates and those who have become unlanded is, however, somewhat curious. The test cases here are the careers of eldest sons, for traditionally younger sons frequently had to make shift to support themselves while eldest sons largely had ornamental or honorific occupations (for example, in fashionable and expensive regiments) to give themselves something to do while waiting to inherit. By the 1920s the conventional wisdom of masters at Eton was that three careers were possible for 'really stupid boys' with good connections: farming, soldiering, or stockbroking.[27] The respectability of stockbroking had been pioneered by the likes of the third son of the 8th duke of Argyll, in the 1870s and 1880s; soldiering is discounted as a profitable occupation in the following analysis, since although it may just about have paid its way as a career by the interwar years it could hardly be relied on to produce a positive net income much before the 1970s; farming is discussed separately.[28]

Setting aside careers in farming or the army, about half the group of title-holders who died between 1951 and 1960—and who thus were in the prime of their active lives in the 1920s and 1930s—had been in gainful employment for some considerable period of their lives; that proportion has risen to more than two-thirds for the 1990 group. The growth of an industrious, or working, peerage and baronetage is even more striking if a distinction is drawn between 'traditional' aristocratic occupations on the one hand—the church, politics, the law, the diplomatic service, and the colonial service—and 'new' occupations in banking, finance, stockbroking, accountancy, engineering, insurance, art dealing, journalism, publishing, film-making, television, and even shopkeeping or teaching. In the first group, the interwar cohort, only

---

[26] Codrington, *Debrett's Distinguished People*; 2nd duke of Westminster, *Burke's Peerage* (1949 edn.).

[27] Quoted in a profile of Lord Carrington, *The Independent*, 16 Nov. 1991, 16.

[28] Lord Walter Campbell, 1848–89, 3rd son of 8th duke of Argyll, was a stockbroker: G. H. Fleming, *Victorian 'Sex Goddess': Lady Colin Campbell* (Oxford, 1989), 101. For farming, see below, 23, and Thompson, 'English Landed Society in the Twentieth Century, IV,' *infra*. III (1992).

twelve per cent had careers in the 'new' category, so that the great majority of those who did anything at all did it in occupations which had long been accepted as entirely suitable for landed gentlemen. In the second group, those living in 1990, fifty-four per cent have occupations of the 'new' variety, so that careers of the traditional kind have become almost insignificant. This is not quite so impressive and conclusive as it may seem. True, a sprinkling of unconventional, even commercially adventurous, jobs are held by those who also still own large estates: the 11th duke of Marlborough may not have moved far from tradition in being chairman of Martini & Rossi, nor the 15th duke of Hamilton in spending some years as a commercial airline pilot, but it is more curious that the 7th earl of Bradford, with a 13,000 acre estate in Shropshire, is running Porters Restaurant in Covent Garden and the Expedier Leisure company. Most of the exotic jobs, however, and of the pin-stripe City jobs, are held by peers and baronets who have been parted from their landed estates, either totally or in substantial part. The figures are striking. Among the group of 110 large landowners who survive in the 1990s less than forty per cent have any occupations of the remunerative kind; and only slightly more than one quarter have had any contact with the 'new' trades and professions, and those are chiefly in the City.[29]

The conclusion to be drawn from this seems to be that the landless and nearly landless hereditary title-holders have managed to save themselves by going out to work, and have thereby in some instances managed to save some part of the old family estate as well.[30] The surviving large landowners, in contrast, do not appear to rely to any great extent on making money by their own exertions in fields not directly connected with their landed possessions. Even company directorships, which at least since the 1880s have been accepted as suitable and convenient sources of outside incomes for lords, are of no great importance to them. No more than ten per cent of the group hold serious collections of directorships, in four or more quoted companies, and most of these are ex-politicians who may have picked up directorships because they have had political careers rather than because

[29] Data on occupations and careers have been drawn from the self-descriptions which constitute entries in *Who's Who* and *Debrett's Distinguished People*, and it is possible that some individuals suppress some information, or consider some periods in their lives not worth mentioning. On the other hand, some, e.g. 11th duke of Marlborough, find it interesting to record details like membership of the 1982 House of Lords bridge team vs. the Commons, suggesting that the self-recording impulse is strong.

[30] There are no reliable sources of information on the current landholdings of former landed families which have sold or parted with much, but not all, of the former estates. Where the present title-holder retains the traditional family seat, or has a house in the same parish, it is reasonable to infer that some of the nineteenth-century estate has survived.

they are landowners.[31] The majority of the landowners, however, have no occupations and no visible means of support outside their estates. That is not intended to suggest that they are an idle lot. The economic, fiscal, and social pressures of the last hundred years have been real enough to have wiped any frivolous leisured class off the land, and these modern landowners are certainly busy people. They are busy with the same kind of unpaid work which occupied the more conscientious and public-spirited of their Victorian forebears, in local affairs, charitable activities, and voluntary associations of many kinds. The main differences are that their official role in local government has declined, while demand for their services on charitable trusts, quangos, and leading local sports clubs has increased. Moreover, participation as trustees, chairmen, and governors of this collection of charities, funds, societies, associations, institutions, museums, galleries, and clubs has become almost universal and is no longer regarded as optional. Some of the voluntary activities, although traditional, have become much more time-consuming: senior stewards and stewards of the Jockey Club, for example, recruited as ever from the ranks of aristocratic racing landowners, have greatly increased responsibilities as the regulating authority for what has become a billion pound industry. On the other hand, some of the new avenues of public service which have opened up for sporting patrons, such as membership of the Horserace Betting Levy Board, do carry with them some remuneration.[32]

They are also busy with their estates. The considerable numbers who deliberately describe themselves as 'landowners', and the number whose education and training have included the Royal Agricultural College, Cirencester, or formal qualification as a land agent or chartered surveyor, or (more rarely) as a chartered accountant, suggest the extent to which owning an estate is taken seriously as a business.[33] It would be extremely interesting to know how far the management of estates includes the management of investment portfolios, for evaluation of

---

[31] There are some cases in which company directorships, and full-blown business careers, have been vital to survival: the 7th lord Camoys has been able to re-purchase the family seat, Stonor Park, and estate because he worked for Rothschilds and has been chief executive of Barclays de Zoete Weld and managing director of Barclays Merchant Bank. More normal are the directorships (G.E.C., and Christie's) acquired by 6th lord Carrington (Buckinghamshire landowner) after his resignation as Foreign Secretary. One of the longest list of directorships belongs not to a landowner, but to Lord (Spycatcher) Armstrong, who holds 14.

[32] Another major difference is that these functions are not monopolised by the 'old' landowners, but are shared with the 'great and the good' in general, who include many large landowners of more recent (post-1885) origins, as well as many non-landowners.

[33] One-fifth of the 1990 large landowners use the description 'landowner' in their entries in *Debrett's Distinguished People*, as do just under 10% of the larger group of 1990 holders of hereditary titles.

the importance of incomes from stock exchange securities is easily the largest gap in the analysis I have presented so far. Alas, the sources for plugging this gap are meagre and patchy even for landowners who died a hundred years ago, and are almost non-existent for today's group apart from the partial evidence which might be extracted from company annual reports which are obliged to disclose the shareholdings of their directors.[34] It may or may not be a fair inference from the mere fact of the survival of a large landed estate that its owner possesses a considerable income from outside sources, and for the present that is as far as it is possible to go. That the administration of the landed estate itself requires more constant and expert attention from the owner and agent than formerly can be more confidently inferred from the complexity of the law, the tax rules, and the regulations affecting agriculture and land use, which has increased almost ceaselessly since just before 1914.

Moreover it is not only the landed estate that has increasingly been treated as a business enterprise: it is the country house also. Badminton is reputed to be the only country house of the first rank which is not open to the public, presumably because the duke of Beaufort is too grand and too wealthy for it to be necessary. All the rest which are in private ownership can be visited, at a price. Country house visiting is largely a post-1945 phenomenon, and it took off in the 1960s. Some of the visiting public sometimes seem to regard the historic houses business as some kind of museum service, but from the suppliers' point of view it is serious, big business. The half-crown houses of the 1950s have become the £2 and £3 houses of the 1990s, and the amateurish management of the early days has been largely replaced by highly professional market-driven operations. The degree of commercialisation varies considerably: Woburn Abbey and Bowood are perhaps at one extreme, with zoos, fun fairs, waxworks, and pick-your-own fruit farms tacked on to the mansions, while at the other end of the spectrum Chatsworth maintains the decorum of a stately home with tearoom and gift shop added. There are costs in opening a house: considerable setting-up costs, and even more considerable running costs, mainly for labour but also for extra maintenance. It is not every country house which is a money-spinner, and some owners make a rational decision to remain closed on the grounds that the prospective flow of visitors

---

[34] Contemporary analyses of the distribution of shareholdings deal, understandably, in anonymous size groups, and do not name names. Historical analysis is dependent on public records that have a very low, and erratic, coverage, and on a handful of private papers which chance to contain relevant information: J. M. Collinge, ' "Probate Valuations and the Death Duty Registers": Some Comments,' *Historical Research*, LX (1987), 240–5. D. Cannadine, *The Decline and Fall of the British Aristocracy* (1990), 130–6, summarises the handful of known cases of diversification into portfolio investments.

would not cover the costs of opening. A case in point is Julian Byng of Wrotham Park, whose location near Potters Bar might not sound as inherently appealing as the Palladian mansion merits.[35]

Running country houses as businesses has an entrepreneurial ring of self-help about it, but it also impinges on outdoor relief of an indoor variety. Opening country houses has become, since 1945, one way of getting at the taxpayer's pocket. For a long time it was possible to get repair and maintenance grants in return for opening a house to the public on one day a week during a stipulated season, and although these were matching grants which implied that the owner spent some of his own money they were still useful outside help from the taxpayer. Then in the early 1970s, when there was a possibility that a Labour government might impose an annual wealth tax that would finally cripple the landowners, the owners got together to form the Historic Houses Association. Almost at once the Association had to mobilise its influence, and in the hands of Commander Michael Saunders Watson, owner of Rockingham Castle (later President of the Association, 1982–8), it conducted one of the most carefully organised and effective parliamentary lobbying campaigns of recent years, at the end of which country houses which were opened to the public for a minimum of sixty days a year were exempted from liability to capital transfer tax, and the establishment of tax-exempt charitable trusts to own country houses while their former owners continued to occupy them was legalised. It was this 1975 campaign, aided by the aesthetic imprimatur of Sir Roy Strong and the architectural wing of the art-historical world, that finally confirmed in the public mind the notion that certain privately-owned houses, art treasures, and family heirlooms are part of the national heritage, and deserve to be preferentially treated and subsidised so that they can stay that way. It became possible to sell pictures or antiques to the National Heritage Fund but to continue to keep them in the houses where they were before; and it became profitable to manufacture fake heritage items, like suits of armour, to equip stately homes which did not possess the genuine articles. The Historic Houses Association has been enormously successful in hitching old landowners to the heritage concept, and in selling the heritage concept to government, the Treasury, industry, and the viewing public.[36]

---

[35] Julian Byng makes his living as a barrister, farmer, and racehorse breeder.

[36] Paxman, *High Places*, 30–9. The V & A exhibition in 1975, *The Destruction of the Country House, 1875–1975*, was an important event in the formation of 'heritage' opinion. In the introduction to the book of the exhibition Sir Roy Strong referred to the buoyant and optimistic decades, for country houses, of the 1950s and 1960s, giving way to gloom and threatened ruin in the early 1970s, and called for 'consideration and justice' for country-house owners, who are 'the hereditary custodians of what was one of the most vital forces of cultural creation in our history,' 8, 10.

While heritage is the key to outdoor relief for the rich man in his country house, the National Trust performs something of the same service for the poor landowner. It was, indeed, the National Trust which first proved the existence of a large house-visiting public, thus establishing that there was a market for private enterprise to supply; but the National Trust had not always been in the business of acquiring, preserving, and opening country houses. The Trust was founded in 1895 as a body which would accept gifts of low-value land that was of exceptional natural beauty, especially on coastlines, and in hill, moor, and mountain country, and preserve them, with regulated public access, in perpetuity. It continued in that way until the 1930s, gradually adding acquisition by purchase to acceptance of gifts and legacies to its operations. Then in the 1930s, through the initiative of lord Lothian, the National Trust abandoned its exclusively open space stand and turned to the preservation of country houses: its 1937 Country House Scheme rapidly received statutory and fiscal ratification, exempting it from taxation and confirming its charitable status. The scheme, scarcely off the ground before 1939, enjoyed great success in the couple of decades after 1945. The main attraction for impoverished landowners who had nevertheless managed to hold on to their houses was that by transferring ownership to the Trust they and their heirs could continue to live in the family seat, while the worry and expense of its upkeep became the responsibility of the Trust. In a sense the National Trust simply became what the trustees of normal strict settlements had always been, the nominal owners of the freehold, but unlike those private trustees also undertook to pay for repairs and maintenance: the extra cost to the landowner and his family was the inconvenience of having the public in their living rooms, but that would have happened anyway if the house had been opened privately. The beautiful simplicity of the system was tarnished from the 1970s onwards, when the National Trust began to refuse offers of country houses unless they were accompanied by endowments, whether in capital or in land, sufficient to pay for the upkeep of the fabric. At that point live-in gifts to the Trust began to tail off; but the National Trust has rescued many landed families and enabled them to go on living in their family homes, just as it has rescued many splendid and much-visited houses.[37]

When they had really gone out of doors in search of outdoor relief the landed aristocracy had traditionally, since the demise of Old

---

[37] There is an in-house, descriptive, history of the National Trust, and an adequately informative centenary history is awaited. Meanwhile the best, and most entertaining, source is in the quartet of James Lees-Milne's diaries: *Ancestral Voices* (1975), *Prophesying Peace* (1977), *Caves of Ice* (1983), and *Midway on the Waves* (1985).

Corruption, looked to the empire. Careers in the Indian Civil Service, or in the colonial service, had perhaps never been very suitable for eldest sons, being much more in the line of younger sons and the gentry, although as many as ten per cent of the peers and baronets with interwar careers were in the colonial service. The ornamental posts at the pinnacle of empire, viceroys, governor-generals, and governors, were a different matter, and several members of the old aristocracy occupied these dignified and well-found positions: it was while his future father-in-law was Governor-General of Canada that Harold Macmillan found his wife.[38] Unsurprisingly, in the light of what became of the colonies, none of the holders of hereditary titles who are now living, and none of the surviving large landowners, have had colonial service careers, either working or dignified; although one or two of the first set do live in Commonwealth countries, as farmers or shopkeepers.

One form of 'outdoor relief for the upper crust', as it has been termed, which did achieve a certain popularity with the aristocracy at about the time the empire was fading has been membership of Lloyds.[39] Lloyds is like a club, and becoming a 'name' requires good connections and personal introductions as well as evidence of wealth. The wealth, however, is merely a pledge, only to be called on in case of disaster. It is not employed as working capital by the underwriting syndicates, and in good times the 'names' simply draw a large annual income without having to lift a finger and while keeping their money free to work elsewhere. Only in the late 1980s did things start to go badly wrong, with some large insurance losses, and some Lloyds' 'names' began to grasp that there are no free lunches as their pledged stakes were called up, and some faced ruin. With a membership of around 30,000 Lloyds is far too large to be an unclusively aristocratic club. But large landowners like the earl of Arran, the dukes of Norfolk and Rutland, and the earl of Lichfield, who can afford to lose half a million pounds or so at a pinch, have cheerfully joined in this superbly effortless way of further enriching themselves, alongside such of the new rich as lords Rothermere and Vestey, or Robert Maxwell, and many of the not so well-heeled cadet branches and the gentrified upper middle-

---

[38] Viceroys and Governor-Generals (of India, Australia, Canada, New Zealand, and South Africa) in the interwar period included, from the ranks of the landed aristocracy: earl of Lytton, earl of Halifax, viscount Goschen, marquess of Linlithgow; duke of Devonshire, earl of Bessborough, earl of Athlone; lord Forster, lord Stonehaven, lord Gowrie; earl of Liverpool, Sir Charles Fergusson, 7th bt, viscount Galway; earl of Clarendon.

[39] The phrase comes from *The Sunday Times*, 'What's in a Name?' 26 May 1991, Section 3, 1.

classes: these last are the ones currently faced with selling up their houses, the main security for their original stake in Lloyds.[40]

So one comes back to the original question: what is the secret of the success of the landowners who have survived? Self-help through chasing rich wives proves to have been of minimal importance, although there is no doubt that some very determined and calculated chasing did take place in the early years of this century. It has been said of the 9th duke of Manchester that 'he brazenly and systematically searched the United States for a rich wife, claiming that he must either marry an Astor or a Vanderbilt or throw in the towel.' He netted neither the one nor the other, and settled in 1900 on Helen Zimmerman, daughter of a Cincinnati railroad magnate: it did neither him, nor the Kimbolton estate, any lasting good.[41] Self-help through going out to earn a living, or at least through collecting a sizeable off-estate income from a non-landed and non-traditional career, proves, not exactly surprisingly, to have been far more important to those old-established families which have lost most or all of their land, than to the survivors; only a minority of the survivors have generated large incomes for themselves by their exertions in business and in the City. Even within that minority it is the descendants of the new-landed of the nineteenth century who stand out as active businessmen, who have carried on family concerns: the 6th lord Ashburton was managing director of Baring Brothers for thirty-four years, after doing a spell in the Scots Greys as a young man, and Samuel Whitbread of Southill Park, Bedfordshire, is chairman of the family brewery.[42] Self-help through turning country houses into businesses, which verges on a form of outdoor relief, has become so prevalent that it must, indeed, rank as a pre-condition of survival, although it ignores that group which have survived as landowners because they have abandoned or demolished their country houses and taken to living in more modest dower houses, farmhouses, and the like on the family estate. In any case, the country house as business usually generates little net profit after taking account of its indispensable contribution to keeping a roof on the place, and serves to conserve the infrastructure of the landed cake rather than to provide any icing. Finally, the classic sources of outdoor relief, in well-paid ornamental

---

[40] *The Sunday Times*, 26 May 1991, mentions that Major Malcolm Gomme-Duncan had already been obliged to sell his family house and small (400 acre) estate at Dunbarney, Perthshire, and that lord Alexander of Tunis (son of the Field Marshal) was faced with selling his home in Wandsworth Common, because of Lloyds' troubles.

[41] Cannadine, *Decline*, 398, quoting from R. Brandon, *The Dollar Princesses* (1980).

[42] Lord Ashburton still owns the Alresford and Stratton Park estates in Hants., and his eldest son has been chairman of Baring Bros. since 1974. Whitbread still owns the Southill Park estate of 10,800 acres: *Debrett's Distinguished People*.

jobs at home or in the colonies, have dried up, and new sources, although lucrative, have been tapped by only a small number.

All these bits and pieces of self-help and outdoor relief undoubtedly add up to a positive contribution to survival, but even so can 'explain' the survival of no more than a small minority of the survivors. The answer might seem to be that there has been no general crisis of the landed order in the last hundred years, because no general response can be detected. Those landowners who have survived, it could be argued, have survived simply because they are landowners; and those landowners who have not survived have been simply the incompetent, inefficient, extravagant, dissolute, and unlucky ones. That, however, is to ignore the largest and most generally available source of outdoor relief for the landed classes, the land itself. That relief has, of course, been forthcoming in the name of agriculture and forestry, and ostensibly has been channelled into the hands of those who farm the land and plant the trees in the form of myriads of subsidies and tax reliefs. Many large landowners, seeing the great flow of public money towards farmers in the shape of farm-price support schemes, crop subsidies, field drainage grants, farm building grants, and the like, have turned themselves into farmers since 1945 and have tapped this largesse at source. Thus, farming is the largest single occupation of the surviving large landowners in 1990, and ranks equal with banking as the largest occupation of the wider group of holders of hereditary titles alive in 1990. An economist might tell them that they need not have bothered, and that all they needed to do in order to obtain a share of the taxpayers' money lavished on farmers was to sit tight and pull it in as rent or as capital value added to the land. Nevertheless, although Ricardo's law plainly has operated, as can be seen in the movement of farm rents and the capital value of agricultural land, it operates slowly and imperfectly because of institutional arrangements, and the farming landowners behaved very sensibly in moving in to take both the tenant's and the landlord's shares of the bounty without waiting for Ricardo. This form of outdoor relief has been available only since 1939 on any scale, and between 1921 when the price guarantees of the First World War were withdrawn and 1939 there was no material state aid to agriculture. The conclusion then is that those landowners who were able to survive the eighteen lean years, whether because they had humps big enough to live on, had no deaths and successions in those years, or for some other reasons, were the ones who entered into the land of milk and honey and have continued to survive and prosper. Whether they were instrumental in turning on the supplies of milk and honey, or simply passive recipients of manna from heaven, are questions that must be left hanging in the air for another twelve months [if you can bear the suspense].

CHARLES I, THE PRIVY COUNCIL AND THE PARLIAMENT OF 1628

By Richard Cust

READ 19 JANUARY 1991

THOSE present in the council chamber around teatime on Friday, 4 April 1628 would have witnessed one of the more hopeful scenes in the politics of the late 1620s. Sir John Coke, Secretary of State, arrived hotfoot from the House of Commons to announce that it had voted to grant the crown five subsidies. The king, who had been waiting for the news, expressed 'joy and contentment, saying he was more happy than any of the kings his predecessors...';

> then asking Sir John Coke farther, by how many voices he carried it, he answered, *but by one voice*. Whereat his Majesty, being at first somewhat appalled, Sir John replied, his majesty had so much the greater cause of joy the whole house being so unanimous as they all made but one voice: at which, they say, his majesty wept.[1]

Whether or not Charles really engaged in such an uncharacteristic display of public emotion, he then proceeded to deliver one of his more gracious pronouncements.

> This contents me that it is not done by any man's labour, but it is the work of the whole House. Another thing that gives me content is this, that although 5 subsidies be inferior to my wants, yet it is the greatest that ever was; and now I see with this I shall have the affections of my people and this will be greater to me than all value. At the first I liked parliaments, but since (I know not how) I was grown to distaste of them. But I am now where I was. I love parliaments. I shall rejoice to meet with my people often.[2]

On this occasion, for once, Charles' characteristic mixture of bluntness and naivety proved very appealing. In spite of what most saw as the Duke of Buckingham's attempt to spoil the occasion by claiming the credit for this new found unity, there was widespread optimism and

---

[1] *Court and Times of Charles I*, 2 vols., ed. T. Birch (1848), I. 337.
[2] *Proceedings in Parliament 1628*, 6 vols., eds. R. C. Johnson, M. F. Keeler, M. J. Cole and W. B. Bidwell (New Haven, 1977–83), II. 324–5.

commentators predicted that the parliament would quickly reach a successful conclusion.[3]

This was to change over the following weeks as it became clear that Charles was simply not prepared to give ground over his right to detain prisoners without showing cause. Nevertheless the episode highlighted an important, but rather neglected aspect of the 1628 Parliament. There is a vast literature on this parliament, but nearly all of it has focussed on the struggle in the Commons and Lords to secure the Petition of Right. In the process its significance for the development of royal policy has been overlooked[4]. Sir Benjamin Rudyerd's oft-quoted statement that 'This is the crisis of parliaments. We shall know by this if parliaments live or die' was not just rhetoric. It expressed real fears and anxieties. Charles' decision to raise the forced loan rather than summon another parliament, in the midst of war, when tradition suggested he should be meeting his people regularly, showed there was a real danger that English parliaments would follow their continental counterparts and cease to exist.[5] This was profoundly disturbing, not least to some leading members of the king's own council. Their struggle to make the parliament work is the main theme of this article.

It was widely supposed that the meeting in 1628 would decide things, one way or another. In the event the outcome was inconclusive, but already one can glimpse some of the tensions and divisions which came to the fore after the failure of the 1629 Parliament and led to the personal rule. Several were apparent on 4 April: for example, in the efforts of Coke to make more than was strictly warranted of what was still only the first stage in the passing of a subsidy bill; in a reference which Buckingham made, albeit slightingly, to those 'projectors and inducers of innovation' who were believed to be turning the king against parliaments[6]; and not least in the obvious struggle within the king's own mind between the desire to meet with and gain the affection of his people and the worries leading to what he called his 'distaste' of parliaments.

The council debate over whether to summon the Parliament of 1628, which lasted from December 1627 to February 1628, was one of the

---

[3] *Ibid*, II. 327; *Court and Times*, I. 338–40; *Cal. State Papers Venetian 1628–9*, 60.

[4] This literature includes: S. R. Gardiner, *History of England, 1603–1642*, 10 vols. (1883–4), VI. 230–338: F. H. Relf, *The Petition of Right* (Minneapolis, 1917); C. S. R. Russell, *Parliaments and English Politics 1621–1629* (Oxford, 1979), 323–89; J. A. Guy, 'The origins of the Petition of Right reconsidered', *Historical Journal*, XXV (1982), 289–312; J. S. Flemion, ' "A savings to satisfy all": the House of Lords and the Petition of Right', *Parliamentary History*, X (1991), 27–44. Gardiner and Russell take most account of the general development of royal policy.

[5] *Proceedings in Parliament 1628*, II. 58; R. P. Cust, *The Forced Loan and English Politics 1626–1628* (Oxford, 1987).

[6] *Proceeding in Parliament 1628*, II. 325.

bitterest and most divisive of the 1620s. This has been discussed at length elsewhere, so there is no need to go over it in detail.[7] Nevertheless it is helpful to highlight some of the themes which became relevant to later proceedings. The debate revealed a council which was basically divided between moderates and hardliners. The moderates, led by senior councillors like Lord Keeper Coventry, Lord President Manchester and the Earl of Pembroke, wanted a meeting of parliament not only to raise much needed revenue, but also to provide a display of national unity which could heal the divisions opened up by the forced loan and boost England's standing abroad. The hardliners, mostly close adherents of Buckingham like the Earl of Dorset, Sir John Savile and Bishop Laud, were opposed to a summons, on the grounds that it was unlikely to produce the requisite subsidies and would offer opponents of the crown an opportunity to agitate. Much better, they argued, to continue to rely on unparliamentary taxation. Through most of the debate Buckingham himself sat on the fence, doing his best to appear in favour of a summons whilst covertly opposing it because of the obvious danger that the Commons would repeat their attempt to impeach him. The decisive factor, as so often in this period, was the view of the king. At first he was adamantly opposed to a summons, insisting that councillors consider alternative means of raising revenue; but it soon became apparent that if he was to continue the war against France, parliament was much the speediest and most straightforward way of raising the huge sums required. Charles was in effect faced with having to abandon his foreign policy unless he summoned a parliament. So, reluctantly, he gave way.

Two themes in this debate were particularly significant in the light of later events. The first of these was the fear, voiced in a memorandum prepared by Laud, that the House of Commons in any future parliament would contain within it 'factious spirits' bent on destroying royal authority. This notion appears to have been part of the mental furniture of privy councillors since James' first parliament of 1604–10, after which Lord Chancellor Ellesmere observed that 'the popular state' had grown so 'big and audacious' that if it 'be suffered to usurp and encroach too far upon the regality, it will not cease until it brake out into democracy.'[8]

---

[7] Cust, *Forced Loan*, 72–85.

[8] *Proceedings in Parliament 1610*, 2 vols., ed. E. R. Foster (New Haven, 1966), I. 276. The earliest instance of this which I am aware of is Robert Cecil's linking of the activities of those agitating against monopolies in 1601 with 'popularity': J. E. Neale, *Elizabeth I and her Parliaments 1584–1601* (1957), 386. Cecil and his allies deployed a similar rhetoric against those MPs who complained about purveyance in 1605–6: P. Croft, 'Parliament, purveyance and the City of London 1589–1608', *Parl. Hist.*, IV (1988), 25, 34n; D. H. Willson, 'The Earl of Salisbury and the "court" party in parliament, 1604–10', *American Historical Review*, XXXVI (1931), 279.

Responsibility for this state of affairs was ascribed not to the Commons as a whole, but to a small minority within it, variously described by councillors as the 'boutefeus', the 'stirring men', the 'popular party' and the 'tribunes of the people'. The terminology was significant because it indicated that the activities of these MPs was assimilated to the familiar idea of a populist conspiracy, emanating from the 'many headed monster' of the 'popular multitude' and aimed at undermining and ultimately destroying monarchy. Small groups of lawyers, puritans and 'free speakers' in the Commons were seen as playing up to the people in challenging the royal prerogative and attacking royal favourites; and their efforts were seen by some councillors as having caused the premature dissolution of most of James' parliaments as well as those of 1625 and 1626.[9]

Laud's memorandum identified this element with those who had disobeyed the king by refusing the forced loan. Such 'factious spirits' he argued 'will studdy revenge, at least unquiet' and 'will take hart if they see the kinge yeeld to them without any submission of theirs as some were seene to laugh outright in the last parliament when they gott their ends upon the kinge'. The only way to defeat them was to deny them opportunities to conspire together and organise, which meant avoiding a summons of parliament.[10]

Other councillors, whilst rejecting Laud's conclusion, nonetheless shared his concern. Moderates like Pembroke and Sir Thomas Edmondes did their best to exclude leading loan refusers from the parliament by interfering in the county elections in Cornwall and Essex.[11] And within a few days of the start of the session councillors were making their habitual calculations about the make up and likely mood of the Commons. Secretary of State, Sir Edward Conway, who had been gloomily pessimistic at the end of the 1626 Parliament, was now much more buoyant, opining hopefully that the 'Lower House ... are composed of graver men and of lesser noyse than at the last parliament, and many signs appear which seeme to foretell a good issue'.[12] Much of the council discussion during the parliament was to hinge around this sort of assessment.

Linked to this, because it determined what alternatives were available

---

[9] For council discussions and memoranda from 1613, 1615 and 1620 in which these views were advanced, see J. A. Spedding, *Life and Letters of Francis Bacon*, 7 vols. (1861–74), IV. 366–73, V, 181, 190, VII. 116; D. H. Willson, 'Summoning and dissolving parliament, 1603–25: the council's advice to James I', *American Hist. Rev.*, xlv (1940), 279–300. For 1625 and 1626, see J. Hacket, *Scrinia Reserata. A Memorial of John Williams D. D.*, 2 parts in 1 vol. (1693), II. 17, 20; Cust, *Forced Loan*, 17–18.

[10] Public Record Office, S. P. 16/94/88.

[11] Cust, *Forced Loan*, 311–14.

[12] P. R. O., S. P. 99/29, fo. 161.

to the king, was the issue of whether or not, in times of necessity, the king had the right to raise taxation without the consent of the subject. The hardliners, in keeping with the doctrine which had come to the fore during the period of the forced loan, insisted that he did; and again this position was stated most trenchantly in Laud's memorandum. Following the notorious sermons by Sibthorpe and Manwaring, Laud argued that royal authority was something which derived almost exclusively from above, owing little to the consent of the subject. This meant that in times of need taxes were due to the king as of right, whether or not a parliament was prepared to agree to them. Parliament's role was restricted to deciding on the manner of making a grant rather than whether a grant should be made, which in turn implied that the king was under no obligation to bargain with a parliament or make concessions to it. Indeed such concessions could be seen as positively dangerous since they diminished the royal prerogative, the ultimate means of exercising royal power. 'By theis bills of grace', Laud argued, 'the flowers of the crowne are parted with and the prerogative soe decreased as I dare not speake of the consequence.'[13] Viewed in such terms the king had little to gain and everything to lose from a parliament; and again Laud's conclusion was that it would be better if it did not meet.

Such views, however, were anathema to the moderates within the council who had gone along with the forced loan in 1626 because of pressure from the king, but had done their best to mitigate its worst effects and ensure that it did not stand in the way of future parliaments. Their basic concern was to uphold customary laws and liberties and strike a balance between the interests of crown and subject, so that government could remain a partnership between the two. These views were set out most clearly in a contribution to the debate, prepared, at the behest of the moderates, by Sir Robert Cotton.[14] This argued that the main danger to the country was the continuing threat of Habsburg aggression, for which the best remedy was a meeting of parliament which would provide not only money, but also a much needed display of national unity. Any repetition of the forced loan would only result in further coercion which had been the source of so much suspicion and division in the recent past. Much better to follow Lord Burghley's maxim, that if you win hearts then you have the people's hands and purses.

The decision at the end of January to send out the writs for a summons showed that for the time being the moderates had won the

[13] *Ibid*, S. P. 16/94/88.
[14] J. Rushworth, *Historical Collections*, 7 vols. (1659–1701), I, 467–72. A manuscript copy of this exists, dated January 1627/8: British Library, Lansdowne MS 254, fos. 258–69.

debate over prerogative taxation; but the essentially conditional nature of their victory was demonstrated on 28 February when the king issued a commission requiring the council to consider impositions or some other means of raising money quickly. The moderates responded by pushing through an immediate resolution that 'there was no way but a parliament to raise monies'; but the discussion did not end there. A decision was also taken to keep the commission in reserve in case the parliament failed to grant supply, and another resolution was passed which stated, according to the Venetian ambassador, that 'unless the Commons grant the money immediately and without further debate, the king will be justified in exercising his prerogative, burdening them with taxes and compelling them'.[15] This was an indication that all was still to play for and that the moderates' struggle to make the parliament work was likely to be as much with their own colleagues and the king as with the House of Commons.

From the council's point of view the parliament can be divided into four phases. The first, which lasted from the opening on 13 March to the council meeting on 4 April, involved the Commons discussing in broad terms the grievances of the previous year and a half and agreeing in principle to grant the king five subsidies. The second phase, from early April to early May, witnessed the beginning of the campaign to prevent imprisonment without showing cause and a serious threat to dissolve the parliament. The third, to 7 June, involved the struggle over the Petition of Right; and the final phase contained the passage of the subsidies, the Commons' Remonstrance against Buckingham and efforts by the king to qualify his earlier concessions.

During the first of these periods most of the council's attention was directed to the House of Commons, where the crown's spokesmen faced two principal tasks. They had to head off any attack on Buckingham which at this stage would probably have been fatal to the parliament; and also extract a statement of the Commons' intention to grant subsidies, which could be used to persuade the king and the hardliners that this was the most straightforward means of obtaining supply. Early indications were that neither task would be easy.

The sermon delivered by Laud at the opening of the parliament emphasised the disruption caused by those who denied obedience to superiors or refused 'to lay down the private for the public's sake'.[16] These were themes which had figured prominently in the sermons of

---

[15] *Proceedings in Parliament 1628*, IV. 241–2; P.R.O., S.P. 16/93/80; S.P. 84/136, fo. 107; *Cal. State Papers Venetian 1628–9*, 10.

[16] W. Laud, *The Works*, 6 vols. (Oxford, 1853), I. 155–82.

Sibthorpe and Manwaring the previous year; and although Laud presented them less aggressively in this context, he could still be taken as supporting the case for extra-parliamentary supply. To judge by his opening speech the king was thinking along similar lines. He began with some comforting enough assurances of his intention to rule through parliament, but then rather spoilt the effect by warning that this was no time for 'long consultation' and that if 'you do neglect your duties herein I must then be forced, for the preservation of the public and that which by the folly of some particular men may be destroyed, to take some other course'. He then added, rather gratuitously, 'I would not have you take this as a threatening for I scorne to threaten any but my equals.'[17] This was not just Charles showing his usual lack of tact in hammering out the implications of statements better left vague. It also indicated that he had barely shifted his ground since the preliminary discussions in council. In spite of the moderates' efforts to persuade him, he remained wary of the disruptive influence of 'particular men' and convinced that he was entitled to take extra-parliamentary supply if the Commons did not co-operate speedily.

Despite this unpromising start, the early stages of the parliament were generally harmonious. They are worth looking at in detail because they give cause to question the long accepted verdict of D. H. Willson, that by the 1620s privy councillors had lost most of their earlier influence in the Commons.[18] During the first phase in 1628 this was emphatically not the case. The star turn for the council was Sir John Coke, characterised by Willson and S. R. Gardiner as 'clumsy' and 'garrulous',[19] but during these debates displaying a tactical awareness and sense of timing which did much to create the right mood. He was effectively supported by Sir Humphrey May and Sir Thomas Edmondes, from within the Privy Council, and amongst the royal officeholders by Sir Benjamin Rudyerd. The latter's significance was enormously enhanced by the fact that he was the acknowledged spokesman of the Earl of Pembroke, the most influential of the council moderates.[20] And, whereas those MPs who were actually members of the council were restricted in what they could do, Rudyerd was able to move relatively freely and offer suggestions and initiatives which guided the Commons'

[17] *Proceedings in Parliament 1628*, II. 8–9.

[18] D. H. Willson, *The Privy Councillors in the House of Commons 1604–1629* (Minneapolis, 1940).

[19] *Ibid.*, 95–7; Gardiner, *History of England*, VI. 239–40, 252. This verdict has been contested in M. Young, *Servility and Service. The Life and Work of Sir John Coke* (Royal Historical Society Studies in History no. 45, Woodbridge, 1989), chap. 11.

[20] Russell, *Parliaments and English Politics*, 13; R. E. Ruigh, *The Parliament of 1624* (Cambridge, Mass., 1971), 178.

leaders over their options if they wished to carry moderate councillors in the Lords.

The councillors' approach during this phase of the parliament was to combine reminders of the disastrous dissolution of the 1626 Parliament with fulsome assurances that the king had banished the doctrine of necessity and would welcome redress of grievances. The first of their two objectives was more or less secured on 22 March, the day on which the Commons decided which course to take in remedying grievances. Whether or not the Commons leaders had already met and decided not to pursue Buckingham, the speeches delivered on this day by Seymour and Eliot look very much like attempts to test the level of support for such a course. The council spokesmen, however, had seen this coming and quickly stepped in. Edmondes reminded the House of the 'lamentable experience' and 'distractions' which had followed impeachment in 1626. May urged them to 'go the right way' and consider a general remedy for grievances. Then Rudyerd weighed in with a long-winded, but timely speech in which he repeated his habitual warnings about the 'crisis of parliaments', reiterated the dire consequences of attacking the duke and left the door open to a different approach by suggesting the need to frame legislation in defence of the subject's liberties.[21] Coming from the mouthpiece of the man who had done more than anyone to make Buckingham's impeachment possible in 1626, the House seemed to take the hint. The speakers who followed confined themselves mainly to discussing general remedies; and in the succeeding weeks, right up to the final stage of the parliament, the Commons as a whole showed remarkable self-restraint in refraining from pursuing any royal servants, let alone Buckingham.[22]

The councillors' second objective proved more of a struggle because, as Tom Cogswell has shown, by 1628 there was a well-established convention that grants of supply should go hand-in-hand with redress of grievances.[23] This slowed down discussion of subsidies considerably. Nevertheless councillors were able to keep things moving along in the right direction by more deft management. Secretary Coke pushed supply to the top of the Commons' agenda with pleas for consideration and a series of messages from the king, which culminated in the

---

[21] *Proceedings in Parliament 1628*, II. 55–65.

[22] Russell, *Parliaments and English Politics*, chap. v. For example on 2 April Phelips carefully steered the House away from Eliot's proposal for considering 'ill counsels': *Proceedings in Parliament 1628*, II. 251. It was also significant that the Commons did not take more vigorous action against Attorney-General Heath after revelations that he had altered the King's Bench controlment roll in the Five Knights Case: Guy, 'Origins of the Petition of Right', 296–9; *Proceedings in Parliament 1628*, II. 231.

[23] T. E. Cogswell, 'A low road to extinction? Supply and redress of grievances in the parliaments of the 1620s', *Hist. Jnl.*, XXXIII (1990), 283–303.

particularly welcome assurance on 4 April that 'we shall enjoy our rights and liberties with as much freedom and security in his time as in any age heretofore... And whether you shall think fit to secure yourselves herein by way of bill or otherwise ... he promiseth ... that he will give way unto it.'[24] All this was again reinforced with hints about what might happen if the Commons did not move promptly. The effect on the House was extremely salutary. Several speakers acknowledged that the efforts of the councillors and the royal messages had helped create an atmosphere of harmony, comparable to what Sir Robert Phelips called the 'good parliament' of 1624.[25] At the same time the Commons' leaders were acutely sensitive to the charge that they themselves were not doing enough to contribute to this and on several occasions stepped in to speed up discussion of supply.[26] Out of this mixture of pressure and reassurance, councillors were able to generate enough momentum to overcome those MPs who wished to delay any offer of supply until after legislation had been framed. The promise of five subsidies made on 4 April was an unprecedently large grant.[27]

Managing the Commons, however, was only part of the moderates' achievement; they also succeeded in managing Charles. The task here was to wean the king away from his initial pessimism and prevent him from poisoning the atmosphere with an ill-judged intervention. The councillors had the considerable advantage that it was they who controlled communications between the king and the Commons. They seem to have reported regularly to him after dinner and were able to present a suitably optimistic picture of the parliament's progress.[28] It was perhaps an indication of the effect this had that by 26 March, when he nominated a series of bishops attending the Lords to preach in his chapel, Charles envisaged the parliament lasting to the end of May.[29] They also prepared more explicit advice on policy. Amongst Secretary Coke's papers there is a memorandum dated 3 April, advising Charles that to keep the ball rolling on supply he should 'yield unto such of' the Commons' demands 'as shall be found just and reasonable'.[30] This was followed by the well-received royal message of 4 April. Finally, and perhaps most significantly, the moderates appear to have exerted a good deal of control over Charles' own pronouncements in this period. The deleterious effect of his bluntness and lack of tact can

[24] *Proceedings in Parliament 1628*, II. 82, 89, 104–5, 228, 245–6, 256, 267, 277–8, 297.
[25] *Ibid.*, II. 126, 131, 246.
[26] *Ibid.*, II. 228, 301–2.
[27] *Ibid.*, II. 301–2.
[28] *Ibid.*, II. 97, 278.
[29] P. R. O., L. C. 5/132, p. 6.
[30] *Proceedings in Parliament 1628*, VI. 106; P. R. O., S. P. 16/100/25.

be gauged from the stunned reaction in the Commons to some of his later messages. It was therefore important that after his opening address the king did not communicate directly with the Commons during this first phase. Instead his views were relayed through messages. Most of these appear to have been drafted, as well as delivered, by Secretary Coke, using the sort of reassuring and emollient language which did not come easily to Charles.[31] The culmination of all this careful groundwork was the royal pronouncement in council on 4 April when, for once, the king struck just the right note.

The Commons' willingness to set a figure on their grant gave the moderates an advantage in the internal council debate which they never entirely lost. In the long term it held out the prospect that if they could just hang on and reach agreement with the Commons, the crown would have immediate access to nearly £300,000, which would go a long way to meeting its most pressing needs. In the short term, it silenced the hardliners and opened up the possibility of settlement on a range of issues.

The king's council table speech of 4 April was quickly printed and widely circulated.[32] As a result, opponents of the parliament found their original position no longer tenable and moved rapidly to make the most of the apparent accommodation.[33] According to Sir Francis Nethersole, adviser to Elizabeth of Bohemia, Buckingham up to this point had been doing his best to persuade the king that parliament was 'not affected' to him, and now had to improvise a quick about turn.[34] Whether or not this was true, the duke certainly displayed his characteristic sense of opportunism in the speech he delivered immediately after the king's on 4 April. It stressed two themes: firstly his desire to see king and people united through frequent parliaments; and secondly his concern that he himself no longer be thought of as 'the man of separation', but rather as a 'good spirit' bent on promoting this unity.[35] According to the newsletter writer Joseph Mead, he also went further and to take away any misgivings over his 'plurality of offices' offered to surrender the Wardenship of the Cinque Ports and the Mastership of the Horse, and serve as Admiral only in peacetime,

---

[31] P. R. O., S. P. 16/98/53; 16/100/21, 48, 69. For a later draft of a royal message by Coke, see S. P. 16/103/8.

[32] *The Duke of Buckingham his speech to the King in Parliament* (1628) (Short Title Cat. no. 24739); *Court and Times*, I. 339; *Proceedings in Parliament 1628*, II. 411–12, 416.

[33] For the reactions of the earl of Dorset and Buckingham's client Sir James Bagge, see: *Proceedings in Parliament 1628*, VI, 205; P. R. O., S. P. 16/100/55.

[34] *Proceedings in Parliament 1628*, VI. 189. Sir Richard Hutton, the Justice of Common Pleas, also recorded in his diary that Buckingham had done his best to get the parliament dissolved: *The Diary of Sir Richard Hutton 1614–1639*, ed. W. R. Prest (Selden Society, Supp. Ser., IX, 1991), 73.

[35] *Proceedings in Parliament 1628*, II. 325–6.

'allowing the council and house of parliament to appoint another for all services at sea'.[36] If the report is correct—and there is a hint from the Venetian ambassador that the idea was at least being canvassed[37]— this represented a striking concession. Buckingham's continued tenure of the post of Lord Admiral, giving him as it did effective oversight of the war effort, was a principal bone of contention not only with the Commons, but also with his opponents at court, chief amongst whom was Pembroke. A compromise over this, which Conrad Russell suggests may well have been on the cards during the impeachment proceedings in 1626,[38] would go a considerable way towards reconciling many of his most powerful enemies to his continuance as royal favourite. Even if Buckingham did not in fact go this far, the publication of his speech, alongside that of the king, made it clear that for the time being he intended to follow the option of working with the parliament rather than trying to get it dissolved.[39]

There was also the prospect of making progress over another divisive issue, the drift towards Arminianism. The council contained a substantial contingent of moderate Calvinists who were disturbed by the direction in which the church had been heading since Buckingham had made clear his support for Arminianism at the York House Conference. This included Coke, May, Carlisle, Manchester and Pembroke.[40] There had been indications during 1627 and 1628 that they were making headway towards reversing the prevailing trend. This had been particularly apparent in the appointment of Joseph Hall as Bishop of Exeter, probably secured by his patron Pembroke and accepted even by Laud.[41] Hall was something of a professional moderate in religion, offering a reassuringly safe version of Calvinism of the sort which needed to be promoted if Charles and the duke were to be enticed back towards resuming the Jacobean status quo. In this respect it was of some significance that Hall and the equally moderate John Davenant, bishop of Salisbury, were chosen by the Lords to preach their fast

---

[36] *Court and Times*, I. 337–9.

[37] *Cal. State Papers Venetian 1628–9*, 59.

[38] Russell, *Parliaments and English Politics*, 296–7.

[39] The two speeches were probably published at Buckingham's behest. He had much to gain from demonstrating that he was in favour of parliaments, as his clients recognised: *Proceedings in Parliament 1628*, II. 277; P.R.O., S.P. 16/108/71. He also took pains to publish accounts of his actions on other occasions: T.E. Cogswell, 'The politics of propaganda: Charles I and the people in the 1620s', *Journal of British Studies*, XXIX (1990), 202–4.

[40] N.R.N. Tyacke, *Anti-Calvinists. The Rise of English Arminianism c. 1590–1640* (Oxford, 1987), 168–70; Cust, *Forced Loan*, 74–5; Russell, *Parliaments and English Politics*, 30–1, 298.

[41] *The Works of Joseph Hall D.D.*, 12 vols. (Oxford, 1837), I. xxiv–v, xxix–x, 361, V. 150, 366; Laud, *Works*, IV. 297.

sermons on 5 April, after a discussion initiated by Pembroke.[42] The addresses they delivered on this occasion were unremarkable, dwelling in general terms on the theme of the imminence of God's judgements unless England turned from its sinfulness. In contrast Jeremiah Dyke's sermon to the Commons on the same occasion launched a frontal assault on Arminianism.[43] But, in the circumstances, Hall and Davenant were doing just what was required, providing a public reminder that Calvinism of the sort sponsored by the Lords and moderate councillors was both responsible and respectable.[44] This offered a solid platform from which Calvinist councillors could move against Arminianism later on in the parliament.

The events around 4 April were the high point of the parliament for the moderate councillors. During the second phase the prospects of a general settlement rapidly diminished as the king grew increasingly distrustful of the Commons. The principal cause was delay in completing the subsidy bill. The king and council expected this to be finalised in a matter of days, in time for Easter, but try as they might they could get the Commons to do no more than approve payment of the subsidies within a year. This was serious because it threatened to undermine the main priority of English foreign policy at this time, the dispatch of a fleet to relieve the Huguenots at La Rochelle. Cash was urgently needed to pay the seamen who were deserting in droves and to furnish grain supplies for the besieged Protestants; and in the circumstances it seemed this could only come from a quick passage of the subsidies. For Charles the whole venture was a matter of personal honour which explains his intense frustration over the delay.[45]

This was compounded by the Commons' stubborn stance over its liberties. It became apparent in the second week of April that in no circumstances would it permit the crown to keep prisoners in confinement without showing cause. Charles adopted an equally inflexible stance. As he declared in a letter to the Lords early in May, such an 'intermitting of the constant rule of government for so many ages within this kingdom practised would soon dissolve the very foundation

---

[42] *Proceedings in Parliament 1628*, V. 97–8. On Hall and Davenant, see P. G. Lake, 'Calvinism and the English Church 1570–1635', *Past and Present*, no. 114 (1987), 32–76.

[43] *Works of Hall*, V. 313–26; M. Fuller, *The Life, Letters and Writings of John Davenant D. D.* (1897), 269–302; J. Dyke, *A Sermon Preached at the Publicke Fast* (1628).

[44] This was particularly important at this time because a high proportion of the Lenten preachers at court, March– April 1628, were anti-Calvinists or Arminians: P. R. O., L. C. 5/132, 'Lent preachers 1627 and 1628'.

[45] Russell, *Parliaments and English Politics*, 360, 391; *Cal. State Papers Domestic 1628–9*, 67–8.

and frame of our monarchy ... without overthrow of sovereignty we cannot suffer this power to be impeached.'[46] The result was deadlock and a rapid deterioration in relations as Charles cast off the restraining influence of the moderates and vented his frustration in increasingly acerbic messages. On 10 April he ordered the Commons to sit through Easter to finalise supply in spite of Coke and May's efforts at mediation.[47] Then two days later, in a message which Coke implied he had been required to deliver verbatim, the Commons were told to 'take heed that we force him not to make an unpleasing end of that which was so well begun', and also warned that 'notice is taken as if the House pressed not upon the abuse of power only, but power itself'. This last remark reduced the House to silence. When it recovered it blamed the influence of those who 'whispered unto his Majesty that we here distaste the government of a monarch' and drafted a resolution to counter this.[48] But the damage had been done and the harmony of the first phase decisively undermined.

Things could well have gone from bad to worse at this point, but on 14 April Charles relaxed the pressure and allowed the Commons to go on with discussion of liberties. The reason for this appears to have been a decision taken on the 12th to order the Rochelle fleet to sail anyway.[49] This removed the immediate panic about cash and provided a breathing space, during which the king and council looked to the Lords to defend the prerogative and persuade the Commons to tone down its demands over imprisonment. The council displayed an impressively united front in support of what appears to have been an agreed strategy. Earlier hardliners like Dorset and Conway were particularly forceful in advocating defence of the prerogative, but they were solidly supported by moderates like Manchester and Pembroke.[50] It was clear, as on other occasions, that when Charles got the bit between his teeth and was determined to hold to a particular line, the council would follow him loyally.

These efforts produced a resolution from the Lords allowing the king to imprison without showing cause when reason of state required; but the Commons rejected this on 26 April.[51] On the 28th, in an attempt to break the deadlock, Lord Keeper Coventry offered the king's personal assurance that he would observe Magna Carta and the supporting

[46] *Proceedings in Parliament 1628*, III. 372.
[47] *Ibid.*, II. 399, 401, 403, 408.
[48] *Ibid.*, II. 430–3; *Court and Times*, I. 311–5.
[49] *Acts of the Privy Council 1627–8*, 375.
[50] *Proceedings in Parliament 1628*, V. 315–16, 321–3, 330; Flemion, 'A Savings to Satisfy All', 32–4, 40.
[51] Guy, 'Origins of the Petition of Right', 304.

statutes. But again the Commons would have nothing to do with it.[52] Finally, in exasperation, Charles resumed the threatening tone of his messages of early April. On 1 May the Commons were asked directly whether they would 'rest on his royal word or no'; on the 2nd they were told that the present session would be brought to an end on 13 May, with the implication that another later in the year would only be guaranteed if they proved more accommodating; finally on the 5th— in a message delivered by the Lord Keeper after hurried consultation with Charles—the House was warned that 'if you seek to bind the king by new and indeed impossible bonds, you must be accountable to God and the country for the ill success of that meeting'.[53] This was alarmingly reminiscent of the king's statements at the end of the 1626 Parliament and it seemed to confirm what most commentators at the time were saying, that the parliament was about to be dissolved.[54]

The events of early May were the crisis point for the 1628 Parliament. This has not been sufficiently emphasised in most accounts where it has been assumed that the message about an end to the session was simply another device to speed supply. That Charles himself was seriously considering a dissolution is demonstrated by an important document which has been largely ignored since Gardiner referred to it in the nineteenth century: this was the draft of a Declaration explaining the king's reasons for dissolving the parliament which was composed between 6 and 12 May by the Attorney-General, Sir Robert Heath.[55] From this one can glean evidence on the otherwise obscure discussions taking place behind the scenes.

To start with it asserted that the king had formally consulted the judges and Privy Council and secured their agreement to dissolving the parliament. In fact, in this respect, Heath appears to have been jumping the gun. None of the other sources available suggest that the council actually agreed to a dissolution. Indeed, statements by Secretary Conway at this time would seem to rule this out.[56] Nonetheless this is good evidence for the belief of someone close to the heart of government that such discussions were about to take place, which in itself was significant.

Heath's draft also indicated that the idea of prerogative taxation was still very much on the agenda. His original version of the declaration

[52] Proceedings in Parliament 1628, III. 125; Guy, 'Origins of the Petition of Right', 305–6.
[53] Proceedings in Parliament 1628, III. 188–90, 212–13, 254.
[54] Ibid., VI. 176, 188; Court and Times, I. 346; The Letters of John Holles, 1587–1637, ed. P. R. Seddon, 3 vols. (1975–86), III. 382.
[55] This document is P. R. O., S. P. 16/138/45i. A full transcript is provided in R. P. Cust, 'Charles I and a draft Declaration for the 1628 Parliament', Historical Research, lxiii (1990), 157–61.
[56] P. R. O., S. P. 77/19, fos. 181–2.

contained an undertaking, in line with councillors' statements in the Commons, not to reimpose the forced loan; however, this passage has an annotation alongside it suggesting that it be removed. This would seem to indicate that someone else close to the king was already anticipating some fresh resort to extra-parliamentary supply. Certainly the way was left open for this by the warning at the end of the draft that 'although we are ... deprived of the ordinary and best meanes for our supplye ... [the Commons] will not suffer us to want this means for ours and ther supply and relief when we shall require the same'.[57] This was reminiscent of a passage in the Declaration issued after the 1626 Parliament which had been conceived as the platform for requesting a benevolence. Who might have been proposing such a course at this time is uncertain, not least because the hand in which the marginal annotations were made has not been identified; but it was certainly in keeping with the advice given earlier by hardliners, and it tends to bear out the fears of contemporaries that there were those about the king who were continually looking for alternatives to supply through parliament.[58]

Once the scope of the Commons' challenge to the prerogative became clear in mid-April, several observers, notably Nethersole and the Venetian ambassador, were convinced that Buckingham, and 'his followers', had once more changed tack and were doing their best to 'break' the parliament. Evidence of the division which still existed in the council was provided in a series of marginal comments by Laud on Rudyerd's speech in the Commons on 28 April. This was part of a concerted initiative from the moderates to keep the parliament going by persuading the Commons to accept the assurances in Coventry's speech earlier in the day. Rudyerd set out to sell this on the grounds that it would pave the way for regular parliaments, something which clearly did not appeal to Laud.[59] Where Rudyerd urged the Commons to 'keep parliaments on foot, for as long as they be frequent there will be no irregular power', Laud noted with obvious disapproval 'the ayme for frequent parliaments' and 'the end of that to make the other power (which he calls irregular) to moulder awaye'. Elsewhere he referred disparagingly to Rudyerd's 'censure of the power used about the loanes'. And when Rudyerd rehearsed the restrictions on the prerogative already secured by the Commons he commented 'Hear's the true ende of deliberations in the lower house'.[60] These were indications that Laud continued to see the Commons' actions as aimed at reducing royal

[57] Cust, 'A draft Declaration', 150, 161.
[58] Cust, *Forced Loan*, 77, 79–80; *Cal. State Papers Venetian 1628–9*, 10, 21, 85; *Proceedings in Parliament 1628*, VI. 175, 189.
[59] *Proceedings in Parliament 1628*, III. 126–9.
[60] P. R. O., S. P. 16/102/43.

power, whilst himself remaining committed to the king's right to tax without the subject's consent. This is not surprising, but it is significant that he should be expressing such views at this point in the parliament and in direct contradiction to the line being pursued by moderate councillors.

The most significant aspect of the draft, however, was the indication that the king's thoughts were moving along the same lines as Laud's. It was similar in form and content to a series of declarations issued in Charles's name to justify dissolving parliaments in 1626, 1629 and 1640. The king does not appear to have drawn these up himself, but relied on trusted advisers who had to try to reflect and anticipate his views and produce a document which he would be happy to approve. Since the last section of the draft provided the text for the letter which Charles sent to the House of Lords on 12 May, it would seem that Heath was successful in this.[61] It is therefore reasonable to use the draft as evidence for the king's views; and here it is very revealing because it suggests that Charles was becoming much more alarmed than previously about the activities of 'ill-affected' MPs in the House of Commons. Whereas in 1625 and 1626 these were described as being motivated by a personal grudge against Buckingham, now they were seen as hostile to monarchy itself. In a striking passage the draft described how 'some of the members of that house, blinded with a popular applause, have under the specious shewe of redeeminge the libertye of the subject indevoured to destroye our just powre of soveraignty'. Moreover, it appeared that these MPs had succeeded in misleading the moderate majority so that the Commons as a whole were now backing resolutions which 'would soe undermine our sov-eraigntye and regall power that we should therby be deprived of means to governe and protect our people'.[62] The references to 'popularity' and anti-monarchical tendencies in the Commons chimed in with the familiar council analysis of the breakdown of parliaments. Once the king accepted this, the obvious course open to him was to order a dissolution and try to raise money some other way.

But the parliament was not dissolved. Instead on 12 May the Lord Keeper made it clear that it would be allowed to continue and the council reverted to its strategy of blocking the resolution over imprisonment in the Lords.[63] Unfortunately there is little evidence for the reasoning behind this decision; however, like most of the council's deliberations in this period it was plainly overshadowed by the need for cash for the Rochelle fleet. This had finally set sail on 27 April and during the first week of May was outside La Rochelle trying to break into the harbour. Early reports persuaded the king and council that it had succeeded. In this case there was an urgent need for reinforcements to consolidate the gains made, and once more any analysis of the financial options would have made it clear that sufficient cash could only be raised quickly through parliamentary subsidies.[64]

The financial arguments for continuing to bargain with the subject were reinforced by councillors' inclinations to go on seeking co-operation and unity. At this stage in the parliament Pembroke appears to have been the most determined exponent of this line, although typically his views emerge not from his own statements, but from those of his clients. Rudyerd's speech on 28 April was a classic expression of this; so too was a remarkable open letter sent to the Commons on the same day by Bishop Hall. It urged them not to 'fear to trust a good king' and reiterated Rudyerd's theme of the importance of securing future parliaments: 'Certainly while parliaments live we need not misdoubt the like violation of our freedom and rights.' This concern for regular assemblies and the subject's liberties had been a theme of moderate councillors in the debates which had preceded the summons of parliament.[65] It presumably remained an important factor in the internal discussions of early May.

There was also a feeling amongst councillors that the Commons could still be persuaded to listen to reason. On 5 May, in a letter to his fellow councillor, the earl of Carlisle, Secretary Conway referred to 'the feares and jealousies of a breach', but at the same time stressed 'the moderacon and discreet proceedings of the House of Commons'. In another letter of 10 May he was even more upbeat, anticipating that the Commons would accept the Lords' amendments to the Petition of Right and that everything would be settled on the following Monday.[66] Coming from a man who had given up hope during the 1626 Parliament, this was a significant assessment.[67] It suggested most councillors had not yet reached the point where exasperation with the Commons overrode the inclination to seek co-operation. In these circumstances they were able to overcome the pressures working towards a dissolution and keep the parliament going.

Once a decision had been taken to continue with the parliament the crown found itself locked in to making considerable concessions. As

[64] Ibid., VI. 176; Cal. State Papers Dom. 1628–9, 120.
[65] Proceedings in Parliament 1628, III. 125–6n. Rudyerd's speech and Hall's letter, were quickly in circulation as 'separates'; ibid., VI. 185.
[66] P. R. O., S. P. 77/19, fos. 181–2.
[67] Cust, Forced Loan, 30–1, 45, 77.

Russell and others have shown, the policy of rallying support in the Lords to defend the prerogative failed, not because of any lack of sympathy for the king's case, but because Charles and Buckingham had been unable to maintain good relations with the nobility. When it became clear that a majority of peers would rather accept the Petition of Right than break off discussions with the Commons, the council conceded and gave it their blessing on 26 May.[68] Charles then attempted to remove what he saw as its most damaging implications by subterfuge. After consulting the judges and meeting with the council to draft a range of answers, on 2 June he delivered the least satisfactory of these, a simple declaration that 'right be done according to the laws and customs of the realm' without reference to the Petition. The Commons were outraged and abandoned their earlier self-restraint to begin drawing up a Remonstrance which named Buckingham as 'the cause of all our miseries'.[69] Once more the outcome of the parliament was thrown into doubt. On the afternoon of 5 June the king and council held a six-hour discussion about whether to dissolve the parliament there and then; but again the decision was taken to continue and on 7 June Charles gave his consent to the Petition in terms which satisfied the Commons.[70]

Given his earlier stance, the king's acceptance of the Commons' demands and his tolerance of the proceedings against Buckingham were remarkable. But he had little choice if he wanted to continue the war against France, and this had clearly become an overriding priority. He interpreted the fleet's failure to breach the French defences as a personal disgrace and on 18 May decided that it must return to La Rochelle immediately.[71] Secretary Coke was sent to Portsmouth to supervise the re-equipping. Almost as soon as he got there, he began bombarding the council with requests for money, to repair ships, provide victuals and pay the deserting seamen. Later in the month when it was decided to wait until the fleet was equipped with fireships, more money was needed to pay for these. And from early June the council faced the added complication that unless it could find money to pay for billeting of soldiers, they would be turned out of their

[68] Russell, *Parliaments and English Politics*, 371–4. I prefer Russell's account of these events to the reinterpretation in Flemion, 'A Savings to Satisfy All', 27–44. Flemion is unable to present any positive evidence prior to the passage of the Petition of Right that the king and council believed that the prerogative would remain untouched by it. On the contrary they continued to argue that it would be a very damaging concession. See, for example, the speeches by Dorset and Buckingham on 24 May: *Proceedings in Parliament 1628*, V 522–6; or the private reaction of the earl of Banbury: P. R. O., S. P. 16/107/89.

[69] Gardiner, *History of England*, VI. 297–306.

[70] *Proceedings in Parliament 1628*, VI. 195; Gardiner, *History of England*, VI. 309.

[71] Gardiner, *History of England*, VI. 291–3.

quarters and dispersed.[72] As was clear from the letters of Buckingham and Conway at this time, everything had to wait on parliament's grant.[73] It was finally completed on 16 June, but such was the council's desperation that it had already begun to spend the money.[74] In the last analysis, then, it was the need for cash which kept the parliament going to its logical conclusion.

During the final phase some of the tension eased as it appeared that everyone was getting more or less what they wanted: Charles received his subsidies; the Commons got the Petition of Right and were allowed to proceed with their Remonstrance; Buckingham and Laud were protected by the king; and the moderate councillors laid some of the foundations for working with future parliaments. But this appearance was deceptive because at the end of the parliament Charles effectively cut himself loose from the moderating influences in council and undercut the concessions granted to the Commons.

The hopes of the moderates were raised by progress over Arminianism and an apparent softening in the attitude of their council opponents. Religious doctrine surfaced as an issue in mid-June. This might have been expected to happen as a result of the case against the Arminian, Richard Montague, which finally emerged from committee on 11 June; but there was insufficient time for John Pym to formulate charges against him before the parliament was prorogued on 26 June.[75] Instead it was the Remonstrance against Buckingham—with its charge that Laud and Neile were 'unsound in their opinions' and favourers of Arminianism—which brought doctrine to the fore.[76] Perhaps the most significant contribution to the debate on this was a statement in the Commons by Pembroke's client, Sir Humphrey May, that in these matters 'the king's hert is right set ... no man shall be preferred by him that is a papist or an Arminian. He hates them both and you shall find that he hates them.'[77] This was intended to draw the Commons away from religion, but it also clearly invited a repudiation of Arminianism by the king. This came a few days later, in a full council meeting, when Charles was moved to declare that 'he did utterly dislike

[72] *Acts of the Privy Council 1627–8*, 429, 451, 473, 484, 490–1, 504; *Cal. State Papers Dom 1628–9*, 116, 135, 138, 140, 148–50; Young, *Servility and Service*, 194–6; Historical Manuscripts Commn., *MSS of Earl Cowper*, 4 vols. (1888–90), I, 346–7.

[73] P. R. O., S. P. 16/106/71; H. M. C., *Cowper*, I. 347; see also, *Acts of the Privy Council 1627–8*, 481.

[74] P. R. O., S. P. 16/106/71.

[75] Tyacke, *Anti-Calvinists*, 160, 180.

[76] *Proceedings in Parliament 1628*, IV. 313.

[77] *Ibid.*, IV. 243.

these novelties', whilst Laud and Neile, 'on their knees with tears in their eyes ... [did] absolutely disavow and protest that they did renounce the opinions of Arminius'.[78] This was probably as much as Calvinist councillors could hope for in the short time that was available to them. It showed the value of pushing forward moderate Calvinists, such as Bishop Hall, and also prepared the ground for the reinstatement of Archbishop Abbot and the condemnation of Montague's *Apello Caesarem* prior to the 1629 Parliament.[79]

Moderate councillors were also prominent in efforts to head off the Commons' attack on Buckingham. Led by May and Rudyerd, a group of courtiers and officeholders were successful in persuading the House to abandon its plan to revive impeachment proceedings.[80] This paid dividends in that during the latter stages, and in the weeks which followed up to his assassination, Buckingham showed every sign of being willing to work with parliaments in the future.[81] A draft reply to the Remonstrance, drawn up on the king's behalf by Laud, also anticipated future assemblies. This contained predictable complaints that the Commons had failed to provide the king with enough money and encroached on the prerogative; but in contrast to Heath's draft Declaration it saw these faults as in the past. The conduct of the present Commons, except insofar as it had attacked Buckingham, was relatively responsible, so much so that the king was made to declare that we 'would be glad hereafter to see such moderate parliaments that we may love them and make them more frequent.'[82] This was Laud at his most politic and restrained, writing to a brief. Even so it was evidence of a mood at the centre of government which was favourable to parliaments.

Part of the reason for the king's confidence in his ability to work with parliaments became alarmingly apparent during the final stages. Once the subsidies were in the bag he seems to have felt he had got

[78] *Commons Debates for 1629*, ed. W. Notestein and F. H. Relf (Minneapolis, 1921), 35, 122.

[79] *Court and Times*, I. 429, 449, 451; P. R. O., S. P. 16/118/33; *Stuart Royal Proclamations*, 2 vols., eds. P. L. Hughes and J. F. Larkin (Oxford, 1973–83), II. 218–20. See in particular John Pory's report of a council meeting in November 1628 at which the king agreed to condemn any Arminian doctrines which did not conform to the 'Book of Articles', something which Pembroke immediately endorsed: *Court and Times*, I. 429.

[80] *Proceedings in parliament 1628*, IV. 245–51, 320; Gardiner, *History of England*, VI. 315; P. R. O., S. P. 16/108/71.

[81] See in particular Buckingham's speech in the Lords on 16 June playing down the significance of a commission to raise extra-parliamentary taxes: *Proceedings in Parliament 1628*, V. 648–9. On Buckingham's preparations for future parliaments, see R. Lockyer, *Buckingham* (1981), 448–9.

[82] *Proceedings in Parliament 1628*, VI. 52–6. A copy of this in state papers is endorsed by Laud, 'This I made by the king's command who then had a purpose to publish it in print ... Who altered the king's mind in this god knowes.': P. R. O., S. P. 16/108/67.

what he wanted and could backtrack on some of the undertakings he had made earlier. He also reverted to a style of dealing with the Commons which was as grating as anything that had gone before. When they presented their Remonstrance, he effectively told them to mind their own business and not interfere with matters which did not concern them. And, in a gesture which was just as disturbing to the Commons, he gave Buckingham his hand to kiss in public.[83] In addition he resorted to his characteristic expedient of resisting attacks on his servants by taking responsibility for their actions onto himself. This was the main theme of Laud's draft reply to the Remonstrance; and the same approach was used to curtail a Commons' enquiry into Sir Edmund Sawyer's proposals for doubling customs rates. This might be effective in the short term, but ultimately it threatened to expose the king himself to the criticisms normally reserved for 'evil counsellors'.[84]

The most disturbing development, however, was the king's attitude to the Petition of Right. His closing speech on 26 June reprimanded those who 'made a false interpretation of my answer to your petition', reminding them that 'my meaning was not to grant any new privileges, but to re-edify your old'.[85] This was applied at the time to those trying to prevent him collecting tonnage and poundage; but the interpretation also had a more general significance, as became clear a few days later. Initially Charles had agreed to allow the petition to be printed and circulated with only the second answer attached, the one which the Commons found acceptable. But on 29 June, apparently without consulting the council, he sent an order to Heath to call in the 1500 copies already printed, 'to be made waste paper'. He then commissioned a second printing which contained his first, unsatisfactory, answer, a series of qualifications to the second answer—saying that parliament could not hurt his prerogative—and his closing speech.[86] In doing this Charles appeared, in Russell's words 'to withdraw all the concessions he made between 2 June and 7 June ... Liberties instead of resting on a secure foundation of law again rested on the king's gracious willingness to execute the law.'[87] No wonder Charles was ready to contemplate the prospect of another parliament. This one had, in effect, given him the subsidies he wanted without damaging the prerogative or seriously threatening his favourite.

[83] Proceedings in Parliament 1628, IV. 352–3; Court and Times, I. 366.

[84] Proceedings in Parliament 1628, VI. 52–6, IV. 393, 406, 408–9. For a discussion of the effects of Charles' habit, see Cust, Forced Loan, 88–9.

[85] Proceedings in Parliament 1628, IV. 482.

[86] E. R. Forster, 'The printing of the Petition of Right', Huntington Library Quarterly, xxviii (1974), 81–3.

[87] Russell, Parliaments and English Politics, 401–2.

Charles' actions brought the parliament to an end on a note of uncertainty. From the point of view of rebuilding good relations with the subject, there were a number of hopeful signs: the Commons had actually completed a grant of supply which at the outset had seemed unlikely; the issue of whether or not the king could raise taxes without parliament's consent had apparently been laid to rest; some progress had been made over the issue of Arminianism; and, not least, Buckingham had shown that in spite of attacks on him, he was still willing to work with parliaments. He seems to have been convinced that he could repeat his success of 1624 and win back the affections of the people.[88] Whilst he remained this at least gave the moderates scope to put the case for regular meetings. However, there were also some disturbing developments in the growing row over tonnage and poundage and the differences in interpretation of the Petition of Right. As far as the future of parliaments was concerned then, 1628 did not settle things in the way many had expected; but it did provide important pointers to the underlying themes and direction of royal policy.

The first of these was the evidence of the crown's need for parliamentary supply in wartime. The council's deliberations, before and during the parliament, indicated that relying on alternatives, such as the forced loan, was simply not feasible. It was not just because these now appeared politically unworkable; subsidies also provided what one of the crown's leading creditors described as a 'perfect security'. Unlike other sources of taxation, they could be used to raise loans and credits as soon as they had been granted, which was particularly valuable when it came to equipping foreign expeditions like the Rochelle fleet.[89] Whilst the war continued then, there was little doubt that seeking supply through parliament would remain the crown's first option.

One of the effects of this was enormously to enhance the bargaining power of the House of Commons. As Cogswell has recently stressed, the argument put forward by Russell, that the Commons was ineffective in using the weapon of withholding supply, is highly questionable.[90] It is not really relevant that Charles reneged on his undertakings at the end of the meeting. During the parliament the Commons and the crown both behaved as if the Petition of Right represented an effective means of redressing grievances and curbing the royal prerogative; and the crown found itself forced into abandoning one defensive position after another. Admittedly Charles' circumstances in 1628, with the

---

[88] Lockyer, *Buckingham*, 180–1, 448–9, 474.

[89] P. R. O., S. P. 16/8/26; 16/106/71; Cust, *Forced Loan*, 15. This point was made by Secretary Coke in the Commons on 2 April: *Proceedings in Parliament 1628*, II. 246.

[90] Cogswell, 'A low road to extinction', 283–303.

clock ticking on his efforts to relieve La Rochelle, were particularly pressing. But such circumstances were not unknown in time of war; and, as again became apparent in 1640–41, they provided excellent opportunities for the Commons to get what it wanted.

Financial considerations were, however, not the only ones to shape royal policy in this period. Just as much depended on the attitude of the king. It was this which usually determined the range of options open to councillors at any particular moment. Here they key was the struggle by the moderates to persuade Charles that the parliament could be made to work. His basic instinct, fortified by the hardliners, was to distrust the Commons and concede as little as possible. But contrary to what has sometimes been argued, Charles did listen to advice and was open to persuasion.[91] In this respect the moderates' handling of him in the tricky first phase of the parliament was a model of how to proceed. The flow of information about what was happening in the Commons was carefully controlled and the king was nudged into making timely concessions by councillors like Sir John Coke, who were adept at reading their master's moods. The problem for the moderates was that the amount of control they could exercise over either the king or the Commons was limited. Thus during the second phase of the parliament, when in spite of their promptings the House refused to compromise over imprisonment, they could not prevent Charles taking offence and undoing much of their earlier good work. In the latter stages it is less easy to discern the pattern of political manoeuvring around the king; but such evidence as there is suggests that the moderates achieved considerable success in persuading the king to make concessions and persevere with the parliament. However, there remained the difficulty, which Russell has emphasised, that although Charles was willing to be counselled over means, he could not be persuaded to alter his ends.[92] In retrospect it appears doubtful whether he ever really intended to abide by the terms of the Petition of Right; and it was this which finally undermined the moderates' efforts to make this parliament the basis for a lasting settlement.

The plight of the moderate councillors, having constantly to work against the grain of Charles' basic political instincts, was perhaps best exemplified by the earl of Pembroke. S. R. Gardiner has cast Pembroke as the Hamlet of early-Stuart politics, someone who was too hesitant and indecisive to be really effective.[93] But this is to overlook the

[91] C. S. R. Russell, *The Causes of the English Civil War* (Oxford, 1990), 189–90.

[92] *Ibid.*, 194–5.

[93] Gardiner, *History of England*, VII, 133. This is not to argue that Pembroke was anything other than a very cautious politician, simply that this was generally the best way he could operate effectively. For some perceptive comments on Pembroke in 1624, see T. E. Cogswell, *The Blessed Revolution* (Cambridge, 1989), 154–6; *idem.*, 'Thomas

problems which he faced. To have any real impact on high politics the earl had to operate within the constraints of what was acceptable to the king. This was always going to be difficult because his views on policy were fundamentally at odds with those of Charles. Moreover, he had been slapped down hard after the attempted impeachment of Buckingham in 1626, and forced to keep a low profile, and surrender much of his local influence, as the price for retaining favour. A new summons of parliament provided Pembroke with the opportunity to mobilise his substantial following in the Commons and reassert himself; but he had to play his hand carefully.[94] This was not the moment to press for the removal of the duke or a war effort against Spain; so instead he concentrated on ensuring future parliaments and suppressing Arminianism. Although his own actions were often rather shadowy, the initiatives taken by his clients—Rudyerd, Bishop Hall and Sir Humphrey May—are clear enough, and made a substantial contribution to the moderates' successes during the parliament. Like Secretary Dorchester in the period 1629–1632[95], Pembroke showed that, in spite of Charles' inclinations, it was possible to make progress towards reinstating the pro-Calvinist/pro-parliament policies which had provided the keynote under Elizabeth and James. But this required considerable political skill, above all in judging when and how to push a particular line and when to concede and give ground.

For councillors like Pembroke and Dorchester, opportunities for influencing policy were closely linked to the prospects for parliament. Indeed the whole moderate strategy for reconciling differences between king and subject depended on regular meetings of parliament. It was therefore particularly disturbing that during 1628 the notion that elements in the Commons were involved in a 'popular' assault on monarchy resurfaced in council debate. Sir Robert Phelips indicated the consequences when he warned the Commons that 'Nothing so endangers us with his majesty as that opinion that we are anti-monarchically affected.'[96] Once the idea had been revived it remained an important factor in council discussions. The parliament was due to reassemble in the autumn, but opinion was divided over whether this was advisable. According to Dorchester, some councillors wanted another meeting straightaway, because of 'a presumed desire the parlement will have to make appeare by theyr faire and moderat

Middleton and the Court in 1624: A Game at Chess in context', *Hunt. Lib. Quart.*, xlviii (1984), 275–6.

[94] Cust, *Forced Loan*, 26–7, 73–5; V. Rowe, 'The influence of the Earls of Pembroke on parliamentary elections, 1625–49', *English Historical Review*, L (1935), 242–56; Russell, *Parliaments and English Politics*, 12–14, 16.

[95] L.J. Reeve, *Charles I and the Road to Personal Rule* (Cambridge, 1989), chaps. 4–8.

[96] *Proceedings in Parliament 1628*, II. 432.

proceeding, the former distempers were rather personal than real'; but others urged postponement on the grounds that Buckingham's assassination had stirred up a potential for popular unrest which must be given time to settle before parliament could be trusted to behave itself.[97] In the event the meeting was put back to January. John Reeve's study of the road to personal rule shows that similar considerations came to the fore after the dissolution of 1629. A climate of opinion was created at court in which even moderate councillors came to adopt the rhetoric of 'popularity' and it became that much harder to argue for a re-summons. It was out of this, Reeve argues, that the policy of rule without parliament developed, by default rather than from any positive, deliberate decision.[98]

Ultimately, of course, it was the king's attitude which more than anything would determine the future for parliaments. In this case we are dealing with something which historians have found elusive; but again this study offers some useful pointers. It suggests that Charles was not opposed to parliaments in principle. His fulsomely expressed feelings of love for them on 4 April were probably rather short-lived. Nonetheless he appears to have been a firm believer in the tradition whereby English kings met with their people and engaged in acts of bargaining and mutual co-operation. The problem was that he also expected them to operate on his terms and display a suitably docile and submissive attitude. When they did not, he began to suspect them of all sorts of disloyal and subversive intentions.[99] In 1626 he spoke of these as being restricted to a few MPs with a grudge against Buckingham.[100] By 1628, however, after experiencing the prolonged disobedience of taxpayers during the forced loan and the Commons' unyielding determination to push through its resolution on imprisonment, he appears to have regarded them in a more sinister light. If Heath's draft Declaration is anything to go by, he was now willing to accept that the House of Commons was in the grip of a group of populist MPs whose aim was to destroy monarchy itself. This was not a settled or permanent conviction, otherwise it would be hard to explain the sympathetic interpretation of the Commons' actions in the draft reply to the Remonstrance, or indeed the summons of the 1629 Parliament. The Commons could still redeem themselves in Charles' eyes if they behaved the right way. However, as a result of their actions in 1628, it became that much harder to convince him of their fundamental loyalty; and his doubts on this score were amply confirmed

[97] P. R. O., S. P. 99/36. fos. 180–1.
[98] Reeve, *Charles I and the Road to Personal Rule*, chaps. 4–8.
[99] Cust, 'A draft Declaration', 143–61. For a different emphasis, see Russell, *Causes of the English Civil War*, 202–3.
[100] Cust, *Forced Loan*, 326–7.

by their conduct in 1629. Prolonged exposure to the Commons in 1628 then, helped to impress on Charles just how dangerous for royal power regular meetings with parliament could be. In many respects this was as significant a legacy of the assembly as the Petition of Right.

IMPROVISED GENOCIDE? THE EMERGENCE OF THE 'FINAL SOLUTION' IN THE 'WARTHEGAU'[1]

by Ian Kershaw

READ I MARCH 1991

THE 'Warthegau'—officially the 'Reichsgau Wartheland', with its capital in Posen (Poznan)—was the largest of three areas of western Poland[2] annexed to the German Reich after the defeat of Poland in 1939. In the genesis of the 'Final Solution' it plays a pivotal role. Some of the first major deportations of Jews took place from the Warthegau. The first big ghetto was established on the territory of the Warthegau, at Lodz (which the Nazis renamed Litzmannstadt). In autumn 1941, the first German Jews to be deported at the spearhead of the combing-out process of European Jewry were dispatched to the Warthegau. The possibility of liquidating ghettoised Jews had by then already been explicitly raised for the first time, in the summer of 1941, significantly by Nazi leaders in the Warthegau. The first mobile gassing units to be deployed against the Jews operated in the Warthegau in the closing months of 1941. And the systematic murder of the Jews began in early December 1941 in the first extermination camp—actually a 'gas van station'[3]—established at Chelmno on the Ner, in the Warthegau.

Despite the centrality of the Warthegau to the unfolding of what the

[1] I would like to express my warmest thanks and appreciation to the following for their most helpful contributions to the research for this article: Christopher Browning, Philippe Burrin, Lucjan Dobroszycki, Gerald Fleming, Czesław Madajczyk, Stanisław Nawrocki, Karol Marian Pospieszalski, and the staffs of the Archiwum Państwowe Poznań, the Berlin Document Center, the Główna Komissa Badni Zbrodni Hitlerowskich w Polsce Archiwum Warsaw, the Instytut Zachodni in Poznań, and the Zentrale Stelle der Landesjustizverwaltungen, Ludwigsburg. I owe grateful thanks, too, to the British Academy and the Polish Academy of Sciences for their generous joint support of the research I undertook in Poznań and Warsaw in September 1989.

[2] The others were West Prussia and part of Upper Silesia. In addition, in the north of Poland substantial tracts of territory were added to the existing German province of East Prussia. In each of the incorporated territories (least in Gau Danzig-Westpreußen, most by far in the Warthegau), the new boundaries included areas which had never hitherto belonged to Prussia/Germany. See Martin Broszat, *Nationalsozialistische Polenpolitik 1939 1945* (Frankfurt am Main, 1965), 36–41; Czesław Madajczyk, *Die Okkupationspolitik Nazideutschlands in Polen 1939–1945* (Berlin, 1987), 30–6.

[3] *Der Mord an den Juden im Zweiten Weltkrieg*, eds. Eberhard Jäckel and Jürgen Rohwer (Stuttgart, 1985), 145.

Nazis called 'the Final Solution of the Jewish Question'—the systematic attempt to exterminate the whole of European Jewry—the precise course of development of Nazi anti-Jewish policy in the Warthegau, though mentioned in every account of the origins of the 'Final Solution', has not been exhaustively explored.[4]

To focus upon the Warthegau in the genesis of the 'Final Solution' can, however, help to contribute towards answering the central questions which have come to dominate scholarly debate on the emergence of systematic genocide: how and when the decision to wipe out the Jews of Europe came about, whether at the moment of German triumph in mid-summer 1941, or later in the year when the growing probability of prolonged war in the east ruled out an envisaged 'territorial solution'; Hitler's own role in the shift to a policy of outright genocide; and whether the 'Final Solution' followed a single order or set of directives issued from Berlin as the culmination of a long-held 'programme' of the Nazi leadership, or unfolded in haphazard and piecemeal fashion, instigated by 'local initiatives' of regional Nazi bosses, improvised as a largely ad hoc response to the logistical difficulties of a 'Jewish problem' they had created for themselves, and only gradually congealing into a full-scale 'programme' for genocide.[5]

The deficiencies and ambiguities of the evidence, enhanced by the language of euphemism and camouflage used by the Nazis even among themselves when dealing with the extermination of the Jews, mean that absolute certainty in answering these complex questions can not be achieved. Close assessment of the Warthegau evidence, it is the contention of this essay, nevertheless sheds light on developments and contributes towards an interpretation which rests on the balance of probabilities.

When the rapidly improvised boundaries of the newly created Reichsgau Posen (from 29 January 1940 Reichsgau Wartheland or, for short, the Warthegau—taking its name from the Warthe, the central river of the province) were eventually settled, they included an extensive area centring upon the large industrial town of Lodz, which had formerly been in Congress Poland and had never been part of Prussian

---

[4] Two essays appeared in Polish in the 1970s, but before much recent scholarly literature on the genesis of the 'Final Solution': Julian Leszczyński, 'Z dziejów zagłady Żydów w Kraju Warty: Szkice do genezy ludóbojstwa hitlerowskiego', *Biuletyn Żydowskiego Instytutu Historycznego* 82 (1972), 57–72; and Artur Eisenbach, 'O należyte zrozumienie genezy zagłady Zydów', *ibid.* 104 (1977), 55–69.

[5] For summaries and evaluations of the debate, see: Saul Friedländer, 'From Anti-Semitism to Extermination', *Yad Vashem Studies* 16 (1984), 1–50. Michael Marrus, *The Holocaust in History* (1988), chap. 2, and Ian Kershaw, *The Nazi Dictatorship. Problems and Perspectives of Interpretation* (3rd edn., 1993), chap. 5.

Poland.[6] The borders of the Reich were thereby extended some 150–200 kilometres eastwards of the boundaries existing before 1918. For Nazi aims at 'solving the Jewish Question', the significance of this extension was that it brought within the territory of the Warthegau—which was to be ruthlessly germanised—an area containing over 350,000 Jews (some 8% of the total population of the region). The most important figures in the Warthegau scene after 1939 were Arthur Greiser, Reich Governor and at the same time Gauleiter of the Nazi Party, and Wilhelm Koppe, the SS and police chief of the region. Greiser, born in the Posen province in 1897, was utterly ruthless and single-minded in his determination to make his region the 'model Gau' of Nazi rule.[7] He called upon a 'special commission', given to him by Hitler personally, whenever he encountered difficulties or obstructions.[8] He also stood high in Himmler's favour, and was given on 30 January 1942 the honorary rank of Obergruppenführer in the SS.[9] Koppe, born in Hildesheim in 1896, nominally subordinate to Greiser but in practice possessing a high degree of independence as the leading SS functionary in the region, had effective control over deportation policy in the Warthegau.[10] He was well up in Himmler's good books and had the ready ear of the Reichsführer-SS. At the same date as Greiser's promotion within the SS, 30 January 1942 and precisely at the point when the killing of the Warthegau Jews had begun, Koppe was

[6] Broszat, *Polenpolitik*, 37–8.
[7] I have contributed a brief character sketch of Greiser to the forthcoming second volume of Ronald Smelser, Enrico Syring, and Rainer Zitelmann (eds.), *Die braune Elite und ihre Helfer*. A character description by the prosecution counsel at Greiser's trial can be found in Zentrale Stelle der Landesjustizverwaltungen, Ludwigsburg (= ZSL), Anklageschrift aus dem Prozeß gegen Arthur Greiser, German translation (= Prozeß Greiser), Bl. 74–82. (A copy of the Polish text is in Polen-365h, Bl. 677–828).
[8] See, for example, Główna Komisa Badania Zbrodni Hitlerowskich w Polsce (= GK), (Archive of the Central Commission for the Investigation of Hitlerite Crimes in Poland, Ministry of Justice, Warsaw), Process Artura Greisera (= PAG), vol. 11, Bl. 52; and see also the comment by Carl J. Burckhardt, *Meine Danziger Mission* (Munich, 1962), 79.
[9] Berlin Document Center (= BDC), Personalakte (= PA) Arthur Greiser, unfoliated, Führer decree awarding the promotion, 30 Jan. 1942. Greiser's telegram to Himmler of the same date, thanking the Reichsführer-SS for his nomination to Hitler, stated that 'I am at your disposal at all times and without reservation in all my areas of work'.
[10] Directly on Koppe, there is Szymon Datner, *Wilhelm Koppe—nie ukarany zbrodniarz hitlerowski* (Warsaw, 1963). Koppe figures prominently in Ruth Bettina Birn, *Die Höheren SS- und Polizeiführer. Himmlers Vertreter im Reich und in den besetzten Gebieten* (Düsseldorf, 1986). There is much valuable information on him in his personal file in the BDC. His trial indictment, ZSL, Landgericht Bonn 8 Js 52/60, Anklageschrift gegen Wilhelm Koppe wegen Beihilfe zum Mord (= Prozeß Koppe), Bl. 49–55, summarises his career and personality. He was said to have been unbureaucratic and unconventional in his work-style—'ruling through the telephone', as one witness put it—and to have combined a propensity for unfolding new, sometimes fantastic, schemes, with pedantic attention to detail. *Ibid.*, Bl. 54.

promoted by Himmler to the rank of SS-Obergruppenführer and General der Polizei.[11] Like Greiser, he was notorious for his cold ruthlessness.

The tone for the administration of Poland was provided by Hitler himself. Admiral Canaris pointed out to General Keitel on 12 September 1939 that he had knowledge that extensive executions (Füsilierungen) were planned for Poland 'and that the nobility and clergy especially were to be exterminated (ausgerottet)'. Keitel replied that this had already been decided by the Führer. The Wehrmacht had to accept the 'racial extermination' and 'political cleansing' by the SS and the Gestapo, even if it did not itself want anything to do with it. That was why, alongside the military commanders, civilian commanders were being appointed, to whom the 'racial extermination' (Volkstums-Ausrottung) would fall.[12] On 17 October, Hitler spoke to a small group of those leaders most directly concerned of a 'hard racial struggle' which did not allow any 'legal constraints' or comply with principles otherwise upheld. The new Reich territories would have to be purged 'of Jews, Polacks, and rabble', and the remainder of the former Poland (the Generalgouvernement) would serve as the dumping ground for such groups of the population.[13] Hitler was involved at an early stage in schemes for a 'solution' to the 'Jewish Question' in Poland, though the ideas themselves emanated from Himmler (presumably in close collaboration with chief of the Security Police Reinhard Heydrich). At a meeting on 14 September 1939, Heydrich explained his own views on the 'Jewish problem' in Poland to the assembled Security Police leaders, adding that suggestions from the Reichsführer were being placed before Hitler, 'which only the Führer could decide'.[14] These were presumably the suggestions which became incorporated in Heydrich's directions to leaders of the Einsatzgruppen on 21 September 1939 for the concentration of Jews in the larger towns as a preparatory measure for a subsequent 'final goal' (to be kept 'strictly secret').[15] The 'final goal' was at this time evidently the eventual deportation of the Jews from Reich territory and from Poland to the intended reservation east of the Vistula, as Hitler himself indicated on 29 September to Alfred Rosenberg.[16] Hitler's views accorded precisely with guidelines which

[11] BDC, PA Koppe, unfoliated, effusive handwritten letter of thanks to Himmler for the latter's good wishes on his promotion, 5 Feb. 1942. The headed notepaper already bore Koppe's new grade, which had been bestowed on him only a week earlier.
[12] Broszat, *Polenpolitik*, p 20.
[13] *Ibid.*, 25.
[14] ZSL, Verschiedenes, 301 Ar., Bl. 32.
[15] ZSL, Polen 365n, Bl. 635-9. Printed in Broszat, *Polenpolitik*, 21.
[16] Hans-Günther Seraphim, *Das politische Tagebuch Alfred Rosenbergs 1934/35 und 1939/40* (Munich, 1964), 99.

Heydrich drew up on that same day. The intention was to create a type of 'Reich Ghetto' to the east of Warsaw and around Lublin 'in which all the political and Jewish elements, who are to be moved out of the future German Gaue, will be accommodated'.[17] The plans for Poland, as they were gradually congealing in September and early October 1939, amounted, therefore, to a three-fold division: of those parts to be incorporated into the Reich and eventually wholly Germanised, and sealed off by an eastern fortification; of a German-run 'foreign-speaking Gau' under Hans Frank outside a proposed 'East Wall', centring on Cracow and coming to be called the 'General Government', as a type of buffer zone; and of a Jewish settlement to the east of this area, into which all Jews from Poland and Germany would be dumped.[18] The initial expectations, both of a Jewish reservation in the Lublin area and of the mass deportation of German Jews to the General Government rapidly, however, proved illusory. The organisational and administrative difficulties involved had been hopelessly underestimated. Eichmann's immediate attempt, in October 1939, to deport Vienna's Jews to the Lublin area was rapidly stopped.[19] And in the event, apart from small-scale deportations from Stettin and Schneidemühl in Pomerania to the Lublin area in February and March 1940—an SS 'initiative' which Frank's administration could not cope with, prompting a protest from the General Governor and a temporary ban announced by Göring on 24 March 1940 on deportation of Jews into Frank's domain[20]—Jews from the Altreich (Germany of the pre-1938 boundaries) were not deported to the east until autumn 1941.[21] From the measures for occupied Poland decided by the central Nazi leadership in September 19349, it can be seen that Hitler set the tone, and provided the ultimate authority for the brutality of racial policy; and that he had far-reaching but imprecise notions of future developments, drawing at least in part on policy initiatives suggested by Himmler, which rapidly proved unfeasible and impracticable. Precisely because Hitler's barbarous imperatives offered no more than broad but loosely

[17] ZSL, Verschiedenes, 301 Ar., Bl. 39–40.

[18] *Verfolgung, Vertreibung, Vernichtung. Dokumente des faschistischen Antisemitismus 1933 bis 1942* ed. Kurt Pätzold (Leipzig, 1983), 239–40.

[19] See Seev Goschen, 'Eichmann und die Nisko-Aktion im Oktober 1939', *Vierteljahrshefte für Zeitgeschichte* 29 (1981), 74–96; and Jonny Moser, 'Nisko, the First Experiment in Deportation', *Simon Wiesenthal Center Annual* 2 (1985), 1–30.

[20] Pätzold, 262.

[21] Some Jews were sent westwards in 1940. On 22–3 Oct. 1940, with Hitler's approval, 6,504 Jews from Baden and the Saarpfalz were deported into Vichy France. Hitler also authorised, at the prompting of von Schirach in October 1940, the deportation of Viennese Jews to Poland. These began in January 1941 but were stopped again in March. See Christopher Browning, 'Nazi Resettlement Policy and the Search for a Solution to the Jewish Question, 1939–1941', *German Studies Review*, IX (1986), 513.

formulated aims and sanction for action of the most brutal kind, they opened the door to the wildest initiatives from agencies of Party and State, and above all, of course, from the SS. The authorities on the spot in the Warthegau did not, in fact, reckon that they would have too much difficulty in tackling the 'Jewish Question', and consequently grossly underestimated the self-created logistical problems. The view prevailed that the real problem was Polish, not Jewish.[22] At the outset of the occupation, the Jews were seen by the Warthegau leadership as a sideshow.[23] The main issue in the Warthegau was thought to be less the 'Jewish' than the 'Polish question'.

Initially, it seemed that things were running more or less according to expectation. In his new capacity as Reich Commissar for the Strengthening of German Nationhood, under powers bestowed on him by Hitler on 7 October, Himmler on 30 October ordered all Jews to be cleared out of the incorporated territories in the months November 1939 to February 1940.[24] On the basis of the discussions on 8 November 1939 in Cracow, at which he was present, about 'the evacuation of Jews and Congress Poles from the Old Reich and from the Reich Gaue of Danzig, Posen' and other areas,[25] Koppe issued instructions on 12 November 1939 for the deportation from the Warthegau between 15 November 1939 and 28 February 1940 of, initially, 200,000 Poles and 100,000 Jews.[26] This appears to have been subjected to slight delay and an amendment of the numbers involved. For on 28 November, Heydrich ordered an initial 'short-term plan' (Nahplan) to deport 80,000 Jews and Poles from the Warthegau to the General Government

[22] A memorandum from the Reichsleitung of the Rassepolitisches Amt of 25 November 1939, for example, establishing guidelines for the treatment of the conquered population 'from a racial-political viewpoint', commented that the Jews in the rump of Poland (Restpolen) posed a less dangerous problem than the Poles themselves. 'The Jews here could certainly be given a freer hand than the Poles,' the memorandum ran, 'since the Jews have no real political force such as the Poles have with their Greater Polish ideology'. ZSL, Polen 365p, Bl. 449, 453.

[23] Already in November 1939, on a visit to Lodz, Greiser spoke of meeting 'figures who can scarcely be credited with the name "person"', but assured his audience that the 'Jewish Question' was no longer a pro blem and would be solved in the immediate future. GK, PAG, vol. 27, Bl. 167.

[24] Instytut Zachodni (= IZ), Poznań, I-441, Bl. 144.

[25] Institut für Zeitgeschichte, Munich (= IfZ), Eichmann 1458; and see Werner Präg and Wolfgang Jacobmeyer (eds.), *Das Diensttagebuch des deutschen Generalgouverneurs in Polen 1939–1945* (Stuttgart, 1975), (= DTB Frank), 6off. The Lodz Jews, however, the greatest number in what became the Warthegau, were not included in the first wave of deportees since it was at this stage not clear whether Lodz would belong to the Warthegau or *Generalgouvernement.*—Christopher Browning, 'Nazi Ghettoization Policy in Poland, *Central European History*, xix (1986), 346 and n.9.

[26] IZ, I-441, Bl. 145–9.

between the 1st and the 16th of December 1939 at a rate of 5,000 per day, to make way for 40,000 Baltic Germans.[27] These expulsions were immediately put into effect. Discussions with Eichmann in Berlin on 4 January 1940 then indicated the goal for the Warthegau as the deportations of 200,000 Jews and 80,000 Poles.[28] But at a meeting in Berlin on 30 January 1940, the first murmurings of complaint from the General Government about the number of expellees being deported from the Warthegau over the border could be registered.[29] By the time Koppe was forced to reply, in spring 1940, to the ever louder complaints, the total number of Jews and Poles deported had reached 128,011.[30]

By February 1940, deep divisions on deportation policy were apparent. While Himmler pressed for speedy deportation of Poles and Jews to make room for the planned influx of ethnic Germans into the annexed territories, Göring opposed the loss of manpower useful to the war effort and was backed by Frank, anxious to block the expanding numbers of expellees being forced into his domain.[31] In April, Greiser's request to deport the Warthegau Jews was deferred until the coming August.[32] But by the summer of that year it was plain that the intended deportations from the Warthegau into the General Government could not be carried out. An important meeting on the issue took place in Cracow on 31 July 1940.[33] Greiser emphasised at the meeting the growing difficulties in the Warthegau. He spoke of the 'massing' of Jews as the construction of a ghetto in Litzmannstadt (Lodz) had concentrated around 250,000 Jews there. This was, he declared, merely a provisional solution.[34] All these Jews had to leave the Warthegau,

[27] IfZ, Eichmann 1460.
[28] ZSL, Prozeß Koppe, Bl. 156. For deportation policy in general, see Robert Koehl, *RKFDV. German Resettlement and Population Policy 1939–1945* (Cambridge Mass., 1957). For the most reliable guide to the numbers of Poles expelled from the Warthegau under Nazi rule, see Madjczyk, *Okkupationspolitik*, appendix, Table 15.
[29] ZSL, Prozeß Koppe, Bl. 158.
[30] ZSL, Polen 179, Bl. 653–4. Koppe to Greiser (17 May 1940), enclosing a 'Stellungnahme' to the complaints, dated 20 April 1940, compiled by the Umwandererzentralstelle Posen. The expulsion figures (which do not differentiate between Jews and Poles) comprised 87,883 persons deported between 1 and 16 December 1939, and 40,128 from the 10 Feb. to 15 March 1940.
[31] Browning, 'Resettlement', 506.
[32] Browning, 'Ghettoisation.', 347.
[33] All following from DTB Frank, 261–4, entry for 31.7.40.
[34] DTB Frank, 261. Greiser had ordered the Lodz Jews to be ghettoised in December 1939 as an interim measure prior to their expulsion—he mentioned a figure of 'some 250,000'—'over the border'. The empty ghetto would then, he added, to burnt to the ground. BDC, PA Greiser, Besuchs-Vermerk/Akten-Vermerk, Stabsleiter of the Reichsschatzmeister, 11 Jan. 1940, Bl. 3. At the establishment of the ghetto, the Government President of Lodz, Dr. Friedrich Uebelhoer, proposed in a communication to party and police authorities dated 10 December 1939 a 'temporary' solution to the problem of Lodz's Jews (which he numbered at about 320,000). He emphasised that 'the

and it had been envisaged that they would be deported to the General Government. He had imagined that the modalities would be discussed at the meeting. But now a new decision—that is, to deport the Jews overseas, to Madagascar—had emerged. Clarification was crucial. The difficulties of feeding the Jews forced into the ghetto as well as the mounting problems of disease meant, he claimed, that they could not be kept there over the coming winter. A temporary solution had at all costs to be found which would allow for the deportation of these Jews into another territory. The Governor General, Hans Frank, reminded Greiser that Himmler had given him the assurance, on Hitler's command, that no more Jews were to be sent into the General Government. Koppe brought the discussion back to the looming crisis in the Warthegau. The position regarding the Jews was deteriorating daily, he claimed, repeating that the ghetto in Litzmannstadt had only been set up on the presumption that the deportation of the Jews concentrated there would commence in mid 1940. Frank replied that the germanisation of Litzmannstadt could not take place overnight and might well last fifteen years. The situation in the General Government, he stated, was in any case worse than that in the Warthegau. Greiser correctly drew the conclusion from the discussion that there was no prospect, even as an interim solution, of the General Government receiving the Warthegau's quarter of a million Jews. It was again stressed, however, by his entourage that there could be no question of the Jews remaining in Litzmannstadt and that 'the Jewish question must, therefore, be solved in some way or other'.[35] On 6 November 1940, Frank informed Greiser by telegram that further deportations of Poles and Jews from the Warthegau into the General Government were impossible before the end of the war. He had informed Himmler of this position, and given instructions to turn back any transports.[36]

Meanwhile, conditions for the Jews in the improvised ghettos and camps of the Warthegau were unspeakable. Outbreaks of epidemic disease were inevitable. At Kutno, where 6,500 Jews were confined in a former sugar factory, spotted fever (Fleckfieber) broke out on 30 October 1940. Breaking up the camp or dispersal of the inmates into buildings in adjoining streets was ruled out for fear of infecting Germans. Even fresh straw for bedding and hot water for delousing could not be provided. It was reported to Greiser that as things stood any possibility of combating the spotted fever in the camp could be ruled out. Worries were expressed about the situation in the coming winter. The epidemic

establishment of the ghetto is, it goes without saying, only a transitional measure'. Jüdisches Historisches Institut, Warsaw, *Faschismus—Getto—Massenmord* (Frankfurt am Main, n.d. [1961]), 81.
[35] DTB Frank, 264.
[36] GK, PAG, vol. 36, Bl. 559–60.

was predictably unstoppable. By the summer of 1941 there had been 1145 cases, 280 of them fatal. The camp was finally closed in March 1942, by which time there had been 1369 cases, 313 leading to deaths.[37] A fate worse than spotted fever, of course, awaited the survivors. In the huge Lodz ghetto, whose Jewish population when hermetically sealed off from the rest of the city on 1 May 1940 numbered 163,177 persons, starvation went hand in hand with disease.[38] The problems of administration and control, of food provision and epidemic containment—that is the difficulties of coping with the internment of the Warthegau Jews which the Nazi leadership both in Berlin and in Posen had been in such a rush to bring about—were only too apparent to Greiser, Koppe, and other heads of the Warthegau administration, not least the Gestapo and the local government leaders in Lodz itself. The pressure which Greiser and Koppe had sought to put on Frank mirrored the pressure they were under from their own subordinates to do something about the mounting and apparently insoluble 'Jewish problem' in the province. But by mid 1941, there was no solution in sight.

It was at this juncture, however, in the summer of 1941, that talk began of new possibilities which might be contemplated. And the first evidence of such possibilities being envisaged can be witnessed in remarks issuing from the top echelon of the Warthegau administration. On 16 July 1941, the head of the Security Service (SD) in Posen, SS-Sturmbannführer Rolf-Heinz Höppner—a man close to both Greiser and Koppe—sent to Adolf Eichmann in the Reich Security Head Office in Berlin a summary, headed 'Solution of the Jewish Problem', of discussions, involving a variety of agencies, in the Reich Governor's headquarters. A possible solution to the 'Jewish Question' in the Reichsgau Wartheland had been broached. This amounted to the concentration of all Warthegau Jews in a huge camp for 300,000 persons close to the centre of coal production, where those Jews capable of working could be exploited in a number of ways with relatively easy policing (as the Police Chief in Lodz, SS-Brigadeführer Albert vouchsafed) and without epidemic danger to the non-Jewish population. The next item addressed the issue of what to do about those Jews incapable of working. A new, ominous, note was struck, offering a

[37] Details in this paragraph based on reports in Archiwum Państwowe Poznań (= APP), Reichsstatthalter 2111.

[38] *The Chronicle of the Lodz Ghetto, 1941–1944*, ed. Lucjan Dobroszycki (New Haven/London, 1984), xxxix, l–li. APP, Reichsstatthalter 1855 contains statistics of disease in the ghetto in 1941. And, for evidence of rocketing death-rates from summer 1940, see also Browning, 'Ghettoisation', 349.

cynical rationalisation for genocide. 'There is the danger this winter', ran the minute, 'that the Jews can no longer all be fed. It is to be seriously considered whether the most humane solution might not be to finish off those Jews not capable of working by some sort of fast-working preparation. This would be in any event more pleasant than letting them starve'. Additionally, it was recommended that all Jewesses still capable of bearing children be sterilised, so that 'the Jewish problem' would be completely solved within the current generation. Reich Governor Greiser, it was added, had not yet commented on the matter. Government President Uebelhoer in Litzmannstadt had, however, given the impression that he did not want the ghetto there to disappear because it was so lucrative. Just how much could be made from the Jews had been explained to Höppner by pointing out that the Reich Labour Ministry was prepared to pay six marks a day from a special fund for each Jewish worker, whereas the actual cost amounted to only eighty pfennige a day. Höppner's covering note asked for Eichmann's opinion. 'The things sound in part fantastic', Höppner concluded, 'but would in my view be quite capable of implementation'.[39]

The Höppner memorandum demonstrates that there were still in July 1941 divergent views—even among the Lodz authorities themselves—about the treatment of the ghettoised Jews, now the ghettos appeared to be a long-term prospect rather than a transient solution.[40] But above all, the memorandum highlights the idea of genocide at an embryonic stage.

By July 1941, events elsewhere were already pushing German policy towards the Jews strongly in the direction of genocide. The preparations for the 'war of annihilation'[41] with the Soviet Union marked, it has been noted, a 'quantum jump' into genocide.[42] Certainly, a genocidal climate was now present as never before. But orders for a general killing of Jews were, recent research indicates, not, as is often presumed, transmitted orally by Heydrich to the leaders of the Einsatzgruppen before the invasion of the Soviet Union. The Einsatzgruppen did not initially behave in a unified fashion, and there was a gradual escalation of killing during the first weeks of the campaign. Only after clarification of the tasks of the Einsatzgruppen had apparently been sought and

[39] GK, PAG, vol. 36, Bl. 567–8v.
[40] See Browning, 'Ghettoisation', 349–51, for disputes between 'productionists' and 'attritionists' in Lodz. Dr. Karl Marder, the mayor of Lodz, signified in a letter to Uebelhoer of 4 July 1941—less than a fortnight before the Höppner memorandum—that the character of the ghetto in Lodz had changed, and that it should remain as an 'essential element of the total economy'. *Ibid.*, 350.
[41] Hitler's description, prior to the invasion of the USSR, as noted by his Chief of Staff, Franz Halder, *Kriegstagebuch*, 3 vols., (Stuttgart, 1962–4), II, 336–7.
[42] Christopher Browning, *The Final Solution and the German Foreign Office* (New York/London, 1978), 8.

provided by Himmler in August 1941, was there a drastic extensification of the slaughter to all Jews, irrespective of age or sex.[43] Outside the Soviet Union, too, the obvious impasses in anti-Jewish policy were, from a number of differing directions, now developing a rapid, and accelerating, momentum towards outright and total genocide.

On 31 July 1941, Göring, who had been nominally in charge of coordinating the forced emigration of German Jews since the aftermath of the great pogrom of November 1938, commissioned Heydrich with undertaking the preparations for the 'complete solution of the Jewish question within the German sphere of influence in Europe'.[44] All Göring did, in fact, was to sign a document drawn up in Heydrich's office, almost certainly drafted by Eichmann.[45] The initiative came, in other words, from the Reich Security Head Office. The Göring mandate has frequently been interpreted as the direct reflection of a Hitler order to kill the Jews of Europe. Such an interpretation is open to doubt.[46] It seems more probable that the mandate still looked to a territorial solution, envisaging the removal of German and other European Jews to a massive reservation in the east—somewhere beyond the Urals. The war, it was thought, would soon be over. The opportunity of such a territorial solution would then present itself. The result, needless to say, would itself have amounted to a different form of genocide in the

---

[43] These comments follow the analyses of Alfred Streim, *Die Behandlung sowjetischer Kriegsgefangener im 'Fall Barbarossa'* (Heidelberg/Karlsruhe, 1981) 74–93; and Philippe Burrin, *Hitler et les Juifs. Genèse d'un génocide* (Paris, 1989) 112–28. The counter-argument, that a general order to exterminate all Soviet Jews was orally given to the Einsatzgruppen leaders before the invasion of the Soviet Union, is most vehemently expressed by Helmut Krausnick, in Helmut Krausnick and Hans-Heinrich Wilhelm, *Die Truppe des Weltanschauungskrieges* (Stuttgart, 1981), 158–66, and in Jäckel and Rohwer, 120–1.

[44] *International Military Tribunal: Trial of the Major War Criminals*, 42 vols., (Nuremberg, 1949), XXVI, 266–7, Doc. 710-PS.

[45] That the document emanated from the *Reichssicherheitshauptamt* is certain, that Eichmann drafted it, very probable: see Raul Hilberg, *Die Vernichtung der europäischen Juden* (Frankfurt am Main, 1990), 1064 n.7; Jäckel and Rohwer, 15; Christopher Browning, *Fateful Months. Essays on the Emergence of the Final Solution* (New York/London, 1985), 21–2; Hans Mommsen, 'Die Realisierung des Utopischen: Die "Endlösung der Judenfrage" im "Dritten Reich"', in Hans Mommsen, *Der Nationalsozialismus und die deutsche Gesellschaft* (Reinbek bei Hamburg, 1991) 207; and Richard Breitman, *The Architect of Genocide. Himmler and the Final Solution* (1991), 192.

[46] See Burrin, 129–34; Mommsen, *Der Nationalsozialismus*, 207; and Arno Mayer, *Why did the Heavens not Darken? The 'Final Solution' in History* (New York, 1988), 290–2. See also Uwe Dietrich Adam, *Judenpolitik im Dritten Reich* (Düsseldorf, 1972), 308–9, though Adam presumes a Hitler directive behind the mandate, for which there is no evidence. Gerald Fleming, *Hitler und die Endlösung. 'Es ist des Führers Wunsch...'* (Wiesbaden/Munich, 1982), 78, Browning, *Fateful Months*, 21–2, Breitman, 193, Krausnick in Jäckel and Rohwer, 201, with differing emphasis, hold to the view that the mandate inaugurated the 'Final Solution'. Hilberg in Jäckel and Rohwer, 137–8, rather agnostically suggests a decision might have been taken around the date of the mandate, but that the evidence is inconclusive.

long run. But it was not the actual 'final solution' which historically emerged in the closing months of 1941 and the beginning of 1942. The territorial solution which was still being pressed for in the summer of 1941 was predicated upon a swift German victory. By September, this prospect was already dwindling. Before this time, Hitler, holding to his notion that the Jews could serve as 'hostages', had resisted pressure, especially from Heydrich and Goebbels, to deport the German Jews to the east.[47] In mid September, a Foreign Office enquiry about deporting Serbian Jews to the east was turned down by Eichmann on the grounds that not even German Jews could be moved to Russia or the General Government. Eichmann recommended shooting.[48] But around the same time, in mid September 1941, Hitler was persuaded to change his mind about deporting the German Jews.[49] In the next months, the crucial steps which culminated in the 'Final Solution' proper were taken. In October and November 1941 the threads of the extermination net were rapidly pulled together.

In this development, events in the Warthegau played a crucial role. Notification of the Führer's wish that the Old Reich and the Protectorate (Bohemia and Moravia) should be cleared of Jews, as a first stage to Poland and then in the following spring further to the east, was sent by Himmler to Greiser on 18 September 1941, four days after Rosenberg's apparently successful intervention in persuading Hitler to deport the German Jews. Evidently because of the immediate implications for the Warthegau of the deportation order, the letter was sent directly to Greiser as head of the province's government and administration. Himmler reported the intention to deport 60,000 Jews to Litzmannstadt for the duration of the winter. Further details, added Himmler, would be provided by Heydrich, either directly or via Koppe.[50] Whether the figure of 60,000 Jews was an error, or was rapidly revised, is unclear. But within a week the number concerned was referred to as 20,000 Jews and now 5,000 Gypsies.[51] Possibly, they were intended as the first 'instalment'. But even this number was far too great for the authorities

[47] Burrin, 136–9; Christopher Browning, 'Zur Genesis der "Endlösung"', *Vierteljahrshefte für Zeitgeschichte* XXIX (1981), 103; Martin Broszat, 'Hitler und die Genesis der "Endlösung"', in *ibid.* XXV (1977), 750.

[48] Browning, *Fateful Months*, 26.

[49] Though impossible to be certain, it is probable that Rosenberg's influence was decisive in pressing Hitler to approve the immediate deportation of German Jews in retaliation for the Soviet deportation of Volga Germans to Siberia. See Burrin, 138–9; Browning, 'Zur Genesis', 103.

[50] ZSL, USA 2, Bl. 310. Both Heydrich and Koppe were in receipt of copies of Himmler's letter to Greiser, which is, in fact, the only direct record of Hitler's deportation order.

[51] *Ibid.*, Bl. 286, Gettoverwaltung to Regierungspräsident Uebelhoer, 24 Sept. 1941, signed by Werner Ventzki, the Oberbürgermeister of Lodz.

in Litzmannstadt. The ghetto administration vehemently protested at the intended influx, and the protest—on the grounds of existing massive overcrowding, provisioning problems, economic dislocation, and danger of epidemics—was conveyed by the Government President of Litzmannstadt, Uebelhoer, in the strongest terms to Berlin.[52] But it was to no avail. Heydrich stated—though his telegram to Uebelhoer was overtaken by events and never sent—that the deportation was 'absolutely necessary and no longer to be delayed', and that Greiser had given his permission to receive the Jews in Litzmannstadt.[53] Himmler demanded the same understanding from Uebelhoer that he had received from Greiser. He sharply upbraided Uebelhoer, for whom Greiser intervened, for his objectionable tone.[54]

From this exchange, it is clear that the pressures for deportation were coming from Berlin, that Greiser was willing to comply despite the already mounting impossibility of 'solving' the Warthegau's own 'Jewish question', and that opposition from Litzmannstadt itself was simply ruled out by Reich Security Head Office. The stated aim, the further expulsion of the Jews the coming spring to the east, does not appear at this point to have been concealing an actual intention to exterminate the Jews in death camps in Poland. Clearly, Uebelhoer knew nothing of any such intention.[55] Hitler himself spoke at the end of the first week in October of transporting Czech Jews directly 'to the east' and not first into the General Government,[56] and both Heydrich and Himmler referred in early October to German Jews being sent to camps in the Baltic.[57] Here, of course, their fate, in view of the murderous onslaught of the Einsatzgruppen in the Soviet Union, would have been all too predictable. The decision to deport Jews into areas where they had already been killed in their tens of thousands was plainly in itself genocidal.[58] By this time, in late September or early October 1941, it would appear that the decision for physical extermination—at least of Jews incapable of working—had in effect been taken, though Russia rather than Poland was still foreseen as the area of implementation. The option of deporting the Jews 'farther east' to the Soviet Union rapidly vanished, however, in the next weeks with

---

[52] *Ibid.*, Bl. 286–309, Gettoverwaltung to Uebelhoer, 24 Sept. 1941; Bl. 277–9, Uebelhoer to Himmler, 4 Oct. 1941.

[53] *Ibid.*, Bl. 280–2, Heydrich telegram to Himmler, 8 Oct. 1941; Brandt reply to Heydrich, same date.

[54] Entire correspondence in the Uebelhoer case in *ibid.*, Bl. 257–85.

[55] Broszat, 'Genesis', 751; Browning's reply, 'Zur Genesis', 103–4, seems weak on this point.

[56] Cited Broszat, 751, n. 24.

[57] Jäckel and Rohwer, 126.

[58] Burrin argues (139–41), correctly in my view, that the deportation decision was tantamount to the decision to kill the European Jews.

first transport difficulties, then the stalling of the German advance and the deteriorating military position in Russia. Far from a quick blitzkrieg victory, the end of the war in the east was nowhere in sight. And towards the end of October Eichmann was making it clear that the mooted further deportation to the east of Jews deported from Germany to Litzmannstadt referred only to Jews 'fit to work'.[59] Since Jews in the east incapable of working were already being earmarked for extermination, the implication was obvious.

New approaches to 'solving the Jewish Question' were meanwhile beginning to emerge. In circles closely connected with the 'Jewish Question', there was now ominous talk of 'special measures' for extermination.[60] Viktor Brack, of the Führer Chancellory and formerly the inspiration of the 'euthanasia action' (whose personnel, after the halting of the 'programme' in the Reich in late August, were now available for redeployment and carried with them 'expertise' derived from the gassing of the incurably sick), offered advice on the potential of poison gas as a means for tackling the 'Jewish problem', again at precisely this juncture.[61] In October, too, the SS commandeered Polish labourers at Belzec in eastern Poland to undertake the construction of the extermination camp there—one of the three camps (the others were Sobibor and Treblinka) which developed into 'Operation Reinhard', directed by the Lublin police chief Globocnik.[62] The former euthanasia personnel dispatched to liaise with Globocnik arrived in Lublin around the same time.[63] The first experimental gassings at Auschwitz (of Soviet prisoners-of-war) took place in late summer and autumn 1941, and construction of the extermination camp at Auschwitz-Birkenau was underway by the end of the year.[64] On 16 December 1941, Hans Frank spoke openly in a meeting of leaders of the General Government about the need to 'exterminate the Jews wherever we find them', pointing out that the Gauleiter of the eastern territories were saying they too did not want the Jews. They were asking why there was not a resort to 'self-help' to liquidate the Jews, rather than sending them to the east. Frank commented that he did not know how the extermination of the 3.5 million Jews in the General Government could come about, since they could not be shot or

---

[59] Fleming, 83, letter from Dr. Wetzel, from the Ministry of the Occupied Eastern Territories, to Hinrich Lohse, Reich Commissar for the Baltic (Ostland), 25 Oct. 1941. The letter states categorically that there are no objections to the gassing of Jews unfit for work.

[60] Browning, *Fateful Months*, 27.

[61] Fleming, 81–3 (see note 59).

[62] Jäckel and Rohwer, 127–8; Browning, *Fateful Months*, 30–1.

[63] Browning, *Fateful Months*, 31.

[64] Jäckel/Rohwer, 172–6; Browning, 'Zur Genesis', 107.

poisoned.[65] A comprehensive plan for the extermination of the Jews had evidently not yet been established. Physical extermination was, however, now unmistakably the intention.[66] The Jewish transports from Berlin, Prague, Vienna, and elsewhere had meanwhile been rolling into Lodz. The first German Jews arrived on 16 October 1941. By 4 November 1941, there had already been twenty transports, and the deportation target was reached.[67] With the number of Jews sharply increasing and the prospects of reductions through further deportations eastwards even more rapidly diminishing, killing the Jews of the Warthegau now emerged as a practical option.

The option was rapidly seized upon. Already in autumn 1941, and weeks before the transports from the Lodz ghetto to systematic extermination at Chelmno began, there were mass killings of Jews at locations in the southern part of the Warthegau. Polish underground sources smuggled out information, published in the United States in 1942, of the slaughter in October 1941 of the entire Jewish population—reputedly some 3,000 persons—of the Konin district, who had been gathered together in Zagarov (a village the Germans renamed 'Hinterberg') and then driven in truckloads into the Kaszimir woods where all trace of them ended.[68] Postwar German investigations corroborated the essence of the report. They concluded that in an indeterminate period, probably between autumn 1940 and late summer or autumn 1941, and in various 'actions', a large number of Jewish men, women and children were driven into the woods between Kazimierz Biskupi and Kleczew and either shot or killed in a gas van. Most of the victims, it was noted, were from Zagarow (Hinterberg), where beforehand a large number of Jewish families from the Konin district had been concentrated. Witnesses said the killings were carried out by police and Gestapo.[69] Further postwar trial investigations in Germany

---

[65] DTB Frank, 457 (entry for 16 Dec. 1941). 'Self-help' was, in fact already being resorted to in the Baltic, where—among many mass shootings—the first German Jews had been shot in Lithuania and Latvia in late November 1941. See Fleming, 14, 77–104.

[66] Further confirmation is the reply from the Eastern Ministry in Berlin, on 18 December, to a request for clarification made the previous month by Gauleiter Lohse, the Reich Commissar in the Baltic, that economic considerations were deemed to be irrelevant to the settling of the 'Jewish problem'. Browning, *Fateful Months*, 33.

[67] *NS-Vernichtungslager im Spiegel deutscher Strafprozesse*, ed. Adalbert Rückerl Munich, 1977, S. 257 n. 39 (henceforth cited as *NS-Vernichtungslager*). APP, Reichsstatthalter 1214, Bl. 7–9 has a statistical breakdown of the 17th and 20th transports on 1st and 4th Nov. 1941. For details of point of origin, date of arrival, and numbers involved, see Dobroszycki, *Chronicle*, lvii.

[68] *The Ghetto Speaks*, 5 Aug. 1942 (Bund Archives of the Jewish Labor Movement, New York), 1. I am grateful to Prof. Lucjan Dobroszycki for a copy of this document. And see Dobroszycki, *Chronicle*, liv (where it is stated they were shot, though this is not stipulated in the report in *The Ghetto Speaks*).

[69] ZSL, Verfahren 206 AR-Z 228/73. I am grateful to Dr. Wacker of the ZSL for providing me with this information.

established that, beginning on 26 November 1941 and lasting several days, an SS extermination squad had killed perhaps some 700 Jews—mainly elderly, ill, or feeble Jews and children—interned in a camp at Kozminek (Bornhagen in German) near Kalisch, by means of a gas van.[70] Probably such killings were envisaged by the security police and liquidation squads as experiments in the extermination techniques which would soon need to be deployed for the far larger numbers in the Lodz ghetto. The major operation was not long delayed. At the beginning of December 1941,[71] regular and systematic extermination began at the site which had been selected specifically for the purpose, Chelmno, by a special 'task squad' which had already accumulated much expertise in gas van extermination.

In the framework of the 'euthanasia programme', which ran in the Reich between autumn 1939 and summer 1941, a 'special unit' under Herbert Lange had operated in the annexed areas of the east from a base in Posen. The most extensive of its mass killings had been the murder, between 21 May and 6 June 1940, of 1,558 mental patients from asylums in and around Soldau in East Prussia.[72] The technique used by Lange's Sonderkommando was the gassing of victims by carbon monoxide poisoning in a large van.[73] Lange's chauffeur, Walter Burmeister, recorded in postwar testimony that he had driven Lange around the Warthegau in autumn 1941, accompanied by other members of the Stapo-Leitstelle of Posen and a guard drawn from the Schutzpolizei looking for a suitable location to carry out killings of Jews. He then, presumably once an appropriate spot had been found, drove Lange to security police headquarters in Berlin and back. In November 1941, shortly after returning from Berlin, Lange's unit—now increased in size—moved from Posen to Chelmno, and at the beginning of December 1941 began the use of two gas vans (a third gas van arrived during the course of the month) sent from Berlin.[74] Thus began the

[70] *Justiz und NS-Verbrechen*, VII, Amsterdam, 1971, no. 231 b-2, 217–18, 230–1.

[71] The date of 5 December 1941 was accepted at the Chelmno trial in Bonn (*Justiz und NS-Verbrechen*, XXI, Amsterdam 1979, 280), and at Koppe's trial (ZSL, Prozeß Koppe, Bl. 218) as the date of the first arrival of transports in Chelmno. Browning, *Fateful Months*, 30, dates the first gassing to 8 December 1941, as does Madajczyk, *Okkupationspolitik*, 380 (apparently, though not explicitly stated, based on early post-war Polish testimony). In a letter he sent me, dated 25 June 1991, Christopher Browning writes: 'I have seen no evidence given for either date, nor have I seen the discrepancy addressed'.

[72] *NS-Vernichtungslager*, 258–9.

[73] The killing was carried out by bottled carbon monoxide gas being released into the van. Lange's unit was to introduce at Chelmno a refined version of gassing, using the vehicle's exhaust. See Browning, *Fateful Months*, 59, 101 n. 8.

[74] Eugen Kogon et al. (eds.), *Nationalsozialistische Massentötungen durch Giftgas* (Frankfurt am Main, 1986), 113–14, 310 n. 10; *Justiz und NS-Verbrechen*, XXI, 246. According to the evidence assembled for Koppe's trial (ZSL, Prozeß Koppe, Bl. 194), the initial drivers of the vehicles were SS men from the unit who were subsequently replaced by two drivers

killing process in the first of the extermination establishments to begin its operations.[75]

Did the initiative to begin the killing come from Berlin, or from within the Warthegau? In one postwar trial, it was accepted that orders for the 'resettlement' (that is, killing) of Jews from the Lodz ghetto to the extermination camp at Chelmno, went directly from the Reich Security Head Office in Berlin to the Gestapo office in Lodz.[76] Even if correct, this could be taken as consonant with a request emanating from within the Warthegau, then sanctioned in Berlin. However, neither a request from Lodz nor a general order coming from Berlin for 'resettlement' of the Lodz Jews could have by-passed the heads of the civil and police administration in the Warthegau, Greiser and Koppe. Moreover, the 'resettlement' of the Lodz Jews began only on 16 January 1942, more than a month after the killings in Chelmno had started.[77] If orders were transmitted direct from Berlin to Lodz, they must have been subsidiary to an initial decision to initiate the genocide in the Warthegau by exterminating the Jews incapable of work. And the balance of probabilities points towards seeing the initial impulses coming from within the Warthegau itself, and not directly from Berlin. The emergence of a genocidal 'solution' in the Warthegau corresponds exactly with the weeks in which the authorities there were having to cope with the reception of 20,000 Jews, accepted only under protest by the local authorities in Litzmannstadt. With the collapse of hopes of deporting the province's own Jews, then the forced reception of Jews from Germany, and finally the cutting off of an exit route for any of the Jews, Warthegau anti-Jewish policy had run ever further into a cul-de-sac.

Killing offered a way out. And, it will be remembered, it had already been talked of seriously among the Warthegau ruling elite as early as July 1941. The means, with the redeployment of Lange's special unit, were by autumn 1941 now to hand to implement what in July had

---

coming from the RSHA in Berlin. Walter Burmeister, Lange's chauffeur, stated, however, that the drivers came together with the gas vans. Kogon, 114.

[75] For the extermination at Chelmno, see above all *NS-Vernichtungslager*, Part 2. An important independent source is the account, compiled in 1945, of the Forest Inspector of the area, Heinz May. Part Three, 'Der große Judenmord', is printed (in German and Polish) in Karol Marian Pospieszalski, 'Niemiecki Nadleśniczy o Zagładzie Żydów w Chełmnie nad Nerem', *Przegląd Zachodni Poznań* 18 (1962), 85–105. I am greatly indebted to Prof. Pospieszalski for providing me with a copy of this article, and with a translation into German of his introduction. An extract in English can be found in Dobroszycki, *Chronicle*, lv–vi.

[76] *NS-Vernichtungslager*, 252.

[77] *Justiz und NS-Verbrechen*, XXI, 280.

been referred to in the Höppner memorandum as 'fantastic notions'. The mention in that memorandum of the names of the Lodz police chief Albert and the Government President Uebelhoer (who came, it will be recalled, in September to protest in the strongest terms about the orders for a new influx of Jews to the Lodz ghetto) indicates the centrality of the Lodz authorities to the internal Warthegau debate on the fate of the region's Jews. It is possible, as has been suggested (though there is no direct evidence to prove it), that when the position, from the point of view of the Nazi bosses in Lodz, became critical following the order to take in the tens of thousands of new deportees from the Reich in the autumn, the suggestion to liquidate them came initially from the Gestapo at Lodz.[78] On the other hand, the Sonderkommando Lange drew mainly for its personnel on the security police headquarters at Posen, where it was based before moving to Chelmno, and continued to liaise directly with the Posen office, not with Lodz.[79] Whatever part was played by the security police authorities in Lodz and Posen, the key role was almost certainly that of the overall head of the security services in the Warthegau, Higher SS and Police Chief Wilhelm Koppe.[80]

Koppe's own version of his involvement in the emergence of a genocidal 'solution' was given in connection with his trial in Bonn in 1960.[81] He portrays himself as the conscience-stricken recipient of orders from Berlin. Quite apart from the apologetics, the account has to be treated with caution. Koppe claimed he heard, either in 1940 or in 1941, that a Commissar (whose name he later learned was Lange) and a special SS unit were to be sent to him from Berlin to carry out the physical extermination of the Jews in the Wartheland. His understanding at the time, he said, was that this would apply only to Jews incapable of work—the impression, he added, also of Greiser. Koppe's view was that the Sonderkommando would carry out 'experiments', trying out gassing methods already devised by Brack of the Führer Chancellory. Koppe was adamant that he had heard of the deployment of the Lange unit from Ernst Damzog, Inspector of the Security Police and SD in the Wartheland, based in Posen, and learnt further from a telephone conversation with Dr. Rudolf Brandt from Himmler's personal office that an 'action' against the Jews was being prepared, and that Brack's

---

[78] As claimed, though he cites no direct evidence, by Madajczyk, *Okkupationspolitik*, 380. Prof. Madajczyk acknowledges in a letter to me, dated 27 August 1991, that the assertion rested on inference. Christopher Browning (letter to me of 25 June 1991) points to the greater role of the Posen Security Police than the Lodz Gestapo in the build-up to the exterminations in Chelmno.

[79] ZSL, Prozeß Koppe, Bl. 194–7; *NS-Vernichtungslager*, 262–4.

[80] The centrality of Koppe's role is taken for granted in Birn, 181.

[81] Printed in Kogon, 111–12. See also, for Koppe's dubious testimony, note 107 below.

gassing experiments, reaching completion in Berlin, were now to be deployed by Sonderkommando Lange, under Brack's direction, in the Wartheland. In a crisis of conscience, alleged Koppe, he consulted Greiser who, it was immediately obvious, was fully in the picture and stated that it was a matter of a 'Führer order' which could not be 'sabotaged' (since Koppe purportedly opposed such 'experiments' as inhumane).

In this account, it seems plain, Koppe is conflating the beginnings of the 'euthanasia action' in the Warthegau with the decision to kill the province's Jews. He could not possibly have heard of a decision to exterminate the Jews of the Warthegau in 1940. But nor did he encounter the name of Herbert Lange and existence of his Sonderkommando for the first time in 1941, and in connection with an 'action' against the Jews. For Lange and his men had by then already been stationed in Posen and at Koppe's behest for over a year, employed in the gassings of mental patients in the annexed areas of Poland. And whether in connection with the 'euthanasia action' or the extermination of the Jews, it seems unlikely that Koppe learnt of the deployment of the Sonderkommando Lange from Damzog, a subordinate. Finally, assuming that the telephone conversation with Brandt took place in autumn 1941 and along the lines Koppe described, it might be still be doubted whether it should be seen as relaying an order from Berlin as opposed to complying with a request from within the Warthegau to deploy the 'Brack methods' to exterminate the Jews. Without minimising the indispensability of empowering orders from Berlin, and accepting that by October 1941 a decision had been taken or sanctioned by Hitler to exterminate European Jewry—certainly those Jews incapable of working—it seems, nevertheless, probable, as we shall see, that Koppe was far more active in initiating the 'action' against the Jews in the Warthegau than his postwar account suggests.

At any rate, for well over a year before the killing of the Jews began, Koppe was in overall command of Lange's unit. Later, when it was renamed Sonderkommando Kulmhof (the German name for Chelmno) and placed under a new leader, Hans Bothman, Koppe had general control of the unit's personnel and economic matters,[82] delegating the practical running of the unit to Damzog's office.[83] In the summer of 1941 Koppe was among the circle of recipients—including by no means

[82] NS-Vernichtungslager, 251, 258. See also ZSL, Prozeß Koppe, Bl. 212, 216–17.

[83] According to one postwar witness, formerly a civil servant in Damzog's office, both Lange and Bothmann visited Damzog on a number of occasions, there was a special file on Chelmno in the office, and reports on the numbers killed were sent there. NS-Vernichtungslager, 252 & n. 22. Written reports of the Sonderkommando on the liquidation of the Jews were sent to Koppe, and Damzog and Bothmann were from time to time summoned by him to present verbal reports. ZSL, Prozeß Koppe, Bl. 197, 211, 216.

all the Higher SS and Police Leaders—of the 'Reports on Events' (Ereignismeldungen), explicitly detailing the killings of Jews in the Soviet Union.[84] He knew, therefore, of the ravages of the Einsatzgruppen in Russia, and, of course, at first hand of the gassings of mental patients in the annexed Polish territories (since he had 'lent out' Sonderkommando Lange for that purpose). He was, as his own testimony shows, aware of Brack's experiments with techniques of mass killing by use of poisonous gas. There can be no doubt that he was involved in the deliberations which led to the Höppner memorandum in July 1941. He was in every way, then, well attuned to the progressively radical thinking on the possible 'solution to the Jewish Question' in the top echelons of the SS and at Reich Security Headquarters in Berlin.

The central role played by the regional command of the security police in the emergence and implementation of a policy of genocide in the Warthegau is obvious. But where did the overlord of the Warthegau, Reich Governor and Gauleiter Arthur Greiser, fit in to the decisions to move to outright genocide? Despite Koppe's assertion that Greiser was supinely carrying out a 'Führer Order' imposed on the Warthegau from Berlin, the evidence suggests, in fact, that the request to begin killing the Jews came directly from Greiser himself. As the letter from Himmler to Greiser of 18 September 1941, informing him of the decision to deport 60,000 Jews to the Lodz ghetto, shows, communication on such matters between the head of the SS and the leader of the Warthegau did not need to pass through the hands of Koppe.[85] Greiser himself had excellent relations with Himmler. But, as Koppe's testimony indicated, the Reich Governor and the regional police chief were of one mind on the 'Jewish Question', while the rounding up of Jews from the smaller ghettos of the Warthegau needed evident close cooperation between the security police and the administrative organs under Greiser's control.[86] It is clear that Greiser contacted Himmler directly in a number of instances relating to Chelmno and the Sonderkommando operating there.[87] And when, after a temporary end to the killing, the work of the Sonderkommando was recommenced in early 1944, it was on the basis of an agreement between Himmler and Greiser in which, it seems plain, the initiative was taken by the latter.[88] Something of Greiser's role can be gathered,

---

[84] ZSL, Prozeß Koppe, Bl. 172.

[85] NS-Vernichtungslager, 252 n. 25.

[86] NS-Vernichtungslager, 252.

[87] NS-Vernichtungslager, 252–3. See, for example, ZSL, USA-1, Bl. 91–4, the exchange of letters Greiser-Himmler. 19–27 March 1943, relating to the end of the operations of the 85 men of Sonderkommando Lange in Kulmhof.

[88] NS-Vernichtungslager, 252–3; BDC, PA Greiser, for correspondence involving Pohl, Greiser, and Himmler, 9–17 Feb. 1944.

too, from references to the killing of the Jews in mid 1942. A report of the Lodz Gestapo from 9 June 1942 noted that 'all Jews not capable of work' were to be 'evacuated'—a euphemism for liquidated—'according to the directions of the Gauleiter'.[89] This is probably to be linked with the killing of 100,000 Jews which Greiser himself had requested and referred to in a letter to Himmler dated 1 May 1942.[90] Greiser spoke in this letter of the completion, within the next two to three months, of 'the action, approved by you in agreement with the Head of the Reich Security Head Office, SS-Obergruppenführer Heydrich, for the special treatment [another camouflage term for killing] of around 100,000 Jews in the area of my Gau'. Although Greiser spoke of the 'action' being completed within two to three months, according to a memorandum from the Reich Security Head Office dated 5 June 1942, a total of 97,000 Jews had in fact already been killed in Chelmno since December 1941.[91] Greiser's request for permission to carry out the 'special treatment' must, therefore, have been made considerably earlier. Indeed, it conceivably marked the actual request to begin the killing before the commencement of operations in Chelmno at the beginning of December 1941.[92] Greiser went on in his letter of 1 May 1942 to request Himmler's approval of a further 'initiative' on his part: the use of the Sonderkommando, directly following on the 'Jewish action', to liquidate 35,000 Poles in the Gau suffering from incurable tuberculosis.[93] The tuberculosis episode is revealing in a number of respects for the light it casts on the likely decision-making process in the killing of the Jews. Greiser's letter to Himmler was immediately followed by a letter to the latter's personal adjutant SS-Sturmbannführer Rudolf Brandt from Koppe, recommending that the case be verbally explained to the Reichsführer and offering his own approval of the

[89] *Faschismus-Getto-Massenmord*, 285; *NS-Vernichtungslager*, 252, 290.

[90] BDC, PA Greiser, Greiser to Himmler, 1 May 1942; printed in *Faschismus-Getto-Massenmord*, 278.

[91] *NS-Vernichtungslager*, 290–1. Possibly, Greiser's request—though not specified as such—related to Jews from the Lodz ghetto, whereas the RSHA figure was a general one for the Warthegau. Around 55,000 Jews from the Lodz ghetto had been killed by 9 June 1942. Attention was turned in the summer to 'clearing' the surrounding rural districts, from where at least 15,000 Jews were transported to their death in Chelmno. A further 15,700, mainly weak and sick, Jews were taken from the Lodz ghetto in September 1942, bringing the total to around 70,000 Lodz Jews killed in Chelmno by the beginning of October 1942. *Ibid.*, 288–90.

[92] This is presumed by Raul Hilberg, *The Destruction of the European Jews* (New York, 1973), 561, and—slightly more cautiously expressed—in the revised German edition (see above, note 44), 508.

[93] BDC, PA Greiser, Greiser to Himmler, 5 May 1942. The number of Poles with tuberculosis was said to be around 230,000, those with the disease in an 'open' condition around 35,000.

'solution striven for by the Gauleiter'.[94] Brandt's reply to Koppe stated that he had passed on Greiser's suggestion for an opinion from Heydrich, but that 'the last decision in this matter must be taken by the Führer'.[95] Soundings were, in fact, taken a week later, on 21 May, from Heydrich, who replied on 9 June, stating that he had no objections, subject to thorough discussion of the necessary measures with the security police.[96] Himmler then wrote to Greiser, using Heydrich's wording as the basis of his own letter, towards the end of June.[97]

There matters appear to have rested until the autumn. Preparations for the 'action' presumably took some time.[98] In November 1942, however, before the 'action' had commenced, Greiser received a letter from Dr. Kurt Blome, deputy head of the Nazi Party's health office (Hauptamt für Volksgesundheit) in Berlin, raising objections on the grounds that it would be impossible to maintain the necessary secrecy, thereby arousing unrest and providing enemy propaganda with a gift. He specifically referred to the lessons to be learnt from the mistakes of such a kind made in the 'euthanasia action' in Germany. Consequently, he thought it necessary to consult Hitler, to ask whether, in the light of the 'euthanasia action' which Hitler had stopped (if only partially) for such reasons, the 'tuberculosis action' should go ahead.[99] Greiser wrote again to Himmler on 21 November in the light of Blome's objections. His comment is enlightening. He wrote: 'I myself do not believe that the Führer needs to be asked again in this matter, especially since at our last discussion with regard to the Jews he told me that I could proceed with these according to my own judgement'.[100] Himmler

---

[94] BDC, PA Greiser, Koppe to Brandt, 3 May 1942.

[95] *Ibid.*, Brandt to Koppe, 14 May 1942.

[96] *Ibid.*, RFSS Persönlicher Stab-Untersturmführer Rutzen, 21 May 1942, with request from Brandt to Heydrich; Heydrich-Himmler, 9 June 1942.

[97] *Ibid.*, Himmler-Greiser, 27 June 1942.

[98] *Ibid.*, Greiser-Himmler, 21 Nov. 1942.

[99] *Ibid.*, Blome-Greiser, 18 Nov. 1942.

[100] *Ibid.*, Greiser-Himmler, 21 Nov. 1942. The date of this discussion between Hitler and Greiser cannot be precisely determined. Gerald Fleming, *Hitler und die Endlösung*, 35, states (though gives no supporting evidence) that Greiser had last seen Hitler on 1 Oct. and 8 Nov. 1942 (the English version of Fleming's book, *Hitler and the Final Solution* (Oxford, 1986), 22, has 11 Nov. 1942, but this seems a translation error). Fleming is followed in this by Friedländer, 'From Anti-Semitism to Extermination', 41, and by Czesław Madajczyk, 'Hitler's Direct Influence on Decisions Affecting Jews during World War II', *Yad Vashem Studies* XX (1990), 63–4. Both the dates mentioned by Fleming were large gatherings—a meeting of Gauleiter and Reichsleiter addressed by Hitler on 1 October, and the annual assembly of the Party faithful to commemorate the 1923 Putsch on 8 November (see Milan Hauner, *Hitler. A Chronology of his Life and Time* (1983), 179). Whether Greiser, presuming he attended both, had the opportunity for a private discussion with Hitler might be doubted. Since Greiser had requested, and been given, Himmler's permission to exterminate 100,000 Jews well before 1 May 1942, and these killings had already taken place before October–November 1942, the purpose of seeking

nevertheless regarded Blome's objections as serious enough to advise against the implementation of Greiser's suggestion.[101]

From this exchange, a number of points seem clear. The initiative for killing 100,000 Jews, and the later suggestion for the liquidation of 35,000 tuberculosis victims came directly from Greiser.[102] Approval in both cases was sought from Himmler, who in the latter case, certainly, then consulted Reich Security Head Office. The Warthegau head of security, Koppe, paved the way for the approval of the 'tuberculosis action' and probably did the same with regard to the 'initiative' on the Jews. It cannot be proved, but seems distinctly possible, that the initial suggestion came from him. In the case of the tuberculose Poles, it was pointed out that a decision could only come from Hitler, whose authorisation was essential, at which point doubts arose leading to Himmler's blocking of an initiative he had earlier approved. It seems inconceivable that the killing of the Jews could have been decided upon without some equivalent blanket authorisation by Hitler.[103] But it also appears plain that, as in the tuberculosis matter, all that would have been required of Hitler was authorisation for the implementation of initiatives coming from others. And, as Greiser pointed out, Hitler's response to his own request for authorisation on 'solving the Jewish Question' in the Warthegau had been to grant him permission to act according to his own discretion. Hitler's role here, as elsewhere, was to set the tone and then to provide the broad sanction for actions prompted and set in motion by others.

In the implementation of genocide in the Warthegau, it can be concluded that responsibility for the personnel and economic matters connected with the Sonderkommando at Chelmno rested with the

---

a mandate from Hitler at such a date is not immediately obvious. The only explanations seem to be: a) that Greiser, for reasons which are unclear but were possibly directly to do with the proposed 'tuberculosis action', was trying at a late stage to obtain Hitler's retrospective dispensation for a free hand in liquidating the Jews; b) that he was asking Hitler for permission to extend the initial figure of 100,000, though it is scarcely imaginable that he would have needed to go beyond Himmler for such permission, nor that any permission at all would have been needed to widen the killing within the scope of what had by spring 1942 emerged as the fully-fledged 'Final Solution' programme; or, c) and perhaps most likely, that his discussion with Hitler relating to the Jews, took place at a significantly earlier date, and was simply being evoked by Greiser in autumn 1942 as a weapon in the tuberculosis matter.

[101] BDC, PA Greiser, Himmler-Greiser, 3 Dec. 1942.

[102] In other policy areas, such as the persecution of the Church, the instigation of draconian measures also came from Greiser and his subordinates rather than from central directives from Berlin ZSL, Prozeß Greiser, 96.

[103] As was necessary—finally even in written form—in the 'euthanasia action' (see Ernst Klee, 'Euthanasie' im NS-Staat. Die 'Vernichtung lebensunwerten Lebens' (Frankfurt am Main, 1983), 100–1) as well as being called for in the case of the tuberculosis victims. The point is made by Burrin, 172.

Higher SS and Police Chief, Koppe, and was delegated by him to the Inspector of the Security Police and SD, Damzog, while general responsibility lay in the hands of Reich Governor and Gauleiter Greiser, operating with the permission of Reichsführer SS Himmler, and head of Reich Security Heydrich, and with the blanket authorisation to act as he saw fit provided by Hitler himself.[104]

This examination of the emergence of genocide in the Warthegau—admittedly tentative in places, and necessarily resting at times on the balance of probabilities—has suggested that improvisation by the German authorities on the spot played a decisive role in the autumn of 1941. It was only in the immediate aftermath of Himmler's order to receive tens of thousands of new Jews into the Warthegau and there into the overcrowded Lodz ghetto—following Hitler's authorisation to deport German and Czech Jews—that earlier 'fantasy' talk of liquidating Jews became transformed into a realisable prospect of extermination. The rapid conversion of the Sonderkommando Lange, conveniently to hand but before that date having no special link with a proposed 'solution' to the 'Jewish Question', into a unit deployed specifically in the systematic extermination of Jews, the prompt search for a suitable killing ground, the initial—seemingly experimental—slaughter of Jews at Zagorow and Bornhagen, and the establishment of Chelmno itself, all smack of improvisation. In this, the initiatives by the Warthegau rulers were highly important. Permission to kill a hundred-thousand Jews was actively sought by Reich Governor Greiser; no order to that effect was forced upon him by Himmler or Heydrich. Such a mandate had been requested by spring 1942 at the latest, but almost certainly well before this time and in all probability before the end of 1941. It is Greiser, too, who discusses the Warthegau Jews with Hitler himself at an unspecified date—at the latest by autumn 1942, but probably earlier—and is told to deal with them as he thinks fit. And, as we have seen, the Gestapo at Lodz recorded the fact that they were acting on Greiser's direct instructions in the liquidation of Jews incapable of work. Greiser was subsequently evidently well informed about what took place at Chelmno, and took a keen interest in the developments and in the work of Sonderkommando Kulmhof.[105] And, finally, it was Greiser, who on 7 March 1944 sent a telegram to Hitler, proudly

[104] NS-Vernichtungslager, 253.
[105] ZSL, Prozeß Greiser, 99–102; USA-1, Bl. 91–4, exchange of letters Greiser-Himmler about Sonderkommando Lange; UdSSR-411, Bl. 13–15, testimony of Hermann Gielow from 15 May 1945 about Greiser's involvement in the work of Sonderkommando Bothmann at Chelmno between March 1944 and January 1945; Prozeß Koppe, 210, 216.

reporting that in the Warthegau 'Jewry [had] shrunk to a tiny remnant'.[106]

Nevertheless, it seems more likely that Koppe, rather than Greiser, took the lead in initiating the move to outright genocide in the Warthegau.[107] Most probably it was Koppe, au fait with the thinking of Heydrich and Himmler, already having cooperated in Brack's gassing experiments through the use of the gas van by Lange's men to kill 'euthanasia' victims, and well aware of the antagonism in Litzmannstadt caused by the order to take in the new influx of Jews—possibly even prompted by the Gestapo there—who suggested to Berlin that a way out of the self-imposed problem would be to deploy the Lange unit to liquidate at least the Jews of the smaller ghettos where the problems in Nazi eyes were even greater than those of Lodz and where the possibility of moving them to Lodz was ruled out. It will be recalled that at the time that Höppner had sent his memorandum, in July, Greiser had not voiced an opinion on the solutions suggested. Evidently they had come from within the Security Police rather than from Greiser himself. And it seems likely that, several months later in the autumn, when the 'fantastic' notions mentioned by Höppner were being turned into reality, it was not Greiser, but Koppe, who was the actual initiator, with the Reich Governor approached when approval at the Gau level was needed.

It would be mistaken to conclude from this that 'local initiatives' acted in independence of central policy in Berlin; and even more so to imagine that central policy merely 'grew out of' practical improvisations at local or regional level.[108] An abundance of evidence has now been assembled, demonstrating beyond reasonable doubt that by the late summer and early autumn 1941 the decision physically to exterminate the Jews of Europe must have been taken by the Nazi leadership.[109] But the contrast between central planning and local initiative can easily be too sharply drawn. Whatever the nature of any

[106] BDC, PA Greiser, (also in IfZ, MA-303) telegram to Himmler, 7 March 1944, thanking him for his generous support and giving the text of the 'proud report' he had sent the same day to the Führer. See also Fleming, *Endlösung*, 34.

[107] Koppe's claims at his trial were both contradictory and incredulous. Having claimed (see above note 81) that he heard in 1940 or 1941 from Rudolf Brandt in Himmler's office of the forthcoming 'action' against the Warthegau Jews, he then alleged that—apart from rumours—he first heard of the 'Final Solution' and of the existence of the extermination camp at Chelmno from Greiser (following a telephone call to the latter from Philip Bouhler at the Führer Chancellor). He went on to claim that he had even successfully persuaded Himmler to end the 'Final Solution', but that Göring and Keitel had opposed it being halted.—ZSL, Prozeß Koppe, Bl. 290–1, 294.

[108] See Broszat, 'Genesis', 753 n. 26.

[109] See Browning, *Fateful Months*, chap. 1, esp. 32; Burrin, chap. 5; Jäckel and Rohwer, 125–98; Breitman, chap. 6–9.

central decision already reached, the fateful developments of autumn 1941 do have, within the overall goal of extermination of the Jews of Europe, an unmistakable air about them of improvisation, experimentation, and rapid adaptation to new policy objectives and opportunities. The 'Final Solution', as it came to emerge, formed a unity out of a number of organisationally separate 'programmes', one of which, arising from conditions specific to the Warthegau and remaining throughout under the direction of the province's own leadership rather than the central control of the Reich Security Head Office, was the extermination programme at Chelmno.[110]

At the time of Hitler's decision in mid September—against his earlier reluctance—to deport the German Jews to the east, knowledge of any already determined central extermination policy was clearly still confined to an extremely small circle of initiates. Plainly, Uebelhoer and the Litzmannstadt authorities were unaware in late September 1941 that the aim of anti-Jewish policy was systematic genocide. Otherwise, the vehemence of the objection to the influx of more Jews to the Lodz ghetto would be hard to comprehend.[111] But Koppe would have known, if anyone in the Warthegau did. His role as the police chief 'on the ground' aware of thinking at the centre was pivotal.

Hitler's own role in the emergence of a policy of systematic genocide was mainly to voice the need for a radical 'solution' to the 'Jewish Question', and to sanction and approve initiatives presented to him by those—above all Heydrich and Himmler—keen to translate the Führer's wishes into practical policy objectives. The evidence from the Warthegau—not least the authorisation to Greiser to act as he saw fit in the 'Jewish Question'—fits the picture of a Dictator whose moral responsibility is not in question but who was content to provide carte blanche for others to turn ideological imperatives into concrete directives for action.

By the date of the Wannsee Conference on 20 January 1942 the killing in the Warthegau had been in operation for over six weeks. By March 1942 the 'Final Solution' as it is known to history was in full swing.[112]

The killings at Chelmno began with the Jews from the neighbouring small ghettos and camps.[113] Transports from the Lodz ghetto began on

---

[110] ZSL, Prozeß Koppe, Bl. 297, emphasised the regional control of the Sonderkommando Lange/Bothmann. The Lodz ghetto was a 'Gaughetto' (*Faschismus-Getto-Massenmord*, 285)—a status Greiser was able to retain in Febrary 1944 when Oswald Pohl, from the SS-Verwaltungshauptamt, was aiming to turn it into a concentration camp (BDC, PA Greiser, Greiser to Pohl, 14 Feb. 1944).
[111] See Broszat, 'Genesis', 751.
[112] Browning, *Fateful Months*, 30–4; chronology in Kogon, 328.
[113] *NS-Vernichtungslager*, 268.

16 January 1942. Some 55,000 Jews from the Lodz ghetto itself had been killed by the end of May 1942.[114] By the end of 1942, the number of transports had declined, and at the end of March 1943 operations at Chelmno were ended and the camp dissolved. Greiser appeared in Chelmno, thanked the men of the Sonderkommando 'in the name of the Führer' for their work, invited them to a festive meal in a hotel in Warthbrücken, and attained through intercession with Himmler their further deployment, according to their wishes, as a unit attached to the SS volunteer division 'Prinz Eugen' in Yugoslavia.[115] The killings were restarted in April 1944, when Bothmann and the Sonderkommando were brought back to Chelmno for a second stint which ended on 17–18 January 1945.[116]

Of the leading provincial perpetrators of Nazi genocide in the Warthegau, Inspector of the Security Police and SD Ernst Damzog was killed in action in 1945. Head of the Posen SD Rolf-Heinz Höppner was sentenced in March 1949 in Poznań (Posen) to life imprisonment and released under an amnesty in April 1956. The Government President of Lodz, Dr. Friedrich Uebelhoer, disappeared after American internment under a false name. The Police President of Lodz, Dr. Wilhelm Albert, died in 1960. The Gestapo head in Lodz from April 1942 and, at the same time, Lord Mayor of the city of Lodz, Dr. Otto Bradfisch, responsible also for Einsatzgruppen shootings in Russia, was sentenced in Munich in 1951 to ten years in a penitentiary, and in Hanover in 1963 to thirteen years, less the time spent from his Munich imprisonment, for complicity in the murder of 15,000 and 5,000 persons. The head of the Jewish desk in Lodz, Günter Fuchs, was sentenced in Hanover in 1963 to life imprisonment for nine cases of murder and complicity in the murder of at least 15,000 persons. The head of German administration of the Lodz ghetto, Hans Biebow, was hanged in Lodz in 1947. Herbert Lange was killed in action near Berlin in 1945. His successor as head of the Sonderkommando Kulmhof, Hans Bothmann, hanged himself in British custody in 1946. Of the 160 men suspected of participating in the Chelmno murders, 105 could not be found; 22 were established as dead or missing in action, and two had been hanged in Poland. A total of 33 were located and interrogated, of whom 12 eventually stood trial in Bonn in 1962. The result of the trial and appeal was, finally, that on 23 July 1965, eight were found guilty of involvement in murder and sentenced to periods of between

---

[114] *Ibid.*, 276–7, and n. 69.
[115] *Ibid.*, 280–2.
[116] *Ibid.*, 282–6. Some 7000 Jews were killed at Chelmno in this second spell, though all between 23 June and 14 July 1944. *Ibid.*, 292–3. There were still at that time over 68,000 Jews in the Lodz ghetto, almost all of whom were, by 28 August 1944, sent to Auschwitz-Birkenau. Dobroszycki, *Chronicle*, lxiii–v.

thirteen months two weeks in prison and thirteen years in a state penitentiary. In another three cases, the involvement was regarded as so slight that no punishment was fitting. The last case was stopped because the accused was unfit to stand trial.[117]

Arthur Greiser was condemned to death by a Polish court and hanged in Poznan in 1946—after a last-minute plea for intercession by the Papacy had failed.[118] Wilhelm Koppe escaped after the war and lived under a pseudonym for over fifteen years as a successful businessman, becoming director of a chocolate factory in Bonn before being captured in 1960 and finally, in 1964, being arraigned for his involvement in mass murder in Poland. He was deemed unfit to stand trial.[119] He died peacefully in his bed on 2 July 1975.[120]

The nearest estimates are that a minimum of 150,000 Jews and about 5,000 gypsies were murdered in Chelmno between 1941 and 1945.[121] Four Jews survived.[122]

[117] *NS-Vernichtungslager*, 246–50, 257 n. 38; letter of ZSL, dated 20 June 1989 to Prof. Dr. Stanisław Nawrocki (State Archives Poznań). I am most grateful to Prof. Nawrocki for a copy of this letter with details of the fate of some of the chief perpetrators.

[118] GK Warsaw, Process Artura Greisera (36 files); ZSL, Prozeß Greiser (transl. of Anklageschrift); Polen-365h, Bl. 677–828, Anklageschrift; Polen-3650, Bl. 88–136, Greiser's final plea. The appeal for papal intercession was reported in *L'Osservatore Romano*, 22–3 July 1946. (I owe this information to the kindness of Dr. Gerald Fleming.) According to Dr. Marian Olszewski of the Instytut Zachodni in Posnań, currently working on a life of Greiser (letter to me from Prof. Nawrocki, Poznań, dated 15 May 1991), Greiser's defence lawyer, Heymowski, wrote intercession letters not only to the Pope, but also to President Truman. No response from either has come to light.

[119] *NS-Vernichtungslager*, 251; ZSL, Prozeß Koppe. On Koppe's arrest, trial, and release on grounds of being unfit to stand: *Quick*, 15 July 1960; *Neue Zürcher Zeitung*, 21 Jan. 1965; *Frankfurter Allgemeine Zeitung*, 29 May 1965; *Allgemeine: Unabhängige jüdische Wochenzeitung*, 17 Feb. 1967 (copies in IfZ, Munich).

[120] Date of Koppe's death according to information from ZSL (see n. 117 above).

[121] *NS-Vernichtungslager*, 288–93. While these figures provide a minimum estimate, they are far more accurate than the figure of 300,000 given at Greiser's trial (ZSL, Prozeß Greiser, Bl. 58).

[122] *NS-Vernichtungslager*, 293 n. 96.

WESTMINSTER AND THE VICTORIAN CONSTITUTION

by Roland Quinault

READ 19 APRIL 1991

THE British constitution is unwritten, but not unbuilt. The character of Britain's government buildings reflects the nature of its political system. This is particularly true with respect to the Houses of Parliament. They were almost entirely rebuilt after a fire, in 1834, which seriously damaged the House of Commons and adjacent buildings. The new Houses of Parliament were the most magnificent and expensive public buildings erected in Queen Victoria's reign. Their architectural evolution has been meticulously chronicled by a former Honorary Secretary of the Royal Historical Society, Professor Michael Port.[1] But constitutionalists and historians have shewn little or no interest in the political character of the Victorian Houses of Parliament. Walter Bagehot, in his famous study, *The English Constitution*, published in 1867, made no reference to the newly completed Houses of Parliament. Likewise most modern books on Victorian political and constitutional history make no mention of the rebuilding.

The Victorian Houses of Parliament have been described by one historian as a symbol of 'The triumph of representative institutions over monarchical and tyrannical authority'. He argued that the Reform Act of 1832 influenced the manner by which parliament recreated the Palace of Westminster.[2] But he did not assess whether the character of the new legislature reflected the constitutional changes effected by the Reform Act. Certainly the new buildings were a much more imposing symbol of parliamentary authority than their predecessors. For the old Houses of Parliament compared poorly with those of other countries and were singularly unsuited for their legislative role.[3] The old House of Commons was so cramped and ill ventilated that it was described as 'The second edition of the Black Hole of Calcutta.' What Gladstone

[1] M. H. Port, 'The New Houses of Parliament', in J. Mordaunt Crook & M. H. Port, *The History of the King's Works, vol. VI 1782–1851* (1973), 573–626; M. H. Port (ed.), *The Houses of Parliament* (1976).
[2] W. J. Rorabough, 'Politics and the Architectural Competition for the Houses of Parliament 1834–37', *Victorian Studies*, XVIII, (1973), 155–6.
[3] E. B. Raylay & J. Britton, *The History of the Ancient Palace and late House of Parliament at Westminster* (1836), xiv.

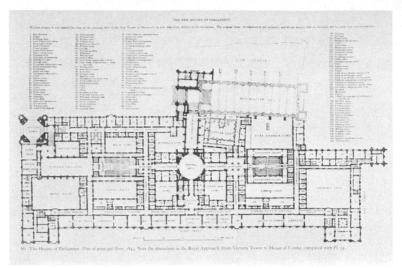

The Houses of Parliament Plan of Principal Floor 1843. From: M.H. Port (ed.), The Houses of Parliament (1976) With the kind permission of Professor Port.

termed its 'Corporeal conveniences' were 'Marvellously small' and unhygienic.[4] A Commons select committee recommended the construction of a new chamber in 1831, but it was not until after the 1834 fire, that parliament and the government decided that rebuilding was necessary.[5]

The new Houses of Parliament which arose, phoenix like, from the flames, were designed and built as a royal palace. The old Palace of Westminster had long been known as 'the Houses of Parliament', but the new building was officially styled 'Westminster New Palace' in 1846.[6] The initial design had been sanctioned by King William IV in 1836, when he was in poor health and did not expect to live much longer. Thus the new palace was planned from its inception for use by William's heir, Victoria. The design was selected, at the suggestion of Sir Edward Cust, by an architectural competition. Cust was closely connected with the family of Princess Victoria, since he was master of the household of King Leopold of Belgium and his wife was bedchamber-woman to the duchess of Kent. He was also one of the royal commissioners who judged the architectural competition.

[4] *Flora Tristan's London Journal*, (English edition, London, 1980), 56–7; John Morley, *The Life of William Ewart Gladstone* (1908 edn.), 75.
[5] *Parliamentary Papers*, 1833, XII, 467.
[6] *Illustrated London News*, 24 Jan. 1846.

The Victoria Tower and the proposed Albert Tower. From A. Barry, Life and Works of Sir Charles Barry (1867).

Charles Barry's winning design for the new Houses of Parliament had a distinctly regal flavour. Barry marked his competition plans with the royal castle emblem—a portcullis topped by a crown—and convinced the royal commissioners that he could 'Carry into effect Your Majesty's Commands, should you be pleased to honour him with your confidence'.[7] The most notable feature of Barry's design was a large square tower, like a castle keep, at the south-west corner of the palace. Barry named it the King's Tower because it stood over the royal entrance to parliament and it aroused much interest before he won the prize.[8] The tower was renamed the Victoria Tower, after the queen's accession. Barry hoped that the tower would be the great feature of the building, by which his name would be best remembered.[9] The size of the tower was criticised by the radicals, but its height was increased to accommodate the records of parliament. When the Victoria Tower was completed in 1858 it was the tallest secular building in the world.

The royal character of the new Houses of Parliament was also evident in its exterior sculpture. Barry wanted to create a 'A monumental history

[7] *Parl. Papers*, 1836 (66) XXXVI.
[8] Port, *The King's Works* 578, 585.
[9] Rev. Alfred Barry, *Sir Charles Barry* (1867), 254.

of England' by inserting statues in the facade.[10] Over three hundred statues were eventually erected: most of which depicted the English kings and queens since the Saxon period. But there was no representation of parliament or parliamentarians on the exterior of the palace. The coats of arms of all the English sovereigns since William I decorated the river front, which was topped by a statue of Queen Victoria. Another statue of the queen decorated the interior entrance of the Victoria Tower, which was also embellished with effigies of her parents, grandparents, aunts and uncles. A bronze equestrian statue of Richard Coeur de Lion, made by Count Marochetti and donated by the nobility and gentry, was erected, rather incongruously, in New Palace Yard, in 1853. The statue was moved in 1860 to its present position in Old Palace Yard, at the suggestion of Prince Albert. Statues of all the monarchs since the Norman conquest were planned for the interior of the palace, but most of them were not executed.

Inside the new palace, the regal theme was most apparent in the House of Lords, which Barry regarded as the Parliament Chamber of the monarch, rather than the peers.[11] The magnificence of the new chamber delayed its completion and prompted protests from peers, but Wellington reminded them of its royal function.[12] The completed chamber was described as 'a scene of royal magnificence as brilliant as it is unequalled' and was personally inspected by the queen.[13] The centrepiece of the new House of Lords was the magnificent throne and canopy designed by Pugin. The wall frescoes depicted the religious, judicial and chivalric virtues of medieval royalty and the stained glass windows depicted the royal lines of England and Scotland. The ceiling was adorned with a medley of royal heraldic devices, including the 'V. R.' monogram. 'Vivat Regina' was inscribed on all the window jambs and 'God Save the Queen' was carved on the gallery panels. Barry also provided the Prince of Wales, who had been born in 1841, with a state chair. The prince's plumes decorated the ceiling of the Lords, whilst the walls had frescoes of Prince Hal and the Black Prince.

The regal character of the House of Lords reflected the importance attached to the monarch's state visits to Parliament. Queen Victoria personally opened parliament almost every year until 1862 and regularly prorogued it until 1855, despite giving birth to nine children that period. The importance of the queen's state visits to parliament has been pointed out by Professor Arnstein, but he ignored the architectural

[10] Rev. Alfred Barry, *Sir Charles Barry* (1867), 258.
[11] *Ibid.*, 248.
[12] *Parl. Debs.*, 1845, LXXXI, 206–8; LXXXII, 1033–4.
[13] *Illustrated London News*, 17 April, 1847.

Interior of the New House of Lords. From: E. W. Godwin, Buildings and Monuments, Ancient and Modern (1850).

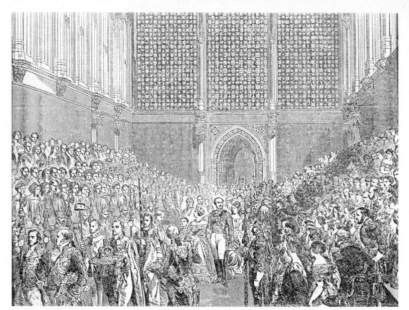

Queen Victoria and Prince Albert progressing through the Victoria Gallery. From: The Illustrated London News, 13 November 1852.

evidence which supports his thesis.[14] Barry aligned the two Houses of Parliament so that the queen could be seen on the throne by the Speaker in the Commons. He also created a new royal approach to the Lords which was the culmination of half a century's architectural assertion of the role of the Crown-in-Parliament. In the eighteenth century, the monarch had walked up an unimposing staircase to the House of Lords, but in 1800, Wyatt designed a new royal entrance and in 1822, Soane added a Scala Regia. Barry rebuilt the royal entrance and staircase in a much more imposing manner.[15] The queen would now dismount underneath the large portal of the Victoria Tower and then ascend the Royal Stair to the Norman Porch and the Robing Room. This was later decorated with latin prayers for the queen's safety, a reminder that Victoria survived three attacks on her life in the early years of her reign.

After the queen's marriage in 1840, Barry revised his plans for the Grand Entrance. The gallery between the Robing Rooms and the Lords was lengthened so that the queen and her husband could

---

[14] Walter L. Arnstein, 'Queen Victoria opens Parliament: the Disinvention of Tradition', *Historical Research*, 63, (1990), 182.

[15] *The Times*, 4 Feb. 1852.

progress, in full regalia, before a select audience ranged in tiers. The length of the Victoria Gallery—the longest room in the palace— prompted criticism that Barry was making 'a mere show of the queen, regardless of her comfort'.[16] So he inserted, between the gallery and the Lords, a private ante-room, the Prince's Chamber, in which was placed Gibson's large statue of Queen Victoria supported by Justice and Mercy. The Grand Entrance was first used by Victoria at the state opening of parliament in 1852. The queen thought that it was 'Magnificent' and bestowed a knighthood on Barry, as a mark of her approbation.[17] Thus Barry was rewarded for emphasising the royal aspect of parliament.

Queen Victoria ensured that the new palace honoured her husband as well as herself. When she married Albert, in 1840, the House of Lords had refused to grant him precedence after the queen. But Victoria issued a royal warrant which ensured that Albert was at her side when she made her state visits to parliament. In 1843, the queen ordered that a chair of state should be set up for Albert in the temporary House of Lords.[18] In 1845, the queen told Peel 'that something must at once be done to place the Prince's position on a constitutionally recognised footing and to give him a title adequate to that position.'[19] By then, Albert had become so identified with the queen's state affairs that he was considered 'king to all intents and purposes'.[20] In the new House of Lords, Barry provided a state chair for Albert which was embellished with his own heraldic badges. He also decorated the ceiling bosses of the Victory Gallery with the spread eagle of Saxe-Coburg, as well as the lion of England.

In 1841, Albert was appointed chairman of the Fine Arts Commission which was to supervise the interior decoration of the palace. For the next twenty years, Albert was an active and influential chairman of the commission. His German upbringing led him to favour the Nazarene style of painting and the use of fresco which was little known in England at the time. When Maclise won the commission to paint the frescoes in the Victoria Gallery, Albert persuaded him to study the waterglass technique at Berlin.[21] German influence was also evident in one of Maclise's frescoes, 'The Meeting of Wellington and Blucher after Waterloo'. Half of the long fresco depicted the Prussian troops, and the theme of Anglo-Prussian alliance was topical when the painting

---

[16] From Lord Sudeley in the Lords: *Parl. Debates*, 1844, lxxiv, 1242–5.
[17] *The Letters of Queen Victoria 1837–61*, eds. A. C. Benson & Viscount Esher, (3 vols., 1907), II, 439: Queen to Lord J. Russell, 4 Feb. 1852.
[18] *The Greville Diary*, ed. P. W. Wilson, (2 vols., 1927), II, 358: 26 Aug., 1843.
[19] *Letters of Queen Victoria*, I, 39–40: Queen to Peel, 18 Feb. 1845.
[20] *Greville Diary*, II, 362: 16 Dec. 1845.
[21] John Charlton in *Works of Art in the House of Lords*, ed. Maurice Bond, (1980), 34.

was commissioned. In 1852, Queen Victoria told the King of Prussia that the 'Powers who acted in concert at the last victory of Wellington and Blucher' should unite again if there were any threat from the Second Empire of Napoleon III.[22] Anglo-Prussian amity was strengthened in 1858 by the marriage of the queen's eldest child, the Princess Royal, to Prince Frederick of Prussia, whose father was a close friend of Prince Albert.

In 1855 Barry proposed to enclose New Palace Yard with an office block and a gateway surmounted by 'The Albert Tower'. Thus the two principle entrances to the Palace of Westminster would have been named after the monarch and her consort. A new direct approach road to the Victoria Tower from Buckingham Palace was also proposed.[23] But these projects were abandoned, partly because the government had to pay for increased military expenditure and partly because Albert died in 1861. The death of the Prince Consort brought the close royal involvement with the New Palace of Westminster to an end. Thereafter, the Fine Arts Commission ceased to award new contracts and the pictorial decoration of the palace was largely suspended. More importantly, the queen abandoned the palace which was so closely associated with her dead husband. For five years Victoria refused to open parliament in person and when she did return, she used the peers' entrance in Old Palace Yard, rather than the Grand Entrance. She never wore her robes again, or read her speech from the throne. In the last twenty years of her reign, the queen only opened parliament once. Thus the raison d'etre for Barry's Grand Entrance and Parliament Chamber was lost until the accession of Edward VII.

There is little iconographic evidence that the new Houses of Parliament were conceived as a temple to Whiggism and parliamentary sovereignty. Yet Barry owed his appointment largely to the Whigs. They had favoured an architectural competition and the chairman of the selection panel was a Whig MP, Charles Hanbury Tracy. He strongly favoured Barry, who had influential Whig patrons, and who, soon afterwards, designed the Reform Club in Pall Mall.[24] But Barry's work at Westminster was supervised by bi-partisan parliamentary committees and the Fine Arts Commission selected hardly any parliamentary scenes for the internal decoration of the palace. Despite the prevalence of medieval

[22] Further Letters of Queen Victoria, ed. Hector Bolitho, (1938), 33: Queen Victoria to the King of Prussia, 30 Nov. 1852.
[23] Barry, Barry, 291–2; Remarks on The Designs proposed for the New Government Offices More Particularly on those for the Block Plans and the approaches to the New Palace at Westminster, By a Practical Man (1857), 30.
[24] Barry, Barry, 67–77.

subjects, no sitting of a medieval parliament was commissioned. Cope's painting of 'Speaker Lenthall asserting the privileges of the House of Commons when Charles I came to arrest the Five Members' depicted a Speaker deferential to the king and MPs gripped by awe, rather than by anger, at the royal intrusion.

The Whig members of the Fine Arts Commission included Lansdowne, Russell and the historians, Hallam and Macaulay. Their reverence for Magna Carta was reflected in the commission's decision to place bronze statues of the barons who signed the charter in the wall niches of the House of Lords. Hallam's proposal that a statue of the archbishop of Dublin should be substituted for one of the bishop of London provoked an unavailing protest from a Tory commissioner, Sir Robert Inglis, that the archbishop had been a rapacious Irish administrator.[25] In general, however, the Fine Arts Commission selected subjects which avoided partisan controversy. The Peers Corridor, for example, was decorated with parallel paintings which illustrated both sides of the constitutional conflict from 1641 to 1689. They included a flattering picture of the 'Whig martyr' Lord Russell. He who was a forebear of Lord John Russell, who was both a member of the commission and prime minister at the time the subject was selected.

Whig influence at Westminster was more apparent in the preservation of the old, than in the creation of the new. The Whigs revered Westminster Hall where the great state trials of Stafford and Charles I had taken place. More recently, the hall had been the scene of Fox's reforming speeches and of the unsuccessful Whig impeachments of Warren Hastings in 1788 and Lord Melville in 1806. But the Whigs had much less affection for the old House of Commons, which had long been under Tory control. So when Lord Althorpe, the Whig Leader of the Commons, heard about the fire in 1834, he remarked 'Damn the House of Commons, let it blaze away; but save, oh save, the Hall.'[26] The hall was saved and it provided shelter for members of the public while they waited to meet MPs after debates in the House.[27]

The radicals had less influence than the Whigs on the character of the new Houses of Parliament. The hopes of the radicals were raised by the 1834 fire, for they had long wanted to move parliament to a more spacious and central site.[28] But the Commons did not debate the location of parliament until after the competition designs for rebuilding at Westminster had been submitted in 1836. Hume then proposed

[25] Parl. Papers, 1847, XXXIII, 282.
[26] The Times, 18 Oct, 1834.
[27] The Parliamentary Diaries of Sir John Trelawny 1858–1865, ed. T. A. Jenkins, (Camden Fourth Series, XXXX, 1990), 84, 300.
[28] Charles S. Parker, Life & Letters of Sir James Graham, Second Baronet of Netherby 1792–1861 (1907), I, 211: Graham to E. G. Stanley, 21 Oct., 1834.

moving parliament to St James's Palace, which was more central and convenient. He was supported by a few Whigs and most radicals, although Attwood, the leader of the Birmingham Political Union, opposed moving 'from a spot so intimately connected with the liberties of the people of England'. Hume's motion was defeated by a large majority of a thin House.[29] Nevertheless the *Westminster Review* argued that since the new Houses of Parliament were intended 'for objects totally different from any appertaining to the feudal system' they should be located on a new site in Green Park. It advocated the use of the Grecian style which it considered 'more expressive, from its associations, of the character of a free people'.[30] But attempts to dispense with Barry's Gothic design proved unavailing. When the Commons again debated the location of parliament, in 1838, work had already begun on embanking the Thames and the radicals were easily defeated.[31]

Radical MPs also failed to obtain a statue at Westminster of their hero, Oliver Cromwell.[32] This lacuna in what Hugh Miller termed 'the Marble History of England' was noted by *Punch*.[33] The suggestion that the arch regicide should be commemorated in parliament was naturally denounced by high Tories.[34] In 1867, the Tory government rejected a Liberal MP's suggestion that a statue of Cromwell should be placed between those of Charles I and Charles II in Westminster Hall. The proposal was rather insensitive, for Charles I had been condemned to death in the hall and Cromwell's head had been set up there on a pole at the Restoration. When the proposal was revived in 1895 by Harcourt, it was fiercely opposed by the Irish Nationalists, who remembered Cromwell's brutality at Drogheda.[35] So the prime minister, Rosebery, privately commissioned a statue from Hamo Thornycroft, which was placed—much to Harcourt's disgust—in the ditch outside Westminster Hall.[36] The statue was unveiled without ceremony, but afterwards Asquith told a Liberal meeting that since Cromwell had beheaded the sovereign, abolished the Commons and reformed the Lords, his statue would serve as a salutary warning to all those who made the laws.[37] However the location of Cromwell's statue *outside* the Palace of Westminster showed that he was still a persona non grata for many MPs.

The new House of Commons met with very little favour from radical

[29] *Parl. Debs.* 1836, XXXI, 236–46.
[30] *The Westminster Review*, XX (July 1836), 412, 418.
[31] *Parl. Debs.* 1838, XLIII, 695–700.
[32] *Parl. Debs.*, 1845, LXXXII, 1256; 1857, cxlvi, 160.
[33] Hugh Miller, 'The Cromwell Controversy' in *Essays* (Edinburgh, 1873), 30; *Punch*, IX, (1845), 151.
[34] *The Croker papers 1808–57*, B. Pool (ed.), (1967), 221.
[35] A. G. Gardiner, *The Life of Sir William Harcourt* (1923), II, 361.
[36] R. Rhodes James, *Rosebery* (1964), 381–2.; Gardiner, *Harcourt*, II, 361.
[37] *The Times*, 15 Nov. 1899.

"IT'S ALL VERY WELL, MR. CROMWELL; BUT YOU CAN'T
LODGE HERE."

Cartoon from: Punch, volume ix, 1845, p 151.

MPs. They disliked its oblong shape which followed the tradition of
the old House of Commons, rather than the semi-circular shape of the
Senate in Washington, or the Chamber of Deputies in Paris.[38] This

[38] *Parl. Papers*, 1833, XII, 547.

seemed to favour the front bench at the expense of back benchers and made no allowance for subtle shades of political allegiance. When the first experimental sitting was held in the new Commons in 1850 'Great complaints [were] made of it in every respect by almost everybody.' One novel feature was the provision of division lobbies around the chamber which reflected the growth of public interest in MP's voting at Westminster. The new lobbies soon had to be enlarged and the debating chamber was also remodelled to improve its poor acoustics. However some backbenchers still found it difficult to hear debates.[39] The natural lighting also proved inadequate and gas illumination was essential. When the House met at noon on 11 May 1864 the debate on parliamentary reform took place almost in darkness, until lights were lit.[40]

Radical MPs also disliked the style and decor of the new House of Commons. In 1848, several MPs complained that the adoption of the phrase 'Westminster New Palace' implied that they were to be accommodated like princes, rather than commoners.[41] Their fears were borne out by Barry's decoration of the new chamber. The front of the gallery was decorated with royal coats of arms, and 'God Save the Queen' was inscribed on the tiled floor of the lobby. MPs variously thought that the ornate design of the Commons was more suitable for a harem, a medieval monastery, or the 1851 Exhibition, than for a modern representative chamber. Hume spoke for many radicals when he observed that 'all tawdry, useless and unnecessary ornament, such as disfigured the House of Lords ... were wholly unfit for the present era.'[42] Benjamin Hall complained that the decoration of the gallery with the shields of parliamentary boroughs discriminated against unincorporated boroughs, like his own constituency of Marylebone, which had no shields to display. But Barry defended the practice, observing that the use of heraldry was 'absolutely essential to the character and the full expression of the Tudor style design adopted by Parliament'.[43]

The new House of Commons provided little more accommodation for MPs than its predecessors. The 1835 select committee had specified floor seating for about 440 MPs and room for the rest in the galleries. But the new Chamber could seat less than half of all MPs on the floor of the House and the gallery seats were disliked. Yet the number of MPs who participated in the business of the House increased markedly, especially after the 1867 Reform Act.[44] Consequently a select committee

[39] Parl. Debs., 1859, CLIV, 1346.
[40] Trelawny Diaries, 278.
[41] Parl. Debs., 1848, XCVI, 579; XCVII, 140.
[42] Ibid., XCVI, 564.
[43] Ibid., 1851, CXVI, 193–4.
[44] Alpheus Todd, On parliamentary Government in England: Its Origin, Development and Practical Operation (1887), II, 400–1.

The interior of the House of Commons as originally designed by Barry. From: E. W. Godwin, Buildings and Monuments, Ancient and Modern (1850).

recommended enlarging the House, and plans for a new chamber were drawn up by Edward Barry. But reconstruction was opposed by the prime minister, Gladstone, in the interests of public economy.[45] In the event, no significant changes were made to the House of Commons until the twentieth century.

The radicals persistently complained about the spiralling cost of the new palace. The estimates were often exceeded and the accounts were inadequately audited, yet the total expenditure on the palace—about £2,500,000 over a quarter of a century—was not exceptionally extravagant by contemporary standards. George IV spent as much per annum on his personal palaces in the 1820s as was spent at Westminster in the 1840s. Far larger sums were raised for railway construction in the mid-nineteenth century than were expended on the parliament where those railways were sanctioned. The palace was also relatively cheap by the standards of some later Victorian town halls such as Manchester, which aped Westminster in many respects. Thus the radicals had some success in limiting the cost of the new Houses of Parliament.

Barry provided virtually no space for government ministers or political parties in the New Palace of Westminster. In his revised 1843 plan, he

[45] *Parl. Debs.*, 1869, CXCV, 259.

allotted one room close to the House of Lords for ministers—about half of whom were peers. But it was not until the end of the Victorian period that separate rooms for senior ministers were provided close to the House of Commons. Barry made no room provision for the Opposition, or for party whips, since neither had official status. However he did allocate a large part of the palace for the residences of eighteen parliamentary offices. The largest of these residences was for the first commoner of the realm, the Speaker. In 1835 it was decided to provide a new residence for the Speaker suited to his situation and salary.[46] Barry allocated space for the Speaker's house at the north-east end of the palace, but he did not work out a detailed plan until 1857. Speaker Denison, who had requested a gentleman's family house, moved into his new residence in 1859. It had over sixty rooms and was lavishly decorated with painting, gilding and stained glass. The Speaker's house was also equipped with an ornate state bed for a future monarch to sleep on before the coronation. This provision reflected the traditionally close ties between the Speaker and the monarch. The Speaker's banquets, held in his large state dining room, were considered 'an important part of constitutional government'.[47] Guests on such occasions wore full court dress—velvet coat, breeches, silk stockings, buckled shoes and sword. Thus accoutred, Joseph Biggar, the Irish Nationalist MP, returned home on a twopenny bus in 1874.[48] But soon afterwards the Parnellites boycotted the Speaker's dinner.[49]

The size and splendour of the Speaker's house reflected the continued importance of the Speaker's role at Westminster. He presided over debates, until 1866 without a deputy, for as long as the House was in session. When he wished to relieve himself, the clerks held up their robes, to give him a measure of privacy.[50] The Speaker was not as impartial as constitutionalists have suggested. In 1834, Speaker Manners-Sutton lost the chair when the Whigs returned to power, because he had helped to engineer Peel's brief Tory ministry. All of the Victorian Speakers, were Liberals, although Peel became a Liberal Unionist. Speaker Denison advised both parties to implement a moderate reform bill in 1866 and he spoke and voted, like an ordinary MP, against the taxation of horses in 1869.[51] His successor, Brand, had been the Liberal

[46] Parl. Papers, 1835 (262), XVIII.; Philip Marsden, The Officers of the Commons 1363–1965 (1966), 146.

[47] Trelawny Diaries, 318.

[48] Arnold Wright & Philip Smith, Parliament Past and Present (1902), I, 57–9.

[49] H. W. Lucy, Diary of Two Parliaments: The Gladstone Parliament 1880–5 (1886), 407.

[50] Disraeli, Derby and the Conservative Party: The Journals and Memoirs of Edward Henry Lord Stanley 1849–69, ed. J. Vincent, (Hassocks, 1978), 201–2.

[51] Rt. Hon. John Evelyn Denison, Viscount Osington, Notes From My Journal When Speaker of the House of Commons (1900), 201–2, 243, 256–7.

Chief Whip and he dealt firmly with both the obstructionist Parnellites and the atheist Bradaugh. Procedural issues and the growth of standing orders ensured that the Speaker's role increased in importance in the later Victorian period.

Around Speaker's Court were grouped the residences of other Commons officials, including the house of the Sergeant-at-Arms. The Sergeant, as the Speaker's deputy, maintained order in the Commons and appointed its minor functionaries. Lord John Russell secured the post for his brother, who appointed old family retainers to his staff. When Sergeant Russell's son became an MP, a Commons official told him that he had helped to bury his grandparents.[52] The Sergeant-at-Arms had a snug above the Commons, where bored MPs sipped scotch, whilst waiting for the division bell to ring.[53] The Clerk of the Commons was also provided with a large house. Erskine May received 600 people there when he became Clerk in 1871. When May fell ill, the Speaker ordered that Big Ben should cease striking and that New Palace Yard should be covered with tan to deaden the sound of carriages. Gladstone told May that his illness had been 'a cabinet question' and gave him prior notice of the dissolution of Parliament in 1874. When the Tories won the election, May 'lost upwards of thirty of my most intimate friends' in the Commons.[54] The Clerk, like the Speaker, was all the more influential because he was discreetly partisan.

Erskine May thought that 'the political centre of the British Empire' was the Central Hall between the two Houses of Parliament. The Fine Arts Commission considered the hall an appropriate place to illustrate the patron saints of the four countries of the United Kingdom. But although the mosaic of St George was unveiled in 1870, that of St Patrick was not completed until after Ireland had left the union. An electric telegraph office was opened in the hall in 1853, which enabled MPs to stay in their clubs or at the opera until a division was called in the Commons. From the Central Hall, a host of lawyers, engineers, councillors, election agents, voters, publicans and others made their way to the numerous committee rooms which occupied a large part of the upper palace.[55] In the early Victorian period, there was a dramatic growth in the number of parliamentary committees, many of which scrutinised railway bills. In 1846, parliament passed 272 railway acts,

[52] George W. E. Russell, *One Look Back* (1911), 5, 197.

[53] Sir J. C. Astley Bt., *Fifty Years Of My Life in the World of Sport at Home and Abroad*, (n.d.), 262.

[54] *Erskine May's Private Journal 1857–82*, ed. D. Holland & D. Menhennet, (1972), 31, 37–40, 51.

[55] Erskine May, 'The Machinery of Parliamentary Legislation', *Edinburgh Review*, XCIX (1854), 252–3; E. M. Whitty, *St Stephen's in the Fifties* (1906), 199.

which were examined in nineteen unfinished committee rooms.[56] In 1848, there were over one hundred select committees which were attended by five or more MPs.[57] Committees usually met between 11 a.m. and the start of Commons business at 4 p.m. Thus some MPs had to spend up to twelve hours at Westminster, and they called for the same limit to their hours of labour which they had granted to textile operatives.[58]

Most of the larger committee rooms were located on the first floor of the palace, along the river front. These rooms were exposed to the bad odours which emanated from the untreated sewage in the Thames and the bone manufactories across the river.[59] In the dry summer of 1858, the stench from the Thames made the library of the Commons 'nearly untenable,' and disrupted the work of the Select Committee on the Bank Acts.[60] Disraeli 'hastened in dismay from the pestilential odour, followed by Sir James Graham, who seemed to be attacked by a sudden fit of expectoration; Mr Gladstone also paid particular attention to his nose'. A fortnight later, Disraeli told MPs that the Thames had become 'a Stygian pool' and persuaded them to subsidise the sewerage scheme of the Metropolitan Board of Works.[61]

Occasionally events in a Commons' committee room overshadowed those in the House itself. This was the case in December 1890, when the Irish Nationalist party decided the fate of its leader Parnell in the cramped confines of Committee Room 15. The first session, attended by 73 MPs and a team of reporters, lasted eleven hours. At night, the room was dimly lit by candles and oil lamps, for there was no gas or electric lighting on the upper floor of the palace. For six days the Irish MPs virtually ceased to attend the Commons, creating a temporary form of home rule at Westminster, which allowed parliamentary business to be expedited.[62] To alleviate the problem of overcrowding, the Grand Committee Room Annexe was constructed at the north-west end of Westminster Hall. It was the scene of the 1897 enquiry into the Jameson Raid, in which both Chamberlain and Rhodes figured prominently.

Informal meetings of MPs also played an important part in the political process at Westminster. It was alleged that the small size of the New House of Commons encouraged vice since MPs who could

[56] Port, *Houses of Parlt.*, 111.
[57] *Parl. Debs.*, 1848, CI, 672–3.
[58] May, *Edin. Review*, XCIX, 250.
[59] *Metropolitan Board of Works: Memorandum by the Chief Engineer on Mr Goldsworthy Gurney's Report Upon the Sewers in the Neighbourhood of the New Houses of Parliament* (1857), 7–8.
[60] *Trelawny Diaries*, 51.
[61] *The Times*, 3 & 15 July, 1858.
[62] H. W. Lucy, *A Diary of the Salisbury Parliament 1886–1892* (1892), 329.

not find a seat, went to the smoking room or slept in the Library.[63] Barry placed the libraries of both Houses on the ground floor, overlooking the terrace, a convenient place for quiet relaxation. The smoking room was another example of the influence of Prince Albert who had made smoking socially acceptable, despite Melbourne's claim that it was a dirty German habit.[64] The smoking room was popular with the Irish party and was also used by John Bright when he informally negotiated with the pro-reform Tories in 1867.[65] But most radical Liberals patronised the tea room and consequently the radical opposition to Gladstone's 1867 franchise proposals was called the 'tea room revolt'.

Before the 1850s, the only eating place for MPs inside the palace of Westminster was Bellamy's Kitchen. This was a small private franchise immortalised by the dying words of Pitt the Younger—'I could do with one of Bellamy's veal pies'—and later by the pen of Dickens. Bellamy's butler opposed giving more seats to London in the Reform Bill since the metropolitan members dined at home. Bellamy's remained a 'corner of the constitution' until it was replaced by Barry's much more spacious and comfortable dining rooms. MPs could now dine as well at Westminster as at their clubs. But the party leaders like Palmerston and Disraeli generally spent only a few minutes over their dinner, before returning to the House.[66]

The Clock Tower became the best known feature of the new palace because it was close to Westminster bridge and had a striking silhouette. Its evolution illuminated several aspects of Victorian politics. Barry borrowed the idea of an overhanging clock case from Scarisbrick Hall, which Pugin designed for a catholic client. Pugin was also directly responsible for the figures on the clock face. But if the clock case was catholic, the clock mechanism was protestant. For the novel escapement was designed by Edmund Beckett, who later became the first president of the Protestant Churchmen's Alliance. Beckett was well known at Westminster, where he was the leader of the lucrative parliamentary bar. But the sound of the new hour bell, 'Big Ben', was not liked by parliamentarians and in 1860, 'Earl Grey in common with all the inhabitants of that part of London in which he lived, rejoiced that the great bell had been cracked.'[67] When Ayrton was the First Commissioner of Works, he ordered the illumination of the west face of the Clock Tower when the Commons was in session. But it was not until 1893 that the 'Ayrton light' was extended to the clock's other faces, after

[63] Parl. Debs., 1850, CXIII, 727, 732–3.
[64] Mark Girouard, The Victorian Country House (Oxford, 1971), 24–5.
[65] The Diaries of John Bright, ed. R. A. J. Walling, (1930), 296.
[66] Illustrated London News, 13 August, 1853.
[67] Parl. Debs., 1860, CLIX, 219.

protests from South Bank MPs that their constituents had as much right as MPs in the West End to know when parliament was sitting.

The New Palace of Westminster was not a People's Palace like that which Queen Victoria opened in the Mile End Road in 1887. For the new Houses of Parliament were designed and built at a time when the great majority of men and all women were unenfranchised. The decision to rebuild the Houses of Parliament on the old site was prompted by several anti-democratic considerations. Westminster was still on the edge of the main London conurbation and remote from that old centre of autonomy and disaffection, the City. The location of the palace on the river allowed escape by water in the event of popular commotion and its cramped site limited the space which could be provided for the general public. In 1835 a select committee called for two hundred public seats in the new House of Commons, but the Whig government was frightened by the example of two French revolutions. Melbourne reminded the King of 'the fatal effects which large galleries filled with the multitude have had upon the deliberations of public assemblies'.[68] In the new chamber, the number of public seats was almost as niggardly as in the old, for Barry took the advice of leading officials. Consequently radical MPs complained that the new chamber 'excluded those whom it professed to represent' and called for more public seats.[69] But after the remodelling of the House there were still only about 130 public seats. Admission to the Strangers' Gallery required an order from either an MP or the Speaker, plus a tip of several shillings to the door-keeper. Public admission became even more difficult after a bomb exploded in the Commons in 1885. Thereafter balloting for public seats was introduced as a security measure.

The general public relied on press reports for its knowledge of parliamentary debates. Since 1803, a few reporters had been reserved places in the public gallery of the old House of Commons and they were dubbed 'a fourth estate of the realm' by Macaulay in 1829.[70] But it was not until 1835 that the press was given separate seating in the temporary House of Commons. In Barry's new chamber, the press occupied boxes in the front two rows of the north gallery, which were tested for audibility by Russell and Peel. Palmerston later complimented the reporters on their accuracy.[71] But the gallery reporters had no

[68] *Lord Melbourne's Papers*, ed. L. C. Sanders, (1889), 214.
[69] *Parl. Debs.*, 1850, CXIII, 734–8.
[70] Lord Macaulay, *Reviews, Essays and Poems* (1890), 134.
[71] *The Times*, 31 May, 1850, 22 Dec. 1859.

official status and could be cleared from the House—as they were during the debates on the Contagious Diseases Acts in 1870. Admission to the press boxes was at the discretion of the Sergeant-at-Arms and Sergeant Russell gave fifteen boxes to the London papers, three to the press agencies and one to Hansard. In 1881, an extension of the press gallery enabled the Scottish, Irish and provincial press to obtain boxes, but foreign and female journalists remained excluded for the rest of the reign.

The Ladies Gallery, The House of Commons. From: The Queen, 21 December, 1861.

The most novel feature of the new House of Commons was the Ladies Gallery. There had been an unofficial ladies gallery in the roof of the old Commons, but there was much opposition to the provision of a proper gallery for women in the new chamber. So Barry placed the Ladies Gallery behind an ornamental grille, which impeded visibility and ventilation and gave rise to the sobriquet 'the Ladies Cage'. Admission to the twenty seats was much sought after, but was restricted to guests of MPs or the Speaker's wife. In 1858, an MP, prompted by 'bitter complaints from many of the ladies of my own constituents', called for increased accommodation, but without success.[72] When Gladstone introduced the 1866 Reform bill, there was intensive com-

[72] *Parl. Debates,* 1858, CL, 1203.

petition for seats in the gallery.[73] One lady was only able to hear the debate by standing in a cellar underneath the Commons. From there she could see Gladstone's feet above her head, while his voice came down like a flood through the ventilator.[74] The presence of ladies in the gallery was believed to influence the tone of debates.[75] In 1867, Mrs Fawcett and her supporters were in the Ladies Gallery when Mill moved his female suffrage amendment to the Reform bill. Josephine Butler frequently visited the Ladies Gallery during her campaign against the Contagious Diseases Acts.[76] When Mrs O'Shea was in the gallery, Parnell signalled to her with his handkerchief to inform her where she could meet him after the debate.[77]

Ladies, in the persons of peeresses and their unmarried daughters, were much more conspicuous in the Lords than the Commons. They packed the unenclosed peeresses gallery when there was an important debate and they occupied most of the floor of the chamber when the Queen opened Parliament. In 1888 ladies were allowed to take tea and supper with MPs and to go on the river terrace. In summertime, the terrace vied with the Lawn at Ascot and the Ladies Mile in Hyde Park as a venue of fashionable Society. Working men and women usually went to the palace for employment, rather than recreation. However New Palace Yard, which was open to the general public, was sometimes used as a democratic forum. It was there that the election of representatives to the Chartist Convention was held in 1838.[78] The yard was enclosed with ornamental railings in 1865, but the general public could still enter it and did so to cheer Gladstone on several occasions.[79] However, when Keir Hardie arrived at the yard after his election for West Ham in 1892, his two horse brake, with a cornet player on the box seat, was refused admission.[80]

The New Palace of Westminster was conservative by design, but radical by construction. About 1,000 men on average were employed in building the palace from 1840 to 1860, and many of them held radical opinions. In 1841, eight stone masons currently working on the Houses of Parliament carried the Chartist national petition to the Commons.[81] When Henry Broadhurst 'roughed-out' the masonry of

[73] William White, *The Inner Life of the House of Commons* (2 vols., 1904), II, 34–5.

[74] *The Letters of Anne Thackeray Ritchie*, ed. Hester Ritchie, (1924).

[75] *Trelawny Diaries*, 210.

[76] *Josephine Butler An Autobiographical Memoir*, eds. G. W. & L. A. Johnson, (1913), 177–9.

[77] Catherine O'Shea, *Charles Stewart Parnell* (1914), I, 177.

[78] *London Radicalism 1830–43: A selection from the papers of Francis Place*, ed. D. J. Rowe, (1970), 190.

[79] *Parl. Debs.*, 1865, CLXXVII, 498–9 & 1866, CLXXXI, 1524. H. W. Lucy, *A Diary of Two Parliaments: The Gladstone Parliament 1880–5* (1886), 481.

[80] K. O. Morgan, *Keir Hardie Radical and Socialist* (1975), 54–5.

[81] David Jones, *Chartism and the Chartists* (1975), 86.

The Terrace of the Houses of Parliament. From: Arnold Wright & Philip Smith, Parliament Past and Present, (London, 1902), volume i, 94.

the Clock Tower in 1865, the bitter north-east wind made it impossible for him to hold a chisel, Broadhurst's dissatisfaction with the mason's lot made him an active trade unionist and he soon worked on the inside of the Houses of Parliament. He became secretary of the TUC parliamentary committee, than a Liberal MP and finally Under-Secretary at the Home Office in 1886. Broadhurst was the first working class minister and his mallet and chisel are now on display in the palace.[82]

When the new Houses of Parliament were built, Westminster was the seat of the judiciary as well as the legislature. The royal courts of justice had been located at Westminster long before parliament. In 1820 the courts were moved from Westminster Hall to new premises alongside, designed by Soane. Their presence generated ancillary services and Parliament Street was lined with law stationers. The proximity of the law courts strengthened the case for parliament remaining at Westminster, for barristers played an important role in the House of Commons.[83] The House of Lords was the supreme court of appeal and

[82] Henry Broadhurst MP, *The Story of his Life from a Stonemason's Bench to the Treasury Bench told by Himself* (1900), 29, 100.
[83] J. A. Thomas, *The House of Commons 1832–1901* (Cardiff, 1939), 4–5.

its Speaker, the Lord Chancellor, was one of the Chancery judges. The judicial role of the Lords was illustrated in Barry's new chamber by Maclise's fresco 'The Spirit of Justice'. In the 1850's it was decided to move the courts of justice closer to the inns of court, but the new Law Courts on the Strand were not completed until 1882.

Barry did not provide a chapel in the palace for the use of MPs. This omission conformed with past practice and the recent decisions of parliament that Nonconformists and Roman Catholics could become MPs. Barry was an Anglican, but he relied on Pugin, an ardent catholic convert, for much of the detailed Gothic decoration of the palace. However no decorative motifs were used which would have been regarded as popish, for suspicion of Catholicism was still strong at Westminster.[84] Pugin's Catholicism effectively debarred him from holding an official post in the rebuilding of parliament.

Radicals regarded the adoption of Barry's Gothic design as evidence of the continued ascendancy of the Church and the episcopacy.[85] Barry provided the bishops with their own robing room and originally intended to give them a separate entrance. He also decorated the Strangers' Gallery in the House of Lords with episcopal coats of arms. The role of the bishops in the Lords was strongly endorsed by Prince Albert.[86] Consequently bishops figured prominently in the Lords' frescoes selected by the Fine Arts Commission. Dyce, who was a protege of Albert and a devout Anglican, was commissioned to paint the central panel above the throne. His subject, 'the Baptism of King Ethelbert'— the first Saxon king to become a Christian—symbolised the union of Crown and Church. The frescoes depicted pre-Reformation scenes and thus avoided giving offence to the Catholic peers. But the emphasis on Christianity was consistent with the strong opposition of the Lords to Jewish emancipation.

The decision to rebuild the palace in the Gothic style was influenced by the propinquity of Westminster Abbey. Barry's adoption of Perpendicular Gothic complemented Henry VII's Chapel which abutted onto Old Palace Yard. Pugin had made drawings in the abbey at the start of his career and he modelled the throne in the Lords on the coronation chair in the abbey. Most of the new palace was literally in the shadow of Westminster Abbey. For Edward the Confessor had positioned the abbey on the highest part of Thorney Island and Henry III had rebuilt it with the tallest Gothic nave in England. The roof of the new palace hardly reached the clerestory of the abbey—which

[84] Charles L. Eastlake, *A History of The Gothic Revival* (1872), 168.

[85] *The Westminster Review*, (July, 1836), 409.

[86] Theodore Martin, *Life of H.R.H. The Prince Consort* (1876), II, 132–3: Albert to the Dean of Westminster, 19 Oct. 1845.

prompted talk of the continued subordination of the state to the church.[87] It was not until the construction of the upper stages of the Clock Tower and the Victoria Tower, in the 1850's, that the abbey lost some of its height advantage over the palace.

The abbey aroused a veneration which was seldom felt for the Houses of Parliament. Disraeli wrote: 'it is something to step aside from Palace Yard and instead of listening to a dull debate ... to enter the old Abbey and listen to an anthem!'[88] In 1851, a London guidebook described the abbey as 'without exception, the most interesting object in London'.[89] Its popularity with the public increased when visitors fees were reduced to 2d a head after criticism by Hume and others in parliament. The abbey was now much more accessible to ordinary people than the Houses of Parliament. When Dean Stanley allowed free admission to the abbey on Mondays, 9,000 visitors came at Easter, in 1870.[90] Stanley thought that the abbey was a monument to the process by which the English constitution had been framed, with 'Church and State inextricably mixed with each other'.[91] He claimed that the close incorporation of the palace and the abbey symbolised the constitutional union of the secular crown with the religious church.[92] Parts of the abbey precinct had long been used by the government for secular purposes. The Chapter House remained a depository for the records of the law courts and the Exchequer until the building of the Public Record Office in 1859. In 1866, parliament voted £7,000 to restore the Chapter House to its original Gothic state, when it had been the meeting place of the early House of Commons.[93] The last part of the abbey to be retained for government use was the Chapel of the Pyx, which housed specimen coins. The trial of the pyx—the quinquennial testing of the coinage by the Goldsmiths' Company— was held at the Exchequer office in Old Palace Yard. The chapel remained under the joint custody of the Lords of the Treasury and the Comptroller of the Exchequer until the trial was transferred to the Mint in 1904.

The abbey church had an important connection with parliament as the burial place of many prominent statesmen. These included Castlereagh and Canning in the 1820's, Palmerston in 1865 and Gladstone in 1898. Their statues (and those of other prominent statesmen not buried in the abbey) were paid for by parliament.

[87] The Westminster Review, IL (July 1848), 468.
[88] B. Disraeli, Sybil (1925 edn.), 235.
[89] The British Metropolis in 1851: A Classified Guide to London (1851), 66.
[90] A House of King's: The History of Westminster Abbey, ed. E. Carpenter, (1966), 288, 307.
[91] The Times, 29 Dec. 1865.
[92] Arthur P. Stanley, Historical Memorials of Westminster Abbey (1868), 35–6.
[93] See: The Times, 30 Dec. 1865.

Gladstone's body lay in state for two days in Westminster Hall, before it was buried next to the statue of his mentor, Peel. The pallbearers included the Prince of Wales and the party leaders in both Houses. Many peers and about 400 MPs attended the service— only the Parnellites being absent.[94] Gladstone had increasingly opposed the union of church and state, but his funeral showed that the union was still strong at Westminster.

Since the Puritan era, MPs had generally worshipped, not in the abbey, but in the parish church of St Margaret's, where there was a special pew for the Speaker. Parliament made regular grants for the repair of the church up to 1846 and the last grant was made in 1876.[95] In the 1840's, one Tory MP worshipped in St Margaret's twice on Sundays when parliament was in session.[96] On Fast Day in 1855, about 150 MPs, including Disraeli and the Speaker attended the service at St Margaret's and in 1887, 400 MPs celebrated Queen Victoria's Jubilee there.[97] Prominent MPs and officers of the Commons were commemorated in the church in the late Victorian period.

Westminster School, which had been established by the abbey and re-founded by Queen Elizabeth, also had close links with Parliament. The school had educated more MPs than Eton in the early eighteenth century and it was still the nursery of many politicians a century later.[98] Several prominent reformers were educated at Westminster, including Burdett, Hobhouse and Graham. The latter was inspired by listening to the parliamentary speeches of Pitt and Fox.[99] The school's Queen's Scholars had reserved seats in the galleries of both Houses of Parliament. In 1848, eight members of the government, including the prime minister (Russell) and the Leader of the House of Lords (Lansdowne) had been educated at the school.[100] Russell recalled that 'physical hardihood was always encouraged' at Westminster and argued that public schools were part of the constitution, because they encouraged 'the democratic character of the English aristocracy'.[101] The tough regime at the

[94] *The Illustrated London News*, 4 June, 1898.

[95] H. F. Westlake, *St Margaret's Westminster: The Church of the House of Commons* (1914), 95, 111, 115–6.

[96] *The Diary of an Honourable Member: The Journal of Henry Broadley MP 1840–2*, ed. John Markham, (Hull, 1987), 4, 140.

[97] Andrew Lang, *Life, Letters & Diaries of Sir Strafford Northcote, First Earl of Iddesleigh* (1891), 73.

[98] Gerrit P. Judd, *Members of Parliament 1734–1832* (New Haven, 1955), 37–8.

[99] *Parl. Papers*, 1864, xxi, Clarendon Commission on Public Schools, 431; Robert E. Zegger, *John Cam Hobhouse: A Political Life 1819–52* (Columbia, Missouri, 1973), 44.

[100] F. H. Forshall, *Westminster School* (1884), vi.

[101] Spencer Walpole, *The Life of Lord John Russell* (1889), I, 9. Lord John Russell, *An Essay on the History of the English Government and Constitution* (1823, edn.), 255.

school provided an ideal preparation for an army career and the Duke of Wellington claimed that his best staff officers came from Westminster.[102] The school educated five out of the seven non-royal Field Marshals created between 1810 and 1856, and Old Westminsters played a prominent part in the Crimean War and the Indian Mutiny. By then, however, prominent families preferred to educate their sons in healthier surroundings than Westminster.[103]

Victorian Westminster was a growing centre of government for the Church as well as the State. The offices and central schools of 'The National Society for the Education of the Poor in the Principles of the Established Church'—the main provider of elementary education in Victorian England—were located in the Sanctuary, across from the abbey. The society's first superintendent, Andrew Bell—the pioneer of monitorial instruction—was a prebendary of the abbey. In the 1890's, Church House was built in Dean's Yard to commemorate Queen Victoria's Golden Jubilee and the blessings conferred on the Church during her reign. It became the administrative headquarters of the Church and the seat of Convocation. In 1903, the Ecclesiastical Commissioners also acquired new headquarters, on Millbank, across the road from the Victoria Tower.

The New Houses of Parliament were not designed to house a new constitution. For neither Barry's buildings, nor the interior decoration approved by the Fine Arts Commission, showed that Britain's ancien regime had come to an end.[104] On the contrary, they were testimony to the truth of Macaulay's observation, in 1849, that the constitution was still mostly old.[105] The new edifice was not a temple to Whig reform or even to the landed interest, but a royal palace which highlighted the role of the Crown-in-Parliament. Barry and Pugin provided a setting of unprecedented splendour for the monarch's state opening of parliament. They also covered the walls, floors and ceilings of the palace with heraldic emblems of the queen and the Crown. The use of the Gothic style also drew attention to the close bond between Church and State at Westminster. Thus it was fitting that Barry was buried in Westminster Abbey and that both he and Pugin were posthumously commemorated on the Albert Memorial.

[102] Parl. Papers, 1864, XXI, 409.
[103] Bernard Cracroft, 'The Analysis of the House of Commons or Indirect Representation', in: Essays on Reform (1867), 327–9; Parl. Papers 1864, XXI, 393.
[104] cf: Jonathan Clark, English Society 1688–1832: Ideology, Social Structure and Political Practice during the Ancien Regime (Cambridge, 1985), 409.
[105] T. B. Macaulay, A History of England from the accession of James II, (n.d.), 27.

The design and decoration of the New Palace of Westminster reflected the substance, as well as the style, of the Victorian constitution. For whereas MPs (of both Houses) were divided by creed and nationality, they all had to swear allegiance to the Crown. Even Daniel O'Connell, the Roman Catholic leader of the Repeal party, professed his loyalty to Queen Victoria. As the 'reign of Victoria and Albert' progressed, it appeared to observers like Macaulay, that the power of the monarchy was increasing.[106] Even after the queen's withdrawal into widowhood, Erskine May noted that republican sentiments were not even whispered in Parliament.[107] MPs also had close links with the Church and the law, since the great majority of them were Anglicans and lawyers held key posts in both Houses.

The exclusive and pre-democratic character of the new Houses of Parliament attracted little criticism until the late Victorian period. In 1890, William Morris—who never became an MP—predicted that the Houses of Parliament would be used as a dung market in the 1990's.[108] This has not *yet* come to pass, but public access is still much restricted, as it was in the Victorian period, by lack of space and concern for security. However television has now made the general public much more familiar with the interior of the palace. The splendour of Barry and Pugin's work has also been revealed by recent cleaning and redecoration. Thus we are now better able to appreciate the truly Victorian character of the New Palace of Westminster and the constitution which it was designed to encase.

[106] *The Spectator*, 23 Feb. 1861.
[107] Erskine May, *Democracy in Europe*, (2 vols., 1877), II, 480.
[108] William Morris, *News From Nowhere* (1912 edn.), 47.

CATHOLIC, ANGLICAN OR PURITAN?
EDWARD SACKVILLE, FOURTH EARL OF DORSET
AND THE AMBIGUITIES OF RELIGION IN EARLY
STUART ENGLAND*

The Alexander Prize Essay

By David L. Smith

READ 17 MAY 1991

THE religion of Edward Sackville, fourth earl of Dorset,[1] foxed his contemporaries, and he has proved an equally slippery customer for those modern historians who wish to see unbridgeable confessional gulfs opening up in the 1620s and 1630s.[2] A detailed study of him reveals ambiguities of position that confused his contemporaries and confound modern categorisation. Those who knew Dorset differed dramatically in their perception of his religion. To one French ambassador, Tillières, he was 'un puritain';[3] while to William Middleton, Lord Fielding's chaplain, he appeared 'strong for Precisians'.[4] By contrast, another French ambassador, Fontenay, believed that Dorset 'n'est pas

*I am most grateful to John Morrill for reading and commenting upon an earlier draft of this essay. I would also like to thank the following for much help, advice and stimulation on the subject of Dorset's religion: John Adamson, Ian Atherton, Gerald Aylmer, David Bevington, Richard Cust, Kenneth Fincham, Andrew Foster, Derek Hirst, Peter Lake, Anthony Milton, Kevin Sharpe, Richard Strier, Nicholas Tyacke, and especially Colin Davis, Sir Geoffrey Elton, Conrad Russell and Peter Salt.

[1] Dorset became a Privy Councillor in 1626 and Lord Chamberlain to Queen Henrietta Maria in 1628. During the Civil War he was a moderate Royalist. For a full-length study, see David L. Smith, 'The Political Career of Edward Sackville, fourth Earl of Dorset (1590–1652)' (unpubl. Ph.D. thesis, Univ. of Cambridge, 1990). For detailed analyses of the successive stages of his career, see also *idem*, 'The fourth Earl of Dorset and the politics of the 1620s', *Historical Research*, LXV (1992), 37–53; *idem*, 'The fourth Earl of Dorset and the Personal Rule of Charles I', *J[ournal] [of] B[ritish] S[tudies]*, XXX (1991), 257–87; *idem*, ' "The more posed and wise advice": the fourth Earl of Dorset and the English Civil Wars', *H[istorical] J[ournal]*, XXXIV (1991), 797–829.

[2] See, for example, N. Tyacke, *Anti-Calvinists: The Rise of English Arminianism, c. 1590–1640* (Oxford, 1987), esp. chapters 6–8; and J. P. Sommerville, *Politics and Ideology in England, 1603–1640* (Harlow, 1986), esp. chapter 6.

[3] P[ublic] R[ecord] O[ffice], PRO 31/3/55 (Baschet's transcripts), unfol.: Tillières to Puisieux, 12 July 1621.

[4] Quoted in William Prynne, *Canterburies Doome* (1646), 429–30. I owe this reference to Anthony Milton.

trop ennemy de nostre religion'[5]; and the papal agent Carlo Rossetti thought him 'assai fautori nell' intrinseco dei Cattolicci'.[6] In 1641 Sir Walter Erle even opposed the re-enfranchisement of Seaford on the grounds that 'the lord of the town [i.e. Dorset] [was] a papist'.[7] Dorset was called everything from a puritan to a papist—and other things besides. In dedicating his 'account of religion by reason' to Dorset, Sir John Suckling wrote that the tract—which was widely condemned as Socinian—'had like to make me an atheist at Court and your lordship no very good Christian'.[8] Whereas Professor Hexter addressed 'the problem of the Presbyterian-Independents',[9] contemporary images of Dorset present the even more bizarre spectacle of a puritan-papist-pagan. Where, that is, they mention his religion at all. For time and again we find that descriptions focus mainly on Dorset's courtly and chivalric qualities. Clarendon portrayed Dorset as 'a man of an obliging nature, much honour, of great generosity, and of most entire fidelity to the Crown'; but made no mention of his religious attitudes.[10] When authors dedicated their writings to Dorset they consistently highlighted these same secular traits: Sir Richard Baker praised his 'publicke vertues', Edward May his 'noble nature'; and even John Bastwick called him simply 'illustrissimus'.[11] Likewise, James Howell's 'elegy upon the most accomplish'd and heroick ... Earl of Dorsett' extolled his 'admired perfections' and 'goodly person', but had virtually nothing to say about his religion.[12] All this material tells us much about how Dorset was perceived during his lifetime. But as evidence of his religious attitudes, the impressions of his contemporaries are of distinctly limited value: either they present conflicting views; or they fail to allude to his religion

[5] P. R. O., PRO 31/3/66, fo. 162v: Fontenay to Bouthillier, Aug. 1630.

[6] P. R. O., PRO 31/9/19 (transcripts from Rome archives), fo. 9r: Rossetti to Barberini, 7 Sept. 1640.

[7] *The Journal of Sir Simonds D'Ewes from the beginning of the Long Parliament to the opening of the trial of the Earl of Strafford*, ed. W. Notestein (New Haven, 1923), 321-2.

[8] *The Works of Sir John Suckling*, ed. A. H. Thompson (1910), 341. For the charge of Socinianism, see also P. R. O., S. P. 16/429/38 (Secretary Windebanke's notes, 27 Sept. 1639). The broad and narrow senses of this term are discussed in H. R. Trevor-Roper, *Catholics, Anglicans and Puritans* (1987), 186–92.

[9] J. H. Hexter, 'The Problem of the Presbyterian Independents', reprinted in his *Reappraisals in History* (1961), 163–84.

[10] Edward Hyde, Earl of Clarendon, *The History of the Rebellion and Civil Wars in England*, ed. W. D. Macray (6 vols, Oxford, 1888), I, 75–6 (Book I, 129–31).

[11] Richard Baker, *Meditations and Disquisitions upon the One and Fiftieth Psalme of David* (1638), sig. 3[v]; Edward May, *A most certaine and true Relation of a strange monster or serpent found in the left ventricle of the heart of John Pennant, gentleman, of the age of twenty-one yeares* (1639), sig. A2[v]; J. Bastwick, *ΠΡΑΞΕΙΣ ΤΩΝ ΕΠΙΣΚΟΠΩΝ, Sive Apologeticus ad Praesules Anglicanos* (1636), 178.

[12] James Howell, *Ah, ha; Tumulus, Thalamus: Two Counter-Poems* (1654), sig. A (B[ritish] L[ibrary], E 228/1).

altogether. This sets the pattern for much of what follows. Dorset's religion proves extremely difficult to reconstruct, for the surviving evidence is patchy, ambiguous and oblique. However, I shall argue that this is itself a clue to his attitudes; and that the problems of retrieval and categorisation which we face today partly reflect the actual nature of Dorset's beliefs three-and-a-half centuries ago.

Let us now turn to the extant records of Dorset's own words. For him—as for the majority of English people in this period—we have little written evidence of religious belief. No diary survives of the kind which illuminates the piety of Ralph Josselin or Thomas Dugard or Robert Woodford.[13] The absence of any indication that Dorset ever compiled one might argue against an introspective 'godliness', although after three-and-a-half centuries the argument from silence is hardly strong. More promisingly, we do possess a will in Dorset's hand dated 23 March 1624/5.[14] Several historians, including Dr Tyacke, have suggested that wills afford some of the most helpful glimpses of religious attitudes in early modern England.[15] So far, two sorts of doubts have been expressed about this deduction: first, that the preambles to wills may reveal the religious position of the scribe rather than that of the testator; and second, that such preambles tended to become mere formulae.[16] Dorset's will, however, prompts a third reservation. For here we have a document, written by the testator, which does not follow a standard formula, yet which consistently strikes a note of studied ambivalence. The preamble reads:

I ioyfully ressigne my sowle unto my creator, confident of its salvation through the mercy and mediation only of that Lambe of God, which taketh away the sinns of the world: vayled over with whose righteousness, my fayth is, thatt by imputative iustice it shall appeare immaculate before the last tribunall, and receave through the intercession of his passion admittance into eternall glory therewith assuredness attendinge the resurrection of my body, with beleefe of reunion, forever to remayne in perpetuall bliss: Lord soe be itt.[17]

---

[13] *The diary of Ralph Josselin, 1616–1683*, ed. A. Macfarlane (1976); A. Hughes, 'Thomas Dugard and His Circle in the 1630s—a "Parliamentary-Puritan" Connexion?', *H.J.*, XXIX (1986), 771–93; J. Fielding, 'Opposition to the Personal Rule of Charles I: the Diary of Robert Woodford, 1637–41', *ibid.*, XXXI (1988), 769–88.

[14] K[ent] A[rchives] O[ffice], Sackville MS, U 269/T83/5.

[15] See esp. Tyacke, *Anti-Calvinists*, 3, 12, 21, 89, 115, 191, 193, 215; also A. Fletcher, *A County Community in Peace and War: Sussex, 1600–1660* (1975), 63–4.

[16] For the first point, see J.J. Scarisbrick, *The Reformation and the English People* (Oxford, 1984), esp. 10; for the second, J. D. Alsop, 'Religious preambles in early modern English wills as formulae', *Journal of Ecclesiastical History*, XL (1989), 19–27.

[17] K. A. O., Sackville MS, U 269/T83/5, fo. 1r.

Clearly Dorset rejected the doctrine of saintly intercession, and this alone should dispel rumours that he was a 'papist'. But equally, there is neither the assurance of election nor the belief in man's innate depravity which usually characterised more 'godly' wills. Little in the preamble is individual: a reliance for salvation on the merits, death and passion of Christ was quite commonplace. Nor does the rest of the will offer any further clues to Dorset's religious beliefs. His bequests—to his wife, children and staff—were apparently not determined by religious considerations. Interestingly, his two executors, Sir Henry Compton and Thomas Middlemore, were both Catholics.[18] But this was probably less important than the fact that both held extensive lands in East Sussex, where Dorset's own territorial base was concentrated.[19] There are even likelier explanations for Dorset's choice. Sir Henry Compton was Dorset's brother-in-law, having married his sister, Cecily Sackville.[20] Thomas Middlemore was a long-standing client of the Sackvilles: he was described in 1600 as 'belongeinge to' Dorset's father[21]; he later became one of Dorset's tenants[22]; and he frequently witnessed Dorset's legal transactions.[23] It seems highly unlikely that Dorset chose Compton and Middlemore as his executors because he shared their Catholicism. While their religion clearly did not dissuade him from appointing them, the positive reasons for his choice were probably that Compton and Middlemore were both powerful and established neighbours, that Compton was a close relative, and that Middlemore was a trusted client, tenant and friend. In short, the religious views expressed in Dorset's will were in many ways conventional and anonymous, and appear to have determined neither his choice of executors nor the pattern of his bequests.

We seem to be little further forward. So far, we have encountered three reasons why the surviving evidence stubbornly refuses to illuminate Dorset's religious attitudes. First, it is necessarily incomplete and helpful material may well have been lost, for example when Dorset House was destroyed in the Great Fire of London in 1666.[24] As in any historical enquiry, it is impossible to know what sources once existed but no longer survive. Second, Dorset's will—where we might expect to find

---

[18] K. A. O., Sackville MS, U 269/T83/5, fo. 8r. For the religious beliefs of Compton and Middlemore, see Fletcher, *Sussex*, 97–8, 100.

[19] Compton lived at Brambletye, near East Grinstead: Fletcher, *Sussex*, 28, 97. Middlemore lived at Rotherfield: *ibid.*, 56.

[20] B. L., Harl. MS 1233 (misc. collections), fo. 91v.

[21] P. R. O., S. P. 12/274/75 (R. Cooke to Mary Goche, 9 Mar. 1599/1600).

[22] E[ast] S[ussex] R[ecord] O[ffice], Add. MS 5729/15 (indenture of 27 May 1628).

[23] See, for example, E. S. R. O., G 23/4 (indenture of 1 June 1618); B.L., Add. Charter 9290 (indenture of 15 July 1629).

[24] K. A. O., Sackville MS, U 269/L4 (papers relating to the destruction of Dorset House, 1666).

a clear statement of belief—gives very little away. Third, Dorset's contemporaries either reached incompatible conclusions about his religion, or preferred to dwell on other, secular characteristics. This last point brings us to another fundamental difficulty: as a peer, Privy Councillor and courtier, Dorset wore several hats besides that of the religious believer. Unlike men such as John Pym and Lord Saye and Sele, Dorset's religious attitudes did not dictate either his political agenda or his public persona. This becomes a serious handicap when we examine his speeches in Star Chamber for evidence of religious belief. On two occasions, Dorset addressed religious or ecclesiastical themes: at Henry Sherfield's trial (February 1633); and at William Prynne's first trial (February 1634). I shall argue, however, that these utterances cannot be treated as manifestations of a personal credo, but rather should be interpreted in the context of Dorset's public offices as Privy Councillor and Henrietta Maria's Lord Chamberlain.

In February 1633, Henry Sherfield, recorder of Salisbury, was brought before Star Chamber charged with smashing a stained-glass window in St Edmund's Church, Salisbury, in defiance of Bishop Davenant's orders. The window depicted God as an old man measuring the world with a pair of compasses, and raising Eve out of the side of Adam. Sherfield allegedly declared that he did 'not like these painted windowes in churches ... they obscure the light, and may be a cause of much superstition'.[25] The case split the Star Chamber. With Charles I's encouragement, Laud, Neile and seven others urged the exemplary punishment of a £1,000 fine. Dorset, by contrast, took a more moderate line.[26] He argued that Sherfield's action was not intrinsically evil: 'if all unlawfull pictures and images were utterly taken out of the churches, I thinke it were a good worke; for at the best they are but vanities and teachers of lies'. But then—just as we hoped to penetrate to the inwardness of Dorset's religion—the secular concerns of the Privy Councillor become predominant. Sherfield's fault, Dorset declared, was that he had acted unilaterally, 'without the Bishop of the place'. Dorset vigorously defended 'the authority of the reverend prelates' on the grounds that 'whensoever that authority goeth downe, or decayeth, the monarchy dieth with it: I thinke they are inseparably ioyned together'. As James I had put it, 'no Bishop, no King'. Dorset believed in a symbiotic hierarchy in both Church and State, and praised Sherfield

---

[25] P. R. O., S. P. 16/183/58 (depositions concerning the smashing of a stained glass window in St Edmund's Church, Salisbury, Jan. 1630/1), fo. 112v.

[26] The most reliable text of Dorset's speech at Sherfield's trial is that in Bod[leian] Lib[rary], MS Tanner 299 (Archbishop Sancroft's transcripts), fos. 116v–117v, from which the following quotations are taken.

for proving 'himselfe a conformitant'. This concern for order also explains Dorset's refusal to punish Sherfield:

> The reason why I shall not sentence him is to avoyd the tumults of the rude ignorant people in the country where this gentleman dwelleth, where he hath beene a good governor ... and noe doubt hath punished drunkennes, and disorders, and then such persons shall rejoyce agaynst him and say, this you have for your paynes and government, this would be noe good reward for him.[27]

Dorset clearly feared the social consequences of a breakdown in ecclesiastical order. Equally, Sherfield himself, 'in going on his owne head without his ordinary to a worke of this nature', had offended against the hierarchy of the Church. It was therefore appropriate that Sherfield should 'make such acknowledgement to my lord Bishop of Sarum, and in such manner, as he shall thinke fitt'; but Dorset did not propose to fine him. However, the influence of Laud and Neile in particular ensured that the Star Chamber sentenced Sherfield to a £500 fine, as well as a public acknowledgement of his fault.[28]

How useful is this speech as evidence of Dorset's religious attitudes? There are certainly some hints of sympathy with the 'godly' attack on ornaments, images, alehouses and drunkenness. But a higher priority still was the preservation of order in Church, State and society. Sherfield had acted on his own initiative, a case of insubordination which had to be punished. On the other hand, too severe a sentence might encourage unruly elements to rebel against a 'good governor'. This commitment to hierarchy, order and good government was surely conditioned by Dorset's position as a senior royal adviser. Throughout his speech we can hear the voice of a Privy Councillor—and one of considerable political sagacity, for Dorset perceived the counter-productive consequences of a harsh sentence far more clearly than Laud or Neile. He may also have wished to restrain Charles I, who was closely involved in Sherfield's case and personally determined the 'publique manner' of his 'acknowledgment'.[29] One of Dorset's most characteristic strategies as a councillor was to try to curb Caroline over-reactions by dropping veiled hints to the monarch. These typically suggested the attractions of a gentler course of action. It seems probable

---

[27] Sherfield's activities in Salisbury are analysed in P. Slack, 'Poverty and Politics in Salisbury, 1597–1666', in *Crisis and Order in English Towns, 1500–1700*, ed. P. Clark and P. Slack (1972), 164–203, esp. 183–7, 191.

[28] Bod. Lib., MS Tanner 299, fos. 121v–122r. For Laud's speech, see *ibid.*, fos. 111v–115v.

[29] B. L., Add. MS 64905 (Coke papers), fo. 117r–v: draft letter from Sir John Coke to the bishop of Salisbury, 15 Feb. 1632/3, with amendments in Charles I's hand. I owe this reference to Kevin Sharpe.

that Dorset's remarks about the symbiosis of episcopacy and monarchy, Sherfield's 'conformity', and the dependence of local order on such 'good governors', were at least partly designed to persuade Charles that the threat posed by Sherfield was less damaging in the long run than the effects of a harsh sentence. In this respect, Dorset's speech was perhaps of a piece with an episode four months later, when

> the Lord Keeper, Sir Tho[mas] Coventry, had a warrant to seale a pardon for the forfeitures of the papists, which he refusing to do, as contrary to law, the King sent for him, called him his Maister, and tooke away the Greate Seale: but upon some words of the Earle of Dorsett, who said, he knew the King would not condemne any man without hearing him, they were restored unto him againe.[30]

Such an approach probably informed Dorset's speech at Sherfield's trial: it is likely that his words express less an individual's private stance on theological and ecclesiological issues than a Privy Councillor's public attempt to preserve order and hierarchy from both 'the tumults of the rude ignorant people' and the hazards of royal heavy-handedness.

Dorset's official hat was even more obvious when he spoke at William Prynne's first trial in February 1634. Prynne's attacks on female actors in his book *Histriomastix* were widely perceived as libels against Queen Henrietta Maria. Dorset—her Lord Chamberlain and hence responsible for her theatrical entertainments—helped to secure Prynne's arrest in February 1633.[31] When he came to be sentenced a year later Dorset was implacable.[32] He condemned Prynne as 'the damner of Prince, people and State', one who 'invades heaven itselfe and flies upon the King's sacred person'. Christ had 'sent out his disciples with an *ite, praedicate*. Then holy men were advanced by humility. They taught obedience, to give unto Caesar that which is Caesar's ... that if there be bad princes we must pray for them; if good, praise God for them'. Again, this was a natural belief for someone in Dorset's position to hold. He then poured scorn on Prynne's religious 'zeale': 'this brittle conscienced brother will sweat at the sight of a surplice, tremble at a cappe, and rather suffer death than putt on womens apparrell'. But Prynne's greatest offence was that he

[30] B. L., Egerton MS 784 (William Whiteway's diary), fo. 94r.

[31] The warrant for Prynne's arrest, dated 1 Feb. 1632/3, was signed by eight Privy Councillors, including Dorset: *C[ommons] J[ournal]*, II, 124. Prynne later claimed that Dorset 'was the chiefe meanes of helping [him] into prison': Hampshire Record Office, Jervoise of Herriard Park MS, 44 M69/XXXIX/88: Prynne to Henry Sherfield, 12 Oct. 1633. I owe this last reference to John Adamson.

[32] The fullest and most reliable text of Dorset's speech at Prynne's first trial is that in Bod. Lib., MS Tanner 299, fos. 130v–131r, from which the following quotations are taken.

hath scandalised the Queenes Majesty, my loving Mistris, or faire Cynthia; one whose vertues noe Orator is able to display, noe Poet able to sett out ... one soe sweetly disposed, that the sunne setts not upon her anger. A woman made for the redemption of all imperfections which men unjustly cast uppon that sexe. She is one that is constant in her devotion; as for confession, she troubleth her confessor with nothing more than that she hath nothing to trouble him withall.

Dorset's robust defence of the queen's 'vertues' was matched only by his intense desire to see Prynne punished. He urged some form of corporal punishment—'his nose slitt, or a brand on his forehead, or ... his eares cutt'—followed by a £10,000 fine and 'perpetuall imprisonment'.[33] This vitriolic reaction is only intelligible in the context of Dorset's status as a Privy Councillor and above all as Henrietta Maria's Lord Chamberlain. As at Sherfield's trial, his views on religious matters—in this case his attitude to 'holy men' and his contempt for Prynne's 'zeale'—were moulded by his tenure of secular offices.

Unfortunately, this public persona continues to block our view of Dorset's private religion when we move out into the provinces. They prevent us, for example, from using his protection of a 'nonconformist' minister, John Brinsley of Great Yarmouth, as evidence of religious conviction. The story is nonetheless of interest. In the early seventeenth century, the right to appoint a lecturer at Great Yarmouth was claimed by both the corporation and the dean and chapter of Norwich, who also nominated the incumbent of the parish church. Dorset was appointed High Steward of Great Yarmouth in 1629, and in April 1631 the bailiffs requested his help in 'the obtaining and injoying of Mr Brinsleye to be our town preacher or lecturer'.[34] Dorset vigorously took up the corporation's case, but the dean and chapter of Norwich stood their ground. The following December they acknowledged Dorset's 'letters in favour of Mr Brinsley', but defended their 'right for choosinge ministers for the towne of Yermouth' as 'mor likly to setle peace and quench facon than for one to be chosen by us and another by' the townsmen.[35] At about the same time, they wrote to the bishop of

[33] This time, the final sentence was marginally less severe than Dorset advocated: Prynne was fined £5,000, pilloried, and had his ears cropped. See House of Lords Record Office, Main Papers, 20 Aug. 1644 (petition of William Prynne).

[34] The lecturer was John Brinsley the younger, a prolific writer whose works are listed in Wing, B 4705–4737. The main documents relating to this episode are printed in H. Swinden, *The History and Antiquities of Great Yarmouth* (Norwich, 1772), 826–56. The bailiffs' letter to Dorset is found at 847–8. See also C.J. Palmer, *The History of Great Yarmouth* (2 vols, 1854–6), II, 158–64; and R. Cust, 'Anti-Puritanism and Urban Politics: Charles I and Great Yarmouth', *H.J.*, XXXV, 1–26.

[35] Bod. Lib., MS Tanner 134 (diocese of Norwich papers), fo. 189r: the dean and chapter of Norwich to Dorset, [?] Dec. 1631.

Norwich reminding him that Chancery had found Brinsley 'a man unfitt
for that place', and urging him not to license 'a man so prejudiced: ' ...
whatsoever is per him or his well willers pretended for his conformitye,
yett are we vehemently suspicious that except they will sett their mynds
uppon some other man they will have no peace amongst themselves'.[36]
The case came before the king and Privy Council on 24 March 1632.
Charles declared himself 'sensible and careful ... of countenancing and
maintaining, as well of ecclesiastical authority and discipline, as of civil
order and government'.[37] Brinsley was forbidden to lecture in the town,
and the chapel in which he had preached was returned to its former
use as a warehouse. Dorset apparently deferred to royal authority and
abandoned the town's case.[38] This shows that he was not so committed to
Great Yarmouth or to Brinsley as to defend them in the face of political
expediency. It seems likely that his earlier campaign was stimulated by
his role as High Steward of the town rather than by any personal sympathy
with Brinsley's religion. Once again, the ramifications of Dorset's offices—
be they national or local—were critical.

Nevertheless, much recent research on early modern England has
demonstrated that many public figures—including those of the first
rank—did have definite and developed religious beliefs. The effects of
high secular office cannot always obscure these. But they do sometimes
mean that we have to look in other, more private, places. In particular,
floods of light have been shed on lay piety by sensitive analysis of the
lay-out and furnishings of private chapels; the choice of domestic
chaplains; and the presentation of ministers to livings. Such highly
personal evidence can give a peculiarly accurate insight into an individual's religious attitudes. Might it therefore provide the key to unlock
the mysteries of Dorset's faith?

The recent work of Pauline Croft on Robert Cecil and of Ian
Atherton on Viscount Scudamore reveals that physical alterations to
private places of worship faithfully reflected developments in spiritual
beliefs.[39] Unfortunately, in Dorset's case we again reach a dead end.
The chapel in his country seat at Knole (Kent) was built in the late
fifteenth century and redecorated in the late sixteenth.[40] The style was
simple but not austere: altar, family pew, pulpit, lectern, font. There is no

[36] *Ibid.*, fo. 184r: the dean and chapter of Norwich to the bishop of Norwich, [?] 1632.
[37] Palmer, *Great Yarmouth*, II, 162; P. R. O., PC 2/41 (Privy Council register), 481.
[38] Cust, 'Anti-Puritanism and Urban Politics', 20, 24–5.
[39] P. Croft, 'The Religion of Robert Cecil', *H.J.*, XXXIV (1991), 773–96; I.J. Atherton,
'Viscount Scudamore's Laudianism: the Religious Practices of the First Viscount Scudamore', *ibid.*, 567–96.
[40] These details about the chapel at Knole are derived from C.J. Phillips, *History of the
Sackville Family* (2 vols, 1930), II, 353–6, 433–4, 449; and V. Sackville-West, *Knole and the
Sackvilles* (1922), 31–2.

evidence of further changes until the 1770s except for the installation—probably at some time during the seventeenth century—of four windows of 'grisaille' work. The date of this feature is apparently unknown, and thus cannot be attributed with confidence to any particular Sackville. The almost total loss of Dorset's private accounts deprives us of information about expenditure on the chapel.[41] Most of these accounts probably perished with Dorset House in 1666. The chapel of that house is also obscure, and no details can be found of its interior, let alone of specific innovations by Dorset. So this window into his soul is sadly blocked.

We fare slightly better with domestic chaplains. Clearly a lay person would regularly experience his/her chaplain's services and sermons, and this therefore looks a very promising line of enquiry.[42] In Dorset's case at least two chaplains can be identified. We know something of the religious attitudes of the first, Brian Duppa, for he later became bishop of Chichester (1638), Salisbury (1641) and Winchester (1660).[43] In the first diocese, 'Duppa's visitation articles of 1638 faithfully mirrored ... Archbishop [Laud's] of three years previously'.[44] It was through Dorset that Duppa had secured his first major appointment, as dean of Christ Church, Oxford, ten years before.[45] But such patronage does not necessarily prove that Dorset shared Duppa's religious views. After all, the two men had almost certainly met at university, for they both entered Christ Church as undergraduates in July 1605.[46] Furthermore, from 1613 Duppa served as chaplain to Dorset's elder brother, the third earl, and was 'inherited' by the fourth earl in 1624.[47] It may well have been this long acquaintanceship and record of family service which recommended Duppa to Dorset, rather than his religious attitudes. For the second chaplain, Charles Beauvois, we have rather less to go on. His presentation in 1638 to the rectory of Withyham—a living which the chaplains to the earls of Dorset seem often to have held in plurality—suggests that he also succeeded Duppa as household chaplain in that year.[48] Beauvois was presented by the king, *pro hac vice*. This

---

[41] For fragments of Dorset's accounts, see K. A. O., Sackville MS, U 269/A1/7–8; U 269/A41/1–2. None of these contains any material relating to the chapels at either Knole or Dorset House.

[42] It bears fruit in, for example, J. T. Cliffe, *The Puritan Gentry* (1984), esp. 135–8, 162–8.

[43] See 'The Correspondence of Bishop Brian Duppa and Sir Justinian Isham, 1650–1660', ed. G. Isham, *Publ. Northants. Rec. Soc.*, XVII (1955), xix–xxxi.

[44] Fletcher, *Sussex*, 81. See also *ibid.*, 90–2; and Tyacke, *Anti-Calvinists*, 206–7.

[45] William Laud, *The History of the Troubles and Tryal of ... William Laud* (1695), 366.

[46] Duppa was admitted to Christ Church on 9 July 1605: *Alumni Oxonienses, 1500–1714*, ed. J. Foster (4 vols, Oxford, 1891–2), I, 434; Dorset on 26 July: *ibid.*, IV, 1298.

[47] Phillips, *Sackville Family*, I, 274–5.

[48] P. R. O., SO 3/11 (Signet Office docquet book), unfol., June 1638; [anon.,] *Historical Notices of the Parish of Withyham in the County of Sussex* (1857), 24–5; *L.J.*, V, 80. I owe this last reference to John Adamson.

may imply that his religious sympathies were at least compatible with the official policies of the later 1630s; which in turn might suggest a certain doctrinal resemblance to his predecessor, Duppa. But in the present state of the evidence this must remain highly speculative. What, then, may be gleaned from Dorset's own presentations to livings? Once again, these can yield persuasive evidence of lay piety, as for example in Barbara Donagan's work on the 'clerical patronage' of the second earl of Warwick.[49] For Dorset we have reasonably full information, and a pattern does begin to emerge. Among the Sackville papers, there survives a list of thirty-nine livings in Dorset's control.[50] By means of the bishops' certificates of presentations to benefices, it has been possible to identify some of the ministers whom Dorset presented.[51] These records are incomplete; in particular, those for the counties of Essex and Middlesex, which both contained Dorset livings, do not survive. This gap can however be filled by the register of the bishops of London.[52] I have traced twenty-two presentations by Dorset, of twenty different ministers. There is explicit evidence for the religious positions of four of these, and clues for a further five. We know most about Brian Duppa, James Marsh, George Blundell and John Tillinghast. Duppa's Laudian attitudes have already been discussed.[53] James Marsh's attitudes were apparently similar: as archdeacon of Chichester from 1640 he reissued Duppa's 1638 articles 'without alteration' for his own visitations.[54] He was sequestered in July 1643.[55] By contrast, the Committee for Plundered Ministers commended George Blundell in 1647 as 'a godlie and orthodox divine';[56] while John Tillinghast is known to have been an Independent in the later 1640s, and possibly a Fifth Monarchist by 1651.[57] Of the other five, Thomas

---

[49] B. Donagan, 'The clerical patronage of Robert Rich, 2nd Earl of Warwick, 1616–1642', *Proceedings of the American Philosophical Society*, CXX (1976), 388–419.

[50] K. A. O., Sackville MS, U 269/Q1.

[51] These certificates are found in P. R. O., E 331. The information about Dorset's presentations derived from them is laid out in Smith, 'Dorset', Appendix 2.

[52] Guildhall Library, MS 9531/15 (register of the bishops of London). I owe this reference to Kenneth Fincham.

[53] See above, 114.

[54] Fletcher, *Sussex*, 81.

[55] B. L., Add. MS 15670 (procs of Cttee for Plundered Ministers), fo. 177r; *C. J.*, III, 161; A. G. Matthews, *Walker Revised* (Oxford, 1948; repr., 1988), 54.

[56] B. L., Add. MS 15671 (procs of Cttee for Plundered Ministers), fo. 216r. In 1657, Blundell received a payment from First Fruits: W. A. Shaw, *A History of the English Church during the Civil Wars and under the Commonwealth* (2 vols, 1900), II, 579. This suggests that his beliefs were again deemed acceptable under the Protectorate.

[57] For Tillinghast's beliefs, see G. F. Nuttall, *Visible Saints: The Congregational Way, 1640–1660* (Oxford, 1957), 147–8, 152–3; and *Dictionary of National Biography*, ed. L. Stephen et al. (63 vols, 1885–1900), LVI, 871. I am grateful to Colin Davis for a discussion of Tillinghast's religious position.

Russell narrowly avoided suspension in 1635 for refusing 'to bowe at the blessed name of Jesus';[58] Richard Gough and Henry Sheppard were sequestered in 1643 and 1644 respectively;[59] and Sheppard together with Robert Baker and Thomas Rogers definitely held Church office after the Restoration.[60] It would be unwise to draw firm conclusions from such partial and incomplete evidence, but the religious positions of these nine ministers look pretty diverse. They certainly ranged from the Laudian to the Independent. I have so far found no sources which throw light on the beliefs of the other eleven,[61] although it seems that none of those still alive in 1660–2 was ejected.[62] There are nevertheless signs of a consistent pattern in Dorset's presentations. Twelve of the ministers apparently graduated from either Oxford or Cambridge, and something of their personal background may therefore be found in the *Alumni Oxonienses* and *Alumni Cantabrigienses*. Ten of these graduates were presented to Sussex livings. In eight cases we know the county in which their father lived, and in seven cases that county was also Sussex.[63] Of the remaining two presentations, the minister at Tooting in Surrey was from Kingston, Surrey, while that at St Dunstan's-in-the-West, London, was the son of a City of London grocer.[64] It thus appears that Dorset

[58] P. R. O., S. P. 16/293/128 (Sir Nathaniel Brent's report of metropolitical visitation, 1635), fo. 15r–v.

[59] For Gough, see B. L., Add. MS 15670, fos. 21v, 59r; Add. MS 15671, fo. 216r. Matthews, *Walker Revised*, 356–7. For Sheppard, see Add. MS 15669 (procs of Cttee for Plundered Ministers), fo. 81r; Add. MS 15671, fos. 32v, 231r; P. R. O., S. P. 46/82, fo. 233r (receipt on Sheppard's behalf, 7 Mar. 1643/4); Matthews, *Walker Revised*, 361.

[60] For Sheppard, see *Al. Oxon.*, IV, 1344; for Robert Baker, *Alumni Cantabrigienses. Part One: from the earliest times to 1751*, ed. J. and J. A. Venn (4 vols, Cambridge, 1922–7), I, 72; for Thomas Rogers, *Al. Oxon.*, III, 1276; *Al. Cant.*, III, 480. It is possible that Robert Man also held office after 1660: *Al. Cant.*, III, 132.

[61] Besides all the sources cited in the other notes to this paragraph, I have also checked the following: P. R. O., S. P. 22/1–3 (papers of Cttee for Plundered Ministers); J. Walker, *An Account of the ... Sufferings of the Clergy* (1714); G. Hennessy, *Chichester Diocese Clergy Lists* (1900); John Le Neve, *Fasti Ecclesiae Anglicanae, 1541–1857*, II (Chichester Diocese), comp. J. M. Horn (1971); W. C. Renshaw, 'Some Clergy of the Archdeaconry of Lewes and South Malling Deanery', *S[ussex] A[rchaeological] C[ollections]*, LV (1912), 220–77; 'The Acts of Bishop Montague', ed. W. D. Peckham, *S. A. C.*, LXXXVI (1947), 141–54; R. Newcourt, *Repertorium Ecclesiasticum Parochiale Londinense* (2 vols, 1708–10); A. Argent, 'Aspects of the Ecclesiastical History of the Parishes of the City of London, 1640–9' (unpubl. PhD. diss., Univ. of London, 1983); H. Smith, *The Ecclesiastical History of Essex under the Long Parliament and Commonwealth* (Colchester, 1932).

[62] No minister known to have been presented by Dorset appears in E. Calamy, *An Account of the ministers ... ejected or silenced, 1660–2* (2 vols, 1727); or in A. G. Matthews, *Calamy Revised* (Oxford, 1934; repr., 1988).

[63] These seven were Edward Kidder, Anthony Midleton, Thomas Rogers, Thomas Russell, George Thetcher, John Tillinghast and Samuel Woods: *Al. Oxon.*, II, 848; III, 1276, 1292; IV, 1469, 1677; *Al. Cant.*, III, 184, 480; IV, 242.

[64] These two were, respectively, Robert Man and James Marsh: *Al. Cant.*, III, 132, 144; *Al. Oxon.*, III, 973.

usually chose local men for his livings.[65] This does not necessarily prove that religion was unimportant, but it does suggest an alternative, secular reason for his presentations.

There is an intriguing codicil to this last point. The whole question of lay presentation to impropriated livings was highly controversial in early Stuart England. This legacy of the Reformation came under growing attack from both right and left, from high churchmen such as Laud and Neile, and from 'puritans'[66] like the feoffees for the purchase of impropriations.[67] On 14 February 1629, Dorset was appointed— along with men as diverse as Laud, Neile and Lord Saye and Sele— to a House of Lords committee 'to draw one bill to prevent the decay of churches, chancels and chapels; and to draw one other bill for sufficient stipends to be allowed unto curates, as well unto curates who serve in churches appropriated as in other churches'.[68] The work of this committee was pre-empted by parliament's dissolution on 10 March. It might however explain a mysterious paper of 1629, now in the Trumbull archive, entitled 'inducements for a generall colleccon to redeeme impropriacons to the Church'. This records that 'the right hon[ourable] the Erle of Dorsett in perticuler hath offered to sell an impropriacon at an under value for the advancement of this good worke'.[69] I have not yet found evidence of whether Dorset actually sold any of his livings. His offer to do so is deeply ambiguous: anyone from Laud to Saye could have praised 'this good worke'. Where did Dorset stand on that spectrum? Is it simply that this particular source fails to tell us? Or was his position genuinely ambivalent? In an attempt to unravel Dorset's motives further, let us explore in turn his attitudes towards Laud on the one hand and 'puritans' on the other.

Dorset's relations with Archbishop Laud are very difficult to reconstruct precisely. Only fragments of evidence survive, but taken together they are perhaps suggestive. In public, Dorset treated Laud courteously.

[65] For a similar pattern among those clergy who were 'sequestered or harassed' during the 1640s, see I. Green, 'Career Prospects and Clerical Conformity in the early Stuart Church', *Past and Present*, XC (1981), 71–115, esp. 89–92. I owe this reference to Ian Atherton.

[66] 'Puritan' is of course a highly complex term, covering a variety of different beliefs. Nevertheless, it remains useful as a general label for those people who disliked the traces of Catholicism in the late Tudor and early Stuart Church (such as bishops, vestments, and the Prayer Book), and who felt that the English Reformation was still incomplete. I use it in this sense throughout the present essay.

[67] On Laud, see esp. J. S. McGee, 'William Laud and the Outward Face of Religion', in *Leaders of the Reformation*, ed. R. L. DeMolen (1984), 318–44; on Neile, A. Foster, 'Church Policies of the 1630s', in *Conflict in Early Stuart England*, ed. R. Cust and A. Hughes (Harlow, 1989), 193–223, esp. 198–201; on the feoffees for the purchase of impropriations, *Activities of the Puritan Faction of the Church of England, 1625–33*, ed. I. M. Calder (1957).

[68] *L. J.*, IV, 31. Cf. Foster, 'Church Policies', 202.

[69] B. L., Trumbull Add. MS 31 (misc. Trumbull papers), unfol.

At the second trial of Bishop Williams of Lincoln in February 1639, Dorset declared: 'my lord of Canterbury is so faithful towards the King, and so upright in his place, that never any that sate in his place before him had cleaner hands than he: he carries himself to the glory of God, the good and welfare of the Church, and the honour of the King'.[70] But such words do not necessarily mean that they were allies, for Dorset then urged far more lenient penalties than Laud. Williams stood charged with receiving letters from Lambert Osbaldeston, the headmaster of Westminster School, which called Laud a 'little ... medling hocas pocas'.[71] The archbishop felt that Williams's offences were 'abominably foul and clearly proved'. Dorset, by contrast, laid the greatest blame on Osbaldeston, and argued that Williams had 'fallen into the limetwiggs of his adversaries'. He therefore advocated a relatively light fine of £3,000: as at Sherfield's trial, he opposed Laud's harsher sentence. Nor were these the only occasions on which Dorset sought to calm the archbishop's temper. In 1640, Dorset rescued five 'young gentlemen of Lincoln's Inn' who had drunk 'a health to the confusion of the Archbishop of Canterbury'.[72] Six years earlier, Dorset may also have tried to protect the celebrated 'nonconformist' minister John Cotton of Boston from prosecution by the Court of High Commission. But as the source for this story dates from after 1700, it must be treated with considerable caution.[73] Only once in his surviving correspondence does Dorset refer to Laud, in terms which suggest no animosity but perhaps some distance between them. 'I conceave as well as you do', he wrote to the earl of Middlesex on 1 October 1636, 'that the little man is turnd up trump. I nether envy his fortune nor malice his person, and am very well I think in his opinion and affections'.[74] The phrase 'turnd up trump' probably referred to Bishop Juxon's appointment as Lord Treasurer in March 1636 and to Laud's highly successful stage-management of the royal visit to Oxford the following summer. None of this diffuse evidence is conclusive. But read as a whole it suggests, perhaps, that Dorset was never very close to the archbishop, and that several times he disagreed with his treatment of specific individuals. It is also worth adding that many within Henrietta

---

[70] The most reliable text of Dorset's speech at Williams's second trial is that in Bod. Lib., MS Tanner 67 (letters and papers of 1638–9), fo. 91r, from which the following quotations are taken.

[71] J. Hacket, *Scrinia Reserata: A Memorial Offer'd to the Great Deservings of John Williams, D. D.* (1693), 131.

[72] John Rushworth, *Historical Collections of private passages of State* (8 vols, 1680–1701), II, ii, 1180; Bod. Lib., MS Eng. Hist. B 204 (Warcup papers), fos. 1r–v, 3r–v. I owe this last reference to John Adamson.

[73] Cotton Mather, *Magnalia Christi Americana* (1702), III, 18–19.

[74] K. A. O., U[ncatalogued] C[ranfield] P[apers]: Dorset to the earl of Middlesex, 1 Oct. 1636.

Maria's entourage were actively hostile to Laud, on social and political as well as religious grounds.[75] It is possible that some of this antagonism rubbed off on the queen's Lord Chamberlain. Indeed, as his speech at Prynne's trial shows, Dorset was so loyal to Henrietta Maria that her dislike of Laud was quite likely to influence Dorset's own behaviour. This may well help to explain his lack of intimacy with the archbishop.

What, then, did Dorset think of Laud's opponents at the other end of the religious spectrum, the 'puritans'? We have already detected one or two signs of sympathy: especially in his favourable view of the 'godly magistrate' Henry Sherfield; and perhaps also in his putative help to John Cotton. The former suggests that Dorset tolerated 'godliness' where it reinforced the existing order and hierarchy in Church, State and society. However, as Richard Cust and Peter Lake have recently shown, during the early seventeenth century a perceived link developed between 'puritanism' and 'popularity'.[76] 'Godliness' increasingly became associated with subversion of religious and political authority. For Dorset—the staunch upholder of order—this was the unacceptable face of 'godliness'. In September 1639 he lamented 'how much liberty and puritanisme rayne in the populace of this people'.[77] A year later he remonstrated with the 'godly' of Rye (Sussex) for 'bread[ing] a suspition in the Kinges people that he was turning papyst', and insisted that 'they should rather helpe to finde out purytynes such as there frend Docktor Downinge of Hackney who preached a sedytious sermon'.[78] The fact that Dorset praised a 'godly magistrate' as a bulwark against 'the tumults of the rude ignorant people', but condemned 'puritanism' when it implied sedition suggests that his variable view of 'godliness' was a function of his consistent defence of the established order. Perhaps understandably in a peer, Dorset's primary aim remained the preservation of unity and degree within the existing hierarchical framework. As he wrote, hauntingly, to the countess of Middlesex on the outbreak of civil war: 'I wowld ... my children had never binn borne, to live under the dominion of soe many Cades and Ketts, as threaten by there multitudes and insurrections to drowne all memory of monarchy, nobility, gentry, in this land'.[79] All this evidence prompts

[75] M. Smuts, 'The Puritan Followers of Henrietta Maria in the 1630s', *English Historical Review*, XCIII (1978), 26–46; C. Hibbard, *Charles I and the Popish Plot* (Chapel Hill, N. C., 1983), 45, 60–4.

[76] R. Cust, *The Forced Loan and English Politics, 1626–1628* (Oxford, 1987), esp. 19–22, 209–12, 327–9; P. Lake, 'Anti-Popery: the structure of a prejudice', in *Conflict*, ed. Cust and Hughes, 72–106, esp. 84–5, 87, 90–1.

[77] K. A. O., UCP: Dorset to the earl of Middlesex, [?] Sept. 1639.

[78] B. L., Harl. MS 383 (letter book of Sir Simonds D'Ewes), fo. 185r: James Dee to Edmund Calamy, 25 Sept. 1640. I owe this reference to Peter Salt.

[79] K. A. O., UCP: Dorset to the countess of Middlesex, [?] Aug. 1642.

the question: how far did Dorset wish to defend the Church of England as part of the existing order?

In his surviving letters and speeches, Dorset never ventures a general opinion of the Church of England. However, there is one vital clue which suggests an attachment to the established Church as it had developed since 1559. In December 1642, Dorset's long-standing friend Sir Kenelm Digby wrote a series of 'observations' on Sir Thomas Browne's spiritual autobiography, the *Religio Medici*. Digby mentions that he had immediately bought this book because Dorset 'gave so advantageous a carecter of it', and describes it as 'a favourite' of the earl's which had 'received the honour and safeguard of [his] approbation'.[80] The *Religio Medici*, written in 1635–6 and published in 1642, contained an eloquent defence of the Church of England, 'to whose faith' Browne professed himself 'a sworne subject'.[81] Dorset's fondness for this work is highly suggestive. Browne's commitment to the Church of England rested, first, on a recognition of the value of reason in religious experience: 'there is no Church ... whose articles, constitutions and customes seeme so consonant unto reason'.[82] Suckling's dedication of his 'account of religion by reason' to Dorset makes it all the more likely that the latter shared this perspective. The second distinctive feature of Browne's religion lay in his deep commitment to unity and tolerance: 'I could never divide my selfe from any man upon the difference of an opinion or be angry with his judgement for not agreeing with mee in that, for which perhaps within a few dayes I should dissent my selfe'.[83] Such a position is extraordinarily difficult to label, for it was an attitude rather than a creed. But it bears a resemblance to what Peter Lake has recently termed the 'conformist caste of mine'.[84] This was a 'moderate' outlook which consciously eschewed extremes and accepted the existence of diverse opinions within the Church of England. It transcended traditional polarities between 'Anglicans' and 'Puritans' or 'Calvinists' and 'Arminians', and thus 'undercut many of the received categories and generalisations' about early seventeenth-century religion.[85] To characterise Dorset as a 'conformist' might therefore explain why he numbered men as diverse

---

[80] *Observations upon Religio Medici, occasionally written by Sir Kenelm Digby* (1643), 2–3 (B. L., E 1113/4).

[81] Sir Thomas Browne, *Religio Medici*, ed. J.-J. Denonain (2nd edition, Cambridge, 1955), 8.

[82] *Ibid.*

[83] *Ibid.*, 9.

[84] P. Lake, *Anglicans and Puritans? Presbyterianism and English Conformist Thought from Whitgift to Hooker* (1988), 6. Cf. John S. Coolidge, *The Pauline Renaissance in England: Puritanism and the Bible* (Oxford, 1970), esp. chapters 1–2. I owe this last reference to Richard Strier.

[85] P. Lake, 'The Calvinist Conformity of Robert Sanderson', *J. B. S.*, XXVII (1988), 81–116, esp. 114. I am grateful to Conrad Russell for a discussion on this point.

as the Catholic Sir Kenelm Digby and the 'puritan' Richard Amherst among his friends. Dorset secured a Court entrée for Digby in 1629, and their relationship remained cordial thereafter.[86] Amherst served until his death in 1632 as Dorset's steward and legal counsel, and rented a large mansion from him.[87] He was also a trustee for the debts of Dorset's elder brother, and acted closely with Dorset in the Chancery disputes over their payment.[88] Anthony Fletcher has described Amherst's will—in which he besought God 'to be gracious unto [him] duringe [his] life' and to 'defend [him] from [his] cruel, subtill, and malitious enemy the Devil and all his wicked spirittes'—as 'distinctly puritan'.[89] Such beliefs are in stark contrast with Digby's devout Catholicism, yet both men were apparently on friendly terms with Dorset. An ecumenical, 'conformist' outlook would also explain why the Catholicism of Sir Henry Compton and Thomas Middlemore did not prevent Dorset's appointing them executors; why the 'godliness' of Brinsley and Sherfield did not dissuade him from publicly defending them; and why he praised the latter for proving 'himselfe a conformitant'. It explains the lack of dogma and extremism in Dorset's religious beliefs: the ambivalence of his will; the cautious approach to several of Laud's decisions and to the more 'scdytious' 'puritans'; the general absence of hard edges. It helps to explain why Dorset's religion left few definite traces. And it may explain why his contemporaries either perceived that religion in diverse ways or felt able to ignore it entirely. This was a man who did not allow differences of religious opinion to affect his political or personal relationships. For all these reasons, it may be helpful to describe Dorset's religious attitudes as 'conformist'.

But people of quite contrasting opinions could claim to be 'conformists' in early Stuart England. By itself the term is still somewhat vague and amorphous. It therefore needs stressing that Dorset was not just a 'conformist'; he was also what I shall call a 'Jacobethan'. I have

[86] P. R. O., S. P. 16/148/99 (Dorset to Viscount Dorchester, 30 Aug. 1629). See also S. P. 16/223/37 (Sir Kenelm Digby to Sir John Coke, 19 Sept. 1632); and New York Public Library, Morgan MS B (letter book of Sir Kenelm Digby), unfol.: Digby to Dorset, 14 June 1633; and Digby to [?] Dorset, 6 Oct. 1633. Digby's Catholicism is discussed in M. Foster, 'Sir Kenelm Digby (1603–65) as Man of Religion and Thinker', *Downside Review*, CVI (1988), 35–58, 101–125.

[87] P. R. O., E 126/3 (Exchequer, King's Remembrancer, entry book of decrees and orders), fos. 159r–160r; E. S. R. O., SAS/P41 (indenture of 22 June 1630); W. H. Godfrey, 'The High Street, Lewes', *S. A. C.*, XCIII (1955), 1–33, at 17.

[88] For Amherst as a trustee for the third earl of Dorset's debts, see B. L., Add. MS 5701 (misc. Sussex collections), fos. 71r–76r. For the main Chancery cases, see P. R. O., C 2 Jas. I, D 14/44, and C 2 Chas. I, M 22/41 (Chancery procs). See also K. A. O., Sackville MS, U 269/L3 (exemplification of Chancery bill, 1625).

[89] P. R. O., PROB 11 (Prerogative Court of Canterbury, copies of probated wills), 161/61; Fletcher, *Sussex*, 63.

argued elsewhere that Dorset's political maxims corresponded far more closely to realities before 1625 than those thereafter.[90] Enough has been said here to suggest that this was true also of his religion. His ecumenical outlook, which avoided extremes and tolerated a plurality of belief within a broad national Church, stamps him unmistakably as someone who reached maturity in the England of Elizabeth I and James I. Kenneth Fincham and Peter Lake have shown that James's ecclesiastical policies perpetuated the delicate balance of the Elizabethan settlement and so furthered the kind of Church which Dorset sought.[91] James was 'a monarch dedicated to the principle of religious unity', and no one doctrinal position was able to dominate the Church.[92] It was otherwise under Charles I. In collaboration with Archbishop Laud, this king significantly narrowed the boundaries of legitimate religious belief and allowed a group of high churchmen to monopolise ecclesiastical preferment.[93] In his hints to Charles—as at Sherfield's trial—and his attempts to restrain Laud's anger, Dorset looks very much like a 'Jacobethan' trying to moderate Caroline policies. His aim was to offer what he later called 'the more posed and wise advice'.[94] In the religious sphere, this advice probably sprang from a 'Jacobethan' vision of the Church of England.

This was the religious counterpart of Dorset's almost obsessive concern with social and political unity.[95] His religious beliefs did not determine his attitudes to politics and society; rather, they reflected and complemented them. This in turn helps to explain why Dorset's religion has left little direct evidence. Undogmatic, ecumenical, 'conformist' values simply did not generate—did not *need* to generate—as much written material as the relentless self-examination which lay behind many 'puritan' diaries. Dorset's faith was part of a coherent package which married the secular and the spiritual. Unfortunately, any ideological conviction manifests itself most clearly—and its strength is easiest to assess—where it conflicts with other motives and then either overrides these or is overridden by them. Thus, Dorset's concern for order and his loyalty to Henrietta Maria were most cogently expressed when he thought they were under threat, as at Prynne's first trial. What never seems to have occurred was the sort of conflict between his religious and secular motives—the sense of being pulled

[90] Smith, 'Dorset and the politics of the 1620s'.
[91] K. Fincham and P. Lake, 'The Ecclesiastical Policy of King James I', *J. B. S.*, XXIV (1985), 169–207.
[92] *Ibid.*; the quotation is found at 187.
[93] For this, see esp. Tyacke, *Anti-Calvinists*; Foster, 'Church Policies'; and J. Davies, *The Caroline Captivity of the Church* (Oxford, 1992).
[94] Smith, ' "The more posed and wise advice" ', 810.
[95] See esp. the correspondence quoted in *ibid.*, 809–12, 816–18.

in opposite directions—which alone would drive such beliefs into the open. There are some striking illustrations of the strength of religious convictions in the summer of 1642: the contrasted Cheshire leaders Sir Thomas Aston and Sir William Brereton dramatically reveal how religious imperatives could overcome constitutional preferences.[96] But for many others, especially perhaps among the Royalists, no such evidence can be adduced. For example, when Edmund Waller defended bishops as 'the counterscarp and outwork' of the whole ecclesiastical, social and political order, can the religious considerations be separated from the secular?[97] Dorset likewise saw episcopacy and monarchy as mutually supportive, but it is impossible to isolate a purely religious motive for his Royalist allegiance. This is what makes the piety of so many people in early seventeenth-century England extremely difficult to reconstruct. The present enquiry has been impeded not only by the effects of fire, water and rats. We have also paid a penalty for the fact that someone three-and-a-half centuries ago possessed what today's jargon would term 'a well integrated world-view'.

This interpretation explains why Dorset's religion never did—never *could*—override his constitutional preferences. They were aspects of a single harmonious outlook, within which they were distinguishable but not separable. Indeed, it is probable that such an approach characterises most of the moderates of the 1640s. Those who gravitated towards the political extremes, especially among the Parliamentarians, were those whose religious beliefs operated rather like an 'override key', those who felt such imperatives so deeply and intensely as to let them dictate their political agendas. Religion often forced such people to jettison conventional seventeenth-century assumptions about an innate symbiosis between Crown and Parliament. But for others, including Dorset, that symbiosis found a precise correlative in the religious sphere. Constitutional unity between monarch and subject, and ecclesiastical unity within a broad national Church, mirrored and reinforced each other. It simply did not occur to people such as Dorset to subordinate secular ideals to religious: how could it when the two were treated as facets of an integrated and indivisible whole?[98]

In that sense, 'ambiguous' may not be quite the best adjective to describe Dorset's religious beliefs. The stem 'ambi-' carries connotations of duality, of trying to have things both ways. In the late twentieth century, which tends to analyse power and authority in terms of checks and balances, of one force *limiting* another, it requires a real empathetic

[96] J. S. Morrill, 'The Religious Context of the English Civil War', *ante*, 5th series, XXXIV (1984), 155–78, esp. 177.

[97] A. Fletcher, *The Outbreak of the English Civil War* (1981), 124.

[98] Cf. Paul E. Kopperman, *Sir Robert Heath, 1575–1649: window on an age* (1989), 194–200.

leap to think ourselves back into the mind-set of someone like Dorset—a mind-set which perceived the world in terms of unity, harmony and order. A division between the religious and the secular, like that between the executive and the legislative, is a modern one and Dorset almost certainly did not perceive it. Where we might see fences on which to sit, Dorset would see seamless garments in need of repair. We are not assisted in this imaginative effort by the relative paucity of the surviving evidence. Yet this in itself tells us something about the actual nature of Dorset's beliefs. The evidential problems which we encounter today arise in part from what apparently went on inside his head in the early seventeenth century. This essay has recounted the search for an historical reality which by its very nature left little explicit evidence. In many historical enquiries, precise and well defined historical realities can only be reconstructed tentatively and with difficulty because the vicissitudes of time have bequeathed few relics to us. In rather fewer cases, a complex, ambivalent historical reality may be reconstructed with something approaching certainty because the relevant material happens to survive. But in this case it seems that the nature of the historical experience itself partly explains the intractability of the available sources. Nevertheless, those sources permit us to discern, albeit dimly, something of that past experience.

THE WAR OF THE SCOTS, 1306–23

The Prothero Lecture

by A. A. M. Duncan

READ 3 JULY 1991

THE life of Robert I, king of Scots, written by John Barbour archdeacon of Aberdeen is the fullest of any medieval king in the west, a chronicle of chivalry in vernacular octosyllabic couplets, on which much of our understanding of the events and ethos of the Scottish war depends.[1] In this paper I discuss some aspects of the king's reign which Barbour ignored: pro-Balliol sentiment which lingered in Scotland and at the French and papal courts; and also aspects of the war where Barbour's narrative is incomplete or misleading, but which illustrate the growth of King Robert's military effort from that of a very uncertain factional rising to one which matched the rhetorical claims (in the Declaration of Arbroath) of a people at war. I shall be treading ground already mapped in Professor Barrow's masterly study,[2] seeking only to point out features to which Barbour has, by omission or commission, drawn my attention.

The war from 1306 to 1323 was only part, if the most active part, of a longer struggle lasting from 1296 to 1560, a part in which aims were more clearly defined and consistently pursued, at least on the Scottish side, than in the later sporadic outbreaks of military activity. The peace of 1328 achieved most of those aims and certainly drew the war to a conclusion for contemporaries; but it left unresolved the rights of many whose ancestors had held land in Scotland before 1286 and hence it contained the seeds of renewed conflict. The war against England which began in 1296 overlapped with another domestic and internal struggle over the right to the Scottish throne (and hence to the heritages of supporters of rival Scottish kings), which first broke into civil war in 1286. This struggle reached a stalemate in 1357 when Edward III, some twenty months after purchasing the rights of Edward Balliol to the kingdom, released 'David Bruce'; by 1363 when he sought the succession to King David, he had by implication abandoned the

---

[1] The poem is some 13,500 lines long. It contains only one year date—1375, the year of composition. I cite it by book and line, using the traditional line numbers of the editions by Skeat and Mackenzie.

[2] G. W. S. Barrow, *Robert Bruce and the Community of the Realm of Scotland* (3rd edn. 1988).

rights of Balliol and all rights dependent upon it. The domestic divisions between adherents of King John and his son on the one hand and King Robert and his son on the other had been resolved in a long civil war, in which the Balliol cause lost all credibility by its compromises with and concessions to the English crown.

Yet when the succession had become an issue in 1290, it was Robert Bruce VI who urged Edward I to assert his lordship, in order to do justice to Bruce's claim that the 'superior lord and emperor' should seat him on the Scottish throne.[3] In 1296 Robert Bruce VII and his son, the earl of Carrick, again petitioned Edward for the throne, and from 1301, with the threat that French troops would occupy parts of Scotland as a neutral force during a truce, and that King John would return to his heritage, not only was Carrick willing to abandon the patriotic cause, but Edward I was prepared to offer him conditional undertakings to re-examine the Bruce right, which at that time reposed in Carrick's father, prudently silent in England.[4] If matters had gone down that road, France and England might have fought a war in Scotland in the names of Balliol and Bruce respectively. Thirty years later they were to fight, but with exchange of Scottish allies.

By 1303 the Scottish hope of French support slumped, and Edward I's campaign north of Forth was a victor's progress, meeting resistance only at Brechin. The brave group of hard-liners who held out in Stirling castle sought leave to contact John de Soules in Paris about surrender, not their king in Picardy.[5] The collapse of morale may be attributable to the failure of King John to move a finger in defence of his kingship or kingdom, for without him leading Scots had no right to vindicate. From 1304 Edward sought to win acquiescence in his regime by a moderate settlement which guaranteed to those submitting, life, freedom, heritage, at the price of fines and in some cases periods of exile. After the death of Wallace, exile was for the most part remitted, the fines were made payable by instalments, and the traditional local offices, with a few important exceptions in the south, were committed to members of the Scottish landed communities.[6] This policy was surely the only one with a chance of success.

The longstanding if imperfect dependence of the Bruces upon English

[3] E. L. G. Stones and G. G. Simpson, *Edward I and the Throne of Scotland, 1290–1296*, (1978), II, 187, 170.

[4] *Johannis de Fordun Chronica Gentis Scotorum*, ed. W. F. Skene, I (1871), 326; *Treaty Rolls*, I, no. 376 (the truce of Asnières); E. L. G. Stones, *Anglo-Scottish Relations, 1174–1328, Some Selected Documents*, (1965), no. 32.

[5] *Flores Historiarum*, III, 118.

[6] *Rotuli Parliamentorum*, I, 212–13 (the submission of 1304); 211–12 (the *forma pacis*, 15 October 1305); Stones, *Anglo-Scottish Relations*, no. 33 (the ordinance for the government of Scotland, September, 1305).

goodwill and the identification of King John's name with the cause of independence were abruptly reversed by the murder of Comyn and Carrick's seizure of the throne. The English government cheerfully accepted its erstwhile enemies as its active agents, but the fact that some Scots now fought with England does not mean that their ultimate allegiance to a Balliol rightful king of Scots had vanished. Within Scotland little is heard directly of support for the Balliol right, which undoubtedly diminished as some families (the Macdougalls of Argyll and Comyns of Badenoch) were exiled, even dying out in the male line (the Comyn earls of Buchan), while the defeats leading up to Bannockburn, the forfeiture of Bruce's enemies and the death of King John late in 1314 changed circumstances, for his son had lived at the court of Edward II; those who might have supported a revival of John's claims now had to recognise that the new Balliol was a creature of England. Bannockburn had split the pro-Balliol Anglo-Scottish community. In varying circumstances David earl of Athol and David Brechin (who seem to have been come over at Dundee in 1312), the earls of Dunbar and Fife, Laurence Abernethy, William de Soules, and the Moubrays found themselves in King Robert's peace.

Sir Ingram de Umfraville, a prisoner taken at Bannockburn, who was not ransomed, is a particularly interesting example of this group, not least because he appears in Barbour's *Brus* as a wise commentator upon events.[7] His descent from the Umfravilles of Prudhoe is something of a mystery, but his mother was probably a Balliol of Redcastle, distantly related to King John, for he was co-heir to that barony, and Ingram was a Balliol name. He helped to make the Franco-Scottish alliance in 1295, served his king as Guardian in 1299, was again in France in 1303 and suffered the longest sentence of exile in the settlement of 1304, so was a leading patriot. In 1306 he became an important commander of the English against King Robert, and it is surprising that as a prisoner after 1314 he compromised his staunch Balliol sympathies. We cannot know how many other pro-Balliol men now decided that their best hope was a reluctant acceptance of the Bruce 'usurper' but they were a not-insignificant addition to the Scottish community of magnates, and the king showed himself concerned to reinforce this new loyalty.

In April 1315 still without a son, though now in hopes of one from

<hr />

[7] *History of Northumberland*, XII, 'Umfraville of Redesdale and Prudhoe' tree identifies him as that Ingram de Umfraville who in 1279 claimed the lands of his father Robert, identified as the Robert born before 1212. It also claims that Ingram's Balliol inheritance came by marriage to a daughter of Ingram Balliol. But his name shows that his mother must have been a Balliol, and since the Guardian died after 1321, his father is unlikely to have been the Robert born before 1212. The matter is not resolved in W. Percy Hedley, *Northumberland Families*, I (1968), 211.

his returned queen, King Robert secured from the magnates a sealed entail of the throne upon his own heirs male, whom failing his brother and heirs male, whom failing his daughter's heirs. Three years later, another entail took account of Edward Bruce's death.[8] But these documents open with a commitment, in the words of 1318, that the magnates 'each and all will be obedient in everything to the lord king and his heirs as their king and liege lord, each according to his estate and condition, and they will faithfully for their strength, help him for the protection and defence of the rights and liberties of the aforesaid kingdom, against all mortals of whatever power, by whatsoever authority, dignity or power they are pre-eminent'. That such an affirmation of loyalty was felt appropriate on both occasions, ten or more years after the king's inauguration, is a sign not merely of external rejection from England and the papacy, but also of a fear of internal division— that the king's supporters now included some of those once loyal to Balliol, who might be willing to accept English lordship.

In a general statement, the same entail recalled 1291 when the law of succession was in doubt and went on to reject explicitly the law of inferior feus (that is the Balliol claim), for succession to the kingdom. Succession went to the heir male whom failing the heir female of line, whom failing the heir male of collateral line. This was simple and consistent, except that it contradicted what was laid down equally confidently in 1315. That was easily dealt with; the new rule is said 'to be sufficiently in agreement with imperial law'—that is with the basis of the Bruce right—though in what respect the king's clerks do not tell us.[9] But the whole passage was a domestic rejection of the judgment of Edward I for John Balliol in the Great Cause. The same parliament of 1318 made open reference to the discords which had arisen on the death of Alexander III between magnates of the realm, as a reason for legislation to maintain peace among or between (*inter*) them and the people, by forbidding breach of the king's peace in pursuit of a civil cause.[10] The ambiguity of the latin obscures this already reticent clause which must refer to tenurial conflicts arising from the complex shifting of allegiances or lordship over many years. Thus Ingram Balliol probably supported King John but on his death Ingram de Umfraville's claim to inherit half of Redesdale was set aside by Edward I in 1299 in favour of Henry Percy, co-heir to the other half.[11] Neither man probably had any sasine even during the brief peace of 1304–6, because after 1314 King Robert, having forfeited Percy, still had to partition

---

[8] *Acts of the Parliaments of Scotland [APS]* I, 464–66; *Regesta Regum Scottorum*, V *Acts of Robert I, 1306–29 [RRS, V]*, (1988), ed. A. A. M. Duncan, no. 58; 560–61.
[9] *APS*, I, 465–66
[10] *APS*, I, 462, c.20; *RRS*, V, 412, c.20.
[11] *Calendar of Documents relating to Scotland [CDS]*, II, no. 1060.

the barony in order to award Ingram his half[12]—the only solid evidence that the latter accepted Robert's lordship though his name occurs as one of the senders of the 1320 Declaration of Arbroath.

Dissent was a recognised danger when the 1318 parliament ordered imprisonment at the king's pleasure for any conspirator, or rumour mongers 'whereby matter of discord could arise between the king and his people'. The reticence of his statute about the nature of the feared plot and rumour is paralleled by our ignorance about the major conspiracy uncovered about June 1320. Our sources for it are wholly narrative and disagree in some respects, notably over who betrayed its leaders. Barbour's highly coloured version of its aims, that William de Soules was to become king, is self-contradictory and improbable to the point of impossibility; the other sources know of no aims.[13] The names of leading conspirators, Brechin, Moubray, Soules and of the (Comyn) countess of Strathearn as a betrayer, however, scarcely permit a doubt that this was a group intent upon forwarding the interests of Edward Balliol; Ingram de Umfraville's request for an English safe-conduct (issued on 20 April 1320)[14] to go on business overseas suggests that the conspirators may have been seeking to use his familiarity with the French court in pursuit of their objectives. They were tried in parliament and would be condemned by an assize, which did not fear to acquit three knights (including the sheriff of Aberdeen) and two esquires; yet King Robert seems to have succeeded in suppressing all wider knowledge of the nature of the treasons committed (just as he had sought to suppress 'rumours'), about which he must have been very sensitive. He feared perhaps that others besides Umfraville would feel some sympathy for the conspirators. The overlap between these events and the dispatch to Avignon of the barons' letter to the pope aroused no comment by fourteenth-century chroniclers for the simple reason that while they knew of the traitors tried in early August 1320, they had no knowledge of this 'Declaration of Arbroath', dated the previous 6 April; but the two events may well have been linked. King Robert's relations with Avignon, recently conducted through the legates Cardinals Luke and Gaucelin, were particularly bad and threatened an interdict upon the whole kingdom. The barons' letter seeking to avert this was

---

[12] *Registrum Magni Sigilli Regum Scotorum*, I, App. 1, no. 76.

[13] *Chron Fordun*, I, 348–49; *Scalacronica*, 144; Barbour, *Brus*, XIX, 76–121. Barbour first says that lords planned to kill the king and reign in his place; Soulis was chief of them. Then that Soulis was to reign in the king's place. He was betrayed by a lady, confessed his plot and was imprisoned. Fordun says that the countess of Strathearn and Soulis were convicted and imprisoned, Brechin and three others executed. The mild treatment of the countess and Soulis suggests that they did turn king's evidence, but makes 'Soulis for king' utterly improbable.

[14] *Cal. Patent Rolls, 1317–21*, 441.

delivered by Sir Adam Gordon, a Berwickshire knight of modest importance, Sir Odard de Maubuisson, a knight of Philip V experienced in Gascony but also an admiral of the Channel fleet in 1303–4, and Mr Alexander Kininmonth, a cleric with experience of the curia.[15] These envoys, probably the first from Scotland to reach the curia since the election of John XXII in 1316, were no mere postmen; they had to break through a wall of curial hostility assiduously buttressed by English monitions and gold, in order to secure the benefit petitioned for (letters adjuring Edward II to desist from attacking the Scots), and were strikingly successful in the task—in contrast to the efforts of the Irish in 1317.

The importance of this mission underlines its weak membership, lacking the usual balance of earl, baron, cleric(s). A fragmentary report from northern England, dateless and largely illegible, does, however, show that at some time after Bannockburn Earl Patrick returned from France with news which caused a turmoil, and that the magnates were going to a council at Scone.[16] Sir Adam Gordon was a knight of Patrick earl of March and had travelled with him to Westminster in 1313 to petition Edward II on behalf of the Anglo-Scottish community of Lothian; but he was not close to King Robert, in the way that a later envoy to Avignon, Sir Robert Keith, was, and his place as envoy in 1320 is puzzling. It becomes much more understandable if the leading envoy had been his lord, Earl Patrick, who turned back from France, with news of 'treasonable' contacts there with Balliol supporters in Scotland, provoking the summons of parliament at Scone to try the offenders. The final and voluntary departure of Ingram de Umfraville from Scotland in 1320, in reaction against the execution of Brechin according to Barbour, was the logical act of a strong Balliol supporter on the failure of the conspiracy.[17] We shall never be sure what lay behind the conspiracy of 1320, but the collecting of seals by the king's chancery, to be appended to the declaration of Arbroath, was, I suggest, its origin.[18] There is a fair possibility that the content of the document

[15] For these ambassadors see Barrow, *Bruce*, 305.

[16] PRO,SC1/49/70. This document was drawn to my attention by Professor Barrow.

[17] Barbour, *Brus*, XIX, 76–121. His safeconduct of 20 April 1320 was vacated and reissued on 4 October, when, however, a significant retinue was included, which he is more likely to have acquired in England than in Scotland. When this was reissued on 26 January, 1321 (*Cal.Patent Rolls, 1317–21*, 555) Ingram was claiming that he had never left Edward's allegiance, but had escaped from the Scots and had secured recovery of some lands (*Cal. Close Rolls, 1318–23*, 288). At Westminster on 29 January, coming from Scotland and going to France, he had a silver gilt cup from the king (B.L. Additional MS. 9951, fo.20r). This leads me to believe his claim and to doubt Barbour's version of events.

[18] A. A. M. Duncan, 'The making of the Declaration of Arbroath', *The Study of Medieval Records, Essays in honour of Kathleen Major*, ed. D. A. Bullough and R. L. Storey (1971), 174–88.

on which they were used was not known to the baronage who appeared as authors of it. This activity may have rekindled the resentment of Brechin and others so that they sought to discover whether Philip V was prepared to do something for Edward Balliol.

The trials of 1320 marked the end of the Balliol party in Scotland until 1332, and the Declaration of Arbroath, in asserting the legitimacy of Robert's kingship, gave no hint of a Balliol claim. The rhetoric of historically-justified freedom was indeed masterly but I am sceptical of its value for judging the political outlook of Scots (or of a section of them) in 1320; it was a statement designed to avert a particular overseas threat to Robert's kingship. In tone it was anticipated by the rhetoric of the declaration of the clergy of 1309–10, the first systematic vindication of King Robert's war, which, like the 1320 Declaration, survived in Scotland but, unlike it, was in all four versions generally addressed to Christ's faithful, and therefore might be seen as a domestic party manifesto.

In fact the declaration belonged to the complex world of international diplomacy, in which Philip IV pressed energetically for a crusade and for the supression of the Templars' Order. His letter taken to Scotland at the end of 1308 invited Robert to join the Crusade, as we can deduce from the reply from the Scottish magnates in a parliament at St Andrews in March 1309, in which they emphatically describe themselves as acknowledging the faith of King Robert and thank Philip for recalling the Franco-Scottish alliance and for his professions of affection for the king. They recall that in the exaltation of Christian princes Christianity benefits, and therefore 'if the estate of our lord [king] .. is uplifted by the grace of your excellency' and freedom and peace achieved for Scotland, then king and subjects will willingly join the Crusade.[19] If the letter be not mere courtesies and rhetoric, if it asks for anything, it asks for these: raising Robert's standing as king, freedom, peace. The first and most attainable, surely refers to his royal title and suggests that the London annals were correct in claiming that Philip's letter did not salute Robert as king.[20]

This refusal of the royal title is made more likely by a second letter from the barons to Philip, now lost, which, however, certainly argued that Robert was true heir of Alexander III and rightful king, [21] as though Philip had shown himself unaware of the fact. These protests by the barons must have reached Philip, for in the summer of 1309 his messenger in England, on the way to Scotland, wrote a letter addressed to Robert earl of Carrick, and carried it in a box, but stitched in his

[19] APS, I, 459–60; for the seals, *ibid.* 289.
[20] *Chronicles of the Reigns of Edward I and Edward II*, I, 226.
[21] APS, I, 289.

belt another version addressed to Robert king of Scots. In July 1309 Philip wrote to Edward II of a king of Scots who troubled the latter, but moderated the offence by leaving the king nameless![22] A failure to style Robert king in 1308 also explains the extraordinary recourse to the holding of a parliament, an institution which proclaimed Robert's royal dignity unmistakeably to the French king. Since an Anglo-Scottish truce was in force, he was able to summon it to the neutral city of St Andrews whose bishop had been released in August 1308, though still forbidden to leave England; the aim was undoubtedly to allow the churchmen whose dioceses ignored political divisions to attend, so that they might receive and act upon bulls sent by Clement V—and react to one not received.

The lost letter to Philip had the same main message as the declaration of the clergy—the right of Robert to be king; the declaration itself was surely, then, also intended for an overseas recipient. Other evidence supports that suggestion and points to the General Council summoned to Vienne for 1 October 1310 as the intended destination.[23] In the bull *Regnans in celis*, of August 1308 the pope had summoned to the council not all bishops, but a selection. The French had proposed from Scotland only the bishops of St Andrews and Whithorn, but the papacy added to the list Robert Wishart bishop of Glasgow.[24] This summons (as was doubtless intended) made it more difficult for Edward II to keep him in prison in defiance of Clement V's claim to jurisdiction in his case; in November 1309 he was released to the bishop of Poitiers and taken to the curia.[25] When King Robert's men learned from *Regnans in celis* that the Scottish church was to be represented by two tools of Edward II and a prisoner, they would wish others to attend the Council. They had to bring the clergy together under royal influence, for which St Andrews was an appropriate place, to take advantage of the permission in the bull for the unsummoned bishops to send proctors.[26] The bishops of St Andrews and Whithorn did not go to Vienne[27] but some others from Scotland certainly did.

[22] *Gascon Register A*, ed. G. P. Cuttino and J.-P. Trabut-Cussac (1975), II, 354, no. 71; *Foedera*, II, 110 = *Treaty Rolls*, I, no. 496, especially n. 3; *Foedera*, II, 79.

[23] For the Council, in addition to Hefele-Leclercq, see J Lecler, *Vienne* (Histoire des conciles oecumeniques, viii (Paris, 1964)), which thinks the crusading plans unimportant. Their significance is shown in S. Schein, *Fideles Crucis*, (1991); see also N. Housley, *The Avignon Papacy and the Crusades, 1305–1378* (1986).

[24] E. Müller, *Das Konzil von Vienne, 1311–12*, (1934), 669.

[25] D. E. R. Watt, *Biographical Dictionary of Scottish Graduates to A.D. 1410*, (1977), 589 gives a full account of Wishart's difficulties at this time.

[26] The full text and various addresses of *Regnans in celis* are in *Regestum Clementis Papae V*, ed. monks of O. S. Benedict (1885–92). The summons of the three Scottish bishops is ibid. no 3631.

[27] Watt, *Biographical Dictionary*, 322–23 for St Andrews; 309 for Whithorn.

A second bull of the same month, *Faciens misericordiam*, came to Scotland in a form addressed to the bishop of St Andrews and the other bishops (unnamed) in the kingdom of Scotland ordering each to enquire into the lives of individual Templars.[28] For most provinces this was to be followed by a provincial council to pronounce absolution or condemnation upon the knights, but in the Scottish bull the bishop of St Andrews was ordered to gather 'all in one' (the pope evidently believed that Scotland had no provincial organisation) for this purpose. This procedure was carefully discharged, for in November 1309 the bishop of St Andrews made the appropriate enquiry in his diocese[29] and in February 1310 a 'Scottish General Council' (i.e. of the church) was held at the Greyfriars just outside Dundee, an English held town but like St Andrews accessible to clergy from all Scotland. *Regnans in celis* had invited the prelates to formulate in writing everything bearing on correction and reform for the guidance of the General Council, and many local synods were held to do so; the council at Dundee was also one of these, meeting after a sufficient interval to enable the complaints of particular dioceses to be collected. The Scottish grievances submitted at Vienne came from 'the church of the kingdom of Scotland'; the clergy used a very similar phrase of themselves, *in regno Scotie constituti*, in the declaration. Both were derived ultimately from the addresses of the bulls of August 1308, evidence that grievances and declaration were alike intended for Vienne.[30]

The declaration had nothing to say about the Templars; it was rather a response to the aspect of *Regnans in celis* which provoked King Robert: it was despatched to every monarch of Catholic Europe from Cyprus to Portugal and Norway, but not to Robert king of Scots.[31] The bull itself did not say so, but Robert would have discovered readily from King Philip's embassy that he had not been summoned, a denial of royal standing which now (as later for John XXII) elicited a carefully organised response, the clergy's declaration. This claimed that John Balliol was only a *de facto* king chosen by the English king in preference to Bruce. It narrated Balliol's deposition, the sufferings of the people, the choice of King Robert and his right to rule, with a rejection of any claim based upon letters sealed in the past under compulsion; the senders have done him fealty and their successors should do the same to him and his heirs. Despite its rather defensive rejection of the sealed

[28] *Foedera*, II, 55 for the text of this bull as sent to Canterbury; *Reg. Clementis V*, no. 3511 for that addressed to Scotland.

[29] *The Spottiswoode Miscellany*, II (1845) 7 16.

[30] *Faciens misericordiam*, and the bull ordering restoration of the Templars' goods were addressed to the bishops *in regno Scotie constituti*, *Regnans in celis* to those *per regnum Scotie constituti*. *Reg. Clementis V*, nos. 3401, 3511, 3631.

[31] *Reg. Clementis V*, nos. 3626–7.

submissions of 1296, the declaration does not dwell upon the wrongdoing of the king of England, and in marked contrast to the 1320 Declaration, the English are not mentioned. This declaration treats English lordship as marginal; central to it is Scottish kingship, a rejection of Balliol, a vindication of Bruce, and in this it responds to the circumstances of the summons to the Council of Vienne. In domestic documents Robert I always resolutely ignored King John, claiming Alexander III as his immediate predecessor—as was done in the lost letter to Philip IV. The acknowledgment here, even in explicit denunciation, of Balliol's kingship suggests that Robert was concerned about more than the failure to call him to Vienne. The bulls to the bishops did speak of the 'kingdom'; who, then had been summoned as king? Robert may have feared that John had been summoned to the Council as king of Scots. This would explain why the clergy's declaration was aimed at the Council, which could exclude John should he attend, and not addressed to the pope who had ignored Robert.

At least two exemplars of the declaration were written by a clerk who served the king;[32] its whole tenour concerns secular politics, so that King Robert was obviously its sponsor. Since the Council's 'reform' of the church, was meant to exclude secular influences, the full version of the declaration, from unnamed bishops, abbots and the rest of the clergy and community in the St Andrews parliament of 1309 was somewhat inappropriate, and an alternative version omitted the community;[33] yet there was still time to submit the declaration to the provincial council at Dundee in February 1310, and produce a version from it, free from all obvious secular taint.[34] All these versions seem to have been sealed by the bishops, including some who cannot have been in Scotland in 1309 or 1310. But these dates are not to be rejected on that account. Rather they show that the king could muster a full complement of episcopal seals and use them for his own purposes. Finally the instruction of *Faciens misericordiam* to unite the bishops 'all in one', was taken up, and a fourth version produced from the bishops only, each named; since demonstrably all could not have met in 1309–10, this version was without place or time date (but was probably of February 1310).[35]

[32] *RRS*, V, 177, scribe 9.

[33] The originals of these are lost; the texts, unprinted are in B. L. Harleian MS. 4694, transcripts by Sir James Balfour of Denmilne (17th century), who notes that some episcopal seals were appended.

[34] SRO,SP 13/4; APS, I, 460; Stones, *Anglo-Scottish Relations*, no. 36.

[35] SRO,SP 13/5; *APS*, I, 460–61. The bishops of Galloway and Sodor were included in this declaration, again a response to the papal letters to the bishops of the kingdom. These two dioceses were in the kingdom, but in the provinces of York and Trondheim ecclesiastically. The declaration of the clergy was first fully discussed by D. W. Hunter Marshall, 'On a supposed Provincial Council . . .' *Scottish Historical Review*, XXIII (1926),

The king had a quite specific destination in mind for the declaration; whether it reached the continent or the Council (which was postponed for a year) is unknown. The presence of so many originals in Scotland might suggest that it was not sent, but that conclusion is unsafe since no two originals were identical, and each may have been a file copy. Clement V seems never to have recognised Robert I. The declaration of the clergy was cogent, but it remains rhetoric and is not a measure of the will of the Scots to maintain war measured by the resources which King Robert was able to muster from his subjects. The evidence suggests that he gathered that support by command and by reward, the recourses needed by any king, whether engaged in conquest or in defence.

In the years following King John's failure to act in 1302, Edward I had done enough to make English rule acceptable not only to his long-term supporters like the earls of Strathearn and Dunbar, but also, at least in the short term, to former Balliol loyalists. When Carrick, now head of the Bruce family, met Comyn on 10 February 1306, it is unlikely that the latter's death had anything to do directly with the Scottish throne. The earliest explanation, that given by Walter of Guisborough, claims that Carrick accused Comyn of damaging his repute and standing with Edward I,[36] a version which fits well with the long reliance of the Bruces upon Edward's goodwill. Certainly in the summer of 1304 the two men had become party to a lost written agreement, which, on the analogy of the contemporaneous agreement between Carrick and the bishop of St Andrews, required mutual support in quite unspecific terms.[37] This agreement, like that with the bishop, was discovered later and made to serve as evidence of Carrick's pre-meditation in his efforts to seize the throne. All the circumstantial evidence is that Carrick blundered into being an accessory to a murder which had nothing to do with reviving the patriotic cause.

280–93, where he takes the view that Greyfriars was so near Dundee castle as to make it an unlikely place for the clergy to agree to the declaration. But it is likely that the bishop of St Andrews was at the Council, which would allay English concern—he was at Lindores with supporters of Robert I on 20 February 1310 (*Liber S Marie de Lundoris*, (Abbotsford Club, 1841) no. 10. More seriously, William Sinclair was at the curia as elect of Dunkeld, and was not yet bishop, as he is called by the declaration (Watt, *Biographical Dictionary*, 496–97). If King Robert used the names of absent bishops, he could well have gambled on Sinclair's consecration at Avignon, not knowing of the rival English 'elect'.

[36] *Chron. Guisborough*, 366.

[37] The agreement was made at Cambuskenneth near Stirling, 11 June 1304 (F. Palgrave. *Documents and Records illustrating the History of Scotland*, no. 146). Although it was thought treasonable in 1306, Edward I did not mention it in his charges against the bishop to the pope. Barbour, *Brus*, I, 484, says that the Bruce-Comyn agreement was made 'as they came riding from Stirling', that is at the time of the siege in the summer of 1304.

There was much uncertainty after the murder. Our only source, a well-informed letter written from Berwick to an administrator at court, shows that Carrick at first made a request to Edward I and told the Berwick government that if it was not granted, he would defend himself with the longest staff that he had. Whatever this request was, 'defend' does not suggest that it was for the title of king; the writer had to warn the court that despite appearances Carrick did intend to become king; and Edward reacted strongly only in April when he heard that Robert had seized the throne. Carrick's request, I suggest, was for a pardon which would protect him from the vengeance of the Comyns and their allies. By the time the letter was written Carrick had seized castles in the south-west, including Ayr, but, unable to man them, had plundered their contents to provision the Carrick castle of Loch Doon and Dunaverty castle, of which he obtained possession by exchange. This deal makes sense only as a preliminary to importing Irish or Hebridean mercenaries to support his defence.

By early March 1306 the impossibility of this position would be apparent; as a manslayer he commanded no significant Scottish support, had a host of Scottish enemies and lacked a response from the English court. Then on a visit to the bishop of Glasgow, when he received the fealty of the people thereabouts and put them on twenty-four hours notice to turn out with arms for him, he made plain that his was now a bid for the throne—for, although not yet a king, he took upon himself kingly authority to command men to perform the army service incumbent upon all free landholders in defence of the kingdom.[38] The decision to become king was certainly taken at the prompting of the bishop, who received his oath to abide by the ordinance of the clergy, gave him absolution, sent him on his way to take his heritage and gave him some trappings for the royal inauguration. The bishop was a patriot; so was Carrick, though neither he nor we may entirely distinguish that sentiment from his interest in the throne. 1306 was a desperately unfavourable moment for both the sentiment and the interest; but Carrick was driven to the throne by the need to command as king, by the search for support.

In 1306 the new-made king had important adherents, notably the earls of Athol and Lennox, the bishops of Glasgow and Moray. In a bid to increase their number he went, in Barbour's words, 'over all the land/friends and friendship purchesand',[39] a description would have sounded ironic to the earl of Strathearn and the bishop of St Andrews. Strathearn was married to a Comyn lady but had kept a very low

---

[38] Stones, *Anglo-Scottish Relations*, no. 34. G. W. S. Barrow, 'The Army of Alexander III's Scotland' in *Scotland in the Reign of Alexander III, 1249–1286*, ed. N. H. Reid (1990), 132–47.
[39] Barbour, *Brus*, II 187–188.

profile between 1297 and 1304 when he was pressed into service by Edward I. King Robert demanded his homage and military service, harried his lands, violated a safe-conduct to sieze him, threatened him with hanging and eventually forced a reluctant homage from him— but Strathearn denounced Athol, whose fealty was 'fragile as glass' and stood by his fealty to the English king until he lost everything when Perth fell to Robert in 1313.[40] The bishop, a patriot until 1304, was likewise harried into joining Robert, though he desperately sought to avoid appearing at the enthronement.

In the following three months leading to the rout at Methven, King Robert progressed north to Aberdeen and perhaps even to the Moray Firth at Banff, a journey which Barbour places quite impossibly after the battle of Methven. Athol was sent to capture Brechin, the bishop of Glasgow to take Cupar, while the king secured Dundee town, from where six foreign merchants were held in his train, probably as security for men and money from the town.[41] Dundee castle was damaged, as were the castles of Forfar, Aboyne and Aberdeen, all held by Scots, while three Aberdeen merchants were added to those from Dundee in the royal train.[42] Sir Richard Siward, taken prisoner by Carrick at Tibbers near Dumfries was later released from Kildrummy, to which place the king probably also took his wife and brother Neil at this time.[43] This progress of King Robert in the north in the spring of 1306 does much to explain the profile of his support among the knights and lairds at the time of Methven as revealed by those forfeited by Edward I. Many came from Ayrshire and Lennox, where he was first active; fifteen came from Perthshire, twelve from Angus and Mearns, twelve from Aberdeen and Banff, and ten from Moray where the bishop preached his cause actively. The Aberdeenshire figure is high for a region which included the Comyn earldom of Buchan.[44]

On the other hand he drew little support from Renfrew, whence James Stewart had been exiled to southern England, from Lanarkshire or Stirlingshire. No doubt some feared to join him, but it is also likely that among those recruited in the north, some joined him through fear. The total size of his army and particularly of its cavalry, even judging by the numbers just cited was not large. The force from Berwick with

[40] Palgrave, *Documents … History of Scotland*, no. 144; Stones, *Anglo-Scottish Relations*, no. 35; C. Neville, 'The Political Allegiance of the Earls of Strathearn during the War of Independence'. SHR, LXV (1986), 133–53.

[41] Barbour, *Brus*, IX, 288–90, where two sieges of Brechin, one by John earl of Athol, are homologated into one; CDS, II, no. 1780 (Cupar); PRO, E101/13/16, fos. 15r, 21r (Dundee, showing that the castle continued to be garrisoned).

[42] PRO, E101/13/16, fos. 11v–15v, esp. 13v, 15v.

[43] PRO, E101/369/11 fo.97v.

[44] E. M. Barron, *Scottish War of Independence*, (2nd edn., 1934), 224–35.

which Aymer de Valence attacked at Methven numbered about 2,200;[45] King Robert's army may have been larger, but probably not by much. It failed from want of prudent generalship and because, as Barbour says, the small folk were defeated. It was an army in which the low ratio of well-armed men to scratch infantry quite outweighed any numerical superiority. King Robert was able to pull out his chivalry, leaving (in Edward I's words) 'the poor commons of Scotland who by force rose against the king' to ransom themselves from his anger; the chivalry was defeated a little later by a contingent of Valence's men at a battle of Loch Tay, unknown to Barbour, and Robert fled.[46] The difficulties which he had over the following year were notorious in his own lifetime. As presented by Barbour they were a triumph over adversities; in reality there was little success and no triumph. His brothers at last brought an Irish contingent to the south-west which was killed or made prisoner before it could contact the king. The battle of Glentrool, a triumph for Robert in Barbour, appears in English sources only as horses lost 'in the chase against Robert Bruce between Glentrool and Glenheur';[47] the battle of Loudoun on 10 May 1307 appears as a Bruce victory in Barbour but also in English chronicles which have picked up a Scottish version of his adventures.[48] It is just possible that Valence came from Bothwell to Loudoun and was waylaid by the king; but the record evidence is that the Treasurer of England, on a tour of supervision of Scottish garrisons, was at Ayr, very probably with Valence on 8 May, and at Bothwell with him on 13 May, returning by Lanark and Dumfries to Carlisle on 18 May.[49] It is likely that the Treasurer had cash with him at least for dire necessities, upon which the King was anxious to lay hands when he met Valence at Loudoun and drove him back to Ayr, as Gray claims. Few were killed and the English made a sensible tactical retreat from ground which they soon recovered.

That conclusion does not square with the English chronicle narrative

---

[45] PRO, E101/13/16, fos 4–9 shows wages paid for some 50 knights, 21 esquires, 140 arbelasters, and 1960 archers.

[46] Barbour, *Brus*, II, 346–445; *Chron. Guisborough*, 368; *Chron. Trivet*, 410; *Chron. Rishanger*, 230; *Scalacronica*, 130; *Chron. Fordun*, I, 341–42. For the battle of Loch Tay, PRO, E101/13/16, fo.16r–v.

[47] Barbour, *Brus*, VII, 488–635; PRO, E101/612/12 m.5, *mortui sunt in chacea super R.B inter Glentruyl et Glenheur ultimo die exercitus in Galwydia.*

[48] Barbour, *Brus*, VIII, 123–358 does not say whence Valence came, but makes him go to Bothwell again after the battle; *Scalacronica*, 132 says Bruce drove Valence to Ayr; *Chron. Guisborough* 378 does not name the battle but says few were killed. I have found no record of horses killed at Loudoun.

[49] *CDS*, II, NOS. 1979,1768 (1307), 1774 (1307), 1928, 1931; iv, no. 1829, and 398. Arrears for the repair of Ayr castle (reoccupied by the English on 6 October, 1306) were paid to Robert Leybourne, sheriff of Ayr, on 24 May, 1307 (PRO E101/13/26).

that three days later Robert bloodily repulsed Ralph Monthermer, earl of Gloucester as one of the Guardians of Scotland to Ayr; Gloucester was said to have been besieged in Ayr till relieved by a royal army.[50] But the whole episode, including Gloucester's presence in Scotland, his guardianship, the siege of Ayr and a relieving force, are entirely unknown to Barbour, not usually silent on a Bruce victory, and also, and conclusively, to English record for the period, which shows that on 17 May Ayr was a busy and open English garrison town in communication with Dumfries and Ireland.[51] The story will have a basis in fact, and I suspect that something like this happened in 1301, when Edward Prince of Wales took Ayr, probably had Monthermer in his army, and found a Scottish force at Loudoun between him and King Edward at Glasgow and Bothwell.[52] In 1301 the Scots were threatening to besiege Ayr; I do not see how they can have done so in 1307.

There can be no doubt that King Robert compelled an English force to withdraw at Loudoun on 10 May 1307, as a letter from Carlisle states,[53] but the battle was of little strategic significance, for the king simply went to ground after it. From mid-July John of Argyll was in command at Ayr with 800 men,[54] and set about hunting Robert with hound and horn,[55] while Edward II in August 1307 brought a small army to Cumnock to search for him. For much of the time he fled alone or with but one or two companions, scarcely able to let down his breeches for fear of the traitors seeking a reward for his death. Yet he did have an army of sorts at Loudoun, and four months later, after the departure of Edward II, he again had a force sufficient to defeat men of Galloway, so that some fled with their cattle to Cumberland, some were compelled to join him against the English, and some, according to Lanercost, paid blackmail to be left in peace.[56] In these months the English named no Scots who were leading men in their communities as having newly joined the rebellion, and I see Robert's force, briefly collected, soon disbanded, as essentially a peasant levy, serving because commanded to do so under threat of the usual pains.

James Douglas, however, had a record in the south considerably more successful than King Robert's. Our knowledge of Douglas's early

[50] *Chron Guisborough*, 378; *Scalacronica*, 132.

[51] *CDS*, II, no. 1774, misdated, of 1307.

[52] J. Stevenson, *Documents illustrative of the History of Scotland, 1286–1306*, no. 611.

[53] *National Manuscripts of Scotland*, II (1870), no. 13.

[54] *CDS*, II, no. 1957. It is astonishing that Barbour gives John's force as 800 men, the figure given in this record.

[55] Barbour, *Brus*, VI, 480– VII, 52; *Chronique de Jean le bel*, ed. J. Viard and E. Déprez, I (1904), 111.

[56] *Chron. Lanercost*, 209–10 (which comments on the 'multitude of people' who adhered to Robert); *Feodera*, II, 8; *Cal. Close Rolls, 1307–13*, 2.

years sowing his oats in Paris, as valet to the Bishop of St Andrews, and seeking from Edward I the lands of his father, a patriot who had died in the Tower, comes wholly from Barbour, who puts him in the king's company at Methven, during the flight and thereafter in Rathlin and Arran. I suspect that these links are Barbour's embroidery, for otherwise he depicts a Douglas who is determined upon one thing— the recovery of his heritage, granted by Edward I to Robert Clifford.[57] Thus in early May 1307 by a ruse, James recovered Douglas castle, slighted it and sent the garrison back to Clifford.[58] A few days later he joined the king at Loudoun, but 'sent and begged' the advancing English force 'that he might be received' to the English peace. then, as he saw the English retreat, 'he chose no longer to keep his word'. Douglas's loyalty was very ambivalent; he came to the king's side in the pursuit of family interest, after seeking terms and on sight of English retreat.

The motivation of Douglas and many others who joined King Robert was undoubtedly patriotic, a compound of outrage at the destruction of Scottish kingship and resentment at the presence of occupying garrisons; but in each case prudence also dictated a calculation of the odds in favour of success. Few found that calculation in Robert's favour during 1307; his support, such as it was, seems to have come from men of humble rank whose motivation, the English said, was fear of Bruce; I see no reason to discount that claim.

On the other hand, when in September 1307, Douglas withdrew to the Forest, emerging in April 1308 to retake Douglas castle and massacre its garrison with particular ferocity,[59] this was the beginning of a long association with the Forest, a description which properly belongs to Ettrick or Selkirkshire, but must have been used more widely of the uplands of Roxburgh and Peebles as well. From the outbreak of Wallace's rising in 1297, when he recruited there, the men of the Forest maintained a sturdy and successful resistance to English forces. Before 1304 English garrisons held Roxburgh, Jedburgh and even Selkirk, where a peel was built to house a large force in rebellious country, but

---

[57] Barbour, *Brus*, I, 415–436, II, 99–112; V, 255–6.

[58] Barbour, *Brus*, VIII, 437–520. The event is dated by the reference to Lanark fair, probably held at Whitsuntide (14 May in 1307); the year is not given by Barbour, but Clifford had a grant to repair the castle on 30 May and clearly reoccupied it in the summer of 1307 (PRO, E101/369/16, fo. 4v.) For Douglas at Loudoun, see *Nat. MSS Scot.* II, no. 13.

[59] Barbour, *Brus*, VIII, 424–427 for the withdrawal to the Forest. The massacre at Douglas Castle, the 'Douglas Lardner', (ibid. V, 335–419) took place on a Palm Sunday, according to Barbour before the battle of Loudoun. But it is not really possible that in March 1307 Douglas massacred Clifford's men and then in May sent them chivalrously back to him. The Douglas Lardner took place after Clifford reoccupied the castle in 1307, on Palm Sunday, 1308.

the sheriff of Peebles had a company of four men at arms, evidence that he occupied no castle.[60] In the rising of 1306, a very significant group of men from Lothian and these upland sheriffdoms broke their faith to Edward I and are listed among those whose lands were redistributed. In particular Aymer de Valence benefitted by a grant of the lands of unnamed tenantry holding of the crown in Selkirk and Peebles, who had rebelled.

Almost certainly the leader of the rebels had been Simon Fraser of Oliver Castle in Peebles-shire, a prominent if occasionally uncertain patriot who deserted from Berwick in spring 1306 and was executed in September with full barbarity in London.[61] He was punished as a major rebel leader, yet he does not figure as present at Methven nor in the flight thereafter, and was captured somewhere between Linlithgow and Stirling. The most likely explanation is that the men of Peebles and the Forest rebelled under his leadership but could not join the king, being contained by the Lothian garrisons, and that they dispersed on the news of Methven and Loch Tay. But it is doubtful if thereafter the English had even islands of authority in the area, for not only did Douglas make the Forest his refuge, source of men for the rousting of an Anglo-Scottish company near Peebles in late 1307[62] and for the Douglas Lardner in April 1308, but as early as March 1309 the king was granting title to land in Peebles-shire, and about the same time at Moffat beyond the head of Tweed, in upper Annandale.[63]

It is true that in September 1310 Edward II marched quickly from Roxburgh by Selkirk and Traquair to Eddleston near Peebles, but the men to the Forest still had to come to his peace when Gloucester brought a force there in 1311.[64] Such allegiance was fleeting; Robert I was able to appear suddenly before the walls of Berwick in December 1312, Douglas before those of Roxburgh in February 1314, only because they had the active support of the men of these Border sheriffdoms, the 'upland men' who in 1313 were arrested on sight by the English

[60] PRO, E101/13/34m. 25. I owe this information to Dr. Fiona Watson.

[61] As late as April 1306 the chamberlain at Berwick wrote to Simon Fraser as though still loyal (PRO, E101/13/16, fo. 29r). He was captured about 10–15 August (the news arrived in Tynedale on 17 August, PRO, E101/369/11 fo. 97v) in 'the battle of Kirkenclyf' beside Stirling' in which a Sir John Lindsay drowned (R. H. Robbins, *Historical Poems of the fourteenth and fifteenth centuries*, (1959), no. 4, lines 91–93). According to another tract deriding him, he was taken at Linlithgow (*Proceedings of the Society of Antiquaries of Scotland*, VII (1884–5), 177–78).

[62] Barbour, *Brus*, IX, 672–725. Douglas captured Alexander Steward and Thomas Randolph; their names are absent from the December 1307 list of English supporters (*CDS*, III, no. 29).

[63] *RRS*, V, nos 5, 387. I now think I was wrong to argue against a 1309–10 date for the latter.

[64] *Chron. Lanercost*, 214: *forestarios receperunt et reliquos de foresta.*

when they came shopping in Berwick.[65] Even the retreating English army of 1322, numbering some 20,000 men, was shadowed by Douglas from the Forest and had its vanguard 'martyred' near Melrose.[66]

By this date Douglas, whose heritage lay in Lanarkshire, had been granted Jedforest and made the chief forester of Selkirk,[67] clearly to reward and support his role as the military chief of the region. The predominantly pastoral economy of these uplands would support a freer small tenantry than the fertile lowlands to north, south and east, and such men were the most ready to turn political sensibilities into action. They also had a particular military skill to offer, as the service of ten archers prescribed for the barony of Manor in Peebles-shire in 1309 bears witness; the beneficiary was Adam the marshall, a name signifying his local military function, similar to that of twentyman or hundredman; he must have served King Robert to some purpose in local command, since he was certainly ousting the rightful laird of Manor from his heritage.[68] The Forest did not differ greatly as a landscape from much of Carrick and Galloway where King Robert had such ill fortune. The difference between them was the adherence of leading families of the latter region, the Macdowells and MacCans, to Comyn and Balliol, as well as the importation of others like John of Argyll to back up the overwhelming power of the English presence. It is indeed surprising that the king found as many supporters as he did; they came, they melted away—and that is more a description of small folk than of their social leaders.

The success of King Robert began with his move north in September or October 1307, into what he may have considered the territory of his enemies the earls of Ross and Buchan.[69] In fact castles there were lost or betrayed to him with surprising ease, only Elgin and Banff offering competent resistance. In their reports to Edward II, Robert's enemies excused themselves with accounts of a large army forcing each into a truce which in fact allowed others to be attacked. But Barbour and other narratives show that his company was highly mobile and suggest that it was very modest, something between fifty and two hundred men, with a king in command who was for a time perilously sick and disabled. He could call on the support of 'freeholders and others'; since his opponents could find and punish them as men of ill repute, many were probably lairds and tenantry provisioning his force, but some willing on occasion to take to arms. A small group of northern

[65] *CDS*, III, no. 337.
[66] Barbour, *Brus*, XVIII, 326.
[67] *RRS*, V, no. 167; *Registrum Magni Sigilli*, I, App. 1, nos. 36, 38.
[68] *RRS*, V, no. 5.
[69] Events in the north are known from the newsletter printed by Professor Barrow and Miss Barnes in *SHR*, XLIX, 57–59.

knights certainly supported the king, and would bring men with them, but the adherence of archers and infantry in numbers sufficient to take castles and force the enemy into truces, cannot be attributed mainly to deference towards, or fear of, the king. There must have been a sympathy for his cause, an appreciation of some meaning for the words 'freedom of the kingdom', among at least some of the peasantry. The harrying of Buchan after the victory of Inverurie was a punishment of the peasantry as well as the lairds for having failed to support or join the king; by implication others elsewhere had joined him. Whether they were the poor who had nothing to lose or the husbandmen who seem to us more likely to form political attitudes, the sources do not tell us. Nor do they tell us whether those who served did so at the command of a lord, or of the king, or of their own volition. They were 'the men of the countryside', 'men of ill repute', 'the small folk'.

The best evidence for patriotic sentiment as the spur to action comes from south of the Mounth, but fits with all the less complete fragments from the north. In May 1307 the sheriff or constable at Forfar had reported that the men of the countryside were waiting for the news of Edward I's death, that Robert, if he came, would find them 'all ready at his will, more entirely than ever'. His letter was prophetic, for a Christmas 1308 the local tenantry crept over the wall with ladders, and overwhelmed and killed the careless garrison.[70] The bailey at Forfar has gone, but the castle survives as a small motte, the top some fifty feet in diameter, and little force would be required to take it with the benefit of surprise. Surprise required the sympathy of the countryside for King Robert, and on the evidence of garrisons taken unawares, he had that aplenty. But no large or well-equipped force was needed to take the castles of Scotland north of the Tay which offered little in the way of strong fortifications; they were motte and bailey structures perhaps with a circuit of stone walls, but probably not of any height, and lacking sophisticated gate-towers. There were exceptions, notably Kildrummy, but it lay burned out and defenceless after the English siege of 1306.

Secondly the garrisons were modest in size, not reinforced and perhaps not regularly paid. Barbour says Forfar was 'stuffit all with Inglis men', but this meant six to ten esquires, ten arbelasters and five archers, perhaps twenty-five men, desperately hoping that their supply line to Dundee would hold. Aberdeen and Coull were in no better state.[71]

[70] CDS, II, 536–37; Barbour, Brus, IX, 310–323; Chron. Holyrood, 179.

[71] PRO E101/13/16, fo. 14v for these garrisons. Aberdeen had 55 men and Dundee 38. The constable of Forfar was John Weston, escheator beyond Forth, and his garrison was strengthened by four men on 1 April 1307 propter superuenienc' inimicorum. It is not known who these Scottish enemies were, but the country was undoubtedly disturbed.

Thirdly, and most importantly, the Anglo-Scottish force defending
Edward II's land was divided and grossly inadequate for its task. In
January 1308, when Sir John Moubray placed men in the castle of
Coull, a solid stone structure, to protect Mar from the king's incursion,
he presumably had to take that garrison from the force paid for by
Edward II in August 1307, to hold Scotland from the Mounth to
Orkney. That force numbered thirty men at arms.[72] To supplement
this he could draw upon the following of the earl of Buchan, and they
in turn could call out the tenantry of the region, as they did when
Robert I seemed pinned down at Slioch. This infantry of 'small folk'
served at Inverurie in May 1308, where it watched the cavalry pull
back as Robert's men advanced. This was enough; the small folk turned
and fled, which in turn broke the morale of the cavalry who rode off
the field.[73] Trying to hold so vast an area with trivial resources meant
that eventually Moubray was bound to have the weaker force when
the king chose to meet him. The king's force probably grew between
January and this defeat of Moubray, but it did not have to be large to
achieve what it did, and the way in which the king played hide and
seek with overstretched and inadequate enemy forces supports a modest
assessment of its size.

By August 1308 the Anglo-Scottish position north of the Mounth had
been destroyed, the king was in control of Aberdeen and Edward II
was desperate to make a truce which would halt his advance. The task
which now faced the Scots was nonetheless formidable, for unlike the
north, Scotland from Perth southward had castles well fortified by
nature and stone walls, although royal castles at Dumfries, which fell
easily to the mob in 1306, Wigtown, Lanark, Rutherglen and Selkirk
were probably little stronger than Forfar. But great private castles like
Carlaverock, Lochmaben, Bothwell and Dirleton greatly strengthened
the English hold, which seemed stable, protected first by a truce from
early 1309 until the summer of 1310, and then by Edward II's presence
at Berwick when some effort was made to strengthen Perth and Dundee.
    King Robert lacked siege engines and had to rely upon numbers
and surprise. His support, assessed by the names of those lords and
lairds known to have joined him, was clearly growing, but there
remained a painful shortage of knights in his forces, which he sought
to remedy by the creation of new knights' feus, imposing, for example,

---

[72] *SHR*, XLIX, 57–59 for the reinforcing of Coull; if this is Aboyne castle, it had a
garrison of 53 men in the first half of 1307. B.L Additional Ms. 35093, fo. 3v for Moubray's
force.
[73] Barbour, *Brus*, IX, 240–293.

a service of eight knights upon the newly created earldom of Moray in 1312.[74] It is doubtful if this can have made much difference. At Bannockburn the only Scottish cavalry are described as 'light horse'; as Edward II and his knights fled from Stirling in 1314, they were pursued much of the way to Dunbar by Douglas and a Scottish squadron which picked off laggards but simply did not have the weight of numbers or horses to attack the enemy.[75] In consequence the victory of Bannockburn could not be completed by the capture of Edward. Even in 1327 Scottish knights and esquires were said to ride on runcins, other folk on hackneys, with no word of a destrier.[76] Similarly the king made numerous grants of land for the service of archers; a total for the reign and the country likely to have been above, perhaps well above, one hundred. Again the contribution to military effectiveness was slight, but the comment upon the deficiency of the army is significant. Incidentally I have found only one reference to what might be the crossbow in use;[77] the Scots were not well provided with this slow but powerful weapon.

The bulk of the army was the infantry summoned to do common army service for their land, following the banner of their province in companies led by their lords serving at the king's command. The depiction of Scottish soldiers in the Carlisle borough charter shows them with bow and arrow, spear or axe,[78] while the Scottish soldier in Liber A has sword and spear.[79] But their armour seems to be limited to a leather cap, and none is shown wearing a mail hauberk, bassinet or even a quilted aketon. Legislation of 1318 demanded that a man with goods worth £10 must have aketon, bassinet and war-gloves, or failing this, hauberk, cap and war-gloves, as well as sword and spear.[80] This, I suggest, was an attempt to improve the front, whether of line or schiltron, the cutting edge of the formation, which was in need of protection from the enemy's cavalry and heavy weapons. Behind these better armed men would be the mass of Barbour's yeomanry. Many of them would have arms, sword or spear, but few armour, and some might have only a staff, mouths to feed but of little military use. These were Barbour's 'rangald' at Loudoun, the 'carriage men and poverale', who were as numerous, he says, as the effective fighting force, and who were placed at the rear, just as at Bannockburn the 'small folk and

[74] RRS, V, 49–50.
[75] Barbour, Brus, XIII, 56, 547–606.
[76] Chron. Jean le bel, I, 54.
[77] RRS, V, 48–49.
[78] C. Tabraham, Scottish Castles and Fortifications, (1986), 16.
[79] T. Newark, Celtic Warriors, 400B.C.–1600 A.D. (1986), 108.
[80] APS, I, 473, c.27; RRS, V, 414, c.27.

poverale' were sent to guard victuals well behind the army.[81] Again the legislation of 1318 sought to extract some of military use from among them by demanding that if they were rich enough to own a cow, they must have lance or bow and arrows. It has nothing to say of those who had more than a cow and less than £10; of them, Barbour tells us that Edward II was advised to make a long truce in 1323 because Bruce's menye were simple yeomanry, who worked with plough and harrow, and would lose their acquired skill in arms.[82] Theirs was a peasant army. Spontaneity could still occur, as with the yeoman who seized Linlithgow in 1313,[83] but after 1310 the king had need of discipline as well as high morale to fulfil his strategy.

But discipline was evidently problematic. Legislation sought to bring to justice those who committed homicide, robbery or theft when travelling through the kingdom to the army.[84] At the taking of Berwick carefully laid plans were ruined when the force which had secured entry ran wildly through the town, as though mad, seizing harness and slaying men, so greedy were they for booty (Barbour's phrase).[85] As a result the castle was reinforced by the fleeing town garrison and held out for eleven weeks. Barbour has the king both urging discipline—do not break formation to take captives—and appealing openly to the cupidity of his men: 'the poorest of you shall be rich and mighty therewithall, if we win'. The behaviour of the rangald in the park in 1314, seeking to join in the battle as it turned in favour of the Scots,[86] suggests that they knew that text better than the now more famous words of the letter to the Pope: 'we fight not for riches, honours or glory'. Cupidity was very ambivalent as motivation.

Those who plundered were reimbursing themselves for the cost of war. Dr Maddicott's analysis of the weight of the burden of war upon the peasantry in England,[87] must, I am sure, be applicable likewise to Scotland. We have no wardrobe, household or exchequer accounts to put figures on the cost of war, but from absence of records we should not conclude that it was lost in a miasma of patriotic goodwill. The king's clearance of Lothian in 1322 would bear heavily upon the

---

[81] Barbour, *Brus*, VIII, 198; XI, 111; XII, 474; XIII, 341 for rangald; VIII, 275, 368; XI, 238, 420; XIII, 229 for poverale.

[82] Barbour, *Brus*, XIX, 158–185.

[83] Barbour, *Brus*, X, 148–250. At line 151 Bunnock is 'husband[man]'; at line 172 his laden wain was led by a yeoman.

[84] *APS*, I, 467, c.4–5; *RRS*, V, 407, c. 4–5.

[85] Barbour, *Brus*, XVII, 95–200. He says (line 199) that the castle held out for six days, but record evidence shows that Gray's eleven weeks is more nearly correct (*Scalacronica*, 144).

[86] Barbour, *Brus*, XII, 240–244, 305–311; XIII, 229–250.

[87] J. R. Maddicott, *The English Peasantry and the Demands of the Crown, 1294–1341* (*Past and Present*, Supplement 1, 1975).

peasants whom he simultaneously swept into his army.[88] Legislation of 1318 piously provided that each lord should come to the army with needful carriage and victuals, those from distant parts with money to pay for victuals so that the country would not be burdened.[89] But burdened it assuredly was, as the concern of the king's acts with exemption from prise and carriage bears witness; these were a grievance of such weight that in 1326, the king gave up the right to them as means of supplying his armies and was able to secure in return the grant of a tenth of rents annually for the rest of his life, a remarkable testimony to their weight and arbitrariness. It was the more so coming from the third year of a thirteen year truce.

The market price paid for purveyance must have been artificially low, but even so the king had to fund it, and his need would be particularly great when a siege was in prospect, for that also implied some payment of the army after forty days service had ended. The funds were provided, at least in part, by the enemy, although Barbour makes no reference to attacks upon England before 1319, nor to the cost thereof. From the departure of Edward II from Berwick in July 1311, Robert showed his determination to drive the recovery of his kingdom by the exaction of blackmail.[90] Striking boldly across the occupied zone, he looted, then took blackmail from the northern counties to be left in peace till Candlemas 1312. With at least some of that money in pocket, in January 1312 he asked Edward II to negotiate a truce, and about the same time laid siege to Dundee. By mid-February the commander, a Scot, had reached an agreement with the besiegers which Edward at York denounced angrily.[91] Fairly strenuous efforts were made to rescue the town, but it surrendered, probably because not relieved, about 12 April. The parliament which King Robert held on 7 April at a small village ten miles from Dundee must have been summoned in late February, when the king was concerned about how he would finance a protracted siege, for its only known business was an agreement with the burgesses that they would negotiate on taxation and military service only with the king's chamberlain.[92]

The obvious next target was Perth. In August 1312 the northern counties were shown a hint of what the Scots might do and agreed to pay for immunity till midsummer 1313. King Robert must have raised some £1500 from them then, a major lift to revenues which were still

[88] Barbour, *Brus*, XVIII, 249–250, 274–290; *APS*, I, 475–76.

[89] *APS*, I, 467, c.5.

[90] *Chron. Lanercost* is the major source for these invasions, on which see J. Scammell, 'Robert I and the North of England', *English Historical Review*, LXXIII (1957), 385–403. She argues that the total amount taken from the north may well have exceeded £20,000.

[91] *Rotuli Scotiae*, I, 107–109.

[92] *RRS*, V, no. 18.

drawn only from north of Tay.[93] So in December 1312 he was able to appear suddenly at Berwick, and just failed to take the English capital of Scotland by surprise. A month later, and perhaps with a different army, he took Perth after a siege of uncertain duration, on 8 or 10 January 1313, and a month after that Dumfries was surrendered to Robert possibly after a siege. Such protracted campaigning cannot have been carried out with only the free service of common army and must have run the king into significant money payments, for which he would have no recourse to Italian bankers.

At midsummer 1313 the mere threat of a visit from King Robert brought the offer of a very great sum from the northern counties for a truce to last until Michaelmas 1314—money that would finance the concerted attack upon English positions in 1314, to which I shall return. Money extracted from Durham in 1314 and again in 1315[94] was probably poured into the bottomless pit of the Irish war, which distracted the king and Moray in 1316–17. But from the recover of Berwick, the last English outpost, in 1318, the strategy was abandoned, clearly deliberately. By 1318 Northumberland was a no-man's-land, Durham gradually sinking into the same state. Armies ravaged, often into the North Riding, in 1318, 1319, and after the truce, devastatingly, in 1322. Some towns were allowed to buy off the Scots, but generally warfare was clearly aimed at destroying English political will by traditional means, devastation and plunder. The truce of Bishopthorpe ended this short destructive phase, which seems to confirm that up to 1317 cash had been the preferred option of King Robert, because it better met his need to finance sustained military effort within Scotland, or, latterly, Ireland.

This funding explains the marked increase from 1311 in the aggressive strikes with significant forces, on a scale which far outranked the king's painful struggles up to 1308. In those early struggles the evidence of popular service—a different thing from support—suggests that it was forthcoming hesitantly, sometimes reluctantly. From 1311 the run of success in the king's favour, the ability to sustain sieges and to raid far into England, suggests that the cost in burdens upon the peasantry was significantly mitigated by funding from northern England. There is no trace of peasant unrest, even during the ill years which began in 1315, no hint in the legislation of 1318 of men avoiding army service, and

---

[93] Stones, *Anglo-Scottish Relations*, no. 37; *RRS*, V, no. 21.

[94] For the 1315 invasion which seems to have raised 1600 marks from Durham for a two-year truce, see *Scriptores Tres*, 96; *Registrum Palatinum Dunelmense*, IV, 159–65; *Chron Guisborough*, 396–97 (under 1312). *Chron. Lanercost*, 230 calls the army which invaded Ireland *maxima comitativa*, and describes the force which assaulted Carlisle in July as Bruce's *tota fortitudo*.

surviving pro-Balliol sentiment found no support among peasant infantry and hobelars. The king's command to serve was willingly obeyed. The successful recovery of Scottish independence was not the result of assault by the Scots only. It owed much to the paralysis of English government by the struggle to oust Gaveston and then to secure the ordinances; so long as that lasted, Edward II was denied the finances which would pay for an expedition to Scotland to recover territory and rebuild the Anglo-Scottish party. By the summer of 1313, when he took the Crusading vow with Philip IV and brought to an end the latter's lukewarm interest in the Scots, Edward's position was improving. But the loyal Scottish community of Lothian and Berwickshire was now at the end of its tether, plundered by unpaid English soldiery and by Robert I with equal enthusiasm. A petition to King Edward laid forth the grievances and was in London by mid-October 1313.[95] It is not certain that Robert I knew of this, but it would explain why, at the end of that month, he held a council at Dundee to force the issue for the Anglo-Scottish community. No source mentions this, but the surviving record of parliament at Cambuskenneth in November 1314, which forfeited all those not then at the king's peace, states plainly that they had been 'often called and lawfully forewarned'. Now Barbour tells of a council after Bannockburn ordering proclamation that all must come to the king's peace within a year or be forfeited. Here is the lawful summons misunderstood by Barbour, the year to be calculated back, not forward, from November 1314. The place and date of the council is indicated by a clutch of royal acts dated at Dundee late in October 1313.[96]

At much the same time Edward II achieved a settlement with his magnates, and early in November 1313 was granted a subsidy for the Scottish war. He announced that he would be in Scotland with an army by midsummer 1314, to muster at Berwick for 10 June.[97] The challenge to King Robert was clear, the danger that he would lose much of his kingdom great; even in 1311 Edward and Piers Gaveston had briefly recovered Angus and Mearns, and an assault on Aberdeen had been planned.[98] With a full English muster, a great deal more was at stake. Robert responded by a triple pre-emptive strike in February 1314. Douglas, perhaps with men of the Forest took Roxburgh, whose garrison had no hint of his coming, by a night assault. Moray besieged Edinburgh which fell to assault in March, and the king and his brother

---

[95] CDS, III, no. 337.

[96] APS, I, 464; Barbour, Brus, XIII, 721–731; RRS, V, nos. 35–37.

[97] J. R. Maddicott, Thomas of Lancaster, 1307–1322, 151, 157; Foedera, II, 237, 245.

[98] In the spring of 1311; PRO, E101/378/30 fo.4r; Bodleian Library, MS Tanner 197, fos. 12r, 13r.

set siege to Stirling, until, in March or April Edward Bruce rashly agreed to its surrender at midsummer if not relieved earlier.

Barbour's history is very different. He claims that Bannockburn occurred at the end of a year's grace agreed for Stirling's relief at a siege begun in the Lent before that, that is in Lent 1313. Such agreements for relief or surrender were quite common, but I have noted no other example where the period to elapse was so absurdly long as a year, and I see no reason to accept this version when three perfectly good and independent English sources place the beginning of the siege in Lent 1314.[99] That makes sense. Edward II did not come north to disaster in 1314 mainly to relieve Stirling; on the contrary, the relief of Stirling was fixed in the knowledge that he had said he was coming—which explains the anger of King Robert at his brother's action in making the agreement. The lasting victory of the Scots in 1314 was the destruction of the English hold upon their only remaining Scottish province, Lothian, by the taking and destruction of three key castles.

Edward came north to follow in his father's footsteps, cross the Forth, take Perth and reduce the rebels to suppliants for peace as he and Edward I had done in 1303–4. Whatever thinking led to the Scottish decision to muster near Stirling in 1314, the battle which was then engaged was an extraordinary risk, one which perhaps a wise general would have refused, particularly when deserted by a key commander, the constable.[100] For if Robert had failed, then far more might have been lost than by a retreat to Lennox, the alternative contemplated by the king.[101] From such a refuge he could have come back to repeat all the advances of the previous four years, and without vast expenditure on castles and garrisons, the English could have done little to stop him. In the similar situation of 1322, Robert cleaned out Lothian and withdrew to Fife to avoid battle, suggesting that he had reached the same conclusion.

The war of the Scots was a search for freedom from occupying garrisons and for peace, not for battle, which settled nothing. Indeed Bannockburn probably made Edward II more determined to continue the war in order to recover a position which reflected his true strength. But the subjugation of the Scots was beyond even that strength, for reasons of morale, cost and geography; inferior resources and geography equally denied the possibility of victory to Robert I. He acknowledged the strategic impossibility of defeating England in 1321 with the offer

[99] Barbour, *Brus*, X, 813–825; *Chron. Lanercost*, 223; *Vita Edwardi II*, 48–49; *Scalacronica*, 140, by implication.

[100] David earl of Athol had come over to Robert in 1312, possibly at the siege of Dundee; he was given the constableship and held aloof from the battle of Bannockburn.

[101] *Scalacronica*, 142.

of a twenty-six year truce; when the English grudgingly settled for one of thirteen years in 1323, this was a mutual recognition that the war, despite a run of remarkable Scottish victories, had become a stalemate. That, I believe, was its inevitable outcome, as it was the outcome of every phase of Anglo-Scottish conflict after 1328.

THE VENETIAN MAINLAND STATE IN THE FIFTEENTH CENTURY

by John E. Law

READ 21 SEPTEMBER 1991

ON 15 April 1483, the young Venetian noble Marino Sanudo set out on a tour of the *stato di terra*, the Republic's mainland state, with his cousin Marco and two other Venetian patricians. Marco and his colleagues were travelling in an official capacity as *auditori nuovi* and syndics of the Venetian government, dispatched to hear appeals from the Republic's subjects, and to investigate the conduct of resident officials. Marino had no such responsibilities, but he left an account of his experiences in the work known as the *Itinerario con i Sindaci di Terraferma.*[1]

The syndics' circuit took in all the larger and most of the smaller communities under Venetian rule. They travelled first to Padua, acquired in 1405. Then they went south to the Polesine di Rovigo, at the time a war zone which the Republic was trying to wrest from the Este of Ferrara.[2] Thereafter the party turned north-west and crossed the south of the *Veronese* which Venice had taken in 1405. They travelled westwards to Brescia (1426), Bergamo (1428) and Crema (1454). They doubled back to follow the shore of Lake Garda which the Republic had secured by 1441, before reaching Rovereto in the *Trentino*, taken in 1416. The party descended the Adige to the city of Verona, acquired in 1402, and travelled on to Vicenza which had surrendered in 1404. After re-entering the *Padovano*, the syndics reached Treviso, which Venice had ruled between 1339 and 1381, and had again acquired in 1387. The party headed into the Dolomites to visit Feltre and Belluno, cities which had finally become part of the *stato di terra* in 1420. That

---

[1] Throughout my references are to the edition by Rawdon Brown, entitled *Itinerario di Marino Sanuto per la Terraferma Veneziana nell'anno 1483* (Padua, 1847). For the place of the work in Sanudo's career, *Diarii di Marino Sanudo*, eds. R. Fulin et al (58 vols, Venice, 1879–1902), I, 14–21; *De Origine, Situ et Magistratibus Urbis Venetae ovvero La Città di Venetia*, ed. A. Caracciolò Aricò (Milan, 1980), IX–XVII.

[2] Venice had held the Polesine as security for a loan to the Este from 1395 to 1438. Sanudo alludes to this when he mentions that 'questo Polexene altre volte fu veneto' and that Bernardo Venier had been *podestà* of Lendinara, a town that returned to Venetian rule on 19 August 1482, *Itinerario*, 43; B. Cessi, *Venezia e Padova e il Polesine di Rovigo* (Città di Castello, 1904); P. H. Labalme, *Bernardo Giustiniani. A Venetian of the Quattrocento* (Rome, 1969), 206–212. The war was ended by the Treaty of Bagnolo of 7 April 1484.

date had also marked the acquisition of the province of Friuli with its centre at Udine; that area was the next to be visited. The Republic did not hold Trieste, but its ascendancy over the coastal cities of Istria had begun in the thirteenth century and had been recognised in 1420. Marino records an uncomfortable sea journey to Capo d'Istria. The party returned, skirting the coast of Friuli, and reached Venice on 3 October. They had been on tour for six months.[3]

The *Itinerario* covers virtually all the territory held by Venice in northern Italy, with the exception of Ravenna—inherited from the Da Polenta in 1441—and Cervia purchased from the Malatesta on 5 May 1463 for 4000 ducats; as Sanudo mentions, military actions in the area of the Po had prevented the syndics of 1483 from visiting these places.[4] After 1483 Venice did make further gains—notably Cremona in 1499—but these were of a transient nature. However, in substance the area treated by the *Itinerario* remained under Venetian rule until 1797.[5]

In common with his many later works, Sanudo's *Itinerario* is full of detail and observations, but a recurring, if not an insistent theme, is his patriotism.[6] Military achievements are recorded.[7] Improvements to defence works and civil buildings are mentioned.[8] Some communities are described as flourishing under Venetian rule.[9] The actions of distinguished members of the Venetian nobility, past and present, are acknowledged.[10] Sanudo notes the coats-of-arms, the inscriptions, the emblems that expressed the continuity and quality of Venetian government. At Rovereto, for example, he mentions the Venetian contribution to the defences, and the new loggia, or seat of civil government. He notes that the emblem of Venice, the winged Lion of St Mark, was painted on that building, with a verse celebrating the Republic's empire on land and sea, and warning wrongdoers of the power of its justice.

---

[3] The best recent study of Venetian history in the period, taking proper account of the stato di terra is G. Cozzi and M. Knapton, *Storia della Repubblica di Venezia della Guerra di Chioggia alla Rinconquista della Terraferma* (Turin, 1986; XII/I of the UTET *Storia d'Italia* directed by G. Galasso).

[4] Labalme, *Bernardo Giustiniani*, 175; Sanudo, *Itinerario*, 157.

[5] For an old but still valuable survey, H. F. Brown, *Venice. An Historical Sketch of the Republic* (1895). With G. Scarabello Cozzi and Knapton have recently completed a further volume for the *Storia d'Italia*, XII/II (Turin, 1992).

[6] G. Cozzi, 'Ambiente veneziano, ambiente veneto. Governatori e governati nel dominio di quattrocento di qua del Mincio', in *Storia della Cultura Veneta* (*SCV*), 4/II (Vicenza, 1984), 505–6.

[7] E.g. the siege of Brescia (1438–41) or the transportation of war galleys from the Adige to the Lago di Garda in 1439, *Itinerario*, 70, 93.

[8] E.g. the palace of the *podestà* in Bergamo and the fortifications of Gradisca, *Itinerario*, 77, 140.

[9] E.g. Brescia and Capo d'Istria, *Itinerario*, 70, 148.

[10] E.g. the exploits of Francesco Tron in Friuli against the Turks in 1482, *Itinerario*, 137–140.

Another piece of propaganda was less intimidating, assuring the inhabitants of the security and protection brought them by the Winged Lion.[11] The message of these two inscriptions and the patriotic tone detectable in the *Itinerario* were not, of course, unique to Rovereto or the writings of Marino Sanudo.[12] Victories and gains on the *terraferma* were cause for celebration in Venice itself, and were proudly recorded in the city's chronicles.[13] The tombs of the two doges in power during the period of greatest expansion, Tommaso Mocenigo (1414–1423) and Francesco Foscari (1423–1457) refer to the Republic's successes.[14] In the sixteenth century, triumphs on land joined those achieved at sea in the celebratory paintings that decorated the council halls of the Ducal Palace.[15] From the previous century, the Republic's admirers and propagandists began to style Venice as a New Rome, an image that was encouraged by the acquisition of an empire on land to balance the empire overseas.[16] Indeed, the word 'empire' began to be used in a positive sense by writers sympathetic to Venice to describe the *stato di terra*.[17] Sanudo uses it in the *Itinerario* to describe both the nature of Venetian authority and the area the city ruled.[18] It may come as a surprise, therefore, that Sanudo says scarcely anything about how that empire was administered. He punctiliously names all the Venetian officials he met, but he says virtually nothing about their administrative role in general, or their activity as individuals. And the same negative point applies to the office of the syndics. He refers to the three Venetian nobles in laudatory terms, Piero Vettore, Giorgio Pisano and Marco Sanudo. He identifies by name some members of their entourage, but the only one he mentions in any detail is 'Pilades scriba', Gianfrancesco

---

[11] Sum Leo quo nullus possedit latius orbe/Imperium: paret terra fretumque mihi,/Et justiciam facio: caveat sibi quisque malorum;/Uliscor scelera qui secat ense meo. The other was: Securi dormite omnes; custodiet urbem/Pervigit hanc, cives, aliger ipse Leo. *Itinerario*, 94.

[12] In general, see D. S. Chambers, *The Imperial Age of Venice* (1970).

[13] For the celebration of victory in Friuli in 1420, J. E. Law, 'Venice and the problem of sovereignty in the *Patria del Friuli*', in *Florence and Italy. Renaissance Studies in Honour of Nicolai Rubinstein*, eds. P. Denley and C. Elam, (1988), 138.

[14] A. Da Mosto, *I Dogi di Venezia* (Venice, 1939), 330.

[15] W. Wolters, *Storia Politica nei Dipinti di Palazzo Ducale* (Venice, 1987), 194, 202–6, 235–6.

[16] Chambers, *Imperial Age*, 12–30.

[17] E.g. in the *proemium* to the statutes of Verona of 1450. For ms versions, Biblioteca Comunale di Verona, MSS 963, 965, 2009. The first printed edition was produced in Vicenza in 1475. Also, Labalme, *Bernardo Giustiniani*, 167–9. Venetian imperialism was bitterly criticised by its enemies, N. Rubinstein, 'Italian reactions to the terraferma expansion in the fifteenth century', in *Renaissance Venice*, ed. J. R. Hale, (1973), 201–6, and below, 159.

[18] *Itinerario*, 21, 43–4, 73, 83, 97–9.

Boccardo, a notary and man of letters from Brescia, regarded by Sanudo as his 'dear companion'.[19]

Near the start of the work, in his description of their entry to Padua, he inserts a comment on the Republic's love of its subjects, as demonstrated by its dispatch of the *auditori* to the *terraferma* at public expense.[20] He mentions their special powers as syndics to refer cases to Venice.[21] He explains briefly that they had to publicise their arrival and their readiness to hear appeals and investigate the conduct of public officials over a ten year period.[22] He mentions the use of inquisition, the interrogation of around fifteen local inhabitants in the attempt to track down abuses, though the procedure is mentioned in action only once.[23] He describes how ducal letters, *ducali*, reached the *auditori* at Riva on Lake Garda, ordering them to attempt to settle a dispute between the commune of Riva and a neighbouring vassal of the prince-bishop of Trent, the count of Arco.[24] Possibly that incident rated a mention because it was a digression to their normal business. More central was their referral of a sentence of the *podestà* of Noale, Pasqualino Querini, back to the Venetian Senate. Unfortunately Sanudo gives no further details, beyond recording that Querini was condemned in his absence.[25]

At Noale, the syndics had lodged in the suburbs with the sons of a builder, a contrast to the flattering reception and comfortable central accommodation 'sopra la piaza' accorded them by the commune of Cividale.[26] Detail of this kind suggests that the syndics of 1483 must have returned to Venice with a varied and vivid impression of the *terraferma*. But this is not suggested by Sanudo when he records the parting of the ways of some of his companions, and his account of the official report of Pisani to the doge and the Senate is brief and matter-of-fact.[27] Sanudo's reticence about the activities of the syndics in particular and the government of the *stato di terra* in general cannot be explained away in terms or youth or inexperience. The same negative conclusion can be reached in the case of a later work, the

---

[19] Sanudo includes a poem celebrating Boccardo's marriage on 22 June 1483 at Salò in the *Bresciano*. Later he describes studying antique inscriptions in his company at Aquileia, *Itinerario*, 15, 17, 87, 145.

[20] *Itinerario*, 23.

[21] *Itinerario*, 14.

[22] *Itinerario*, 22–3.

[23] *Itinerario*, 130.

[24] Riva had once been held by the counts. An outlawed member of the dynasty married to a Venetian lived at Riva under the Republic's protection, *Itinerario*, 91–2.

[25] *Itinerario*, 115.

[26] *Itinerario*, 138.

[27] *Itinerario*, 157.

De Origine, Situ et Magistratibus Urbis Venetiae.[28] Nor can Sanudo's silence on the nature and government of the *stato di terra* be put down to a lack of perception in one observer. The acquisition of the *terraferma* state made relatively little impact on Venetian political thought in the fifteenth century.[29] One cannot say that it had no impact. In his funeral oration for the doge Francesco Foscari delivered in 1457, the Venetian noble and humanist Bernardo Giustiniani justified the Republic's intervention on the Italian mainland in terms of providence, self-defence and the defence of Italian liberty.[30] Around 1464 another Venetian noble sought to defend Venice and its territorial gains against criticism in Italy and beyond in terms of legitimate self-defence. For Paolo Morosini, the Republic was never the aggressor, and frequently showed restraint in the face of communities and provinces eager to surrender, though in the case of Treviso he claims that the tears and prayers of all its citizens moved the Republic to accept them as subjects.[31] In the context of the administration of the *stato di terra*, towards the end of the century Marc'Antonio Sabellico wrote a short treatise on the role of the *podestà*, dedicated to the chief magistrate of Vicenza, Antonio Corner.[32] Questions relating to government and defence were touched on in another brief work, the *De Reipublicae Venetae Administratione*, written around 1492 by one of the Republic's Friulian vassals, Count Jacopo di Porcia.[33] More centrally, and certainly at much greater length, jurists at the University of Padua—notably Paolo di Castro and Bartolomeo Cipolla—gave their verdicts on the nature and extent of Venetian sovereignty, and on the relationship between Venetian law and procedures and the statutes and privileges of its subject cities.[34]

Of course, it has been argued that Venetian political thought and historiography were slow to develop, but even in the sixteenth century

---

[28] Above n. 1.

[29] J. E. Law, 'Verona e il dominio veneziano: gli inizi', in *Il Primo Dominio Veneziano a Verona* (Verona, Accademia di Scienze, Lettere ed Arti, 1991), 17. C. C. Lopez has observed that Renaissance commentators showed little interest in the office of the *auditori nuovi*, 'Gli auditori nuovi e il dominio di terraferma', in *Stato, Società e Giustizia nella Repubblica Veneta*, ed. G. Cozzi, I (Rome, 1980), 261–2.

[30] The oration is published in G. A. Molin, *Orazioni, Elogi e Vite Scritte da Litterati Veneti Patrizii in Lodo di Dogi ed altri Illustri Soggetti* (Venice, 1795–6), 21–59. For commentary, Labalme, *Bernardo Giustiniani*, 112–124.

[31] Paolo Morosini, 'Defensio Venetorum ad Europae principes contra obtrectatores' and 'De rebus et forma reipublicae venetae', both published by J. Valentinelli in *Bibliotheca Manuscripta ad S. Marci Venetiarum*, III (Venice, 1870), esp. 218–227 and 238–241.

[32] Marc'Antonio Sabellico, 'De praetorio officio' in *Epistolae familiae necnon orationes et poemata* (Venice, 1502?), 105r–108v.

[33] Published at Treviso, probably in 1492.

[34] A. Mazzacane, 'Lo stato e il dominio nei giuristi veneti durante il "secolo di terraferma"', *SCV*, 3/1 (Vicenza, 1980), 577–650.

the attention paid to the *terraferma* state in this kind of source material remained marginal.[35] The most compendious legal examination of Venetian claims to sovereignty, written by the Corfiot jurist Tommaso Diplovatazio and presented to the government in 1523, considered the *stato di terra* as an afterthought.[36] The same is true of the most famous Venetian account of the Republic's constitution, the *De Magistratibus et Republica Venetorum*, written by Gasparo Contarini between 1523 and 1524.[37] One is tempted to conclude that what has recently been called—rather inelegantly—'urbanocentrism', and what is more familiarly known as *campanilismo*, prevented, or long delayed, the development of a new concept of the Venetian state to match its greatly expanded frontiers.[38] However that most certainly does not mean that Venice and the *terraferma* had no impact on each other.

One area of impact was on the political life of Venice itself. The acquisition and extension of the mainland state were not always viewed with enthusiasm. As early as 1381, the Republic's chancellor, Raffaino de' Caresini, urged the nobility to shun the dangers and intrigue inherent in the land and concentrate on the sea, the city's traditional source of wealth and greatness.[39] Doubts and opposition followed the growing military, fiscal and political burdens that attended the Republic's increasing involvement on the *terraferma*, and which characterised the controversial dogeship of Francesco Foscari (1423–57).[40] In the early years of the sixteenth century, traditionally-minded patricians like Domenico Morosini and Girolamo Priuli were critical of the place the *terraferma* had acquired in the public and private life of Venice.[41] They echoed and amplified the warnings of Caresini, seeing the mainland as distracting the patriciate away from the values and sources of wealth associated with the sea. This strand of doubt and criticism may explain

---

[35] E.g. W.J. Bouwsma, *Venice and the Defense of Republican Liberty (Berkeley and Los Angeles, 1968)*, esp. chaps 2–4; A. Ventura, 'Scrittori politici e scritture di governo', *SCV*, 3/III (Vicenza, 1981), 513.

[36] Mazzacane, 'Giuristi veneti', 622–650.

[37] First published in 1543 and translated as *The Commonwealth and Government of Venice* by Lewis Lewkenor (London, 1599). References to the *auditori nuovi* are in bk IV and to the *terraferma* in bk V.

[38] J.S. Grubb, 'When myths lose power: four decades of Venetian historiography', *Journal of Modern History*, LVIII (1986), 72–4.

[39] I. Cervelli, *Machiavelli e la Crisi dello Stato Veneziano* (Naples, 1974), 168.

[40] H. Baron, 'The anti-Florentine discourses of the doge Tommaso Mocenigo', *Speculum*, XXVII (1952), 323–42.

[41] G. Cozzi, 'Domenico Morosini e il "De Bene Instituta Re Publica"', *Studi Veneziani*, XII (1970), 415, 418, 434; C. Vivanti, 'Pace e libertà in un'opera di Domenico Morosini', *Rivista Storica Italiana* LIV (1972), 619; A. Tenenti, 'The sense of space and time in the Venetian world of the fifteenth and sixteenth centuries', *Renaissance Venice*, 20–26; Cervelli, *Machiavelli*, 168, 182–6, 302.

why the *stato di terra* never acquired the standing of the *stato di mar* in the myth of Venice.[42]

More certainly, Venetian disquiet and opposition were paralleled—and possibly also encouraged—by the mounting hostility the Republic's expansion aroused in Italy and Europe.[43] The volume and efficacy of anti-Venetian propaganda increased as the Florentines became alarmed at the extent of Venetian ambitions in Lombardy around 1450, but earlier and later gains were made at the expense of a number of powers. Prominent among these were the Empire. Most of the Republic's acquisitions lay within the *Regnum Italicum*, and were at the immediate expense of the emperor's vassals and clients: the della Scala of Verona; the Carrara of Padua; the Visconti of Milan; the prince-bishop of Trent; the patriarch of Aquileia.[44] The loss of territory and jurisdiction experienced by the last two also offended the papacy, whose suspicions of Venice grew as the Republic expanded in the Romagna, a province of the Papal States. Further acquisitions in Lombardy and the Romagna around 1500 intensified hostility towards Venice on a European level, as did the Venetian occupation of the more important ports of Apulia in the kingdom of Naples.

In 1506, a Belgian visitor to Venice, Jean Lemaire, was shown two winged lions in the mosaics of St Mark's. One was fat, with most of his body in the sea; the other was thin and was mostly standing on the land. Lemaire was told that Joachim of Fiore had designed these mosaics to warn the Venetians that their prosperity lay with the sea, while desolation lay with the land. The fears of the Belgian's guides appeared realised when the powers of Europe isolated the Republic with the League of Cambrai of December 1508.[45]

However, the Republic's emergence, for better or worse, as an imperial power was a gradual development, and the Lion's early steps on the Italian mainland were cautious. The acquisition of Vicenza, Verona and Padua were prompted by the renewed threat posed by the

---

[42] Tenenti, 'Space and time', 25–6; Cervelli, *Machiavelli*, 331. This may also help to explain why the study of the *stato di terra* remained until relatively recently a cinderella subject in Venetian studies, A. Ventura, introduction to 'Dentro lo "Stado Italico". Venezia e la Terraferma fra quattro e seicento', *Civis*, eds. G. Gracco and M. Knapton, 8 (1984), 165–175; Grubb, 'Myths lose power'.

[43] N. Valeri, 'Venezia nella crisi italiana del Rinascimento' in *La Civiltà Veneziana del Quattrocento* (Florence, 1967), 25–48; Rubinstein, 'Italian reactions'.

[44] I have tried to explore these issues in 'Venice and the problem of sovereignty', and in 'A new frontier: Venice and the Trentino in the early fifteenth century', *Atti della Accademia Roveretana degli Agiati*, ser. VI, 28 (1990), 159–180.

[45] M. Reeves, *The Influence of Prophecy in the Late Middle Ages* (Oxford, 1969), 97–9; Cervelli, *Machiavelli*, 215; Mazzacane, 'Giuristi veneti', 634; O. Niccoli, *Prophecy and People in Renaissance Italy* (Princeton, 1990), 22–5. However, the Lion could appear more confidently amphibian, Wolters, *Storia Politica*, 225–7.

Carrara of Padua to dominate the Republic's hinterland and strangle its trade routes. Similar fears led to the seizure of Friuli, to deny that strategically important area to Sigismund, king of the Romans, and his allies. But the Republic's rather *ad hoc* penetration of another potentially vital area, the valley of the Adige in the *Trentino*, stopped deliberately short of Trent itself. In 1409, and possibly on other occasions, Venice turned down the offer from some of its inhabitants to surrender that city.[46]

Political pragmatism rather than respect for the authority of the prince-bishop probably informed that particular decision. Similar calculations also lay behind the Republic's readiness to encourage cities and smaller communities elsewhere to surrender to its representatives on terms.[47] Whatever the precise circumstances surrounding the stages of Venetian expansion, a constant theme propagated by the Republic itself was of the welcome accorded to its representatives by its new subjects, and the willingness with which they accepted Venetian rule. When the Veronese formally surrendered to Venice in the Piazza San Marco on 12 July 1405, the ceremony was designed as one of celebration rather than humiliation, and the doge assured his new subjects that a people that had walked in darkness had seen a great light.[48] That biblical imagery must have appealed to the Republic: later in 1405 the Paduan embassy of surrender drew on it, and Sanudo noted the theme expressed in a painted inscription in Rovigo.[49] More generally, Venetian apologists like Lorenzo de' Monaci and Francesco Barbaro argued that the Republic had not entered the Italian mainland as a conqueror, but as a liberator.[50] In his *Itinerario*, Sanudo tends to describe previous regimes as tyrannies.[51]

The accuracy of such claims may be doubted. If the Republic had

[46] Law, 'New frontier'. Caution had also characterised Venetian policy before the acquisition of Treviso in 1339, M. Knapton, 'Venezia e Treviso nel trecento: proposte per une ricerca sul primo dominio veneziano a Treviso', in *Tomaso da Modena e il suo Tempo* (Treviso, 1980), 46.

[47] For much of what follows, I am indebted to the work of A. Menniti Ippolito: 'Milano e Venezia nel bresciano nel primo '400', *Studi Veneziani*, n.s., 8 (1984), 37–76; 'La dedizione e lo stato regionale. Osservazioni sul caso veneto', *Archivio Veneto* (*AV*), ser. v, 162 (1986), 5–30; 'La "fedeltà" vincentina e Venezia. La dedizione del 1404', in *Storia di Vicenza*, eds. F. Barbieri and P. Prodi, III/i (Vicenza, 1989), 29–43; 'La dedizione di Brescia a Milano (1421) e a Venezia (1427): città suddite e distretto nello stato regionale', in *Stato, nella Repubblica Veneta*, II, 17–58.

[48] J. E. Law, 'Verona and the Venetian state in the fifteenth century', *Bulletin of the Institute of Historical Research*, LII (1979), 14.

[49] J. S. Grubb, *Firstborn of Venice. Vicenza in the Early Renaissance State* (Baltimore and London, 1988), 17; *Itinerario*, 45.

[50] Labalme, *Bernardo Giustiniani*, 117–122, 169, 280–2; Menniti Ippolito, 'Le dedizioni', 10; Ventura 'Scrittori politici', 543; Grubb, *Vicenza*, 15.

[51] E.g. the Este, and the della Scala, *Itinerario*, 39, 46, 57, 60, 97, 104.

rarely to use force to take its subject cities, with a few exceptions their surrender had followed sustained military campaigns, as in the case of Verona and Padua in 1405, Udine in 1420 and Bergamo in 1428.[52] Moreover, on occasion the Republic and its apologists could choose to justify the city's gains in terms of a just war, expense, effort and self-defence. According to the Mantuan chronicler Bonaventi Aliprandi, Venice rejected Sigismund's demands that Padua, Vicenza and Verona be surrendered in 1414 on the grounds of the hostility of the Carrara towards Venice and the great expense incurred by the city in the subsequent war.[53] Ambassadors to Rome in 1421 were instructed to defend the acquisition of Friuli in similar terms.[54]

However, the preferred justification accepted and offered by the Republic was that of the free and willing surrender of its new subjects. Nor was this preference abandoned as Venetian expansion accelerated; in the *Trentino*, the *Bresciano* and the *Bergamasco*, Venetian gains were marked by a mass of *privilegia*, as communities came 'freely' under her rule. Returning to the case of Verona, on 24 June 1405, the Republic informed its own officials on the mainland that Venetian forces had entered the city 'with the goodwill and agreement' of its population.[55] In 1407, the duke of Milan was told that the Republic's claim to the city was based on 'force of arms, involving great expense and effort, as well as on a just, lawful and legitimate war'. However that war had been directed at the Carrara who had seized the lordship of the city in 1404, whereas the Venetians had entered Verona 'with the consent and goodwill of the populace ... as is clear from public instruments, and as everyone is well aware'.[56] It is the spirit of the end of that statement that was to inform the historiography of both Verona and Venice in the centuries that followed, as it did in the cases of Padua, Bergamo and other major and minor centres.[57] Vicenza exploited its early surrender of 1404 as the 'firstborn' of Venice; it sought formal

---

[52] S. Rota, 'La politica di Venezia nei confronti del territorio bergamasco nel primo secolo di dominazione', in *Bergamo Terra di S. Marco*, 2, *Venezia e le Istituzioni di Terraferma* (Bergamo, 1988), 71–2.

[53] 'Chronicon Mantuanum', in *Rerum Italicorum Scriptores*, ed. L. A. Muratori, 24 (Milan, 1737), col. 1239.

[54] Law 'Problem of sovereignty', 138–143. Sanudo justified taking Este in the *Padovano* in these terms, *Itinerario*, 29. More rarely, purchase could be cited as justification, Morosini, 'Defensio', 220–1, 226 and 'De Rebus', 239.

[55] G. B. Verci, *Storia della Marca Trivigiana e Veronese* (20 vols, Venice, 1789–91), XVIII, documents, 79.

[56] Law, 'Verona and the Venetian state', 11–12.

[57] E.g. the *proemium* to the Veronese statutes of 1450. More generally, F. Gaeta, 'L'Idea di Venezia', *SCV*, 3/III (Vicenza, 1981), 590–1; R. Avesani, 'Verona nel quattrocento. La civiltà delle lettere', in *Verona e il suo Territorio*, IV/III (Verona, Istituto Storico Veronese, 1984), 99–105, 185.

recognition for its exemplary loyalty, and the church of Santa Maria della Misericordia was built to commemorate the city's resistance to the hated Carrara.[58]

Other aspects of the appearance of Venetian rule point in a similar direction. In 1406, the archives of the Carrara of Padua were removed to Venice, and the same thing happened to the records of the patriarchs of Aquileia, the rulers of Friuli, in 1420.[59] But the Venetian aim was to identify its enemies and secure its rights. There was no looting of the subject cities, no carrying off of relics to enhance the shrine of St Mark has had followed the crusade of 1204; indeed local cults flourished unchallenged, and could be patronised by Venetians.[60] In the secular sphere, orders were issued for the destruction of the arms of the Carrara family, but these were only partially carried out.[61] Memorials to the della Scala of Verona remained untouched in the centre of the city despite the presence of active claimants to its lordship at the imperial court.[62] More generally, the Republic had no objection to use by its subject cities of their own coats of arms and emblems on banners, seals and public buildings.[63] After an ambitious experiment in monetary imperialism, the Republic reintroduced local currencies distinguished by traditional patron saints and coats of arms.[64] As such examples suggest, the introduction of a Venetian imprint was gradual, piecemeal and incomplete. It could take the form of the inscriptions, emblems and coats of arms noted by Sanudo on his travels.[65] St Mark's day and the anniversary of a city's surrender to Venice were celebrated,[66] but the Republic did not insist on the annual, irksome, centralised acts of homage which Florence demanded of its subject communes.[67] As Sanudo noted, without a trace of indignation, the Paduans commemorated their surrender with a horse race on 18 November.[68]

---

[58] *Itinerario*, 108; Grubb, *Vincenza*, 132; G. Ortalli, 'Cronisti e storici del quattrocento e cinquecento', in *Storia di Vicenza*, III/I, 354–80; Menniti Ippolito, 'Le dedizioni', 20–1, 25 and 'La fedeltà', 29–41.

[59] Law, 'Problem of sovereignty', 138.

[60] As with the cult of San Zeno in Verona, Avesani, 'Civiltà delle lettere', 96–100.

[61] Archivio di Stato di Venezia (ASVen), *Consiglio dei Dieci (X)*, 'Misti', reg. 8, 126v; *Senato*, 'Secreta', reg. 2, 179v and 'Misti', reg. 48, 64r. I am indebted to Benjamin Kohl for information on this subject.

[62] J. E. Law, 'Venice, Verona and the della Scala after 1405', *Atti e Memorie della Accademia di Verona*, ser.VI, 29 (1977–8), 157–185.

[63] G. Da Re, *Documenti sull'Antico Sigillo di Verona* (Verona, 1896), 12–17.

[64] R. Mueller, 'L'imperialismo monetario veneziano nel quattrocento', *Societa e Storia*, 8 (1980), 294; Grubb, *Vicenza*, 116–7.

[65] Though on 28 March 1409 *rettori* were banned from displaying their arms in subject cities, ASVen, *Senato*, 'Misti', reg. 48, 64r; Grubb, *Vicenza*, 156.

[66] ASVen, *X*, 'Misti', reg. 9, 121v; Law, 'Verona and the Venetian state', 14.

[67] D. Hay and J. E. Law, *Italy in the Age of the Renaissance.* (1989), 117.

[68] *Itinerario*, 25.

Finally, the subject cities were wont to send embassies to greet the election of a new doge, but the underlying aim was to petition for personal and collective favours. In 1476, an exasperated Republic tried to place limits on the size of such delegations and the length and number of their orations.[69] When in a more charitable or ingratiating mood, Venice addressed its subjects as its children, though they could be more forward. In 1477 Francesco Corna described Verona as the sister of Venice rather than her daughter.[70]

Why did the Republic accept and perpetuate such a non-triumphalist view of the extension of its authority on the *terraferma*? In the first place, the policy was less risky, damaging and expensive than relying on force of arms. Even when its subject cities chose, or were forced, to abandon Venetian rule, as during the War of the League of Cambrai, the Republic confined its retribution to the most outstanding traitors, and was ready to accept the contrite, rediscovered loyalty of the majority.[71] Secondly, to insist on the free surrender of the subject population was to claim for Venetian rule an acceptable legitimacy it otherwise lacked. After all, the Republic had no historic title or claim to rule the mainland cities. A few apologists, like Lorenzo de' Monaci in the fifteenth century and Gasparo Contarini around a century later tried to argue that the Republic was simply re-occupying the Roman province of *Venetia* from which the Venetians had been driven by the barbarian invaders of the Empire, but this ingenious antiquarian argument was neither sustained with much force nor received with much conviction.[72]

Again, the Republic had a hereditary claim to a few lordships in the *Trentino* and the city of Ravenna, but these did not impress either the prince-bishop of Trent or the papacy.[73] The Republic did come round to securing an imperial investiture for its gains in the *Regnum Italicum* from Sigismund in 1437, but this remained incomplete and did not put the jurisdictional position of Venice on a formal, regular footing.[74] Later in the century Paduan jurists argued that Venice, as a sovereign power, had inherited the rights of the empire in Italy, but this flimsy argument was never used by the Republic which also refrained from styling its territories or authority in imperial terms.[75] The word 'empire' appears on the tomb of doge Francesco Foscari in the Frari church, but this

[69] D. Queller, *Early Venetian Legislation on Ambassadors* (Geneva, 1966), 55; Labalme, *Bernardo Giustiniani*, 224.

[70] Grubb, *Vicenza*, 25–6; Avesani, 'Civiltà della lettere', 185.

[71] A. Ventura, *Nobiltà e Popolo nella Società Veneta* (Bari, 1964), 244–374; Grubb, *Vicenza*, 185–6.

[72] Menotti Ippolito, 'Le dedizioni', 15–16; Gaeta, 'L'Idea di Venezia', 588–9, 637; Grubb, *Vicenza*, 16, 27.

[73] Law, 'A new frontier', 164; Cozzi in *Storia della Repubblica di Venezia*, 38–9.

[74] Law, 'Verona and the Venetian state', 10–11.

[75] Grubb, *Vicenza*, 41.

was a family rather than a state monument, and the Republic did not style itself as an empire in the period.[76]

It is probably for these reasons that no explicit title to the *stato di terra* appeared in the formulae of the Venetian chancery or on the coins and seals of the Republic.[77] And it is for these reasons that the Republic put more store by the idea that its lordship was willed and accepted by its loyal and faithful subjects. In the fourteenth century, the lawyer-doge Andrea Dandolo (1343–54) arranged for a ceremony marking the spontaneous surrender of Treviso in 1344, four years after the city had come under Venetian rule; similar calculations were probably present in a period of much greater territorial expansion.[78]

Such conclusions may appear to conflict with Venice's high regard for herself as a sovereign power, not to mention its track record as an empire builder in east and west.[79] And it may be thought that the Republic's willingness to accept the surrender of its new subjects was to make its authority over them all the more binding. Indeed this is an interpretation that has been given to the pacts drawn up between Venice and its subject cities on their surrender. In general, these were composed in a hurry. The Venetian representatives to whom they were presented could accept them only provisionally. When ratified in Venice, they were rarely accepted in their entirety; the Republic regarded them as petitions and not as treaties. Though documents that sought to define relations between rulers and ruled, many of their clauses were concerned with immediate political and economic issues. Further sighted requests—asking that there be no increases in taxation or that fortresses be demolished, for example—could be rejected or ignored. All such pacts recognised without equivocation or condition the lordship of Venice.[80] On the other hand, these collections of *capitula* proved to be of more than transitory significance.[81] In the case of the major cities, the Republic authenticated them with a gold seal, conferring on them an authority that recalls the golden bulls granted Venice by the Byzantine empire centuries earlier. They were attached to the statutes of the subject community, remaining there without modification or gloss. Venetian officials were repeatedly ordered to respect them, even when they were contrary to Venetian interests. And their authority

[76] Da Mosto, *Dogi*, 330. As Nicolai Rubinstein has pointed out, the adoption of the word 'empire' could have proved politically embarrassing for Venice, 'Italian reactions', 201–6.

[77] Law, 'Verona and the Venetian state', 9.

[78] Knapton, 'Venezia e Treviso', 46.

[79] Mazzacane, 'Giuristi veneti'.

[80] Law, 'Verona and the Venetian state', 14–5; but see above all the work of Menniti Ippolito, above n. 47.

[81] M. Berengo, 'Il governo veneziano a Ravenna' in *Ravenna in Età Veneziana*, ed. D. Bolognesi, (Ravenna, 1986), 31–2.

could be defended by jurists like Paolo di Castro.[82] In some cases, like Vicenza, vague general clauses promising to respect local statutes were given a wide interpretation which could take in subsequent editions of these statutes and privileges granted by Venice; opportunistic petitioners from the subject cities could cite their golden bulls as a form of bluff, to give authenticity to non-existing statutes.[83]

It has been suggested that these lists of *capitula* are the nearest the *stato di terra* came to a constitution.[84] If that is the case, the structure they suggest is a very vague one, full of uncertainties unresolved both at the moment of surrender and subsequently. However, analysis of the privileges issued to Vicenza and other cities suggests that they laid the foundations for a much broader autonomy than had been enjoyed under previous regimes, for example in such important areas as the administration of the *contado*, the city's jurisdiction outside its walls.[85] Moreover, such *capitula* were bilateral, linking Venice to individual communities, or groups of communities in the case of some rural districts. This gave the *stato di terra* the character of an accumulation of territories rather than as a unified whole.

In many respects Venice did little to change this situation; indeed the Republic continued to refer to its *terraferma* acquisitions in the plural, and only outlaws from Venice or those guilty of treason and other serious offences were banned from all Venetian territories.[86] As is clear from the *Itinerario*, the provinces of the *stato di terra* followed, by and large, the frontiers of the previous political and jurisdictional map, and the subject cities strove, largely successfully, to preserve their territories and their own conditions of citizenship.[87] When the Republic modified the boundaries within its frontiers, the net result was an increase in the number of communities enjoying or claiming bilateral or privileged relations with Venice. For example, in 1406 Bassano and Cologna were

[82] Menniti Ippolito, 'Le dedizioni', 28–9; Mazzacane, 'Giuristi veneti', 586f.

[83] Grubb, *Vicenza*, 8–13. For instances of Verona trying to broaden the scope of its golden bull, Archivio di Stato di Verona (ASVer), *Antico Archivio di Commune (AAC)*, reg. 60, 25v–26r (1450); Law, 'Verona and the Venetian state', 15 (1475).

[84] Berengo, 'Governo veneziano', 31–2.

[85] Grubb, *Vicenza*, 8–13.

[86] The nomenclature of the five *savi di terraferma*, an office created to advise the Senate on mainland matters, took time to settle down. On 2 June 1423 their responsibilities were described as being 'super factis Patrie Forojulii et aliarum terrarum et locorum de novo acquisitorum', ASVen, *Senato*, 'Misti', reg. 54, 78r. On outlawry, *Senato*, 'Misti', reg. 57, 82r; ASVer, *AAC*, reg. 10, 47r–v, 51v; Grubb, *Vicenza*, 103, 106–7, 165, 174–5.

[87] J. E. Law, 'The Commune of Verona under Venetian Rule' (D. Phil. thesis, University of Oxford, 1974), 101–132; J. S. Grubb, 'Alla ricerca delle prerogative locali: la cittadinanza a Vicenza 1404–1500', ' "Stado Italico" ', 177–192; Menniti Ippolito, 'Dedizioni di Brescia', 46–7; Berengo, 'Governo veneziano', 54–5, 59.

detached from the jurisdictions of Vicenza and Verona.[88] In the *Bresciano* and *Bergamasco* Venetian rule strengthened the privileges enjoyed by feudal landowners and some rural communities at the expense of the cities' authority.[89] Such concessions can be explained to a certain extent in terms of Venetian initiatives; for example the Republic sought to cultivate the loyalty of communities like the Valpolicella in the *Veronese* and the *Sette Comuni* in the *Vicentino* because of their economic and strategic importance.[90] On the other hand, the opportunism of the subject communities should not be overlooked. Sanudo records how Cologna had asked to be directly dependent on Venice.[91] The Valpolicella carefully preserved its growing body of administrative and fiscal privileges.[92]

This picture, of Venice accepting and even encouraging the proliferation and fragmentation of the provinces under her rule, might appear to conflict with the character and structure of the Republic's imperial administration. This can appear to be assertive, highly centralised and growing. Certainly the researcher is immediately struck by the growth of Venetian archival material in the fifteenth century, with the deliberations of a key body, the Senate, being divided into two series, *Terra* and *Mar*, in 1440. From 1423, the Republic moved from styling itself as a commune in favour of the terms *dominium* or *signoria*, better to express the nature and extent of its authority.[93] When the Republic indulged in political imagery and talked in terms of the body politic, the *terraferma* cities were the limbs and Venice the head. In official correspondence, even major centres like Vicenza could be addressed as 'communities' rather than as cities or communes.[94] Only occasionally did Venice see its *terraferma* subjects other than as foreigners; for example on 29 October 1408 the Veronese were told that they were 'no less dear than our own nobles and citizens' while on 21 June 1428 they were described as 'Veneti proprii'.[95]

There was no decentralisation of the powers of the central organs

[88] Verci, *Storia*, XIX, documenti, 5; Grubb, *Vicenza*, 176–7. This policy helps to explain the loyalty of such communities to Venice in the War of the League of Cambrai, Cervelli, *Machiavelli*, 53.

[89] J. M. Ferraro, 'Feudal patrician investments in the Bresciano and the politics of the estimo', *Studi Veneziani*, n.s., 7 (1983), 31–2; G. Scarabello, 'La Repubblica di Venezia: Signoria di uno Stato o di una Città?', in *Venezia e le Istituzioni di Terraferma*, 27.

[90] Law, *Commune of Verona*, 157–163; Grubb, *Vicenza*, 64.

[91] *Itinerario*, 105–6.

[92] Decentralisation at the expense of the authority of Treviso had been a feature of Venetian rule in the *Trevigiano* in the fourteenth century, Knapton, 'Venezia e Treviso', 49.

[93] Law, 'Verona and the Venetian state', 20–1; Grubb, *Vicenza*, 20–23.

[94] Tenenti, 'Space and time', 18; Grubb, *Vicenza*, 173, 181 and 'La cittadinanza', 180.

[95] ASVen., *Senato*, 'Misti', reg. 48. 41v; reg. 57, 13r; ASVer, *AAC*, reg. 52, 8r–v.

of government, and the admission of representatives from the *terraferma* to sit in the Greater Council, the Senate, the *Collegio* or the Council of Ten was never contemplated. Of course, the subject communes sent frequent embassies to Venice, and from the later fifteenth century they tended to appoint resident ambassadors in the capital whose correspondence can reveal them to have been skilled, well-informed lobbyists, but they were not seen as part of the Venetian government.[96] Some leading *terraferma* families were granted Venetian nobility, and with it the right to hereditary membership of the city's sovereign body, the Greater Council—in his *Itinerario* Sanudo mentions the Cavalli of Verona in this connection—but the number was very small and the award was seen as largely honorary, and not as a means of widening participation in Venetian government.[97] And the partial citizenship, citizenship *de intus*, granted to many of the subject cities carried economic rather than administrative and political privileges.[98]

However, additions and modifications were made to the Venetian constitution to take account of the *stato di terra*.[99] The introduction of various avenues of appeal, presenting opportunities and procedures previously denied the *terraferma* cities, had a considerable impact on Venetian magistracies; in 1410 the office of the *auditori nuovi* was introduced to hear appeals from the *terraferma*.[100] In 1421 the small committee of five *savi di terraferma* was made permanent, to advise the government on policy.[101] New fiscal offices were introduced. The *terraferma* was one of the areas where the Council of Ten—originally entrusted with matters of internal security—steadily extended its competence.[102] Cases of treason and other serious crimes were handled centrally, and the issues of usury and gambling came increasingly to the attention of the central government, which also had the power to pass legislation and issue decrees for general application throughout the *stato di terra*.[103]

The impression of centralisation can be confirmed when the nature of the Republic's administration on the *terraferma* is considered. Venetian nobles were the *rettori*, the *podestà* and *capitano*, in charge of the administration of justice, the collection of revenue and local defence in

---

[96] C. Scroccaro, 'Dalla corrispondenza dei legati veronesi: aspetti delle istituzioni veneziane nel secolo quattrocento', *Nuova Rivista Storica*, 70 (1986), 625–636.

[97] *Itinerario*, 97–8, 103; Law, *Commune of Verona*, 87–99.

[98] Grubb, 'La cittadinanza', 179–80; *Vicenza*, 22, 173; Rota, 'Politica veneziana', 76.

[99] M. Knapton, 'Le istituzioni centrali per l'amministrazione e il controllo della terraferma', in *Venezia e le Istituzioni di Terraferma*, 35–56.

[100] Lopez, 'Auditori nuovi'.

[101] ASVen, *Senato*, 'Misti', reg. 53, 100v.

[102] M. Knapton, 'Il Consiglio dei Dieci nel governo di terraferma', in *Venezia e la Terraferma attraverso le relazioni dei Rettori* (Milan, 1981), 237–260.

[103] Lopez, 'Auditori nuovi', 272–3; Grubb, *Vicenza*, 102–4, 134–5.

the individual cities. Venetian nobles were also appointed to subordinate posts: as *camerlenghi*—chamberlains—for the collection and dispatch of revenue; as castellans of major, and an increasing number of minor, fortresses; as *podestà* of some of the subordinate communes. All these officials were elected centrally, and their commissions, which could be detailed and exacting, insisted on their obedience to the central government. In addition to these resident officials, the Republic dispatched a growing number of nobles with special responsibilities to the *stato di terra*: to settle boundary disputes; to inspect defence works; to supervise the armed forces; to audit accounts; to attend to matters of internal security. A few non-Venetians of proven loyalty were given wide powers, especially in military organisation.[104]

And finally, for an imperial power the problems of administration were in certain important respects much less than were encountered in the *stato di mar*. Distances were shorter. As is clear from the *Itinerario* communication by water and land were relatively easy.[105] Though it is difficult to generalise, business could be transacted relatively quickly. A decision taken by the councils of Verona on 22 October 1408 was considered by the Venetian Senate on 27 October and the ducal letters expressing its decision were issued on 29 October. On 6 May 1412 the Venetian magistracy of the *avogari del comun* wrote to the *podestà* of Verona asking for information in a land dispute and ordering one of those involved to appear with the information on 16 May. On 19 May, the *avogari* wrote again marvelling at the *podestà's* delay, dismissing his excuse that a revolt in the city on 2 May had held up business and giving him until 25 May to send the required information under threat of a 500 lira fine.[106] And communication was easier in the *stato di terra* in other respects. Only on the northern and eastern frontiers were there linguistic problems with German, Ladino and Serbo-Croat speakers; more generally an Italian heavily influenced by Venetian dialect was spoken.[107] And, with the exception of a few small Jewish communities, all the Republic's subjects of the *terraferma* were Roman Catholic.[108]

In addition to these points, it has been argued that as the product of an undying corporation, the Republic's rule had a more burdensome and cumulative quality than experienced by its subjects under previous regimes.[109] However, in practice the Venetian government was less

[104] M. E. Mallett, in Mallett and J. R. Hale, *The Military Organisation of a Renaissance State* (Cambridge, 1984), 101–113.

[105] Only in the *Trentino* did Sanudo complain about the roads, *Itinerario*, 92–3.

[106] ASVen, *Senato*, 'Misti', reg. 48, 41v; *Avogaria del Comune*, 'Lettere', reg. 166/2; ASVer, *AAC*, reg. 52, 8r–v, reg. 56, 110r.

[107] Cozzi, 'Ambiente veneziano', 498, 501.

[108] *Itinerario*, 60, 117, 129.

[109] Ventura, *Nobiltà e Popolo*, 49.

centralised, watchful and consistent than might at first appear. The burgeoning archives of that government, both in Venice and in the subject cities, are as much a record of resistance, opportunism, non-cooperation and bloody-mindedness as of Venetian initiatives.[110] At times the Republic was clearly infuriated by the flood of miscellaneous yet persistent litigation and complaint reaching the capital, and attempts were made to control the number, size and role of embassies arriving in Venice.[111] Within the Ducal Palace itself there were long-running disputes over such issues as: fiscall administration, the relationship between the *auditori nuovi* and other magistracies; where responsibility lay for the protection of the privileges of the subject cities.[112] The *savi di terraferma* were generally men of wide experience in government, but that did not necessarily include *terraferma* office. Their term as *savi* was only six months and their deliberation were not confined to the *stato di terra*, but frequently covered diplomatic and military affairs.

The *auditori nuovi* held office for sixteen months. They were expected to go on circuit as syndics every year, but their visitations of the *terraferma* were on a less regular and frequent basis.[113] They did not necessarily have a legal training; only one of the three 'sindaci' in 1483, Giorgio Pisano, had been trained in law, which was perhaps why he was assigned the task of making the formal report to the Senate.[114] Whatever their legal backgrounds, their role in hearing and forwarding appeals in civil disputes was circumscribed by the frequently reiterated obligation to respect the statutes and procedures of the *terraferma*, and not to meddle in an expanding area of inappellable cases.[115] This was the legal world of the doctors of law Sanudo describes in a later work, who 'attended the *auditori nuovi* as advocates because of the many cases

[110] Berengo, 'Il governo veneziano', 33, 55–6.

[111] For a principal area of petition and complaint, J. E. Law, ' "Super differentiis agitatis Venetiis inter districtuales e civitatem": Venice, Verona e il Contado nel '400', *AV*, ser. v, 116 (1981), 5–32. On embassies, Queller, *Early Legislation*, 55, 99, 127–8; Grubb, *Vicenza*, 151.

[112] G. Cozzi, 'Authority and law in Renaissance Venice', in *Renaissance Venice*, 303–5 and 'La politica del diritto nella Repubblica di Venezia', in *Stato, Società e Giustizia*, i, 116–7; Lopez, 'Auditori nuovi', 271; Grubb, *Vicenza*, 143–5, 149–51.

[113] ASVen, *Maggior Consiglio*, 'Leona', 198r; Biblioteca Nazionale della Marciana, Lat. V, 67(2518), 'Capitolare Auditorum Novorum Sententiarum'; 37r, 94r. Also of value is the sixteenth century account of the office published by Rawdon Brown in his edition of the *Itinerario*, III–VI. Law, 'Verona and the Venetian state', 17–19; Lopez, 'Auditori nuovi'.

[114] *Itinerario*, 21, 157.

[115] 'Capitolare', 37v–39v and *passim*; Grubb, *Vicenza*, 110–2, 147–8. The *auditori nuovi* were not the only guilty parties in this regard. Complaints on similar grounds were addressed by the councils of Verona to the Council of Ten (20 November 1452) and the *avogari* (26 January 1455), ASVer, *AAC*, reg. 60, 161v–162r.

and matters of civil law (before them)'.[116] The *Itinerario* mentions these professionals, if only in passing. One, Silvestro Rambaldo, was a Veronese lawyer who had acquired a Paduan doctorate around 1480. He has recently been identified as serving the commune of Verona for almost sixteen years as its 'defensor et advocatus' in Venice.[117]

In view of the presence of such men, and the variety of business coming before the office, it is unlikely that the *auditori* were able or expected to challenge the legal autonomy of the larger subject cities.[118] Unfortunately, conclusions on the role of the office in Venice and on the *terraferma* must needs be of a provisional nature; to date studies of the office have been based on Venetian legislation rather than on 'case law'. However, if the evidence of the first reveals the confusion and controversy that could surround the office, the impression given by the latter is that much of its activity was generated from below. After all, it was pressure from the *terraferma* that led to the institution of the office in 1410, and it would probably be wrong to see the *auditori* in the fifteenth century as agents of a centralising programme designed to achieve legal conformity or the ascendancy of Venetian practice.[119] The impression given by the Veronese records supports this interpretation: the judgements queried by the *auditori nuovi* were more often those handed down by the resident Venetian officials in the city.[120] Moreover, when subject cities revised their statutes, no place was explicitly accorded to Venice in the hierarchy of legal authorities. Returning to the case of Verona, when statute and custom proved deficient, recourse had to be made to Roman Law and the opinion of the glossators. In the event of contradictions arising from these sources, the gloss most acceptable to Venice was to be followed.[121] More generally, it was recognised that an appeals procedure had to respect the practice of the courts of first instance.[122]

The short terms of duty that were a feature of the office of the *auditori nuovi* were also characterised the resident officials of the *stato di terra*. In the *Itinerario* Sanudo tends to remark on unusually long periods

---

[116] *De Origine, Situ et Magistratibus*, 126–7, 259–60.

[117] *Itinerario*, 157; Scroccaro, 'Dalla corrispondenza'.

[118] It was only in 1492 that the *auditori* were instructed to keep detailed records of their decisions, Lopez, 'Auditori nuovi', 289–90.

[119] P. S. Leicht suggested that from the fifteenth century Venetian practice Gradually became the 'common law' of the *stato di terra*, 'Lo stato veneziano e il diritto comune', in *Miscellanea in Onore di Roberto Cessi* (3 vols, Rome, 1958), I, 207. Recent studies would put the emphasis on 'gradually', e.g. G. Cozzi, 'Considerazioni sull'amministrazione della giustizia della Repubblica di Venezia', in *Florence and Venice*, eds. S. Bertelli et al, II (Florence, 1980), 105–7.

[120] These observations are based on the collections of *ducali* and other letters in registers 9 to 11 of the *Antico Archivio di Comun* of the Archivio di Stato of Verona.

[121] From chapter 137 of the second book of the statutes of Verona.

[122] Mazzacane, 'Giuristi veneti', 597.

of office, of between two and three years.[123] Such appointments were usually held by castellans who had a very restricted administrative role, and whose offices were increasingly regarded as sinecures rather than as responsibilities.[124] Only in periods of international tension did the castellans of urban fortresses command a serious number of troops. The *podestà* and the *capitano* of a city were normally appointed for a year, rising later to sixteen months, which was followed by a four year *contumacia*, or ban on re-election. For the principal cities of the *terraferma*, these officials tended to be men of experience, on the higher rungs of the Venetian *cursus honorum*; when Treviso was the major *terraferma* city held by Venice in the fourteenth century, it tended to be administered by fairly senior statesmen; when outranked by Padua, Verona and Brescia in the fifteenth century it was no longer regarded as a top posting.[125] Sanudo proudly records the various appointments held by his uncle, Francesco, in the cities of the *stato di terra*, but Venetian nobles were rarely reappointed to a position.[126] The aim of their detailed and steadily elaborated commissions was to achieve honest, conscientious but detached government.[127] When Vinciguerra Zorzi was elected as *podestà* of Ravenna in 1502 the appointment was an unusual one in that he had property in the area; but Ravenna was in a war zone and the Republic's choice was possibly made in the hope that an interested party would be all the more committed to defending a valuable but endangered frontier city.[128]

Some Venetian office-holders, often those with humanist interests, tried to strike a proconsular stance, and were encouraged to do so by admiring men of letters, and even by events. Francesco Barbaro is a good example. He held a large number of important governorships. He was *capitano* of Brescia during a long and at times epic siege from 1437 to 1440. His achievements aroused the flattering admiration of his correspondents and from career-conscious men of letters like Flavio Biondo.[129] Others sought to avoid such risks; Leonardo Giustiniani, as

---

[123] E.g., Sanudo records that the castellans of Ponte della Torre and Peneda held office for three years, as—unusually—did the *camerlengo* of Bergamo and the *rettore* of Martinengo, *Itinerario*, 36, 79, 83, 92–3.

[124] J. E. Law 'Lo stato veneziano e le castellanie di Verone', in ' "Stado Italico" '

[125] Knapton, 'Venezia e Treviso', 48.

[126] Francesco had been posted to Asolo (1430) and Bassano (1454); he then graduated to higher office as *podestà* of Vicenza and Verona, and *capitano* of Brescia and Padua, *Itinerario*, 59, 70, 97, 108, 112, 114, 119, 134. On seeing a portrait of his uncle in Verona, Marino was moved to compose a verse tribute to Francesco' patriotism, 97–8. He died on 27 November 1482 after falling ill while in command of a fleet on the Po, 16.

[127] Law, *Commune of Verona*, 168–170; Grubb, *Vicenza*, 156f.

[128] Berengo, 'Governo veneziano', 35–6.

[129] F. Gaeta, 'Storiografia, conscienza nazionale e politica culturale nella Venezia del Rinascimento', *SCV* 3/i (Vicenza, 1980), 30–5; M. King, *Venetian Humanism in an Age of Patrician Dominance* (Princeton, 1986), 55, 60, 323–5.

luogotenente of Friuli from 1432 to 1433 looked for tranquillity and the chance to pursue his literary interests.[130] Noble *rettori* who sought to enhance their reputations on the *terraferma* did so as conciliators, as initiators of public works, as patrons and protectors of their subjects, and not as innovators. In 1441, on his second term of office in Verona, Francesco Barbaro was hailed as 'Pater Patriae'. In return he assured the Veronese that he was their 'father, guardian and perpetual defender'.[131] This was not necessarily empty rhetoric. Some ex-*rettori*, and lesser officials, were clearly seen as useful agents in the capital. Nicola Trevisano was *capitano* of Verona from 1490 to 1491. In October 1491 he wrote to express 'the love and singular affection I have for your magnificent city and the obligations I feel towards it'.[132] And subject cities could be eager to cultivate the good will of ex-*rettori* who rose higher in government. In the fourteenth century, Treviso sent large embassies to Venice to congratulate those newly elected doges who had served in their city.[133]

As Trevisano's assurances of 1491 suggest, the freedom of action of a Venetian *rettore* could be curtailed by more than his commission. In every aspect of administration he depended on the cooperation of the local citizenry: from the organisation of defence to the maintenance of the records of government; from the assessment and collection of taxation to the administration of justice.[134] As regards the last, for all the *arbitrium* invested in a Venetian *podestà* he was unlikely to be well-versed in local statutes and customs, and the principles of Roman law that informed them. Even if he was, the practical extent of his jurisdiction was limited by the obligation to observe local statues and procedures. He depended on the professional lawyers in his own entourage, or *familia*,—for the most part citizens of the *stato di terra*—and even more on the jurists appointed by the commune to preside over its courts.[135] Studies of some of the major centres of the *terraferma*—Vicenza, Verona and Bergamo—suggest that their judicial autonomy increased at the expense of the power of the *podestà* in the period.[136] And although Venice claimed the right to approve new compilations

[130] Labalme, *Bernardo Giustiniani*, 54.
[131] Law, 'Verona e il dominio veneziano', 24–26.
[132] Scroccaro, 'Dalla corrispondenza', 633. For Sanudo's Veronese attachments, D. S. Chambers, 'Marin Sanudo, camerlengo of Verona', *AV*, ser. V, 109 (1977), 52–8; G. M. Varanini, 'Altri documenti su Marin Sanudo e Verona', *Studi Storici Veronese Luigi Simeoni*, 30–1 (1980–1), 8–13.
[133] Knapton, 'Venezia e Treviso', 48, n. 52.
[134] Grubb, *Vicenza*, 119–124.
[135] Law, *Commune of Verona*, 170–4.
[136] Cozzi, 'La politica del diritto', 104 and 'Considerazioni', 107–9; Grubb, *Vicenza*, 55–62; Varanini, 'Altri documenti', 9; Rota, 'Politica di Venezia'; 75–6. Sanudo himself noticed the juridical autonomy of Verona and Vicenza, *Itinerario*, 108.

of statutes, and such collections often sang the praises of the presiding *podestà*, the actual work was carried out by local experts. The statutes of Vicenza of 1425 paid fulsome tribute to Francesco Barbaro, but all the work was carried out by native citizens.[137] Moreover, Venetian officials could be compromised as agents of central government for other reasons. Self-interest, inefficiency, errors of judgement, petty and more serious corruptions could undermine Venetian rule.[138] For example, malpractices, delays and inefficiency associated with the *auditori nuovi* could cause alarm. In 1489, one of their number, Marco da Ca' Pesaro, was jailed and disgraced for insulting a widow in Bergamo 'essendo syndaco fuora'.[139]

Lastly, even if the *stato di terra* was more accessible than the *stato di mar*, problems of scale—albeit of a different kind—faced the Republic and its representatives. Padua, Verona and Brescia were of considerable size. If at the end of the century Venice had a population of around 100,000, Verona was almost half that figure.[140] Vicenza, a city of the second rank, had around 20,000 inhabitants.[141] Centres of this scale could not be policed or controlled in the longer term by the few Venetian officials and small garrisons normally in position. And distance from Venice was a factor. For most of his journey, the only Venetians Sanudo encountered were officials, though the Venetian presence in terms of office-holding in church and state, and landownership, was more marked in very accessible areas like the *Padovano*.[142] Sanudo was particularly impressed by Venetian properties at Noventa on the Brenta,[143] though he does not record the resentment caused by the high level of Venetian investment in the area.

From this it can be deduced that the impact of Venetian rule was uneven, being felt more clearly in areas like the *Trevigiano* and the *Padovano*, closer to the city, than in the more distant and less familiar *Bresciano*, *Bergamasco* and *Trentino*.[144] It therefore comes as no surprise that at the end of the fifteenth century Paduan sources described the

---

[137] Law, 'Verona and the Venetian state', 15–17.

[138] Chambers, 'Marin Sanudo', 46–52; Law, 'Verona e il dominio', 23–4.

[139] Lopez, 'Auditori nuovi', 287, 298–302; G. Soranzo, *Parte Inedita della Cronica di Anonima Veronese* (Verona, 1955), 49.

[140] D. Herlihy, 'The population of Verona in the first century of Venetian rule', in *Renaissance Venice*, 91–120.

[141] Grubb, *Vicenza*, 75.

[142] Cozzi, 'Domenico Morosini', 417 and 'Ambiente veneziano', 503, 508; M. Knapton, 'Il fisco nella stato veneziano di terraferma', in *Il Sistema Fiscale Veneto*, ed. G. Borelli, (Verona, 1982), 19.

[143] *Itinerario*, 29, 114. He also records Sanudo property at Piove di Sacco and at Sanguinetto in the *Veronese*, 17, 30, 59.

[144] Law, 'A new frontier', 170–3.

government of Venice as that of three thousand tyrants.[145] In 1498 the commune threatened to return its gold-sealed privileges as a sarcastic comment on the weight and insistence of Venetian demands.[146] It is for reasons of this kind that some historians—often those most familiar with the Paduan source material—see Venetian rule in terms of mounting exploitation and intervention. That the Venetians as governors and private individuals turned increasingly to the *terraferma* can hardly be denied. But to insist on exploitation as a principal characteristic of the *stato di terra* ignores its survival, and the extent of positive support for Venetian rule in the War of the League of Cambrai.[147] These phenomena confound the views of some hostile contemporary commentators who thought that a Republic could not govern an empire, and that Venice had been mistaken to embark on mainland conquests. They can confound the modern historian for whom Venice failed to create a modern state.[148]

Partial explanations for the survival of the *stato di terra* can be found in the stability and security of Venice itself, in the skill of its diplomacy, in its military resourcefulness and in the divisions of its enemies. But any equation seeking to explain the survival of the mainland state must take into account positive qualities within the *stato di terra* itself. These would include the accessibility, flexibility and decentralised nature of its supposedly closed government. They would also include a pragmatism whose cause and effect was the survival of the mainland state as a multiplicity of provinces.

---

[145] Cervelli, *Machiavelli*, 47, 57. For the fiscal impact of Venetian rule on Padua, M. Knapton, 'I rapporti fiscali tra Venezia e la terraferma: il caso padovano nel secondo '400', *AV*, ser. V, 117 (1981), 5–65.

[146] M. Knapton, 'Capital City and Subject Province: fiscal and military relations between Venice and Padua in the late fifteenth century' (D. Phil. thesis, University of Oxford, 1978), 234.

[147] Cervelli, *Machiavelli*, 38, 344–6, 362–408.

[148] Tenenti, 'Space and time', 17; Grubb, 'Myths lose power', 74–80; G. Ortalli, 'Terra di San Marco; tra mito e realta', in *Venezia e le Istituzioni di Terraferma*, 9–19; Law, Verona and the Venetian state', 21–2 and 'Verona e il dominio', 31–2. More generally, B. Guenée, *States and Rulers in Later Medieval Europe* (Oxford, 1985), 4–22, 49–66.

THE CREATION OF BRITAIN: MULTIPLE KINGDOMS OR CORE AND COLONIES?

by Jenny Wormald

READ 21 SEPTEMBER 1991

It is merely idle and frivolous, to conceive that any unperfect Union is desired, or can be granted: It is no more unperfect, as now it is projected, than a Child, that is born without a Beard. It is already a perfect Union in me, the Head ... It is now perfect in my Title and Descent, though it be not accomplisht and full Union; for that Time hath all the Lineaments and Parts of a Body, yet is it but an Embrio, and no Child; and shall be born in his due Time; when it is born, though it then be a perfect Child, yet it is no Man; it must gather Strength and Perfection by Time; Even so is it in this case of Union. The Union is perfect in me; that is, it is a Union in my Blood and Title; yet but *in embrione* perfect. Upon the late Queen's Death, the Child was first brought to light; but to make it a perfect Man, to bring it to an accomplisht Union, it must have Time and Means; and if it be not at the first, blame not me; blame Time; blame the Order of Nature.

THUS said King James, in his speech to the English parliament on 2 May 1607. It is a powerful metaphor, which would later find sumptuous expression in Rubens' magnificent idealisation on the ceiling of the Banqueting Hall. But it was also an appeal, and an appeal which was shot through by despair; and out of despair and burning frustration came threat. 'I confess', said the king,

it is good to be sometimes far from the Prince's Court: *Procul a numine, procul a fulmine* ... if you find that my Residence here doth Harm, I will make Two Offers: One, I will keep my Seat *alteratim* in the several Countries: I will stay one year in Scotland and another here; as some other Kings do, that have several kingdoms: the other is, I will keep my Court nearer Scotland: at York: at some Place thereabouts; so as you and Scotland shall both be alike *procul a fulmine*: And I protest. I will do either of these, if you think it for your Good; and if I shall not see this Union likely to go forward, I will do it howsoever ... Something must be done, you all confess; the Devil himself cannot deny it ... I am your King; I am placed to govern you and shall answer for your Errors. I am a Man of

Flesh and Blood, and have my Passions and Affections as other men:
I pray you, do not too far move me to do that which my Power
may tempt me unto.[1]

It was an outburst which had been heralded, three weeks earlier, in
the Venetian ambassador's report that it was said that James would
turn the stalemate of the Commons' obstinacy into checkmate, by
dissolving parliament and summoning another in York, which would
be so inconvenient for both Houses that they would despatch the
business the sooner; indeed, because of the malignity of certain individuals, he was even considering pushing it through 'by his own absolute
authority'. Meanwhile from the north came the sounds of offended
pride and complaint, as the Scots bombarded him with pleas to desist;
they could never, they said, agree to Union with a people who showed
them only contempt. And already the ambassador had reported their
demands that either the king or Prince Henry should reside in Scotland.[2]

The threat to move to York had a Scottish precedent. In December
1596, James had had a triumphant victory over the extreme presbyterian
ministers, hounding him in Edinburgh, by announcing that he, his
court, and his government would move out. The godly merchants and
burgesses of Edinburgh promptly remembered that capitalism counted
as well as Calvinism, and rushed to demonstrate their love and
obedience to their king. But Edinburgh, even at the end of the sixteenth
century, did not have the grip on the kingdom of Scotland that London
did on England. It was just conceivable that James VI might indeed
move from Edinburgh; James I suggested an unthinkable outrage.
Here, at least, Scottish tactics were only a stark reminder to English
subjects of the unacceptability of non-English habits, traditions—and
people. Fortunately, James I himself moved. In May 1607, a happier
occupation than threatening the English parliament was the exchange
of Hatfield for Salisbury's Theobalds, and by the 22nd he was there
watching an entertainment put on by Ben Jonson.[3]

Probably, despite perennial complaints about his penchant for leaving
London, it was on this occasion as well. If the threat to move king and
government was deeply disturbing, even worse was the reference to 'my

[1] *Commons' Journal*, I, 367.
[2] *Calendar of State Papers Venetian 1603–7*, 484, 485. The issue of residence in Scotland
continued; on 30 May 1607, Giustinian reported that the Scots were still insisting that
the king should spend more time in Scotland, but that they were not likely to be gratified:
ibid., 501.
[3] M. Lee Jr, 'James VI and the Revival of Episcopacy in Scotland, 1596–1600', *Church
History* 43 (1974), 53–4; David Calderwood, *The History of the Kirk of Scotland* (8 vols.,
Wodrow Society, Edinburgh 1842–9), V, 443–535; John Nichols, *The Progresses, Processions
and Magnificent Festivities of King James the First, His Royal Consort, Family and Court* (4 vols.,
London, 1828), II, 126–31

Power'. Both the French and Venetian ambassadors were impressed, in this very year, by the extent of the king's authority. On 10 March 1607, lamenting James's impatience to leave London for a month, de la Boderie asserted that 'c'est sans doute que s'il pouvoit rester ici un mois entier, ladite union se résoudrait beaucoup plûtot; car tant qu'il est présent, il y en a peu qui osent parler.' And Nicolo Molin claimed that he summoned parliament only 'out of modesty'; for parliament had once been strong, 'but now that the Sovereign is absolute, matters move in a very different fashion' and James had now reached 'such a pitch of formidable power that he can do what he likes, and there is no one who would dare, either in Parliament or out of it ... even to make the smallest sign of running counter to his will.'[4] These are notable comments. Of course they were exaggerated; James's one ardently desired policy, the perfect Union, was visibly in tatters. But they are a stark reminder that within four years of his accession, the one effect of his dramatically radical solution to the problem of multiple kingdoms and provinces, the move towards the kingdom of Britain, was to raise the hideous twin spectres of royal neglect in Scotland and terrifying abuse of power in England. The union of the crowns of England and Scotland had produced not the child of peace and harmony, but the monstrous progeny of fear and distrust.

Yet when the king complained that he had been misled by his advisers, who had encouraged him to think that union would be an easy matter, if only because the naturalisation of the Postnati, if accepted, would lead automatically to union, and that these advisers 'committed him to a labyrinth, in which his honour is involved', he was making a very valid point. He left no-one in doubt about his own view of the union, and the divine obligation laid upon him by God to perfect it. It is admirably laid out in his proclamation of 20 October 1604:

> As often as we call to minde ... the blessed Union, or rather Reuniting of these two mightie, famous and ancient Kingdomes of England and Scotland, under one Imperiall Crowne: So often doe We thinke, that it is our dutie, to doe our uttermost endeavour, for the advancement and perfection of that ... which God hath put together ... an uniformitie of constitutions both of body and minde ... A communitie of Language, the principall meanes of Civil societie, An unitie of Religion, the chiefest band of heartie Union, and the surest knot of lasting Peace: What can be a more expresse Testimonie

[4] *Ambassades de Monsieur de la Boderie en Angleterre* (5 vols., Paris, 1750), II, 101; *C.S.P. Venetian 1603–7*, 509. Molin's lengthy analysis of the state of England and its monarchy and government, from which this assertion comes, is conflicting; he also refers to James's laziness and preference for hunting rather than governing. But on the basis of some very dubious parliamentary history, he is in no doubt about the king's power.

of Gods authoritie of this worke, then that two mightie nations, having bene ever from their first separation continually in blood against each other, should for so many yeres immediately before our Succession, be at peace together, as it were to this end, That their memory being free from sense of the smart of former injuries, their minds might, in the time of Gods appointment, more willingly come together ... Wherefor Wee have thought good to discontinue the divided names of England and Scotland out of our Regal Stile, and doe intend and resolve to take and assume unto Us ... the Name and Stile of KING OF GREAT BRITTAINE...

The lion and the leopard would now lie together in peace and harmony—according to God's will, and by proclamation of the king. And the world outside would see what had happened; after the royal proclamation of 12 April 1606, and ferocious heraldic debate about how to create it without reducing either England or Scotland to a place of subservience, the royal and merchant ships of 'South and North Britaine' would fly the new British flag, the Union Jack.[5]

It was an ideal very quickly given the authority of history. As early as 26 March 1603, only two days after Elizabeth's death, no less a figure than that remarkable scholar and antiquary Sir Robert Cotton put all his learning and weight behind it, in a discourse setting out the arguments for the name Britain, which he thought should content both the states which now desired peaceful union, 'so as to appease the former spoils and enmytie of both kingdomes'. Using arguments which anticipated James's own, in his proclamation and in his pleas for union in his speeches to the English parliament in 1604 and 1607, Cotton invoked shared language, religion, descent, similar laws, geography, in support of the idea of a united Britain; and he turned to history, for James's intention, he said, was 'to reduce theis two potent Kingdomes to that entier state wherein it stood of old, and that neither may suffer under a seeminge servitude but fellowlike (as it might if either name shold conteyne or precead the other)'. This in itself made the ancient name of Britain the obvious choice, that name with a pedigree going back 2000 years, to Aristotle.[6] But perhaps we should not be surprised by the speed with which Cotton produced his treatise for the kingdom. He had already established his own Anglo-Scottishness, with a genealogy which showed his descent from the great King Robert Bruce; he had

[5] *C.S.P. Venetian 1603–7*, 485; *Stuart Royal Proclamations*, eds. J. F. Larkin and P. L. Hughes (Oxford, 1973), I, 94–5 and 135–6; Bruce Galloway, *The Union of England and Scotland 1603–1608* (Edinburgh, 1986), 82–4 and plate at 88.

[6] P.R.O., S.P. 14/1/3, 'A Discourse of the Descent of the K's Mty from the Saxons'; K. Sharpe, *Sir Robert Cotton, 1586–1631; History and Politics in Early Modern England* (Oxford, 1979), 114–5. For James's speeches, *The Political Works of James I*, ed. C. H. McIlwain (reprint, New York, 1965), 271–3 and 290–305.

rebuilt the Bruce castle in Huntingdonshire; and from 1603 he called himself 'Robert Cotton Bruceus', signing his books RCB. Here was a very proud inhabitant of the kingdom of Britain, and he got his reward, being knighted by James in 1603; although given the number of people knighted by James in 1603, it was perhaps less of a signal reward for this notable Anglo-Scot, called 'cousin' by the king, than he might have expected.

Outwardly, leading English politicians and lawyers seemed to share the view of this authoritative English savant, in their apparent support of union and their desire to please their Scottish king by praising the Scots. Lord Chancellor Ellesmere's reference, in a speech of 1608, to the 'learned, grave and reverend Judges' of the Scottish judiciary, and to the Scottish privy councillors as 'so many honorable wyse & worthy persons as are not inferior to any counsell of State whatsoever' had a note of sonority which was strikingly unusual. It was not one which Englishmen were accustomed to sound when speaking of their despised and backward northern neighbours. It shows the outward change of attitude, which goes right back to the beginning of the reign. On 10 April 1603, Cecil and three others of the council wrote to James 'to give his Majesty humble thanks for sending so grave and judicious a man amongst us as my lord of Kinloss, who is already so good an Englishman...'[7] The tact may seem a little heavy-handed, but at the time it suggested the integration which James so ardently desired.

But behind the mask so carefully shown to the king lay the very different face of English hostility. That other impressive scholar, if ultimately rather less than impressive statesman, Francis Bacon, went even further than Cotton when in a letter to Ellesmere, he not only appealed to history in support of the idea of Britain, but appealed for a history of Britain; recalling the 'worthiness of the history of Britain ... and the partiality and obliquity of that of Scotland', he pointed to the need for 'this island of Great Britain, as it is now joined in monarchy for ages to come', to be 'so joined in history for times past, and that one just and complete History (be) compiled of both nations'. This letter was written by one strong public supporter of union to another. Yet in private a warning note was being sounded, a note not of course yet heard by the king. The distinction between British worthiness and Scottish obliquity may suggest a certain ambivalence in Bacon's commitment to Britain. But it is Ellesmere's endorsement of Bacon's letter which shows just how ambivalent that ardent supporter of union, the Lord Chancellor, was. Here is Ellesmere writing to his king in July 1606, on the usual theme of his declining years: 'I praye God I may

---

[7] Henry E. Huntington Library, Bridgwater and Ellesmere MSS, EL 1210, ff. 4r–v; P.R.O., S.P. 14/1/18, f. 38r.

have yet a whyle ... to serve you a litle longer, as a poore Labourer in the effectings of that blessed worke the Union, which I have long wished & desired to see perfecte & complete before I die.' And here he is in April 1605, endorsing Bacon's letter with its plea for British history, to underwrite that long-desired Union: 'Sir Francis Bacon touching the Story of *England*. It is a lovely example of deeply engrained Englishness wrestling with the British vision demanded by the new king of England; and it is presumably one of the earliest examples of that habit which infuriates inhabitants of the other parts of the British Isles to this day: the habit of using 'England' as synonymous with 'Britain'.[8]

It also demonstrates how far James's famous hope of a union of hearts and minds had produced only confusion of hearts and minds. Moreover, the ambivalence created by the Scottish king was not confined to the instinctive response to threatened English morale in the private comment of an endorsement. Reading the draft hand of Lord Chancellor Ellesmere is an appalling experience. Even so, one can only sympathise with Ellesmere when turning to decipher the even more appalling hand of Thomas Erskine, viscount Fenton, in his flattering letter to Ellesmere of March 1606. Moreover, Ellesmere not only had the difficulty of reading it; he also had to cope with Erskine's Scottish dialect. And of course he had to read the letter; for Erskine was very close to the king, and was writing to tell the Chancellor what he desperately wanted to know, of James's enthusiasm for his great English servant. And there, surely, is a major problem of the Union admirably illustrated: suddenly the leading figures of the last years of Elizabeth's reign found themselves hanging on illegible letters from despised Scots to hear of the approval of the king of England.[9]

Confusion about just what had been created by the Union of the Crowns was, of course, far more than personal and individual. In 1608, even after the final collapse of James's perfect union, Salisbury, Ellesmere, Bacon and Coke were devoting immense time and energy to Calvin's Case, that carefully fixed case which established the legal status of the Post-Nati.[10] It did so by testing the right of a Scot to hold land in England, and prove his title in the English courts, instead of being debarred as an alien—which was fair enough, for it was much

[8] Francis Bacon to Ellesmere, EL 126; the text of the letter but not the endorsement, is printed in *The Life and Letters of Francis Bacon*, ed. J. Spedding (7 vols., London 1861–74), III, 249–52. For Ellesmere's letter to the king, EL 162 f. 1r.

[9] EL 160, f. 1r. Fenton at least recognised the limitations of his literacy; in a letter to John earl of Mar on 4 October 1616, in which he acknowledged a letter from Mar's son lord Erskine, he pointed out that 'if I culd reid his letter he shuld have an answere. I thank God one of the name wrets noe better then my selfe': *H.M.C. Mar and Kellie Supplement*, 69. Such disarming frankness, however, can hardly have consoled those who had to struggle with his own handwriting.

[10] For admirable discussion of this case, see B. Galloway, *Union* 148–57.

more likely that Scotsmen would press for their legal privileges, not to mention land, in England than the other way round. The question of naturalisation was, of course, deeply contentious. It seemed to offer a way of achieving union by the back door. And quite apart from grave doubts about allowing the Scots to sneak into the blessings of Englishness, Scotsmen were by act of the Scottish parliament, long irrelevant but still on the statute book, naturalised Frenchmen; they seemed to be climbing in everywhere.[11] English foot-dragging over the question of naturalisation was indeed the context of James's outbursts in the spring of 1607. But because the wider issue of unification of the laws of the two kingdoms failed utterly, all that naturalisation really amounted to was a few individuals claiming it, and being carefully excluded from the English parliament when they got it. In its own right, therefore, Calvin's Case signified much less of a victory for those pursuing the cause of union, or defeat for those who opposed it, than might have been expected.

Much more important were the fundamental arguments used; for they tried to establish the nature of James's kingship over his English and Scottish subjects, and the basis of their respective—or common—allegiances to him. Yet this supreme and utterly focused attempt to clarify and define that kingship only created huge problems. The case for Calvin rested on the argument that allegiance was to the natural body of the king, and not to the body politic. It was therefore impossible to separate the allegiance owed to King James by his Scottish and English subjects; 'If the Kinge be one, the subiects & Kingdomes can not be dyvided in allegiance.' If James, as king of England, went to war, the Scots would be called in to assist the English; what justification could there be for this, other than their allegiance to the king of England? Conversely, the king could not be at war with himself; there could therefore be no wars between the king of England and king of Scotland—an argument which sounded logical enough, but would later be strained to breaking point when politics got in the way of con-stitutional theory, and the king of Great Britain went to war in 1639, as king of England, against his Scottish subjects.[12] And in the later seventeenth century, the demand for Scottish involvement in English wars against Scotland's trading partners, the Dutch and French, would bring the whole concept of union into bitter question.

More immediately, this approach involved very considerable diffi-culties; for its insistence on allegiance to the natural body of the king

---

[11] *C.S.P. Venetian 1603–7*, 485; *Acts of the Parliaments of Scotland*, eds. T. Thomson and C. Innes (12 vols., Edinburgh, 1814–75), II, 507 and 515–6. The English were well aware of this legislation of 1558; it was included in the list of hostile laws whose repeal was another contentious issue: EL 1865, f. 1r.

[12] EL 1215, Notes on Calvin's Case, f. 3v; also EL 1868, f. 3v.

and not the body politic put the natural body into a potentially very frightening position. Ellesmere took the most radical stance, denying altogether the theory of the King's Two Bodies.[13] But it was not necessary to go as far as Ellesmere to advance dangerous ideas. Bacon asserted that

> allegiance is of a greater extent than laws or kingdom, and cannot consist by the laws merely; because it began before laws, it continueth after laws, and it is in vigour where laws are suspended ... That it is more ancient than law appeareth by that which was spoken in the beginning .. that kings were more ancient than lawgivers, that the first submissions were simple, and upon confidence to the person of kings and that the allegiance of subjects to hereditary monarchs can no more be said to consist by laws, than the obedience of children to parents.

This was saying something very similar to one of James's more terrifying claims, in *The Trew Law of Free Monarchies*, that

> The Kings therefore in Scotland were before any estates, or rankes of men within the same, before any Parliaments were holden, or lawes made ... And so it follows of necessitie, that the Kinges were the authors & makers of the lawes, and not the lawes of the Kings.

And it was reinforced with devastating clarity in Fleming's judgement, when he succinctly stated that 'the liga is to the king's person not to the law. Common law is to yield to the law of nature. The king hath an absolute power ... above the law by which he may commaund when and where he will.'[14] Admittedly much emphasis was put on the reciprocal bond between king and subject, and the fact that allegiance was owed only so long as the king could offer defence and protection. But it was not enough to offset the fear evoked by the theory of the king being above the law, a fear which in any case James's own delight in continental political theory, and its Scottish version which he had written himself, had already instilled.[15] It illustrates nicely the great

---

[13] Ellesmere's speech is printed in L. A. Knafla, *Law and Politics in Jacobean England: The Tracts of Lord Chancellor Ellesmere* (Cambridge, 1977), 202–53; see also *ibid.*, 66–8.

[14] *The Works of Francis Bacon*, ed. J. Spedding (7 vols., London 1858–61) VII, 665–6; James VI, *The Trew Law of Free Monarchies*, in *The Minor Prose Works of King James VI and I*, eds. J. Craigie and A. Law (Scottish Text Society, Edinburgh, 1982), 70; P.R.O. SP 14/34/10, f. 24.

[15] Jenny Wormald, 'James VI and I, *Basilikon Doron* and *The Trew Law of Free Monarchies*: the Scottish context and the English translation', J. P. Sommerville, 'James I and the divine right of kings: English politics and continental theory', and Paul Christianson, 'Royal and Parliamentary Voices on the Ancient Constitution, c. 1604–1621' in *The Mental World of the Jacobean Court*, ed. Linda Levy Peck (Cambridge, 1991), 36–54, 55–70 and 71–95.

paradox, that those who won in Calvin's Case, and brought James at least a little of what he wanted, did so by using arguments which only succeeded in portraying the kingship of Great Britain in terms utterly unacceptable to many of his British subjects.

The arguments of the losing side were no less problematic. For their case rested on the argument of allegiance to the body politic, and that forced on them the admission that Scotland, far from being the vassal state beloved of English thinking, was a fully sovereign kingdom. Naturalisation in England depended on being subject to the crown, laws and government of England. 'But Scotland is of it self an absolute kingdome, an absolute governmente and hath absolute lawes whereunto they are subiects: and are not subiects to the crowne government and lawes of Englande: and therefore not naturalized... The pollitick bodie of a kingdome consisteth of a heade, which is the kinge of a bodie which are the subiects, of a lief which is the lawes, of a soule which is the execution of them: But the people of Scotlande are noe parte of this politicke bodie ... and therefor not naturalized...' Thus 'Scottishmen are subiect *to him that is king of England*, but not subiecte to the kinge of England.'[16] Just as Coke, Bacon and Ellesmere had used arguments which echoed the dangerous theorizing of a Scottish king, so the defence in Calvin's Case were acknowledging the status of the Scottish kingdom with which every Scottish lawyer and writer of tracts on the Union agreed, but which by no means found general acceptance among English ones.[17]

The real difficulty lay in the fact that legal definitions, which were in any case conflicting, could never resolve the fundamental political question posed by the Union of the Crowns. It was all very well, in 1603–4, when the Scots had not yet begun to feel the chill of neglect, and could bask in the sunshine of having provided their aggressive and powerful southern neighbour with a king, having successfully resisted every attempt by that neighbour to impose a king on them, while the English could feel a sense of profound relief that the succession had gone through quietly, providing them with an adult protestant male, with a family, even if with the wrong accent; and that relief initially obscured the fact that the new king was going to force intolerable questions on them. The full implications of the Scottish succession were clearly not yet understood. One way of remaining blind was

---

[16] EL 1215, f. 2r.

[17] Thomas Craig of Riccarton, *De Unione Regnorum Britanniae Tractatus*, ed. and trans. C. S. Terry (Scottish History Society, Edinburgh, 1909), and *Scotland's Sovereignty Asserted*, ed. G. Ridpath (Edinburgh, 1695). *The Jacobean Union: Six Tracts of 1604*, eds. B. R. Galloway and B. P. Levack (Scottish History Society, 1985): the three Scottish tracts, by Robert Point and John Russell, and the anonymous 'Treatise about the Union of England and Scotland', 1–142; also 241–4 for a summary of other Scottish tracts.

Northumberland's; he had simply assumed, as he told James, that the king would recognise that his real honour lay in being king of England, and that Scotland would sink into second place.[18] Much less offensive—indeed, all too positive, for King James—was the reaction seen in Ellesmere's notes for his speeches opening the sessions of James's first parliament, which with remarkable outspokenness hammered away on the theme of the blessings given by God to England in the person of the Scottish king who had succeeded Elizabeth and united the kingdoms. Orbity and old age were starkly contrasted with a thriving royal family and mature wisdom; religious dissensions and the fear of Rome had given way to security of faith, safe in the hands of 'Godds instrument & minister'. 'Never people so depely obliged to theyr soveraigne. Never people so happye, yf wee have grace to see & feele our own happines.' No wonder he was so horrified by the Gunpowder Plotters, and burst out that 'I am ashamed they be English, I am ashamed they be Christians.' There is a certain disarming appeal about Ellesmere's sense of priorities. But at least they 'be but Roman Christians'. There was no let-out for their Englishness.[19]

Union, therefore, brought a safety which England alone could never enjoy: safety against foreign princes, safety against Romish tyranny. And it brought peace: peace with Spain, freedom from the threat of war with Scotland. All that was wrong with all this was that as yet no real thought was given to what union actually meant. What could have produced consideration of the nature of the state which would become a central issue in the course of the seventeenth century, was used instead as the opportunity for a wonderful outburst of debate about that much more fascinating subject, the nature of the English constitution; even the less constitutionally minded Scots were forced to climb uneasily and defensively aboard the constitutional bandwagon. And definition of the English state—let alone the new 'British' one—continued to languish in obscurity. No-one except King James, apparently, was particularly interested in 'state formation'; and by 1607, such was the reaction to the king's unthinkable 'perfect union' that the most strenuous opponents of union could turn to the simple expedient of adopting his concept in order to destroy any hope of the reality.

'Perfect union' was too extreme, and indeed was never to be achieved. What was wholly lacking in 1603 was any less radical model which might provide a viable alternative. For the Union of the Crowns was not simply the bringing together of two kingdoms, although that was

---

[18] *Correspondence of King James VI of Scotland with Sir Robert Cecil and Others in England*, ed. J. Bruce (Camden Society, London, 1861), 56.

[19] EL 451, ff. 1r, 1v; 473 f. 1r, 1v; 455 f. 1r, 2r; 458 f. 2r. 451 were the notes for 1604, 473 and 458 for 1605, and 455 possibly for 1604, or for 1607.

how it was described, but the addition of another kingdom to the multiple kingdoms of England and Ireland, with the dependency of Wales thrown in. It was the inclusion of Scotland which introduced the idea of 'Britain' into the political language of the day, and made the creation of 'Britain', in whatever form, potentially realisable. But England, unlike Scotland, was already experienced in the business of multiple kingdoms and unions. The difficulty was that its solutions were not actually notably successful, and certainly offered no model which the Scots would accept.

Among the notes made about Calvin's Case is one which, echoing James's appeal to time in his speech of May 1607, refers to 'The kings desire to have one Crowne, & one Lawe so farre as maye be, and one government. But tyme must work yt. Nota for Wales how yt did grow.'[20] The last point was, of course, entirely irrelevant as far as the king and his Scottish subjects were concerned; incorporation was on no agenda that they would accept. Nor was Ireland, despite the status of kingdom accorded to it by Henry VIII in 1541. Bruce Galloway has pointed out that the recognition of Scotland in Calvin's Case as an independent sovereign state had implications for Ireland also; but they were not implications which anyone bothered to think about, and Ireland's position, far from offering an exemplar, was so ambivalent as to create nothing but disquiet.[21] It was far from clear whether Ireland was indeed a kingdom or in fact a colony. The modification of Poynings Law by Irish statute in 1557, which removed the English council's control of Irish legislation, had little practical effect, and none at all in its right to advise the king on Irish judicial matters; and the existence of Lieutenants and Deputies who were far more often English than Irish hardly encouraged Irishmen to feel that they had autonomous status under the king of Ireland. James himself was entirely happy to think of himself as king of Ireland; but his extension of his policy of settling lowland Scots in the Western Isles of Scotland, as a civilising process, to planting them in Ulster had all the signs of the colonial administrator rather than the king. As Russell, Clark and Perceval-Maxwell have demonstrated, the strains of the early 1640s showed all too clearly the muddled thinking about Ireland; crisis turned a rather vague notion of multiple kingdoms into clear assertions of Ireland's dependant status, as Irish constitutionalists sought the protection of the English parliament, and the case against Strafford was based on Ireland being 'a portion of the English crown'. Moreover, one possible source of unity,

[20] EJ, 1215, f 3v
[21] Galloway, *Union*, 157. H. Wheeler, 'Calvin's Case (1608) and the McIlwain-Schuyler Debate', *American Historical Review* LXI (1956), 587–97, also discussed the relevance of the case to Ireland, and went on from there to argue for its appeal to the American colonists of the eighteenth century.

the church, did not work for Ireland as it could, and did, do under James VI and I for Scotland and England—and indeed, in terms of creating profound fear and hostility, and ultimately providing common cause for rebellion, it continued to do under Charles I.[22] But amongst all the muddle and confused thinking, one section of the British Isles saw the issue very clearly. As subjects of a somewhat ill-defined 'free monarchie', the Scottish estates told King James in 1607 that they would consider a 'trew and freindlie Unioun'; but they would not become 'a conquered and slavishe province to be governed by a Viceroy or Deputye'. The parallel they used was the king of Spain's provinces. They were equally well aware of the parallel at home.[23]

There was, therefore, nothing in the multiple kingdoms already existing within the British Isles to suggest a solution to the inclusion of Scotland. Indeed, if England, from an undoubted position of strength, had failed to resolve the problem of multiple states with Ireland and even Wales, the chances of any kind of satisfactory unifying settlement with Scotland were slender in the extreme, whatever King James, his leading politicians seeking to comply with the king's wishes, or even the Devil himself thought of the matter. 'Trew' union was not on the political agenda; and even a 'freindlie' one was unlikely. For beyond the soothing cocoon into which James was initially wound by English statesmen lay no more than a marriage of necessity between two partners filled not with love but mutual suspicion and even hate. Such attitudes represent a far more enduring response to the historical and theoretic perceptions of England and Scotland which for three centuries had stressed antagonism to the point where it was regarded as the

---

[22] Conrad Russell, 'The British Problem and the English Civil War', *History* 72 (1987), 395–415, 'The British Background to the Irish Rebellion of 1641', *Historical Research* 61 (1988), 166–82, and *The Causes of the English Civil War* (Oxford, 1990) and *The Fall of the British Monarchies, 1637–1642* (Oxford, 1990), *passim*. Aidan Clark, 'Ireland and the General Crisis' *Past and Present* 48 (1970), 79–99, 'The History of Poynings' Law', *Irish Historical Studies* 18 (1972), 207–22, and chapters IX and X in *A New History of Ireland*, eds. T. W. Moody, F. X. Masters and F. J. Byrne, (Oxford, 1976), III, 243–69. M. Perceval-Maxwell, 'Ireland and Scotland, 1638–1648' in *The Scottish National Covenant in its British Context*, ed. J. S. Morrill, (Edinburgh, 1990), 193–211 and 'Ireland and the Monarchy in the Early Stuart Multiple Kingdom', *Historical Journal* 34 (1991), 279–95. On the church, see Morrill, introduction to *The Scottish National Covenant*, 7–11.

[23] *The Register of the Privy Council of Scotland*, eds. J. H. Burton and others (Edinburgh, 1877–), VII, 536. This letter, written in August 1607, was still reiterating the appeals put forward by the Scots in the spring, that the king would divide his time equally between his two kingdoms. The letter and the Act anent the Union passed by the 1607 parliament show a profound unease, very different from the confident pride of the earlier act of 1604, which asserted 'That as the present Age is Ravisched in Admiration with sa fortunat begynning sua the Posteritie may rejoice in the fruitioun of sic ane effectuall unioun of twa sa famous and Ancient kingdomes Miracoulouslie accompleisched in the blude and persone of sa Rare ane Monarchie': *A.P.S.* IV, 366–71 (1607); 263–4 (1604).

natural order, than the efforts made by the politicians, the theorists and the flatterers of 1603 to replace the curse of enmity with the blessing of peace. For would-be unionists, the sad fact was that the common ground in Anglo-Scottish thinking about the advantages of harmony only underlined the impossibility of finding an acceptable way of achieving it. Edward I and Edward III, Henry VIII and Somerset, would undoubtedly all have agreed with the basic argument put forward by King James or his great Scottish lawyer Thomas Craig or John Major, that early-sixteenth century Scottish theorist who first suggested to an astonished and unsympathetic world the advantages of good relations between England and Scotland; within the confines of the British Isles, it would have suited them infinitely better had England and Scotland been at peace.[24] Where they profoundly disagreed was in the nature of the Anglo-Scottish relationship. The 'two mightie nations' of James's proclamation were, in English eyes, nothing of the sort; there was one mighty nation, England, and its vassal kingdom, Scotland. It was certainly true, as Arthur Williamson has established, that there was an 'Edwardian moment' when men contemplated the idea of Britain, and that one theme in the flood of union tracts which have been so admirably discussed and edited by Bruce Galloway and Brian Levack, the concept of Britain as divinely ordained by God, arose from an apocalyptic tradition going back to that 'moment'. But it was very brief; the ideas of 1547–48 were not sustained, and were not fully revived in 1603. The Scottish tracts consistently write about two equal nations. The English group has been divided by Galloway into two: those clearly written to please the king, which he calls 'Royal tracts', and those which discuss union in terms of the superior and inferior nation. An Anglo-Scottish union on the lines of the Anglo-Welsh one would have been entirely acceptable; a union of equal partners was not.[25]

The touchiness which the Scots were displaying by 1607 in response to English reluctance to admit equality should not, however, obscure the fact that in relation to Scotland the English, suddenly presented with a unique problem which could not be resolved in their traditional, imperialist fashion, were in a position of profound weakness. Hostility to the Scots was rooted in failure to conquer them. It was, of course, also the case that the English had failed in their wars with France and

---

[24] Craig, *De Unione Regnorum Britanniae*; John Major, *A History of Greater Britain*, ed. and trans. by A. Constable and A. J. G. Mackay (Scottish History Society, Edinburgh, 1892).

[25] A. H. Williamson, 'Scotland, Antichrist and the Invention of Britain' in *New Perspectives on the Politics and Culture of Early Modern Scotland*, eds. J. Dwyer, R. A. Mason and A. Murdoch, (Edinburgh, 1982), 39. Galloway, *Union*, 48–51. Knafla, *Law and Politics*, 87, suggests that Ellesmere regarded union with Scotland 'in the same light as the previous union with Wales.' Understandably, this was an attitude not made clear to King James.

Spain, which is one reason why Agincourt and the Armada loom so large in English self-consciousness, just as Bannockburn looms large in Scottish, the difference being that Bannockburn was, unlike the English victories, decisive in ensuring the ultimate outcome of the war. But from the English point of view, wars with France and Spain meant wars with equals. The war with Scotland had a colonial purpose. It had failed in the past; and in the more pacific circumstances offered by the Union of 1603, it failed now. King James never realised his vision of creating the kingdom of Britain. But his was not the only failure. The model which would have satisfied the English, not multiple kingdoms but core and province, or colony, was equally unrealised. How does one define a colony? At the very least, it must surely have rulers sent in by the colonising power, and it must have settlers; and it involves the imposition of the values and mores of the colonising power. That was precisely the model which Edward I and Edward III had both tried to impose. Now, the ruler, and the settlers, came out from the second-rate territory and showed every sign of taking over the would-be controlling power. That is the context for Nicholas Fuller's astonishing assertion, in the parliament of 1610, that it was the duty of the Commons to tell the king of England what he could do.[26] How redolent that is of what scores of native rulers must have been told, in the days of the British empire, by their British masters. How redolent is the virulent anti-Scottish literature of the early seventeenth century, with its recurrent theme of backwardness, lack of civility, parasitism, of attitudes of British colonists of the nineteenth and early twentieth centuries to the natives of the colonies which enjoyed British rule.[27] How many Indians living under the British Raj would have instantly recognised that theme? The twist to the story in the early seventeenth century, is that the English had lost their desire to colonise Scotland directly; they had no desire whatsoever to go there. What they wanted was to train the 'native' ruler who had, against the odds, become their king, in their values, to turn him into an acceptable king of England. They were therefore trapped in an impossible position. For how does one colonise one's king?

[26] *Proceedings in Parliament, 1610*, ed. Elizabeth Read Foster (2 vols., New Haven, 1966),II, 109. A less polemical example of the English belief that a king of Scotland needed instruction in his new and greater role is the advisory letter written by Sir Edmund Ashfield on a wide range of subjects, from the common lawyers to foreign policy, before James's accession: B. L. Cotton MS Julius F VI, ff. 139r–141r.

[27] For example, Francis Osborne, *Traditional Memoyres of the Raigne of King James the First*, and Anthony Weldon, *A Perfect Description of the People and Country of Scotland*, in *The Secret History of the Court of James I*, ed. Walter Scott (2 vols., Edinburgh, 1811), I, 1–298, and II, 75–89. Even an author more favourable to the king was highly critical of the disorderly and beggarly covetousness of his Scottish subjects: Godfrey Goodman, *The Court of King James*, ed. J. S. Brewer (London, 1839).

The harsh reality was that it was impossible to do so. But equally, *any* move towards an incorporating union of the kingdoms as well as of the crowns was, and had to be, made far too quickly, especially for English susceptibilities. Perhaps the most appropriate symbolism of the union, therefore, was not the extolling of Britain, in James's triumphal entry into London in 1604, but the fact that Thomas Dekker's intention that the king should be met, as he approached the city, by St Andrew and St George riding together, was never realised, because of the confusion and the crowds and the noise.[28] A fundamental reluctance to allow St Andrew equal place with St George, was far more deeply embedded in English minds than any consideration of Time or the Order of Nature. This most divinely favoured of kingdoms was being asked to admit another into that favour. This most constitutionally minded of people was being faced with a constitutional revolution of horrifying proportions. Moreover, however sensitive the king might be to the question of giving time for union to mature, the very concept of *una grex, una lex* as well as *unus rex* was in fact terrifyingly far ahead of its time. For the real problem was that this was not just an Anglo-Scottish, let alone a British matter. Elizabeth's dynastic failings pushed both England and Scotland into an already all too familiar European trap: the trap of composite kingdoms. And if the experience of the composite kingdoms of England, Wales and Ireland provided no help in resolving the problem created in 1603, neither was there as yet any model in Europe which might offer a clear way forward.

Contemporaries were well aware of this. Running through the tracts, in greater or lesser detail, was discussion of other unions: Norway and Sweden, Poland and Lithuania, Castile and Aragon, Castile and Portugal and so on. There was no shortage of models. There was every shortage of a model which could be regarded as completely successful. Late sixteenth century Europe, indeed, seemed rather to demonstrate the virtual impossibility of sustaining effective composite kingship. The astonishing careers of Charles V and Philip II raised the spectre of universal monarchy; and Philip was a stark reminder of the effect of absentee kingship. The Netherlands were in revolt; Portugal was an unwilling—and temporary—addition to the Spanish Monarchy; and Aragon was visibly resentful of royal neglect. In time, the idea of 'king of all and king of each' would provide a relatively workable *modus vivendi*, but in 1603 it was what they regarded as the imperial rule of the Spanish kings which antagonised the Scots and worried even the English. In the same period, two attempts by Poland to establish multiple kingdoms, with France and Sweden, failed completely; indeed,

---

[28] G. Parry, *The Golden Age Restor'd: the Culture of the Stewart Court, 1603–1642* (Manchester, 1981), 6–7.

the dual rule of Henri de Valois lasted only for the time it took him to escape from Poland on the death of his brother Charles IX. Poland's composite monarchy with Lithuania, created in 1386, had certainly lasted, and became, by the Treaty of Lublin in 1569, an incorporating union. Yet the treaty created considerable opposition, and a backlash in Lithuania where, in 1588, the Third Lithuanian Statute asserted the separate sovereignty of the Duchy.[29] A union based on an entirely conflicting constitutional position was unlikely to appeal to the inhabitants of Britain. Moreover, theory had as little to offer as practice. Grotius and Pufendorf were yet to write; the ideas of 'ius gentium' and reasons of state, the concept of the impersonal power of the state, the growth of imperial monarchies ruling over dependant provinces, were developments of the seventeenth and early eighteenth centuries.[30] The British 'state'—like British Trade Unionism—had the problem of beginning life too early.

Yet that was by no means its only problem. For uniquely, the Anglo-Scottish union began the wrong way round, as the king of the lesser power came to rule the greater, creating paroxysms within the English body-politic. As a direct result, the English response was to think fearfully, and to think very small. The result was dramatic. In this age of colonisation, and with centuries of expansionist imperial ambition behind it, the kingdom of England restated Henry VIII's definition of 'empire' as a kingdom free from outside influence or interference, not this time to resist the mighty claims of the Papacy, but to deal with a little domestic matter, the infiltration of the Scots. At one end of the spectrum, in the early seventeenth century, were the Holy Roman Empire and the Spanish Monarchy. At the other was England. In 1600, Sir Thomas Wilson listed the claimants to the 'absolute Imperiall Monarchy' of England. That, not the title Emperor of the Whole Island of Britain which graced the accession medal of the Scottish claimant, was what mattered. Cotton's 'glorious Empier ... of Great Brittane' would not exist; Jonson's prophetic 'empire (as) a world divided from the world' was horribly re-interpreted.[31] James could be neither British king nor British emperor, for the empire of England had closed in on itself. It would be another foreign king, William III, who would drag it out of its hermetic

---

[29] Norman Davies, *God's Playground: A History of Poland* (2 vols., New York, 1982), I, 115–55, 322–3, 413–20, 433–7.

[30] John Robertson, 'Union, State and Empire: the European Context of British Union in 1707', to be published in *A National State at War*, ed. L. Stone, (forthcoming). I am extremely grateful to Dr Robertson for allowing me to cite his important paper before publication, and for discussions from which I have learned much.

[31] Sir Thomas Wilson, *The State of England (1600)*, ed. F.J. Fisher (Camden Miscellany 16: Camden Society, 3rd ser., LII, 1936), 1. The accession medal is illustrated in *Mental World of the Jacobean Court*, ed. Peck, plate 1 at 178. SP14/1/3, f. 9r–v; Parry, *Golden Age Restor'd*, 7.

isolation and open the way to the world of the far-flung British empire—in which the Scots would play a disproportionate part.

When James VI and I died in 1625, he left to the second king of Britain the old problems of England and Ireland, and his ancient, separate and distinct kingdom of Scotland, integrated neither as kingdom nor as province, and with no desire to become even the first, let along the second. Even at the level of possible mutual cooperation between the ruling élites and the institutions of England and Scotland, there was singular lack of enthusiasm. In 1615 and 1616, the duke of Lennox, sitting in the English council, listened to the debates of the English councillors. The subject was the king's finances; the solution seemed to be another parliament, and the real issue how to avoid another Addled Parliament. But Lennox certainly reacted when it was suggested that one answer was a Scottish parliament, which could demonstrate that loving subjects supported their king. An English parliament he agreed with; but 'for a parlement in Scotlande, they have alredy gyven example'[32] Indeed they had—back in 1612. Scotsmen with even longer experience than the English of the financial disaster that was James VI were not going to add to their difficulties, in order to assist the worried subjects of James I. Nothing, it seemed, would fundamentally affect the determined separation of the independent kingdoms of England and Scotland. And nothing, in these early years, indicated the emergence of any pattern for the future.

What did happen was that the multiple kingdoms of Britain continued to break such rules as there were for multiple kingdoms.[33] Indeed, it can be argued that even cautious integration, and the move towards core and province—as far as England and Scotland were concerned— never really happened, although there was of course great fear that it would. The union created in 1707 was certainly very different from that of 1603. But the underlying balance between the constituent parts of the kingdom of Britain remained fundamentally unchanged—except that Scotsmen on the make happily turned themselves into self-styled 'north Britons' (not, incidentally, a name which implies any kind of inferiority) where earlier they had cheerfully acted the part of northern Europeans.

---

[32] EL 2628, f. 2v.

[33] Recently Mark Greengrass has pointed out that while, by the eighteenth century, it is possible to see what he calls 'a kind of political Darwinism' at work, in which the weaker went to the wall, the approach which concentrates exclusively on state-building from the centre misses the crucial dimension of awareness of the caution with which rulers dealt with deeply ingrained regional identities and differences; and this is surely a very fruitful revision: *Conquest and Coalescence: The Shaping of the State in Early Modern Europe*, ed. Greengrass, (1991), introduction, especially 4–7. Britain can be seen as an extreme case of regional identities, which has until now survived even incautious rulers.

That argument depends on how one interprets 'the British Problem' of the seventeenth century. That there was a British Problem, no-one can now doubt; mid-seventeenth century England will never again be seen in the old, insular terms.[34] But that was a problem primarily of Charles I, admittedly with considerable help from intransigent Scottish Covenanters and confused Irish.[35] In other words, a particular concatenation of personalities and political and religious circumstances might create an international problem within the British Isles; but it was not a fundamental and essential consequence of the composite monarchy of seventeenth century Britain. The Solemn League and Covenant of 1643 did revive king James's concept of 'the blessed union'. Ensuring the 'happiness' of Charles I apparently meant allowing him to preside over the kirk in Scotland preserved and the churches of England and Ireland reformed, as a king of three kingdoms in which 'the Lord may be one and His name one'; but neither the English nor the Scots seriously envisaged closer secular bonds, and in any case their commitment to their common cause was visibly strained within a year.[36] Indeed, to put the point in a rather different way, arguments for or against union itself—its fact and its nature—were, after the first decade of the seventeenth century, sporadic in the extreme, and almost inevitably the product of political crisis. There is a vast difference between the Cromwellian Union, imposed as part of a wholly novel crisis in government, and the Union of Parliaments itself, which was the undoubted product of intolerable, short-term strain on Anglo-Scottish relations, and the vague rumblings about union in 1670, which William Ferguson described as 'an attempt at union so mysterious that it has to date defied explanation'.[37] The fact is that there was very little

[34] This is due to the seminal work of Conrad Russell and John Morrill; see references in n. 21 above.

[35] On the Scots, D. Stevenson, *The Scottish Revolution: The Triumph of the Covenanters* (Newton Abbot, 1973); M. Lee, Jr, *The Road to Revolution: Scotland under Charles I, 1625–1637* (Illinois, 1985). To these can now be added the ground-breaking book by A. I. Macinnes, *Charles I and the Covenanting Movement* (Edinburgh, 1991), and P. H. Donald, *An Uncounselled King: Charles I and the Scottish Troubles, 1637–1641* (Cambridge, 1990).

[36] *A.P.S.* VI, pt. i, 150–1; David Stevenson, 'The Early Covenanters and the Federal Union of Britain' in *Scotland and England, 1286–1815*, ed. R.A. Mason (Edinburgh, 1987), 163–81.

[37] W. Ferguson, *Scotland's Relations with England: a Survey to 1707* (Edinburgh, 1977), 152–7. The comment, on p. 152, is exaggerated; M. Lee, Jr, *The Cabal* (Illinois, 1965), 43–69, has a very lucid account of this episode, and shows quite clearly the economic strains which lay behind it, a point which Ferguson in fact recognises. It was, however, an extremely limited affair, pushed hard by the dominant Scottish politician, Lauderdale, but a matter of indifference to everyone else, including, it appears, Charles II. For an admirable survey of all the plans put forward for union in the seventeenth century, B. P. Levack, *The Formation of the British State: England, Scotland and the Union, 1603–1707* (Oxford, 1987).

interest indeed in consolidating and integrating the kingdoms of Britain into a British kingdom. The main parties were almost entirely indifferent, except on these rare occasions when the security of both was threatened at the same time; and then, like a seismic shock, there was a British Problem.

That is a pattern of sorts, but not one which lends itself to definitions of either multiple kingdoms or core and colonies. Despite the superior wealth of England, and the undoubted dominance of London, despite even the suppression of the Scottish parliament in 1707, it has never been possible to characterise Scotland in colonial or provincial terms. A separate church, law and educational system are not the hallmarks of colony or province; and although those who sought a federal solution failed in 1707, their existence raises serious doubts about whether 'incorporating union' is really an accurate description either. And that leaves one final question: why did this messy and inchoate Union survive at all? The answer is surely not because of enthusiasm, or any kind of inevitability, but *faute de mieux*. In England, the cause of instability in the fifteenth century, the excessive number of potential monarchs, gave way in the sixteenth to an embarrassing lack of them. The English therefore had to accept a king from Scotland, and were tied to the Stuart line. But once the Scots had provided that king, what alternative was there for them? They had given away the source of their independent status. Thus when the execution of Charles I broke the personal union, the Scots unilaterally proclaimed Charles II; but they proclaimed him as king of Great Britain. When that experiment failed, waiting in the wings was an English country gentleman, to whom there was no alternative. Scotland and England, throughout the seventeenth century, were simply short of potential rulers.

That was dramatically and finally highlighted in 1703. Exactly one hundred years after the Union of the Crowns, the Scottish parliament passed the Act of Security, stating that if Anne died childless, the estates would choose her successor, who would not be the same as her successor in England, unless Scotland was guaranteed the independence of its Crown, the freedom of its parliament, and liberty of religion and trade. This denied the Hanoverian succession established by the English Act of Settlement, leaving the Electress Sophia disconsolately referring to her great love of the Scots, because she was of the blood of Scotland.[38] It was not entirely bluff. It was an expression of profound anger about the way in which Scotland had been treated in the 1690s by a Dutch king largely indifferent to English internal affairs, and wholly so to Scottish ones, and about the high-handed action of the English parliament in determining the succession without consulting the Scots.

[38] Ferguson, *Scotland's Relations*, 219.

And had it not been for one fatal element of unreality, it might have been put into effect. But the unreality was crucial: for who could be the non-Hanoverian king? The Act insisted on a successor to Anne of the royal line of Scotland, and the true Protestant religion. That cut out the senior line of Stuart. And the sad fact was that the duke of Hamilton, the one candidate who might satisfy both conditions, was only a historical hang-over. In the mid-sixteenth century, an inept head of the great family of Hamilton dreamed empty dreams of the crown; in the early eighteenth, it happened again. Minds were clarified, on both sides of the border; and a new union came into being. It fell far short of the perfect union sought by King James. It did not conform to the pattern of imperial monarchies of seventeenth-century Europe. But it worked, precisely because it forced that most constitutionally minded of nations, England, into pragmatism, and allowed the anomaly of Scotland, neither independent kingdom nor province, to continue.

In 1733, George II and Queen Caroline climbed the scaffolding in the Banqueting House to gaze admiringly at the recently cleaned ceiling which commemorated that moment when an independent Scottish king took over the extraordinary combination of English multiple kingdoms and provinces, and created a new combination which defies ready classification, and which has survived for almost four centuries. There is much to complain about, and many who complain; but no-one who has just witnessed the wholly unexpected outcome of the General Election of 1992 can be left in much doubt about the passive but stupendous power of this ill-defined but deeply embedded British fact of life. The theme of Anglo-Scottish relations since 1603 is one which has regularly required redefinition. The ingrained reluctance to ask, let alone answer, fundamental questions about the nature of Britain has been, and remains, constant.

ANGLO-PORTUGUESE TRADE IN THE FIFTEENTH CENTURY

by Wendy R. Childs

READ 11 OCTOBER 1992

MY concern in this paper is essentially the complementary commercial links of the two countries against the background of political friendship. Eighty years ago Miss Shillington[1] put forward a very positive picture of the strength of Anglo-Portuguese trade, and apart from some work by Professor Carus-Wilson[2] and Dr Livermore,[3] not much has been done on this trade since, although almost all other aspects of Portuguese activity in northern and Mediterranean markets and in exploration have been considered, and the relationship of northern trade in Portugal's seemingly dramatic expansion into colonial adventure has not infrequently been raised.[4] Writers may passingly refer to Anglo-Portuguese trade as vigorous, regular, modest, increasing or decreasing: but on what scale? Is vigorous trade two, five, or ten ships a year in

[1] V. M. Shillington and A. B. Wallis Chapman, *The Commercial Relations of England and Portugal* (1907: reprinted 1970). The quality of this pioneering work is illustrated by the scarcity of new work and by the decision to reprint the book in 1970.

[2] E. M. Carus-Wilson, 'The overseas trade of Bristol in the fifteenth century', in *Studies in English Trade in the Fifteenth Century*, ed. E. Power and M. M. Postan (1933). Work on specific ports and areas also allows the Portuguese role on England's overseas trade to be set in a clearer framework: see W. R. Childs *Anglo-Castilian Trade in the Later Middle Ages* (Manchester, 1978); *The Overseas Trade of London. Exchequer Customs Accounts 1480–1*, ed. H. S. Cobb, London Record Society, 27 (1990).

[3] H. V. Livermore, 'The "Privileges of an Englishman in the Kingdoms and Dominions of Portugal"', *Atlanta*, 2 (1954); see also P. E. Russell, *English Intervention in Spain and Portugal in the Time of Edward III and Richard II* (Oxford, 1955).

[4] J. Heers, 'L'expansion maritime portugaise à la fin du moyen âge: la Mediterranée', *Revista da Faculdade de Letras, Lisboa*, 2nd ser., 22 (1956); H. H. de Oliviera Marques, *A History of Portugal*, 2 vols. (New York, 1972); *idem*, *Hanse e Portugal na Idade Media* (Lisbon, 1959); *idem*, 'Navigation entre la Prusse et le Portugal au début du XVe siècle', *Vierteljahrschrift für Social- und Wirtschaftsgeschichte*, 46 (1959); *idem*, 'Notas para a Historia da Feitoria Portuguesa na Flandres no Século XV', *Studi in Onore di A. Fanfani*, ed. A. Guiffre, II (Milan, 1962); V. Rau, 'A family of Italian Merchants in Portugal in the XVth century: the Lomellini', *Studi in Onore di A. Sapori*, I (Milan, 1957); C. Verlinden, 'Deux aspects de l'expansion commerciale de Portugal au moyen âge', *Revista Portuguesa de Historia*, (1949); for colonial expansion C. R. Boxer, *The Portuguese Seaborne Empire, 1415–1825* (1969) remains the starting point; G. V. Scammell, *The First Imperial Age* (1989) provides a recent synthesis, and *idem*, *The World Encompassed. The First European Maritime Empires c. 800–1650* (1981), 298–300 also provides a useful bibliographical note.

the context of Anglo-Portuguese trade?[5] I first became interested in Portuguese trade years ago as I wrote on Castilian trade, when it seemed to me that, despite good political relations Anglo-Portuguese trade was modest, while the Basque and Castilian trade flourished in much less welcoming political circumstances. The approach of 1992 with its promised closer commercial links in the European community (now including Portugal) seems a good time to review England's medieval links with what is commonly called her oldest continuous ally and trading partner. What I intend to do in this paper is at once limited (to examine England's trade with Portugal and the Portuguese role in it) and very broad (to sweep a whole century to provide a context for this activity).

Straightforward access, good political relations, and attractive commodities should make this a strong trading partnership. The Atlantic seas were hazardous but familiar to Portuguese and English. The opening of the regular sea route between the Mediterranean and the Channel at the end of the thirteenth century tied them ever more tightly into the trade networks of Europe. The English control of Gascony, and regular carriage of pilgrims between England and Corunna for Santiago reinforced English familiarisation with the Bay of Biscay. The fifteenth century *Instructions for the Circumnavigation of England*[6] describes the most frequent Atlantic routes, showing the direct crossing of the Bay of Biscay to be common: from Ushant, the Scillies, or Cape Clear in Ireland to Cape Ortegal or Finisterre. Scores of ships plied the routes each year. The English ships were predominantly from Bristol, London, and the west country (especially from Dartmouth), with some as far afield as Hull. About eighty-five per cent of Portuguese vessels came from Lisbon and Oporto, with others from Viaña, Setubal, Villa do Conde, and Faro. Lisbon was the main English landfall.[7]

---

[5] Earlier writers spoke of exploration as underpinned by a flourishing trade with England and Flanders. More recently emphasis has been put on the importance of royal and aristocratic investment in exploratory and colonial voyages, and the northern trade has, more realistically, been seen as modest. This still leaves questions of precise scale unanswered. Slowness in providing a scale for Portugal's northern trade has not, in the last few years, been due to lack of interest but rather to scarcity of good serial sources. No customs accounts or similar serial material seems to survive in Portugal until the early years of the sixteenth century, and few survive in her northern markets with the exception of England. English customs accounts themselves pose problems of interpretation, rate of survival, and reliability, but there are enough of them to provide a fairly clear idea of the normal trade between England and Portugal at various periods, and to give adjectives such as flourishing, vigorous, or modest a more precise meaning.

[6] *Sailing Directions for the Circumnavigation of England and for a Voyage to the Straits of Gibraltar*, ed J. Gairdner, Hakluyt Society, LXXIX (1889).

[7] At Bristol in the late fifteenth century about 85 per cent of the shipping movements to and from Portugal were to and from Lisbon and about 10 per cent to and from the Algarve.

Sailings took place in all months but summer outward sailings tended to predominate, and inward sailings sometimes bunched in December as fruit and sweet wines were brought in for the winter festivities. Political relations were particularly close at the beginning of the fifteenth century. They had generally been good since the English Crusaders helped with the Reconquest but had recently been tightened by the treaty of Windsor of 1386 and the marriage of Lancaster's English daughter Phillippa to the successful usurper João I of Portugal. Phillippa, her household, and her family kept up very close contacts with England for nearly thirty years until her death in 1415. Her three eldest sons all became Knights of the Garter, and her daughter Isabella, wife of Philip of Burgundy, was to become deeply involved in Anglo-French-Burgundian diplomatic negotiations with her half-uncle, Cardinal Beaufort. Phillippa's second son, Pedro duke of Coimbra, later Regent for his young nephew Afonso V, was the member of the family most familiar with England, and Anglo-Portuguese relations were probably closest while he remained in power. He came to England as part of a European tour in 1425 and became a very successful mediator in the quarrel between the duke of Gloucester (his cousin) and Henry Beaufort, bishop of Winchester (his half-uncle).[8] In 1428 he was back for his installation as Knight of the Garter at Windsor, and in 1429 he attended the coronation of Henry VI. At that time he may also have met his sister Isabella who was blown to England on her way to her Burgundian marriage.[9] After Pedro's disgrace and death in rebellion against the new court faction around Afonso V in 1449, it was to England that Isabella turned to find careers and sanctuary for his sons, her nephews.[10] The royal links were deepened by others. Phillippa encouraged the marriage to Thomas FitzAlan, earl of Arundel, of João's illegitimate daughter Beatriz, who came to live in England with a Portuguese household in 1405. João Vaz de Almada and his son Alvaro did well under the Lancastrians, and Alvaro, a supporter of Pedro of Coimbra, was created count of Avranches by Henry VI in 1445.[11] The impact of royal and aristocratic links on trade can be seen

[8] 'William Gregory's Chronicle of London', in *The Historical Collections of a Citizen of London in the Fifteenth Century*, ed. J. Gairdner (1876), 159–60. On this visit he was given two golden jars decorated with precious stones and pearls valued at £700; *Proceedings and Ordinances of the Privy Council of England, 10 Richard II–33 Henry VIII*, N. H. Nicolas, ed., 7 vols. (1834–7), III, 180.

[9] *Foedera; Conventiones, Litterae...*, ed. T. Rymer, 4 vols. (Record Commission, 1816–69), IV, iv, 140, 151; 'Gregory's Chronicle', 165.

[10] *Calendar of Patent Rolls* (hereafter *CPR*) 1446–52, 121, 520, 521.

[11] For this family's later claim to English blood, see Carlos Guilherme Riley, 'Da Origem Inglesa dos Almadas: Genealogia de uma Ficção Linghagística', *Arquipélago*, Revista da Universidade dos Açores, serie Historia, XI (1989), 153–69. I am indebted to Dr Anthony Goodman of the University of Edinburgh for this reference.

in the mercantile use of royal and aristocratic ships, and in the use of English merchants as royal factors. Links inevitably grew more slender as generations passed, especially after the political eclipse of Phillipa's sons in 1449. Old links between the houses of Lancaster and Aviz did not stop the king of Portugal recognising Edward IV in 1461, and suggestions of further Anglo-Portuguese marriages for Henry VI, for the sister of Edward IV, and for Richard III, came to nothing. Even at the beginning of the century relations had not been entirely smooth. The unpaid debts of João I's ambassadors from the 1380s led to reprisals even up to 1405. Individuals' attitudes were always unpredictable, and piracy, robbery, and fraud occurred. João de Porte found himself imprisoned in Honiton and threatened with death in 1434 as he tried to reach London to sue those who had robbed him in Devon,[12] and when Henry May's ship rescued a Portuguese vessel from pirates the English master was heard to say that if he had known the pirates were English he would not have bothered to save the Portuguese, and since these had not paid him a penny for his trouble he was disposed to wash his hands of them.[13] Moreover, no treaty worked in isolation. Anglo-Portuguese relations were constantly affected by Anglo-French, Anglo-Castilian, and Anglo-Burgundian relations. Problems occurred when the Anglo-French war caused the Portuguese to be arrested for English war service or checked for enemy alien goods. Arrests could lead to violence. Seakeeping could be a cover for piracy. In such circumstances safe-conducts were sought, and kings warned their subjects to honour the treaty of Windsor, but offences still occurred and reprisals might be exacted. On the other hand Portuguese merchants, as suppliers of Iberian goods, benefited when open war meant that Castile, as a French ally, became an enemy alien and withdrew from English ports. Conversely they suffered when the customs privileges of the new Anglo-Castilian treaty of 1466–89 gave Castilians the economic edge. Anglo-Burgundian conflicts also influenced the trade. Isabella's marriage to Burgundy in 1429 encouraged both Portuguese trade with the Low Countries and a triangular trade between the Low Countries, England and Portugal, but conflict and Burgundian embargoes on English cloth in 1436–9 upset it, and forced Portuguese merchants to choose one side or the other.

Nonetheless, the treaty was confirmed throughout the century at every change of monarch. The two countries remained familiar ground and the Portuguese immigrant Edward Brampton, who made a very

[12] CPR 1429–36, 469; PRO, C1/9/177–8; SC8/6719.
[13] E. M. Carus-Wilson, The Overseas Trade of Bristol in the Later Middle Ages, Bristol Record Society, VII (Bristol, 1937).

successful career under Edward IV, was not the only Portuguese to acquire denization papers in the 1470s.[14]

Vigorous trade depended not only on peace but on mutually attractive goods. Although it is sometimes said that Portugal had little to offer the international market until colonial sugar and slaves made strong appearances in the later fifteenth century, contemporaries thought otherwise. Several English treatises provide approving lists of goods. The *Libelle of Englyshe Polycye* of about 1436 recorded:

> They bene oure frendes wyth there commoditez...
> Here londe hathe oyle, wyne, osey, wex and greyne,
> Fygues, reysyns, hony and cordeweyne,
> Dates and salt hydes and suche marchaundy.[15]

Complaints by English merchants in the 1450s about the overcharging of duties on wine exports from Portugal refer to a variety of wines, largely from the Lisbon area.[16] The English treatise on overseas markets known as the *Noumbre of Weyghtes* confirms the role of wine and amplifies descriptions of other goods. 'Also in Portyngale the cheffe merchaundyse is swette wyne that growe within the land, that is to say bastard, capryke, osey, raspey, reputage, and land wyne; ther is also oyle olyffe growyng wiche is most holsummyst for mann ys mette and medicins, and where ytt is old yt is good woll oyll; ther is also wax, hony, datys, and fygges, poundgarnett, oryngys, lytomse, pomsyders; also there is a mowntayne that is called Rocke Seyntoure [Mt Cintra] and there on groweth grete plente of the beste grayne that is to grayne cloth with; ther is also grete salt'.[17]

Contemporaries clearly paid attention to Iberian wines. True, imports from Portugal were not high, but they offered a change from unalleviated Bordeaux and were significant at Bristol where imports were *regularly* around 200 tuns a year, and in 1465–6 and 1492–3 passed 500

---

[14] *CPR 1467–77*, 357, 359, 362, 509; for Brampton see R. Horrox in the revised *Dictionary of National Biography* (forthcoming).

[15] *The Libelle of Englyshe Polycye*, ed. G. Warner (Oxford, 1924), lines 130, 132–34. A similar list which includes a greater variety of wines, 'osseye, ryptage, bastarde, caprike' is provided by the treatise *The Commodyties of England*, sometimes attributed to Sir John Fortescue, ed. Rev. T. O. Payne for Lord Clermont (1863), 6.

[16] 'Ribatejo, e dallmadãa, e dazoya de villa lõgua, e pedra da estrema, e Ribas dallmaquer'; cited by the English in their petition of 1458. See G. Schanz, *Englische Handelspolitik gegen Ende des Mittelalters*, 2 vols (Leipzig, 1881), II, 520; Livermore, 'The "Privileges of an Englishman" ', 72. Ribatejo, Almada, Alenquer are all around Lisbon. Wine of Azoia was also sent to Flanders and Germany; Oliviera Marques, 'Feitoria portuguesa', 469.

[17] British Library (hereafter BL), Cotton MS. Vespasian E IX, fos. 100v–101. For part of the text see H. Hall and F.J. Nichols, eds., 'Select Tracts and Table Books relating to English Weights and Measures, 1100–1742', *Camden Miscellany XV*, Camden Society 3rd ser., XLI (1929).

tuns.[18] Sometimes two hundred tuns reached Southampton and London. More important industrially however would have been the oil and dyes for the cloth industry.[19]

These treatises are all too early to record sugar as a major Portuguese import, but it makes a considerable impact at the end of the century with the full exploitation of Madeira. It appears by the case and hundredweight in customs accounts from the mid-fifteenth century, together with a little powdered sugar, sugar loaves, and odd barrels of molasses. Most came through Lisbon, but in 1486 some came to Bristol directly from Madeira.[20] Of interest also is evidence that some still needed refining and that this could be done in London. One refiner, Arnald White or de Witt, possibly from the Low Countries, agreed to refine from brown sugar, making comfets and syrups with the residue, but found himself sued by an English sugar supplier who insisted on having the same weight of refined sugar as he had given in brown. Whether this was ignorance or sharp practice is unclear.[21]

By the end of the fifteenth century, alongside the traditional bulk cargoes came succade, marmalade, litmus, orchell, bay berries, almonds, oranges, pomegranates, grain of Paradise, and parrots. With the last, colonial goods began to make an impact on London's social if not economic life well before the sixteenth century.

The *Noumbre of Weyghtes* advised that good return cargoes were English cloth and the horses and hawks of Ireland.[22] Customs accounts show no hawks and horses but plenty of cloth. Alongside broadcloths Portugal took many lighter cloths for herself and her new markets: from Bristol she took a higher level of the lighter Welsh cloths than did Spain and Gascony, and London cargoes too included Welsh cloth, kersies, worsteds, Norfolk, London and Winchester coverlets, and cotton russetts. Portugal probably took the full range of colours England could offer; certainly colours for the king of Portugal in 1428 included red, green, white, blue, black, mustervilliers, and a marbled effect.[23] This cloth trade was the most clearly complementary since Portugal provided oil and dyes for the cloth industry. There was also some export of corn, and (under licence) of arms for Portuguese expeditions in North Africa. London sent regular small shipments of tin and pewter pots, basins, dishes, brass mortars, salt cellars, pins, knives, bells, and re-exports of Prussian tables. Bristol sent occasional alabaster carvings.

[18] PRO, E122/19/4, 20/9. For Castilian wines see Childs, *Anglo-Castilian Trade*, 126–36.

[19] Oil does not appear to be such a frequent import to the Low Countries: Oliviera Marques, 'Feitoria portuguesa', 465.

[20] PRO, E122/20/5.

[21] PRO, C1/61/580.

[22] BL, Cotton MSD. Vespasian E IX, fo. 101.

[23] *Calendar of Close Rolls* (hereafter *CCR*) 1422–9, 368.

This combination of access, friendship and good commodities should support a healthy exchange, but the picture was a mixed one. The fifteenth century trade was based on long but sometimes fragile antecedents. Portuguese commercial activity in England had been weak and intermittent until the mid-fourteenth century. The Trastaramaran usurpation in 1369, which severed Anglo-Castilian trade and cut their Castilian competitors from English ports,[24] had offered the Portuguese a particular opportunity to expand trade, but their reaction was not as dramatic or as sustained as might have been expected, and their trade soon dropped back to modest levels of four or five ships a year.[25] It was the English activity in Portugal which was most strengthened. English merchants rarely visited Portugal until the 1350s when some began to keep permanent factors in Lisbon,[26] but, unable to acquire Iberian goods through Castile, they took full advantage of Portuguese opportunities in the 1370s and 1380s, and were encouraged by further privileges in 1389.[27] By the fifteenth century, Anglo-Portuguese trade was regular, and much more solidly based on mutual activity than it had been a century earlier. Encouraged by the treaty of Windsor and intermittent Anglo-Castilian hostility, the trade was maintained in a period not especially propitious for international trade, although the Portuguese role continued to be less than might perhaps have been expected, and for much of the time it was overshadowed by Anglo-Castilian trade despite bumpier relationships between England and Castile.

The fifteenth century trade falls into three phases: it continues at a modest level through the early century, drops during the mid-century recession, and increases in the general trade expansion of the late fifteenth century. Within the trade the activity of Portuguese merchants reflects these movements in an exaggerated way, reflecting political factors as well as the economic pressures of the fifteenth century. From 1400 to the 1440s alongside continued English activity, their trade is highly visible and peaks in the 1430s. In the late 1440s and 1450s

[24] Childs, *Anglo-Castilian Trade*, 33, 40–43.

[25] See particularly the Bristol customs accounts and the Butler's accounts of alien wine imports: PRO, E122/15/8, 16/2, 4, 5, 9, 11, 13, 15, 17–22, 26, 28, 30, 34, 40/12; E101/80/20, 22, 23, 25.

[26] *CCR 1349–54*, 491.

[27] Livermore, 'The "Privileges of an Englishman" ', 65–6. See also Shillington, *Commercial Relations*, 53–4. Her analyses of Bristol accounts need minor corrections. In 1378–82 the balance of Portuguese to English ships overall is nearer 1:1 and in 1390–1 there were 21 ships laden with cloth, of which 17 were Bristol owned, three were from the Low Countries, and one was probably of Oporto; in all 9 cloths belonged to Portuguese merchants.

Portuguese activity drifted downwards even before the full return of the Castilians, leaving English activity even more visibly dominant. In the 1480s and especially in the 1490s Portuguese activity rose again but could not compete with the Castilian activity in England.

In the busiest years of the first period there might be overall a dozen or so Portuguese ships in Southampton, London, and western harbours. Numbers were modest up to about 1405,[28] then rose. The Butler's accounts of alien owned wine imports for 1400–1420 show the changing pattern. One to five Portuguese ships unloaded wine each year in the first decade, then six to ten in the second. Most wine trade was with London but some reached Ipswich and Yarmouth.[29] The activity, albeit modest, then quite outweighed Castilian movements and continued to increase in the 1420s. In the 1430s Portuguese shipping movements remained twice as active as the Basques, although Basque cargoes might be more valuable.[30] In the 1430s Southampton was clearly their preferred centre with three to eight serious trading voyages a year.[31] The cargoes were mainly oil, fruit (oranges, pomegranates, figs, and raisins), wax, and wine, with small shipments of leathers, vinegar, salt, and grain for cloth. The shippers were mixed. Two fifths of vessels carried Portuguese shippers only, the same proportion carried Portuguese and English dealers, and a fifth carried also for Italians. The high number with Portuguese shippers alone is probably due to passing trade, but the English trade was strong. The Englishmen were drawn

[28] For instance in 1403–4, Bristol saw 1, Southampton 5, and Exeter 1; no account survives for London that year. PRO, E122/17/9, 10, 12, 18/13; 139/4, 7; Devon Record Office, Exeter local customs roll, 5–6 Hen. IV.

[29] PRO, E101/81/1, 3, 5, 8.

[30] In the 40 year period 1420–1460 surviving customs accounts show altogether 124 Portuguese vessels and 67 Spanish ones in English ports. See note 34.

[31] PRO, E122/141/21–23, 25, 29, 31, 209/1, 140/62; *The Local Port Book of Southampton for 1435–36*, ed. B. Foster, Southampton Record Series, VII (1963), 8, 14, 30, 46, 50, 60–2, 66; *The Local Port Book of Southampton for 1439–40*, ed. H. Cobb, Southampton Record Series, V (1961), 15–17, 22, 30, 48, 104–5, 107, 109. Portuguese ships and cargoes are as follows:

Date	No. of ships recorded in	Cargo value	Wine (tuns)	No. of ships recorded out	Cloths exported
1432–3	7	£398	23	10	404
1433–4	8	£402	41	4	14
1435–6	7	—*		6?	111 [minimum]
1437–8	3	£627		5	22
1438–9	3	£517	8	2	179
1439–40	13	—*	12?	—	
1442–3	3	£100	54	3	26
1443–4	1	nil	1	0	0
1447–8	3	£ 5	78	2	58
1448–9	2?	£ 98	147	3	43

* Information in the local accounts does not allow accurate estimates of cargo values.

from the port's major municipal figures—Walter Fetplace, John Emery, Peter James, Robert Aylward, and Nicholas Billett—and their investment was much higher than that of the Portuguese. Eighty per cent of Portuguese shipments were valued at under £10 compared with only fifty-seven per cent of English; but few of either nationality had shipments worth over £30 in Southampton. The Italians involved were usually members of the Lomellini family, some of whom had settled in Lisbon and owned Portuguese ships.[32] Some Portuguese vessels were clearly large: in 1438 João Afonso's ship carried at least 160 tuns of cargo, and during that decade at least two Portuguese ships were described as carracks.[33]

Southampton (unlike London and Bristol) also picked up passing trade to Low Country markets. Ships, perhaps sheltering from bad weather or needing repairs or victuals, were often in port only two or three days, selling and buying little. In 1433 one ship loaded only eighteen yards of cloth and tin worth 13s 4d.[34] Similar patterns are sometimes seen in other channel ports, as at Exeter in 1410–11 when eight Portuguese ships unloaded only one tun of wine and goods worth £12 13s. 4d.[35] Sailing patterns at Southampton show some Portuguese developing the Low Country connection further, to form a triangular trade between Portugal, England and Flanders in the early 1430s. João Afonso's carrack entered Southampton in February 1433 to unload Portuguese goods worth £111.16.8 and 14¾ tuns of wine; it returned in May, unloading cargo worth £78 clearly from Flanders; it left within four days having loaded 144 cloths, and was back in September with another Portuguese cargo worth £149.17.6. It is not recorded out, but was back in November with Flemish goods worth £34.[36] Afonso was making two major round trips a year, taking in Southampton and Flanders. English commentators were well aware of this aspect of Channel trade and deplored it; the author of the *Libelle of Englyshe Polycye*, written c. 1436, recorded the Portuguese as among those likely to want 'to Flaundres passe forthe bye', whose trade should be brought to England.[37] It was probably an awareness of this general feeling, and

[32] Rau, 'A family of Italian merchants', *passim*; PRO, C76/134 m. 12.

[33] PRO, E122/141/22, 23.

[34] PRO, E122/141/21. Portuguese ships can be outstripped by smaller number of Spanish ships. In 1435–6 for instance seven Portuguese ships exported at least 111 English cloths, but the three Castilian ships exported 330 cloths; their imports of over 431 tons of iron worth at least £863 were similarly certainly larger than those of the Portuguese; Foster, *Port Book*, 36, 52–4, 58–60.

[35] PRO, E122 40/30; see also E122/126/12, 36–8 (Sandwich), 139/4, 7, 8 (Southampton); DRO, Exeter local customs rolls, 5–7 Henry IV. Others put into Dartmouth for shelter, *CPR 1436–41*, 515.

[36] PRO, E122/141/21, 22.

[37] *Libelle*, l. 135.

the piracy of five ships sailing from Portugal to Flanders in 1435, quite as much as the Anglo-Burgundian war itself, that made the masters of six Portuguese ships lying in English harbours in 1436 buy safe-conducts for their voyages to the Low Countries, which they now made to Middelburg.[38]

The pattern in London was different. Without the passing trade, total numbers of Portuguese ships were often lower,[39] but cargoes were always of at least moderate size, and vessels stayed in port for one or two months. The imports were mainly the same as at Southampton but with a little more variety, including cork, bowstaves, and fig-cakes. Some of the large ships at Southampton came on up to London: João Peris's vessel brought 206 tuns of wine and oil in 1431,[40] but like the Italians the Portuguese sent no carracks there.[41] Compared with Southampton, more vessels carried shipments for Italian and London merchants. As in Southampton over 80 per cent of the Portuguese shipments were under £10, although here some reached £60, but English investment was higher. Only thirty-eight per cent had shipments of under £10, and larger consignments reached to £100 and beyond. This pattern of per capita investment is of considerable significance and underlines the relative weakness of Portuguese merchants in investment throughout the period. It is sometimes exaggerated in records, when members of Portuguese crews—carpenters, caulker, mariners, and pilots—used their freight allowances to trade in small amounts of under £1, but the pattern remains clear.[42]

The surges of Portuguese activity in the second and fourth decades of the century were affected by complex Channel politics. In 1413–1418

---

[38] *CPR 1429–36*, 527; PRO, C76/118, mm. 3, 7.

[39] PRO, E122/73/10, 12, 20, 23, 25, 76/34, 38, 77/1, 3, 4, 203/1, 2, 3. Portuguese ships and cargoes were as follows:

Date	No. of ships recorded in	Cargo value	Wine (tuns)	No. of ships recorded out	Cloths exported
1431–2	1	£239	185	0	
1432–3	0			2	96
1435–6	5	£443		4	87 [+ 71]
1437–8	1	£ 44		1	70 [+ 149]
1438–9	1	£132		2	15 [+ 89]
1439–40	0			1	
1442–3	0			0	
1445–6	4	£442	14	1	228
1449–50	2	£360	13	2	147

Cloths in brackets are those belonging to English merchants shipped on Portuguese vessels. No account is taken of small amounts of worsted exported. In the poundage accounts, 1438–9 and 1442–3, English ships are also recorded to and from Portugal.

[40] PRO, E122/77/1.

[41] Goods were sent to a carrack at Sandwich 1437–8; PRO, E122/77/3.

[42] PRO, E122/76/34.

Henry V's campaigns upset Anglo-Castilian trade since Castile was still a French ally, and probably encouraged Portugal as a supplier of Iberian goods. In the 1430s, however, it was not the removal of Castilian competition, but the Anglo-Burgundian conflicts which influenced their activity. Triangular voyages disappeared from the records, but while some Portuguese shippers possibly chose Bruges, the Burgundian embargo on English cloth from 1436–9 probably encouraged others to come to England for supplies. Numbers of Portuguese merchants in Bruges were certainly low in these years.[43]

At its height in the 1430s and early 1440s Portuguese activity meant that in some years up to a dozen ships, hundreds of seamen, and tens of shippers might be found on English quays. Over a generation hundreds of names of Portuguese shippers are found recorded in customs accounts and chancery rolls, yet relatively few are recorded more than once. The page is not entirely blank. Shipmen such as João Afonso, João Peris,[44] and João Ferreira,[45] returned several times, and in 1441 Fonsu Martin (probably a merchant) was in London long enough to be caught, as a non-householder, by the alien subsidy.[46] But in general the Portuguese showed no inclination to settle in any English port, as they did in Bruges, or as the English did in Lisbon. They rarely seem to have left permanent factors to trade for them. There is no evidence of hiring houses and warehouses, and little of merchants living in the native community for long. Impermanence was not necessarily a hindrance to enterprise since the English mercantile community in Lisbon could provide them with contacts. In London between 1435 and 1455 at least 150 English shippers dealt with Portugal, and a score or so of these formed a close knit group apparently well known to the Portuguese. In 1439 Robert Shirburn received in a deed of gift all the assets of Martim Gonçalves of Lisbon who needed some financial protection.[47] Peter Alford and William Thorn hosted the seven

---

[43] See below, note 85.

[44] For Afonso see above, 203. There are two masters named John Peres. Both were in London in December 1431; one or other of them was back in February 1432; at Southampton in April 1433; in London on 2 September 1433. This last was probably the same ship which then left Southampton on 12 September, including in its shippers William Saxby of London and Alvero Vasques who had also been included among the London shippers of 2 September. The ship was back at Southampton on 20 December 1433. There is of course difficulty of clear identification with a common name such as John Peres. PRO, E122/77/1, 203/1, 141/21, 22.

[45] PRO, C76/134 m. 12 (St Marie Grace of Lisbon, owned by Marco Lomellini and Dominico Scoti), 139 m. 22, 142 m. 25 (Holy Spirit, 110 tuns) With the Anglo-Portuguese treaty in force such safe-conducts were legally unnecessary, but it was sometimes safer to obtain them.

[46] PRO, E179/144/54.

[47] CCR 1435–41, 381.

Portuguese merchants who arrived in 1440–41.[48] Alford and John Brampton acted as guarantors for Luis Vasques and Nono Gonçalves in 1458.[49] John Adam of London, who also acted as attorney before the council for Portuguese merchants robbed at sea, went into partnership with Pero Fernandes in buying a Dartmouth ship from Thomas Gille which was also attacked in 1452.[50] Lisbon trader, Henry May of Bristol, when asked for help by João de Veilho, sent him to John Chirche, Stephen Stichmersh, and Alford.[51] All these merchants were regular London–Portuguese traders. The contrast between Portuguese and Castilian merchants as well as with the English in Lisbon is marked. Both before the disruptions of the Hundred Years War, and in the later decades of the fifteenth century when trade was reasonably safe again, Castilians (mainly Basques) traded repeatedly, obtained special grants and privileges, and left factors in England. Even during the war it was possible to find them making regular applications for safe-conducts and sailing repeatedly into English ports under truces.[52] Perhaps the Portuguese did not need to stay because the English community served them so well, yet the impression remains that, even in the busy period of the 1430s and 1440s, their trade was too small to need long residence and many saw England as only an occasional market, despite the much vaunted treaty of Windsor.

The size of the English community in Lisbon is difficult to assess. Privileges and protection gained in the fourteenth century were enhanced in the fifteenth.[53] Individual careers show long and deep involvement. John Chirche, London mercer, traded in Iberia for at least twenty years and was particularly busy in Portugal in the 1430s: in 1438 he was described as factor of the King of Portugal, exporting wool to Florence in exchange for cloth of gold.[54] Henry Logan, Stephen Stichmersh, Bartholomew James, Peter Alford, William Abraham, and William Saxby similarly regularly traded over decades using Portuguese and English ships. English factors probably continued to stay for years in Lisbon as they had in the fourteenth century, and Portuguese merchants called John Inglis and John Bristowe imply English fathers, who settled there. Bartholomew James, a steady trader, who became alderman and mayor of London seems to be the same man who was

[48] PRO, E101/128/33.

[49] CCR 1454–61, 300.

[50] PRO, E28/82, 9 March 30 Hen. VI; CPR 1446–52, 536; ibid. 1452–61, 61, 165.

[51] E. M. Carus-Wilson, The Overseas Trade of Bristol in the later Middle Ages (1937), no. 87.

[52] The treaty of Windsor meant Portuguese merchants would not appear in some records where Spaniards are recorded as enemy aliens, but this does not affect customs accounts, local London records, and many legal records.

[53] Livermore, 'The "Privileges of an Englishman"', passim.

[54] PRO, C76/119 m. 5, 120 m. 4, 123 m. 18; E122/73/12, 76/38, 77/3.

born of an English father in Portugal and who, although always treated as a denizen by customs collectors, clearly felt it necessary to buy formal denization papers in 1445 at a time of increasing xenophobia.

The numbers of English ships engaged might be small, often only one a year from Southampton, but two or three from London, and possibly half a dozen from Bristol, but in all ports the investment of English merchants was heavy compared with that of Portuguese merchants. Few Portuguese ships carried Portuguese owned cargoes worth more than £150 (the largest before 1500 was £360 for a factor of the King of Portugal), and most were well under £100. In contrast, two English ships arriving in London from Portugal in 1442–3 unloaded cargoes both valued at about £770, and one had also 58½ tuns of wine aboard, worth perhaps £234 at customs valuation.[55] There were of course small shippers among the English, but also considerable numbers of large dealers. In 1442–3 Bartholomew James imported oil and kermes worth £115 on one ship and oil, wax, and wine on the other; Peter Alford imported oil, wax, and oranges worth £93 on one, and in 1445 brought fruit worth £60 on the ship of Lopo Eanes (Janus). Such cargoes illustrate the greater capital outlay of the English, whose average per capita investment was about double that of the Portuguese.

It is a pity that we have no surviving Bristol customs accounts to illuminate the scale of trade there, but the interrelation of London and Bristol merchants is frequently indicated. For instance, the *Nicholas* of Bristol unloaded Portuguese salt and oil in London in 1440, and the May brothers, Henry and Richard, operated from both.[56] Of the other west country ports Dartmouth men (among them Thomas Gille) and ships, well known for their carrying trade, were most active in Portuguese navigation.[57]

*　　*　　*

[55] For London see PRO, E122/73/10, 12, 20, 23, 25, 74/11, 76/34, 38, 77/1, 3, 4, 203/1, 2, 3. Of the English cargoes one, for 25 Englishmen and Jeronimo Spinola, included 140 tuns of oil (£606 13s. 4d.), kermes (£104 18s. 4d.), wax (£47), and small amounts of oranges, salt, vinegar, and bowstaves; the other, for 37 Englishmen, was also predominantly of olive oil (136 tuns, £585), with wax (over £151), small amounts of cordwain, oranges, salt, and 58½ tuns of wine: E122/77/4.

[56] No national accounts for Bristol survive; shipping movements at Bristol in 1432, cited in a fraud case, show no Portuguese ships, and only two locals sailing for Lisbon (PRO, E159/210 Recorda Mich. m. 34); a local account for 1437–8 shows only one possible Portuguese ship, *Bristol Town Duties*, ed. H. Bush (Bristol, 1828), 17–25. For the London connection see PRO, E122/76/38; and above, 206 and n. 51.

[57] *CPR 1429–36*, 351; for more on Dartmouth carrying trade see W. R. Childs, 'The Overseas Trade of Devon in the later Middle Ages', in *A New Maritime History of Devon*, I, ed. M. Duffy et al. (Conway Maritime Press, forthcoming); for Gille see P. de Azevedo, 'Comércio anglo-português no meado do sec. XV', *Academia da Sciências de Lisboa, Boletim da Segunda Classe*, VIII (1913–14), 55–6.

In the second phase, from the late 1440s to the 1460s, Portuguese ships in English harbours declined. London and Southampton occasionally saw one, but generally none. Bristol in the 1460s saw similarly few apart from 1465–6 when five appeared. There were several possible causes: first the general economic recession was probably pushing a small community to the wall; secondly, increasing Castilian competition may again be a problem as in all the customs accounts Castilian activity is much higher; and thirdly, if a choice had to be made by Portuguese merchants with limited resources, Bruges seems to have won, despite the cloth embargoes of 1447–52 and 1464–7.[58] Although instability in the Channel affected trade to England and Flanders equally, the seizure by the English of six Portuguese ships in 1455 and two more in 1456 might have been a deterrent to sailing into English ports. The trade of the English merchants, however, was maintained. Although its exact scale remains difficult to assess, and there is more friction, it is illuminated by increasingly interesting documentation. Of eighteen safe-conducts and other grants known to me for the period 1438–88,[59] fourteen were granted in the 1450s and early 1460s. Of the thirteen named English merchants in these grants between 1438 and 1462 at least eight were Bristol men, and some were certainly well entrenched. Nicholas Broun seems to have lived in Lisbon for ten years, as his grant of 1438 to live tax free in Lisbon was confirmed in 1448. John Stokker, John Collins, and John Redy were favoured enough to be allowed individually to bear arms, although the King would not allow this to the English generally.[60] To this period also belong the petitions of English merchants made in 1454 and 1458 against the abuses in the Lisbon customs house, already analysed by Miss Shillington and Dr Livermore.[61] These show the routines of business and the frustration of petty bureaucracy for the English in Portugal, but also show the king of Portugal willing to uphold their general privileges.

The third phase came at the end of the fifteenth century when Portuguese activity increased again in English harbours. Economic causes were dominant now, as the Portuguese took part in the general European revival of trade, to which their colonisation of the Atlantic Islands and exploration of West Africa gave further impetus. The expansion of their trade with England was, nonetheless, fairly slow

---

[58] Numbers of Portuguese there increased at this time. Oliviera Marques, 'Feitoria portuguesa', 458; see below, 216.

[59] PRO, PRO31/8/153, fos 632–64, 671–2; Azevedo, 'Comércio anglo-português', 53–66.

[60] Azevedo, 'Comércio anglo-português', 61, 65–6; PRO, PRO31/8/153, fos. 632, 640; Schanz, *Handelspolitik*, 511–13.

[61] Shillington, *Commercial Relations*, 68–9, 113–26; Livermore, 'The "Privileges of an Englishman" ', *passim*.

until the early 1490s, when their activity increased in many European areas. Their trade shows a shift in geographical concentration towards London, but there is still only limited evidence of Portuguese commercial settlement in England. Three Portuguese became denizens in 1472: one of these was Martin Deniz who continued to trade with Portugal from London in the 1470s, but another was Edward Brampton whose career is far more than that of a merchant.[62] The account of Roger Machado, one of the English diplomatic envoys to Spain and Portugal in 1489 and probably himself Portuguese in origin, confirms the contrast with Castile. In Laredo and Burgos he sought out and lodged with Castilian merchants such as Diego de Castro, well known to him (and us) from trade in Southampton and London, but in Lisbon, apart from lodging with Edward Brampton, he turned to resident Bristol and London merchants for help.[63]

The surge of the early 1490s is visible in several ports.[64] At Southampton in 1491–2 three ships entered.[65] In Bristol in 1492–3 four sailed in.[66] But London was their centre: four Portuguese ships were there in 1477–8, eight in 1480–1, at least seven in 1487–8, six in 1490–1, and the exceptional number of nineteen arrived in 1494–5. These unloaded 120 tuns of wine, and other cargo worth an unprecedented £2964, and exported 440 cloths and some kersies. Numbers remained high in 1502–3 when ten vessels lay at London's quays.[67]

Changes other than scale appear in London. Sugar was big business now and Portugal instead of Italy was the main provider. By 1494–5 Portuguese ships dominated the trade, carrying 1081 cases, while English ships carried forty-four cases and Spanish ships only thirty-four. Although Italians still took part in the Lisbon sugar trade, and in 1494–5 nearly half the sugar was still imported in the name of Giovanni Batista on the ship of Luis Eanes (Lodowicus Johannis), much of it was now owned by the Portuguese themselves. More luxury goods also appear alongside oil and wine, again often in the hands of the Portuguese themselves. Cargo values on Portuguese ships were in consequence regularly much higher, often more than double those of

[62] See above note 14; PRO, E122/194/23 shows Deniz exporting on ships of Andree Perus and Gonçalvo Fons in May 1478.

[63] *Journal of Roger Machado*, ed. J. Gairdner, Rolls Series, X (1856), 333–6, 364–5; I am indebted for discussion on the origins of Machado to Dr Michael Jones of the University of Nottingham.

[64] PRO, E122 *passim*; DRO Exeter local customs rolls, Edw. IV–Hen. VII; *The Port Books or Local Customs Accounts of Southampton for the Reign of Edward IV*, ed. D. B. Quinn and A. A. Ruddock, Southampton Record Society, 37–8 (1937–8); Southampton Civic Centre, Local Port Books for 1484–5 and 1494–5.

[65] PRO, E122/142/11.

[66] PRO, E122/20/9.

[67] PRO, E122/194/23, 24, 78/7, 9, 79/5, 80/3.

fifty years earlier, but even here, they never came to dominate the Iberian route. Their activity in London in 1494–5 was matched by eight English ships bringing southern Iberian cargoes worth £2757 and 128 tuns of wine and, despite the loss of their customs privileges in 1489, outstripped by twenty-four Castilian ships exporting 3039 cloths and twice as much kersey as the Portuguese, and bringing goods worth £5172 and 289 tuns of wine. The Castilian share of the *southern* market was less than this total suggests, since only £1062 was invested in oil, fruit, and cork on six ships from the south, but Castilian activity was more widespread than was Portuguese. Apart from trade on their own ships, Castilian merchants also imported goods worth £4735, largely woad, and sixty tuns of wine on ships of other nationalities, while Portuguese merchants were rarely found in such complex relationships. Although London was the centre of Portuguese interest in England, except in the case of sugar, they were clearly not the only suppliers of Iberian produce there. Nonetheless, with imports of over £3000 on their own ships compared with some £5200 aboard all Spanish ships and £2700 on English ships from Iberia, they carried well over one quarter of London's direct Iberian trade in the exceptional year of 1494–5.

Bristol records reveal a sharply contrasting picture.[68] Portuguese shipping was much less active than English shipping, and cargo values were lower. Typically one or two Portuguese ships arrived in a year. Alongside these, five or six English ships were regularly recorded as sailing to Lisbon or the Algarve, and Spanish and Breton ships joined them. Here, the Portuguese generally handled far less than a quarter of Bristol's Portuguese trade, let alone her total Iberian trade.[69] Yet Portuguese trade as a whole was more important to Bristol than to London, which had other markets on its doorstep. Bristol men needed Portuguese trade more than did the Londoners, and about forty-five per cent of Bristol's merchants who engaged in Continental trade sent some goods to Portugal. Among them were many of the aldermanic class; again a different picture from London where the top rank of merchants more often dealt with Castile, Italy, and the Low Countries. Nevertheless, despite the wide interest in Portugal, as in London, Castilian trade was more important. In the 1480s and 1490s, between twenty-five per cent of Bristol's cloth exports were recorded as for Portugal but sixty-two per cent for Castile; eighteen per cent of Bristol's

---

[68] PRO, E122/20/1, 5, 7, 9.

[69] Overall they handled about 14% of general imports, 15% of wine, and 10–14% of cloth exports, but in 1492–3, with some large sugar cargoes, they brought 38 per cent of imports from Portugal by value and 37 per cent of Portuguese wine; they still took only 10 per cent of the cloth sent to Portugal, leaving the bulk of the trade in the hands of the English.

wine came from Portugal, but thirty-two per cent from Castile.[70] A closer look shows complexity. The Algarve attracted several ships but provided mainly fruit, and was greatly overshadowed by the Lisbon market, which could supply sugar. However, the value of general goods from these two markets was more important than those from Andalusia. On the other hand, Andalusia supplied twice or three times as much wine as Portugal, which brought her total value up to and beyond that of the Portuguese market. The Basque trade pushed the Castilian value even higher. Nonetheless, although the trade of Portugal is clearly smaller than that of Castile, it should not be undervalued. A market normally taking a fifth to a quarter of Bristol's exports and supplying fifteen per cent of imports was an extremely useful one.

Apart from an increase in scale, I have also pointed to changes in the shape of trade. First, new colonial goods especially sugar were brought from Portugal. Secondly more cargoes of mixed semi-luxury goods appeared on Portuguese ships in London. This is so regular as to look planned. Possibly small amounts of attractive goods with a fast turnover suited Portuguese commercial resources better than the heavy outlay for large quantities of oil or wine which might take longer to move from the warehouse. These traditional cargoes were left to the English.[71] Portuguese investment per capita was considerably higher: only forty-two per cent now had cargoes valued at under £10, and five per cent had cargoes over £60, with the greatest reaching £212. The average cargo value had doubled since the 1440s, and at the bottom end of the scale investment was not far from the English level. In 1487–8 and 1494–5 English ventures from southern Iberia[72] showed thirty-five per cent of English shipments under £10, but twenty-five per cent over £60, and seven per cent over £100. English merchants' investments were still greater, but the gap had narrowed. Thirdly, the shippers aboard Portuguese vessels in London became almost entirely Portuguese, although carrying for Italians and English never disappeared.[73]

[70] It should of course be remembered that the destinations given in the accounts may not indicate the only market, and that ships sailing to Andalusia might call at Lisbon too.

[71] A shortage of capital is also evidenced by all really expensive cargoes being in the hands of Italians or Englishmen.

[72] Trade with Portugal and Andalusia is impossible to disentangle if ships and all shippers are English. I have used data from 11 ships with cargoes of wine, oil, and other southern goods, but they may be from either area.

[73] In 1487–8, and 1494–5 they still carried single consignments of sugar worth £403 and £555 for individual Italians, but this is becoming a smaller amount of the trade they carry, [33% in 1487–8, 19% in 1494–5]. In 1480–1 they brought sugar worth about £430 for Alessandro Portinari, a Genoese who traded much with the Burgundian court, but

Two thirds of vessels carried only Portuguese shippers. Most of the others had only one denizen aboard, and that might be the naturalised Martin Deniz or Edward Brampton. A similar shift was apparent in Bristol, although the sample is very small. There in the 1460s ninety-five per cent of the goods on Portuguese ships had belonged to English merchants, but in 1492–3 the Portuguese owned one hundred per cent of general goods and seventy per cent of the wine on their ships. Fourthly a new aspect appears which suggests that the Portuguese were beginning to engage more heavily in the Mediterranean carrying trade. In London and Bristol from the 1470s they imported for English and Florentine merchants occasional large shipments of alum, probably from the Tolfa mines, and in 1480 they brought a large shipment of woad to London for eight Genoese. Until then, the Portuguese do not seem to have sought a carrying trade in the same way as the Basques. The Italians and Englishmen for whom they had previously carried goods had been those directly interested in the Lisbon market, but this carrying decreased at the end of the century, when Portuguese merchants, benefiting from their new colonies, built up their own capital, and played a larger part in the direct trade between Portugal and England.

This paper concerns mainly direct Anglo-Portuguese trade, but the alum carrying reminds us of the complexity of medieval trade. Anglo-Portuguese trade was part of a network on which complex journeys were planned and executed by a number of nationalities. The Bristol accounts show Portuguese ships involved in the Irish trade. Breton ships involved in the trade from Madeira, and Basque ships sailing to Lisbon. Elsewhere Italian and Flemish merchants handled Portuguese goods. Calculations however show that the total amounts of these goods were not enough to distort seriously the picture of general patterns and trends, although absolute figures should be treated with care.

Over the century (apart from the dip in the middle), the Portuguese did quite well: shipping movements about doubled, Portuguese owned goods increased sixfold, and their cloth exports fourfold, although their wine imports remained steady. Their trade was still modest and their expansion not as impressive as that of the Basques in the same period, but nonetheless the total direct Portuguese trade, including that handled by English merchants, had significance not only for individual ports but also in England's overall trade. At the end of the fifteenth century

the Italians engaged in direct Anglo-Portuguese trade are more often those domiciled in Lisbon; Rau, 'A family of Italian merchants'; C. Verlinden, 'La colonie italienne de Lisbonne et le developpement de l'économie metropolitaine et coloniale portugaise', *Studi in onore di Armando Sapori*, I (Milan, 1957); J. Heers, *Gênes au XV siècle*, Ecole Pratique des Hautes Etudes, Vle section, Centre de Recherches Historiques, Ports, XXIV (Paris, 1961), 485–7.

the Portuguese market took perhaps 3000 cloths a year from England, about five per cent of exports. Portugal supplied up to 600–700 tuns of wine, about six to twelve per cent of imports. Other goods were valued by customs collectors at well under £10,000 a year, but this constituted about ten to twelve per cent of imports by value.[74] The market was limited but noticeable. The goods were welcome. Merchants and seamen made profitable livings. Yet overall the close political relationships, although helpful, had not promoted a trade of the depth visible in Anglo-Castilian connections despite the difficult political relations there. English merchants moved westwards and set up resident factors in Lisbon, but Portuguese merchants did not take full advantage of the opportunity to push into English markets, and were nearly always surpassed by Basque activity. Why?

In answering this question three points may be considered. Portugal's resources; her voyages of exploration; and her trade elsewhere. Portugal was a small and mountainous country, with a population after the Black Death of perhaps a million, and with therefore a limited market. Its shipping, concentrated above all in Lisbon and Oporto,[75] suggests a country with few areas economically active on a large scale. However, the south had resources of wine, oil, fruit, salt, cork, and dyes, which were eminently saleable in the north, and which attracted permanent English and Genoese communities. Contemporary impressions are shown in the commodity lists above, and in the views of visitors. On the same journey in 1466 two of Leo of Rozmital's followers had very different impressions: Tetzel constantly talked of barrenness and poverty; Schaseck marvelled at the many fruit trees and the fertile vineyards.[76] Access to Spain in truces and peacetime also increased its hinterland.

Moreover being a poor and mountainous country need not be a total handicap to commerce. It has been argued in the case of Genoa that an unpromising hinterland forced her to the sea. The regular use

---

[74] Total annual cloth exports to Portugal from Bristol were c. 1000–1500. Exports by Portuguese themselves reached 440 at their peak in London, but were counted in scores in southern ports; supplements on English ships from these ports ran into hundreds. For totals see E. M. Carus-Wilson and O. Coleman, *England's Export Trade 1275–1547* (Oxford, 1963); for Spanish totals see Childs, *Anglo-Castilian Trade*, 89–90. Portugal supplied 200–250 tuns of wine and sometimes 500 tuns a year to Bristol; Childs, op. cit., 133 (where the final figure for Portugal should read 499). It rarely supplied over 100 tuns and frequently none to southern ports. The Portuguese themselves brought only 117 tuns to London in their peak year. For total wine imports see M. K. James, *Studies in the English Wine Trade*, ed. E. M. Veale (Oxford, 1971). The import values of general merchandise can be estimated only roughly from customs particulars, as numerous adjustments have to be made to petty custom and poundage totals.

[75] In English records for the fourteenth and fifteenth centuries, of the Portuguese ships identified by a home port name, 45% came from Lisbon, and 45% from Oporto.

[76] *The Travels of Leo of Rozmital*, ed. M. Letts, Hakluyt Society, 2nd ser., CVIII (1957), 100–107, 119, 123.

of the sea route between northern and southern Europe saw Portuguese seamen uniquely well positioned to secure some of the carrying trade if they wished, but they clearly did not make the most of their chance here. Shipowning was a high risk enterprise, especially in the economic recession of the fifteenth century, and Portuguese merchants possibly had not the capital resources to risk. English records of Portuguese ships show the same high ratio of royal and noble shipowners here as elsewhere.[77] However the Portuguese did better than the Andalusians, who were perhaps more dominated by the great Italian companies, although less well than the Basques, with whom comparison is interesting. Basques competed strongly in both England and the Mediterranean, yet in neither area were they obviously better placed than the Portuguese. In the Mediterranean the Basques could use Andalusian ports freely, but after 1415 the conquest of Ceuta gave the Portuguese an adequate base, and their journeys from home bases on the Algarve were in any case shorter than those for the Basques. Commercially Basque iron helped to maintain their hold in the north, but the Portuguese in England should have had a positive political advantage over the Basques until 1466 when the Anglo-Castilian treaty granted the latter merchants customs privileges. From then their economic edge over Portuguese merchants is clear, but even before 1466 the Portuguese had not moved with any permanence into English trade.

The matter of Portuguese exploration can be dealt with quickly. Long ago Miss Shillington suggested ships and interest were drawn away from the north into exploration, thus helping to explain the way in which English merchants moved into Portugal and obtained privileges in the fifteenth century. It is now well established however, that exploration was largely financed by the royal house and the aristocracy not by merchants; that it was discontinuous and patchy until the late fifteenth century; and that it was 'remarkably economic of resources'.[78] Portugal's traditional trade would not be drained, but rather would

---

[77] In 1384 the *Holy Ghost* belonging to the king of Portugal was seized by English pirates off Harfleur, and a ship of his brother, João, Master of Aviz, was wrecked off the Isle of Wight. In 1416 the *Katherine* of the king of Portugal was in England ready to sail to Calais. In 1439 pirates robbed a ship of João Alvar, a Portuguese knight, in Mountsbay. In 1445 Alvaro Vaz d'Almada, count of Avranches, owned a ship which arrived in London. In 1454 Alvaro de Cayado, knight of the Order of Christ, owned a carvel which sailed into Southampton and possibly also owned another carvel of Setubal. In 1455 a knight of Portugal, named as Albuquerque (Alvokyrk), was recorded as owner of one of six Portuguese ships taken at sea. A few cases where Portuguese knights are included among shippers may indicate an interest in the vessel as well as the goods. *CCR 1381–5*, 358, 380; PRO, C76/99, m. 21; *CPR 1436–41*, 409; PRO, C76/128 m. 2; E28/84; *CPR 1452–61*, 172, 254, 281.

[78] P. Chaunu, *European Expansion in the Later Middle Ages* (Eng. trans., Amsterdam, 1979), 309; and see note 4.

increase alongside explorations by both providing markets for colonial goods and obtaining cloth and metal goods for trade in Africa and the Atlantic islands. The most important consideration must be their greater interest in other markets, which might draw attention away from England. Certainly they traded widely, but the evidence suggests that activity all over the north remained modest until the very end of the fifteenth century. Only Flanders can have been regularly busier than England. Ireland was a landfall regularly visited by the Portuguese from the later fourteenth century, but it is unlikely that the trade was in excess of or even equalled that with the larger market of England.[79] In Gascony the surviving Bordeaux Constable's accounts for wine duties show only one Portuguese ship there in the whole century.[80] At La Rochelle researchers have drawn a blank for Portuguese activity until 1536.[81] Their trade in Breton ports is better substantiated, although extremely modest in the records.[82] Normandy was probably their main French centre, where their first privileges at Harfleur predated the Castilian ones, but surviving materials for Rouen and Dieppe show very limited activity before the sixteenth century.[83] The Low Countries were of course their most important destination. This was only to be expected given the international importance of Bruges.[84] Their activity was well established by the later thirteenth century; they established a small colony in the fourteenth century, and in the fifteenth they had a resident royal factor. Wider privileges were formulated in 1411, and the merchants were permitted their own consuls in 1438. England rarely offered special conditions to aliens, although the Carta Mercatoria offered general basic provisions. The link was strengthened by the marriage in 1429 of the Infanta Isabella to Burgundy, who by this time had inherited not only Flanders, but also Hainault, Holland, Zeeland, and Brabant, and this more recent political tie superseded that with

[79] W. R. Childs, 'Ireland's trade with England in the later middle ages', *Irish Economic and Social History*, 9 (1982), 9–10, 30, 32–3; W. R. Childs and T. O'Neill, 'The Overseas Trade of Ireland in the later Middle Ages', *A New History of Ireland*, II, *Medieval Ireland 1169–1534*, ed. A. Cosgrove (Oxford, 1987), 489, 498, 507–8, 511.

[80] PRO, E101/184/19, 185/7, 9, 11, 188/12, 14, 190/6, 191/3, 192/1, 194/3, 195/19; BL, Additional MS 15524; M. G. Ducaunnes-Duval, 'Registre de la Comptablie de Bordeaux 1482–3', *Archives Historiques du département de la Gironde*, L (1915), 1–166.

[81] E. Trocmé and M. Delafosse, *Le Commerce rochelais de la fin du XVe siècle au début du XVIIIe* (Paris, 1952), pp. 69–72; see below, 216 and note 89.

[82] H. Touchard, *Le Commerce maritime breton à la fin du moyen âge* (Paris, 1967), 143–4, 150, 210–14.

[83] Verlinden, 'Deux aspects de l'expansion commerciale', 177–9; M. Mollat, *Le Commerce maritime normand à la fin du moyen âge* (Paris, 1952), 15–16, 43, 217–26; idem, *Comptabilité du port de Dieppe au XVe siècle* (Paris, 1951), 94, 97.

[84] For detail about many of the following points see Oliviera Marques, 'Feitoria portuguesa', 440–5, 453–60, 475–6.

England. The attraction of Bruges also lay in its supply of armaments for the Portuguese Crown, and metal goods for the colonies. Yet the scale of this Flemish trade in numbers of ships, numbers of merchants, and size of annual cargoes remains difficult to establish, and was perhaps often not much greater than that with England. Names drawn from a variety of sources by Oliviera Marques when working on the Portuguese factory in Bruges show a low presence (only in tens) in the 1430s when they were active in England. However, regular merchants were numbered in scores in the 1450s and 1460s, exactly at the time they faded from England.[85] Evidence for the number of ships is slight and late. In 1486–7 out of seventy-five arrivals in Sluis six were by Portuguese ships but thirty-three by Basques; in 1499 only one was Portuguese and in 1500 only four.[86] However by this time Portuguese activity was moving to Antwerp, and Sluis is no longer a good indicator of their Low Country activity. Nonetheless, six in 1486–7, a time when Bruges was trying to woo the Portuguese back, is not out of line with the small convoys of ships sheltering in English ports earlier in the century apparently on the Flanders voyage. Elsewhere, the Portuguese had an interest in Middelburg, where they were briefly offered privileges in 1390, and which they used in 1436 when Anglo-Burgundian troubles made Bruges impossible, but they did not move in in force until the sixteenth century.[87] The Portuguese made no attempt to move beyond Burgundian lands into the Baltic.[88] Although Bruges lost its importance, the Low Countries as a whole did not, and the 1498 sugar quotas reflect the perceived importance of markets. Of the 56,000 *arrobas* allocated for northern markets, Flanders was expected to take 40,000, England only 7000, Rouen with its access to Paris 6000, La Rochelle 2000, and Brittany 1000. Portugal itself was expected to take 7000, and 57,000 arrobas were to go to the Mediterranean.[89]

However, the Mediterranean was not drawing maritime energy away from the north. Portuguese goods other than sugar were less attractive there, and until the end of the period proven activity was low. Sources for Barcelona and Genoa show Portuguese trade there to be negligible.[90] Some reflection of increased western Mediterranean trade may be found in the imports of alum on Portuguese ships from the 1470s

[85] *Ibid.*, 458. See also J. Finot, *Etude historique sur les relations commerciales entre la Flandre et l'Espagne au moyen âge* (Paris, 1899), 141–6, 195–203, 209–12.
[86] *Ibid.*, 217–220, 232–3.
[87] Verlinden, 'Deux aspects de l'expansion commerciale', 202–09.
[88] Oliviera Marques, *Hanse e Portugal*, *passim*.
[89] V. Rau and J. de Macedo, *O Açúcar da Madeira nos fins do século XV. Problemas de Produção e Comércio* (Funchal, 1962), 14.
[90] C. Carrère, *Barcelone: centre économique à l'époque des difficultés, 1380–1462*, 2 vols. (Paris, 1967), 557–8; Heers, 'L'expansion maritime portugaise', *passim*.

mentioned above,[91] and a marked change appears in the last decade of the century, when a Genoese customs account shows ten Portuguese ships there in 1495.[92] This increase, however, coincided exactly with increased activity in England in the early 1490s and does not suggest that Mediterranean activity drained interest and energy from northern markets.

Where does this leave us in explaining why Portuguese activity, although frequent, was modest, despite good political relations and the temporary abeyance of Basque competition, and why Portuguese merchants did not settle in London? Each traditional explanation seems insufficient, but a combination of small resources and rival markets in the particular economic and political circumstances of the mid-fifteenth century is perhaps adequate.

Portugal *was* a small country, with a relatively small market and limited commercial and seafaring classes, despite the apparent encouragement to these with the change of dynasty in 1384. Its goods were not exclusive, and trade was likely therefore be modest, unless carrying services or colonisation extended it. The first did not happen on any scale; the latter was not in full flood before the end of the fifteenth century. Yet in the light of Portugal's very rapid expansion in the sixteenth century, the small advantage her seamen and merchants took of English opportunities still remains a little surprising. The trade was regular, provided work for hundreds of seamen, traders, and ship-builders, and was attractive enough to draw resident English merchants to Lisbon. The Portuguese role cannot be explained by small resources alone, but limited resources in men, capital, and ships, possibly meant Portugal could not easily service *two* major northern markets at once. It is highly suggestive that numbers of Portuguese merchants in England and Bruges rose and fell out of phase in the mid-fifteenth century.[93] Choices might have to be made if circumstances became difficult. Circumstances did become difficult in the general economic recession of the mid-fifteenth century. To this was added Anglo-Burgundian clashes and trade embargoes in 1436–9 and 1447–52. In the first, ports of Holland and Zeeland remained friendly to England and open, but the second was much more effective.[94] By then the Low Countries

[91] PRO, E122/194/20, 22, 24.

[92] Heers, 'L'expansion maritime portugaise'; *idem*, 'Le commerce des Basques en Méditerranée au XVe siècle (d'après les archives de Génes)', *Bulletin Hispanique*, LVII (1955).

[93] See above note 85.

[94] J. H. Munro, *Wool, Cloth, and Gold. The Struggle for Bullion in Anglo-Burgundian Trade 1340–1478* (Toronto, 1972), 115–17, 134–7.

offered better political conditions with the marriage of 1429, and the fall of the English party in Portugal in 1449. Choices had to be made and many chose the Low Countries. Similarly the failure of Portuguese seamen to increase their wealth by breaking into the Atlantic carrying trade in the fifteenth century, despite Portugal's apparently ideal situation between the Channel and the Mediterranean, was also due not just to inadequate resources, but to these in the face of well established Italian and Basque competition, strong enough to beat off newcomers in a period of economic difficulty. Italian shipping efficiency increased; Basque competition, strong from the fourteenth century onwards with Basques always ready to sail into any harbours under truce, increased its competitive edge in England with the Castilian customs privileges 1466–1489.[95] It was limited resources exacerbated by the European trade depression and the acute shortage of bullion and credit in mid-century which curtailed their activity. Problems of shipowning and of investing in international cargoes hit all nations as capital could be tied up for long periods with little return. It was particularly small merchants who could not bear such burdens, as the smaller English wool staplers found when confronted by similar cash flow problems under the Partition Ordinance in the 1430s. Portugal's dramatically unstable currency exacerbated problems. The extreme debasement of silver between 1384 and 1435, which accompanied political instability and wars, hit landlords more than merchants, but did not ease the path of commerce either.[96] England, on the other hand, as a whole did rather better. Her wool and cloth exports kept her international trade in balance. Bullion was not as short as elsewhere, and debasement was not a problem. If the Portuguese currency and balance of trade was not similarly good in mid-century, then English merchants would continue to have the edge over Portuguese merchants in investment capacity. It is not therefore surprising that the English maintained a higher profile in the trade than did the Portuguese throughout the period.

The conclusion in the end is not surprising, but has I hope provided a more precise picture of Anglo-Portuguese trade, and of the Portuguese activity in that. The trade was attractive, but fluctuated. It was no doubt helped by the treaty of Windsor, but this could not outweigh other political pressures and commercial factors. The Portuguese possibly had

[95] Childs, *Anglo-Castilian Trade*, 53–65.
[96] Reforms and revaluation were also uncomfortable for commercial classes; V. Magalhães-Godinho, *L'économie de l'empire portugais aux XVe et XVIe siècles*, Ecole Pratique des Hautes Etudes, VIe section, Centre de Recherches Historiques, Ports-Routes-Trafics, XXVI (Paris, 1969), 147–67. For comment on a similar relationship of bullion shortage and political problems, see A. MacKay, *Money, Prices and Politics in Fifteenth Century Castile* (1981), 40–1.

limited resources, but, probably more important, their interest in England waned in Bruges' favour. Embargoes on cloth supplies there might draw some back to England, but generally if a choice had to be made, the Low Countries would draw them from England. The English, and particularly the Bristol merchants, on the other hand, had sufficient resources and wide enough interests to make the Portuguese market a most fruitful one. The bulk of the trade therefore came to rest in their hands.

PROBLEMS OF COMPARING RURAL SOCIETIES IN EARLY MEDIEVAL WESTERN EUROPE

by Chris Wickham

READ 13 DECEMBER 1991

THERE is surprisingly little early medieval social history being written. In recent years, more specifically economic history has had a remarkable rebirth, thanks to the (largely unconnected) efforts of archaeologists on the one side and Belgian and German historians on the other[1]; but the study of society in general, outside the restricted spheres of the aristocracy and the church, has been neglected. I speak schematically; obviously, there are notable exceptions.[2] But it is significant that no-one, in any country, has thought it worthwhile to attempt a synthesis of early medieval European socio-economic history as a whole that could replace those of Alfons Dopsch or, maybe, André Déléage.[3] It would be hard; but people have tried it for the centuries after 900, with interesting (even if inevitably controversial) results.[4] Why not earlier? Richard Sullivan recently lamented the conservatism of most

---

[1] I thank Leslie Brubaker, Steven Bassett, Paul Fouracre and John Haldon for commenting on drafts of this article, and Wendy Davies, Timothy Reuter and Ian Wood for advice. The arguments owe much to a decade's discussions with the Bucknell group.

[2] Notes for this article will have to be almost arbitrarily selective. For the archaeologists, see e.g. R. Hodges, *Dark Age Economics* (1982); K. Randsborg, *The First Millennium A.D. in Europe and the Mediterranean* (Cambridge, 1991). For historians, see the detailed bibliographical survey by W. Rösener in *Strukturen der Grundherrschaft im frühen Mittelalter*, ed. *idem* (Göttingen, 1989), 9–28—the whole book is the most recent of several analyses of one major economic issue, the great estate in Francia. The French have been slower, with few exceptions, e.g. S. Lebecq, *Marchands et navigateurs frisons du haut moyen âge* (Lille, 1983); P. Toubert, 'Le part du grand domaine dans le décollage économique de l'Occident', *Flaran*, X (1988), 53–86.

[3] One exception is the history of early Byzantium, for which see e.g. E. Patlagean, *Pauvreté économique et pauvreté sociale à Byzance* (Paris, 1977); J. F. Haldon, *Byzantium in the Seventh Century* (Cambridge, 1991). Another is 'new cultural' history: e.g. P. R. L. Brown, *The Cult of the Saints* (1981); P. Fouracre, 'Merovingian History and Merovingian Hagiography', *Past and Present* cxxvii (1990), 3–38. Surveys: A. Dopsch, *The Economic and Social Foundations of European Civilisation* (1937); *idem*, *Die Wirtschaftsentwicklung der Karolingerzeit* (Cologne, 1962); and the unjustly neglected A. Déléage, *La vie économique et sociale de la Bourgogne dans le haut moyen âge* (Mâcon, 1941).

[4] E.g. R. Fossier, *Enfance de l'Europe* (Paris, 1982); S. Reynolds, *Kingdoms and Communities in Western Europe* (Oxford, 1984); H. Fichtenau, *Living in the Tenth Century* (Chicago, 1991).

Carolingian scholarship[5]; in the arena of social history, he could easily have extended his complaints back to 500.

Recently, I came sharply up against this problem when writing a summary chapter on Carolingian rural society for the *New Cambridge Medieval History*; to say anything about Europe as a whole, I virtually had to start from scratch. I ended up by comparing four very different small-scale societies taken from different parts of Carolingian Europe, the Catalan Pyrenees, the Breton march, the middle Rhineland above Mainz and the Lombard plain east of Milan, as micro-examples that could act as the basis for a (strictly partial) synthesis. But the format of the *CMH* does not exactly encourage musing about the methodological problems involved in constructing such a survey. Here, I want to reflect on some of these; and, in the second half of the paper, offer some proposals for how to construct models for at least part of the social history of the West between 500 and 900.

Much of the problem is historiographical: the research paradigms people have been governed by do not lead usefully to synthesis. One of these paradigms is national identity. (I will come on to a second, law, in a moment.) The period following the end of the western Roman empire has been analysed in different countries by national historiographies that have little or nothing to do with each other, and which cannot easily be brought into a comparative framework. Only at the end of our period, with the impact of the Carolingians in the ninth century, and, after 900, with the modern arguments about the concept of feudalism, have historians tended to recognise a common western European development that could usefully be discussed as a whole. Such discussions are often far from perfect, for they have privileged the charmed circle of the lands between the Rhine and the Loire, the rest of Europe being often dismissed as more or less marginal[6]; but, for the period between the Romans and the Carolingians, recent history-writing has lacked even this element of common ground.

When I say 'national identity', I do not mean it in the sense of outright national chauvinism, which has not been common in the field, at least in western Europe, since 1945. But each country in Europe continues to have its own characteristic historical preoccupations—the growth of the united nation in England, its failure in Germany, the vitality of city autonomies in Italy, the effect of the Arabs on the history of the Iberian peninsula, and so on—which have remained at the

---

[5] R. E. Sullivan, 'The Carolingian Age: Reflections on its Place in the History of the Middle Ages', *Speculum*, LXIV (1989), 267–306, at 297–304.

[6] The remit of 'classic feudalism' has recently been extended southwards, by *Structures féodales et féodalisme dans l'Occident méditerranéen* (Rome, 1980).

centre of national debates, and which the historians of each country as a result still regard as being of surpassing interest.[7] Many of these preoccupations have roots in the early middle ages, a period tailor-made for theorising on the basis of modern concerns, given its poor documentation, and given that the national communities of modern western Europe are nearly all seen as deriving, somehow, from the societies of the post-Roman world. Whole debates have sometimes appeared (and, often, disappeared again) in an individual country without historians elsewhere being even aware of them: *Königsfreie* theory in Germany, multiple estates in England, the Carolingian land tax in France are only some examples. The restriction of these theories to one country partially derives from the linguistic limitations of many historians; but it is also, I think, the result of their lack of resonance in other national communities: the theory that the Carolingians exacted the land tax, for example, might make little sense to someone who did not wish to see Frankish Gaul, i.e. France, as the principal heir in the West of the unchanging structures of the Roman empire.[8]

Another example of this sort of cultural solipsism is the issue of 'free peasants', that is to say (to use a less loaded phrase) direct cultivators who possess their own land with more or less full property rights. It used to be believed, on the basis of the law codes, that the Germanic tribes were composed of free peasants (*Gemeinfreie* in German), who settled on the land in the fifth and sixth centuries in egalitarian communities, without aristocracies; only later did aristocrats and land-lordship develop, with peasants commending themselves to lords for economic and military protection, and full-blown feudalism as the next step. The question of the truth underlying this model is a very complex one; I will come back to it later. But the fate of the model in different countries is another matter entirely. The West Germans abandoned it first, in the 1940s and '50s, as a result of a series of hostile responses to the easy Romantic ideal of original Germanic freedom; its replacement, *Königsfreie* theory, in its most extreme forms denied that peasant proprietors ever existed, and put in their place no-one except the noble and the unfree. These views have been more or less abandoned as well, as a result of a series of sharp critiques, particularly in the 1970s;[9]

[7] I have discussed this point elsewhere too, e.g. in J. W. Fentress and C. J. Wickham, *Social Memory* (Oxford, 1992), 127. The relationship of the whole issue to the current vogue for historiography and discourse theory should be obvious; I hope that literary analysis does not recede from the discipline before properly deconstructing early medievalists.

[8] The most recent statement of the theory, with bibliography, is J. Durliat, *Les finances publiques de Dioclétien aux Carolingiens* (Sigmaringen, 1990).

[9] E.g. H. K. Schulze, 'Rodungsfreiheit und Königsfreiheit', *Historische Zeitschrift*, CCXIX (1974), 529–50; J. Schmitt, *Untersuchungen zu den liberi homines der Karolingerzeit* (Frankfurt, 1977)—which includes a full bibliography of previous critiques (see esp. those of Müller-

but what has remained among a good number of historians is a considerable unease about recognising peasant owners anywhere. Unless peasant proprietorship can be clearly demonstrated (which is seldom), it is assumed that documents, even for small pieces of land, usually emanated from aristocrats.[10]

This argument has some plausibility; but its urgency derives only from fear, the fear that one will somehow fall back into Romanticism if one identifies free peasants too unwarily. This is not necessarily going to make much sense to people outside Germany, and indeed does not. The French and the Italians have for long happily assumed that aristocrats and independent peasants co-existed in the seventh and eighth centuries, and the issue is rarely discussed there at all (too little in fact). At the other extreme, Catalan and Castilian historians have remained, in large part, *Gemeinfreie* theorists, with an image of peasant freedom at its height in the ninth and tenth centuries and declining graphically thereafter. The date is later because it is the invasion of the Arabs, not of the Germanic Visigoths, which is seen as the great break in the Peninsula (the Visigoths are generally seen to have continued Roman social structures, with a strong aristocracy and lots of slaves).[11] It is not, indeed, at all unlikely, as we shall see, that peasants were fairly independent in Catalonia or Castile; but the theory is as closely associated with local images of history and nationhood as it is in Germany—in this case, largely the liberty of the Christian frontier, a very specifically Hispanic image, which has more resonance in the Americas than it has elsewhere in western Europe. In reality, one could argue that in, say, Catalonia and East Francia (central Germany), the documents themselves show societies not nearly as different as they appear in these national historiographies. There was a stronger aristocracy in the latter than in the former, and the two can be contrasted as a result, but they were not fully different in *kind*, and there were both aristocrats and peasant owners in each.[12]

One could go on: no country is immune. The German uneasiness about free peasants has often been matched in France by an uneasiness

---

Mertens and Tabacco); F. Staab, 'A Reconsideration of the Ancestry of Modern Political Liberty', *Viator*, XI (1980), 51–69.

[10] E.g. F. Staab, *Untersuchungen zur Gesellschaft am Mittelrhein in der Karolingerzeit* (Wiesbaden, 1975), 261–81; and even his critic, M. Gockel, in a review of *ibid*, in *Nassauische Annalen*, LXXXVII (1976), 309–15. The issue does not worry everyone; but recent German historiography on peasant owners remains hesitant.

[11] A bibliography of major theorists, such as Sánchez-Albornoz, Pastor, Bonnassie, can be found in the most recent survey, J. A. García de Cortázar, *La sociedad rural en la España medieval* (Madrid, 1988), 1–54. See below, nn. 28–9.

[12] See C. J. Wickham, 'Rural Society in Carolingian Europe', in *New Cambridge Medieval History* II, ed. R. McKitterick (Cambridge, forthcoming).

about any economic development in the Carolingian period that will somehow undermine the great leap forward of the 'grands défrichements' of the eleventh and twelfth centuries—a worry which the Germans, this time, are more detached about.[13] Italian history-writing on the seventh to eleventh centuries is riven by debates about whether enough people lived in cities, and whether they behaved in sufficiently 'civic' a way, to make Italian historical development qualitatively different from that everywhere else. (I should add, lest it be thought that I wish to present myself somehow as above these preoccupations, that this is a debate I have happily contributed to.)[14] Much English writing on the Anglo-Saxons, secure in the presumption that England was fundamentally different, at least before 1066, has not noticed the existence of any of these debates at all, whether they are relevant this side of the Channel or not; and the arguments of the 1960s about the precise impact of the Norman Conquest seemed so important for the general issue of national development that they were often conducted in tones little short of hysteria.[15]

Why does all this need saying? It is, after all, illusory to imagine that national historiographies will ever go away, so that, as Lord Acton said, the battle of Waterloo will be described in the same way whether by a British, a French, or a German historian;[16] nor would this be in any way desirable. But, again speaking broadly, these particular idées-fixe seem so prevalent in early medieval historiography, and so seldom recognised, at least in print. If we are to avoid talking past each other, the simple existence of such deep-rooted national preoccupations needs to be identified and discussed. We cannot talk them away; but we can, at least in part, correct for them.

Nearly all the theories I have so far referred to have at least one laudable aspect: they are conceived in opposition to the traditional,

[13] See e.g. the classic short synthesis of early medieval economic history, G. Duby, *The Early Growth of the European Economy* (1974), 104–11; and, further, R. Fossier, 'Les tendances de l'économie: stagnation ou croissance?', *Settimane di studio*, xxvii (1979), 261–90; *idem* in *Flaran*, X (1988), 182–4; contrast, e.g. *Untersuchungen zu Handel und Verkehr der vor- und frühgeschichtlichen Zeit in Mittel- und Nordeuropa*, III, IV, eds. K. Düwel *et al.* (Göttingen, 1985–7), and now, for the French, Toubert and Lebecq, as n. 2.

[14] See e.g. R. Bordone, 'Tema cittadino e "ritorno alla terra" nella storiografia comunale recente', *Quaderni storici*, LII (1983), 255–77; or the recent debate in *Archeologia medievale*, XIII (1986), 31–78; XIV (1987), 27–46; XV (1988), 105–24, 649–51. It should be noted that 'foreign' historians tend to adopt the conceptual framework of the country they write on, and, if they do not, they are often ignored.

[15] See, for pathological examples, H. G. Richardson and G. O. Sayles, *The Governance of Medieval England* (Edinburgh, 1963), 22–41; R. A. Brown, 'The Norman Conquest', *Supra*, ser. 5, XVII (1967), 109–30. More recently, things have partially improved.

[16] Quoted in E. H. Carr, *What is History?* (1964), 9.

long dominant, paradigm for understanding early medieval society, that of legal history. Legal history is, one must recognise, a paradigm that makes comparison relatively straightforward, at least inside the Germanic kingdoms, for their law codes and capitularies can easily be related to each other; most of the clearest 'international' analyses of early medieval society are essentially based on them, such as Brunner's *Rechtsgeschichte*, or Ganshof's pieces for the Société Jean Bodin, or Njeussychin's Engelsian analyses of the end of peasant freedom, or even much of Dopsch.[17] The trouble here is that the picture of society that one can derive from such laws is based on a false premise: that a simple reading of a law code can give in any sense an accurate or representative picture of real social behaviour, as if early medieval codes, with their dozens or at most hundreds of provisions, could be meaningfully compared to the legislation of the modern world, and as if (mostly) illiterate judges and law-finders, far from royal palaces and assemblies, could be assumed to be bound by the same respect for written procedures as that supposedly found in the Crown Courts.[18] Actually, of course, even modern social rules (let alone what people really do) cannot be reduced to those enshrined in written law; in the early middle ages, such belief is nonsense. Law codes are not valueless, by any means, as we shall see when we come back to the issue of peasant society. They are, however, simply normative texts, like sermons or chronicles, and were written for specific, interested, reasons; they should be analysed as such.

Most people know this by now. But the knowledge has not had much effect on the way people compare societies; indeed, a good deal of more locally focussed history-writing still depends heavily on the law codes as well. To a large extent, this is inescapable: before the appearance of documents in relatively large numbers in parts of Europe in the later eighth and ninth centuries, law codes are almost our only source for many major issues in social history, such as stratification or family structure, and they remain our principal source for what we would now call crime for a good deal longer. In the seventh century, say, we are therefore in large part restricted to studying social theory

[17] H. Brunner, *Deutsche Rechtsgeschichte* (Leipzig-Munich, 1906–28); F. L. Ganshof, e.g. 'Le statut de la femme dans la monarchie franque', *Recueils de la Société Jean Bodin*, XII (1962), 5–58; A. I. Njeussychin, *Die Entstehung der abhängigen Bauernschaft* (Berlin, 1961); for Dopsch, see above, n. 3.
[18] See *The Settlement of Disputes in Early Medieval Europe*, eds. W. Davies and P. Fouracre (Cambridge, 1986). By the ninth century, some judges were literate and knew the codes reasonably well, as R. McKitterick, *The Carolingians and the Written Word* (Cambridge, 1989) has strongly argued for Francia; indeed, the capitularies sometimes had immediate administrative consequences—see J. L. Nelson, 'Literacy in Carolingian Government', in *The Uses of Literacy in Early Mediaeval Europe*, ed. R. McKitterick (Cambridge, 1990), 258–96; but the point remains.

rather than practice, at least in these fields (although archaeology can tell us something about stratification, and, increasingly, even about families).[19] In the ninth, however, in some of Europe we do have documents, which tell us more directly about practice; and when substantial numbers of charters survive for a single area, their authors, local owners both rich and poor, can be seen relatively clearly in at least part of their daily lives, as they sell land to each other, give to local churches, lease to tenants, or go to court to make claims against opponents.[20] These charters allow wider sorts of questions to be asked than can be asked of law: about what sorts of people give land to the church in a given society, and what sorts of people do not; how support tends to be built up when people go to law, and whether they seek victory or compromise; what are the relationships between the possession of land and the construction of political power and social status; what is the difference between female and male access to the public arena; and so on. We are thus able, when we are lucky, to dispense with the misleadingly simple norms of the codes—or (better) to analyse the contrasts and convergences of theory and practice, so as to enhance our understanding of both; and the best local social history does precisely that.[21] But, even for the ninth century, these local histories cannot yet be added up to a Europe-wide whole; when comparison begins, the codes and capitularies are still dominant.

The reason for this, I think, is that the issue of *how* to compare has not been satisfactorily faced outside the legal history paradigm. Rules are indeed easier to compare than practices. As a result, even social history that is not exclusively based on an analysis of legislation often does much the same sort of thing: it reconstructs rules (whether to supplement, or to 'correct', the codes), often from isolated examples of practices, rather as classical sculptures used to be reconstructed from fragments of noses and knees. What is wrong with this is again a basic presupposition: that there was, across any given society, Wessex or Alemannia or whatever, a set of fixed rules, which everyone normally followed. It cannot have been like that. The early middle ages were far too localised, locally varying, inconsistent, conflict-ridden, weak in their political systems, for such a set of fixed rules to be usefully adduced anywhere. We have to abandon the legal history paradigm, and do it quite consciously. Instead, we have to confront the harder task of

---

[19] See, for surveys with bibliography, E. James, 'Burial and Status in the Early Medieval West,' *Supra*, ser. 5, XXXIX (1989), 23–40; H. Steuer, 'Archaeology and History: Proposals on the Social Structure of the Merovingian Kingdom', in *The Birth of Europe*, ed. K. Randsborg (Rome, 1989), 100–22.

[20] See further Wickham, 'Rural Society'.

[21] E.g. W. Davies, *Small Worlds* (1988); Staab, *Untersuchungen*; G. Rossetti, *Società e istituzioni nel contado lombardo durante il medioevo: Cologno Monzese*, i (Milan, 1968).

comparing, not rules, but the sets of local practices that constituted whole societies. The experts in comparison of this kind are sociologists and (for our purposes, above all) social anthropologists; they have generated the categories most useful for comparing whole societies, and have made the comparisons most explicitly. We must construct a rural sociology, in the widest sense, for ourselves.[22] In fact, historians already use sociological categories, often without realising it; words like 'aristocracy' and 'peasantry', not to speak of 'feudalism', are not real phenomena, unproblematically present in our evidence, but our own abstractions from the data. (Is a *nobilis* an 'aristocrat', or a *servus* a 'peasant' rather than a 'slave'? When, and why?) Many are, in fact, ideal types in the Weberian sense: abstractions that are not even supposed to be simple descriptions of a really-existing society somewhere, but that are set out simply as points of reference for the comparison of such societies—Marc Bloch's famous characterisation of feudalism in *Feudal Society* was one such, and is still one of the best.[23] We need to recognise that we are using such categories, and, in the light of this recognition, make them more consistent, more useful for our own analyses. This does not have to be impossibly difficult, although it does require us to be more systematic as historians than we often are.

None of these points are particularly new as a series of exhortations; it may be more useful to show how they can work in practice. To do so, I will take two socio-political examples, from northern Italy and Catalonia. In the areas of Europe ruled by the Carolingians, the local organisation of society varied greatly from place to place. In northern Italy, for example, we find a complex network of landowning, with greater and lesser estate-owners (who formed an as yet ill-defined 'aristocratic' stratum), larger and smaller ecclesiastical establishments, and rich and poor peasant owners, all owning side by side—often, thanks to a high level of fragmentation of property, all in the same village. Inside the village, smaller owners cultivated lands intermingled with those cultivated by free and unfree tenants, and a wide stratum of peasants who owned some land parcels, leased others from landlords, and maybe rented others yet out to their neighbours.[24] This intricate structure, itself varying in detail from place to place, underpinned a

---

[22] See, for a stimulating framework, the historical models in W. G. Runciman, *A Treatise on Social Theory*, II (Cambridge, 1989).

[23] M. Bloch, *Feudal Society* (Cambridge, 1961), esp. 443–7.

[24] E.g. Rossetti, *Società e istituzioni*, 42–140; V. Fumagalli, *Terra e società nell'Italia padana* (Turin, 1976); R. Balzaretti, 'The Lands of Saint Ambrose' (Ph.D thesis, University of London, 1989); C.J. Wickham, *The Mountains and the City* (Oxford, 1988), 40–67.

public world of considerable coherence. Counts, public officials based in the cities, ran the army and pronounced judgement in court; bishops, often their rivals, had their own legal powers and acted as the focus for a provincial politics that united diocesan landowners round the city (where a good proportion of larger owners themselves lived).[25]

How stable was this system? The political coherence of Italy would suffer considerable strain in the tenth and eleventh centuries, when the kings were weak or absentee, legal tribunals became more ritualised and more often disregarded, and counts and bishops slowly came to seek (indeed, seize) private political powers for themselves focussed on castles and, after 1000, private justice. These are standard European developments, in fact; and one must add that counts were already exceeding their powers, the poor were expropriated, justice was denied, and private influence outweighed public responsibility under Charlemagne as well. One might see, as a result, a constant decline in public power from 800 at the latest to a nadir in the eleventh century, and many people have indeed argued this. The first point that can be made in reply is that these developments did not lead in Italy to the unmediated triumph of the aristocracy, as for example in much of France.[26] In particular, for all the pressure of the powerful on the poor, the intricate structure of private landowning persisted in Italy, without any substantial change in kind, for centuries. Aristocrats and churches did not manage, or maybe even try, to root out the independent peasantry; it may have been enough to have them as in some sense their clients, and eventually subject some of them to private justice, without absorbing their land. Eleventh-century charter collections for the most part show the same complexity of landowning as do those of the eighth. The continuance of this network must have been one of the reasons for the greater survival of the public world in Italy than in France, too: law-courts did at least continue to exist in most cities right up to the development of a new urban communal politics in the twelfth century; seigneurial lordship, too, however widespread in Italy, was in most places relatively restricted by the standards of France or Germany.[27] Civil society, that is to say, whether in the country or the city, remained too complex for private relationships, however much they grew in importance, adequately to encompass it.

[25] The basic survey is G. Tabacco, *The Struggle for Power in Medieval Italy* (Cambridge, 1990), 116–36; a good local study is H. M. Schwarzmaier, *Lucca und das Reich bis zum Ende des 11. Jahrhunderts* (Tübingen, 1972).

[26] Tabacco, *Struggle for Power*, 151–208; cf. H. Fichtenau, *The Carolingian Empire* (Oxford, 1963), 104–55; and, for France, J.-P. Poly and E. Bournazel, *La mutation féodale* (Paris, 1980).

[27] E.g. Wickham, *Mountains*, 238–344; J.-P. Delumeau, 'L'exercice de la justice dans le comté d'Arezzo', *Mélanges de l'Ecole Française de Rome. Moyen âge*, XC (1978), 563–605.

This much is generally agreed, and I would not wish to argue with it. But it is also often assumed that the oppressions of great landowners in Italy, already in the ninth century, at least show that the public world as a whole was in some sense under threat. Here a comparison with Catalonia may point us in other directions. What is now called Catalonia was in the ninth century certainly dissimilar to northern Italy. It was, for a start, as already noted, a region of unusually independent peasantries. It was a frontier, in part conquered by Charlemagne from the Arabs; indeed, its southern half remained under Arab hegemony, leaving the Carolingians with little more than the Pyrenees and the coastal valleys between Barcelona and Perpignan. The peasantry were, as a result, highly militarised, and this helped their independence. This latter should not be overstressed; there were certainly aristocrats as well, notably the comital families, who not only effectively controlled local royal land, but were themselves (unusually in lands conquered by the Carolingians) of local origin, thus indicating that they had their own family lands in the area as well. The counts had their own entourages of militarised notables, too, as elsewhere in Europe. And, perhaps separate from this group (but not necessarily), there was, at least in the Pyrenees, an important category of village notables, *milites* or priests, who led their poorer neighbours around 800 in their collective activities, such as church-building: villages were coherent and confident enough as communities to build their own churches, but their leaders characteristically gave the largest gifts, and often became the priests of the new churches. Nonetheless, really large lay owners are relatively rare in texts before 950, except for the counts themselves. And the public world that Catalonia shared with the rest of the Carolingian lands was as coherent as that in Italy, probably as a result of the local survival of well-structured Visigothic institutions. The judicial system was particularly highly organised; and ruling counts gave considerable political space to the village communities, apparently considering them valuable as defences not only against the Arabs, but also, increasingly, against a slowly coalescing aristocracy.[28] It was not until the 1030s that the aristocracy sought power directly, over local areas, for themselves. When they did, on the other hand, a generation of civil wars ensued, which left public institutions in ruins and crystallised private seigneurial power over a now largely dependent peasantry. When in the twelfth century the count of Barcelona re-established a

[28] P. Bonnassie, *La Catalogne du milieu du Xe à la fin du XIe siècle* (Toulouse, 1975–6), esp. 215–42; *idem, From Slavery to Feudalism in South-Western Europe* (Cambridge, 1991), 243–54; J.-M. Salrach, *El procés de feudalització* (Barcelona, 1987), 153–252, with bibliography; R. Martí, 'Els inicis de l'organització feudal de la producció al bisbat de Girona' (doctoral thesis, Barcelona, 1987); for the judicial system, R.J.H. Collins, '*Sicut lex Gothorum continet*', *English Historical Review*, c (1985), 489–512.

hegemony over the aristocracy, its basis was private lordship, not public power.[29]

Catalonia's move away from a political structure of a Carolingian type was sudden and violent; much more sudden than that in the Po plain, and much more complete. Why? It is evident that the social groups that came together in the eleventh century as the aristocracy had already been accumulating power at the expense of the peasantry across the tenth; by 1100, as Bonnassie has argued, peasants would have largely lost their lands and been reduced to being tenants.[30] This would undoubtedly have led anyway to the sort of involution of the public that the Italians partially avoided. But the violence of the shift throws into relief a different point: the unusual feature of Catalonia was not that the strata of the aristocracy dominated political life in 1100, but that they did not in 850. The political practices of the ninth century in the Catalan counties privileged the direct link between public officials and the whole of free society which legal theory favoured, a link which in the particular military situation of the Arab frontier made some sense, but which in heartlands of Carolingian political authority such as northern Italy was decidedly unreal. In reality, in Italy the aristocracy already controlled the political system of the ninth century, in part illegally perhaps, but in an established manner. Although that system could still yield more power to them, and would do so, it was not in their interests to destroy it entirely. It was the relative exclusion of aristocratic privilege from the political structures of Catalonia, despite its increasing force on the ground, that led to their overthrow. Institutionalised corruption and oppression in Italy led, by contrast, to relative stability for the institutions concerned.

This sort of pattern of comparison seems to me useful, and capable of being extended more or less indefinitely; whole societies, alike in certain respects but unlike in others, can be set against each other, to see how both similarities and differences originate and develop, and how they can be explained—as well as, and not least important, how they should not be explained. Stepping back from these two case studies, however, allows another point to be made. I took my examples from Carolingian Europe, and indeed, Carolingian southern Europe, because in these areas one can be sufficiently sure that there was enough common ground for the comparisons to be meaningful. Both Catalonia and Italy had systems of fragmented land tenure, which means that land transactions, the normal focus of charter evidence, can give a denser picture of local society than in those parts of northern

---

[29] Bonnassie, *Catalogne*, 539–733; *La formació i expansió del feudalisme català*, ed. J. Portella (Girona, 1985–6).
[30] Bonnassie, *Catalogne*, 816–17.

Europe where the only evidence for a given village is a single text in which a king gives it to a church. Furthermore, both these regions had a concept of property that was, for the most part at least, governed by the presuppositions of 'Vulgar' Roman law, as enunciated for us by Ernst Levy in the 1950s.[31] The charter form itself derives from the Roman world, and presupposes the same law; in southern Europe one can assume that charters mostly meant what they said. One cannot make the same assumption in, say, England, where early land grants by kings are supposed by many scholars from Maitland onwards (and correctly, in my view) to denote not the transfer of ownership in a Roman sense, but rather the granting of certain royal rights over land to third parties, usually churches—even though the charters themselves are couched in strictly Roman legal terms, and mostly talk only about transferring property. What these rights were, when they changed into more 'orthodox' concepts of property, and what the real régime of land tenure was in England in 700 or so (let alone earlier) remains obscure, and hotly argued over, not least because Anglo-Saxon evidence also makes clear that charters ('books') in themselves changed the legal status of land tenure, and land without charter was, somehow, organised differently.[32]

I will come back to this daunting example of Heisenberg's Uncertainty Principle shortly, for the fact that the problem exists is in itself significant, whether it can be easily resolved or not. But it is introduced here as an illustration of the limits of easy comparison. Charters are texts, just as hagiography or legislation is; the structures of their discourse have to be unpicked too, even for such a mundane enterprise as being sure one is comparing like with like. Societies in early medieval western Europe were not at all similar in their basic structures, in fact; and I would argue that Italy, for example, was genuinely different from England in crucial ways. If we are to understand European social development as a whole, we need to develop a more generalised understanding of the differences, as well as the similarities, in its basic patterns. The second half of this paper will be spent sketching out one of these: how we distinguish, and how we should analyse, those parts of early medieval Europe which do not seem to have been dominated by aristocracies.

If one reads the early Germanic law codes as if they were objective

---

[31] E. Levy, *West Roman Vulgar Law. The Law of Property* (Philadelphia, 1951). For exceptions to the hegemony of Roman law, e.g. C.J. Wickham, 'European Forests in the Early Middle Ages', *Settimane di studio*, XXXVII (1990), 479–548, at 483–99.

[32] F. W. Maitland, *Domesday Book and Beyond* (1960 edition), 272–90, 374–97; see further below, nn. 37–9.

accounts of early medieval social behaviour, then one can see how easy it was for historians to come up with the model of 'primitive Germanic' society, with no lords or major landowners: i.e. no-one but kings and *Gemeinfreie*, 'common freemen'. The free man (and, to a considerably lesser extent, woman) is there right through the sixth-century *Pactus legis Salicae*, as in the seventh-century codes of Ine in Wessex or Rothari in Italy; aristocrats, by contrast, are rarely mentioned, except for specially-privileged king's dependents, and the occasional allusion to higher-status groups with higher wergilds, the 'twelve-hundred' men of West Saxon law or the privileged *genealogiae* of Bavarian law.[33] When, however, more recent historians pointed out that there was scarcely any other type of source in, for example, Francia that did not mention powerful lords with their own armed followings and their own extensive landed properties, cultivated by both free and servile dependents, who could certainly be thought of as aristocrats, legal-historical logic meant that the law-codes themselves presented a problem. The free men in them were reinterpreted as aristocrats themselves, or else as a special category of the free under royal protection: *Königsfreie*, in other words. This is not good enough. The *Pactus* tells us about theory, not practice; but its theory is revealing. It spends a great deal of time discussing agricultural offences, the theft of pigs and cattle, or vegetables and flax, or the cutting down of trees, that are not obviously in the field of interest of aristocrats. As a set of norms, it presupposes a peasant society. And while one can show, easily, that this imagined society had rich and poor among its free inhabitants, and a large under-class of slaves, the point of reference is nonetheless that of 'a small face-to-face community', as Ian Wood has called it, in which norms dealing with direct cultivation were of immediate relevance to people.[34] Whoever the early sixth-century compilers of the *Pactus* were, this is what they thought significant to elaborate on; their social theory did not need to encompass, and rarely even took note of, the society of large landowners readily visible in the *Histories* of Gregory of Tours or the will of Bertram of Le Mans or the Formulae, or the sharp hierarchies of wealth (and the logically consequent networks of dependence) that are transparent in any major Merovingian-period cemetery. Why this was so we cannot consider here; but the laws would be senseless even just as idealisations if their peasant world was entirely invented.

---

[33] *Pactus legis Salicae*, ed. K.A. Eckhardt (Hanover, 1962); Ine, cap. 19, 70, Alfred, cap. 10 (in *Die Gesetze der Angelsachsen*, I, ed. F. Liebermann, Halle, 1903); *Lex Baiwariorum*, cap. 31, ed. E. von Schwind (Hanover, 1926).

[34] For *Königsfreie*, see above, n. 9. For aristocrats, the best recent survey is H. Grahn-Hoek, *Die fränkische Oberschicht im 6. Jahrhundert* (Sigmaringen, 1976), with bibliography. For the quote, I. N. Wood, 'Disputes in late fifth- and sixth-century Gaul', in Davies and Fouracre, *Disputes*, 7–22, at 11.

With this in mind, we can look for the traces of this 'peasant-based' society in the early medieval sources that tell us most about practice, charter collections. On the borders of the Frankish world, we have already seen it in Catalonia; it has also been analysed in, among other places, Brittany, Burgundy, and the Auvergne.[35] And even in the Frankish heartland, Carolingian-period documents show it, or at least its shadow. In the villages of the middle Rhineland, which are visible thanks to the thousands of gifts of land to the great East Frankish monasteries of Lorsch and Fulda between 750 and 840, it is admittedly true that most donors about whom we can say anything at all were demonstrably large landowners. Their lands were substantially divided up, however, as in Italy; gifts of single fields were commoner than cessions of blocks of land with servile dependents. Mixed in with these fragmented estates, there were smaller properties; their owners gave relatively few gifts to the monasteries, but consistently occur as groups in village witness-lists—consistently enough in some cases for their periods of public activity to be traced with some precision.[36] Rhenish village societies often seem to have been made up of three levels: at the top, great owners, usually absentee, involved in the political patronage networks of the monasteries; at the bottom, their servile dependents; and, between these two extremes, a cohesive group of locally-living free families, whether poor or rich (i.e. whether direct cultivators or 'medium landowners' with their own dependent cultivators), with a public role for their menfolk. These latter in practice dominated the village itself, insofar as it acted as a community. Sometimes, indeed, they probably had a fairly autonomous role, where the society of great lords was distant, or relatively unconnected to them. Here, inside the interstices of aristocratic society, the agrarian world described three centuries earlier in the *Pactus legis Salicae* may have kept a certain resonance for people. To this limited extent, one must recognise a certain move of the pendulum back to a version of the *Gemeinfreie* model.

I would guess that variants of this tripartite picture fit most of the Carolingian world, from the considerably autonomous communities of Catalonia across to the peasantries of Italy, which were often by now more fully incorporated into aristocratic hierarchies. The dialogue between theory and practice that is at its base may also help to put into perspective the situation in Middle Saxon England. Ine's code, like the *Pactus*, focuses on a world of free cultivators. This, however, contrasts sharply with seventh- to ninth-century English documents,

---

[35] Davies, *Small Worlds*; G. Bois, *La mutation de l'an mil* (Paris, 1989), 63–114; C. Lauranson-Rosaz, *L'Auvergne et ses marges* (Le Puy, 1987), 397–404.

[36] Wickham, 'Rural Society'; cf. Staab, *Untersuchungen*, 262–78.

which show kings giving village-sized blocks of land to churches with what are referred to as *manentes* and *cassati,* normal Latin terms for dependent tenancies, on them. In well-documented counties like Hampshire and Worcestershire, these blocks of land adjoin other blocks with considerable regularity, so much so that recent historians with a topographical bent have been able, with the help of Domesday Book and late medieval parish boundaries, to construct networks of interlocking territories extending over virtually the whole of southern England. If these territories were 'estates' in a Roman law sense, then Ine and his contemporaries as kings in England were landowners on a scale undreamt of by William the Conqueror, and everyone else except a few aristocrats and, increasingly, churchmen, must have been their tenants; the *Gemeinfreie* community would dissolve into a world of dependent cultivators, simply taken over (in the opinion of the most extreme adherents of this model) from Romano-British estates.[37]

There are a number of problems with such a model; but, once again, one of the main ones is that it makes no sense of Ine's code. If the only people of significance in society were lords, it simply would not be necessary to assume in one's law code, however ideal a picture it painted, that the 'common freeman' (*ceorl* in Anglo-Saxon) was heavily engaged in agriculture. The problem cannot be got around by recognising that legally free cultivators could also be tenants, however true this undoubtedly is, for the size of these territories implies that all, or nearly all, *ceorls* would have to have been tenants. (Compare the public law of England in the late twelfth and early thirteenth century, when free peasants were certainly mostly tenants: it focuses on disputes about feudal tenure and élite military obligation. The more mundane agricultural issues could be safely left to manorial courts.) The presuppositions of Ine's code imply more independence for *ceorls* than that; one must conclude, I think, not that (some or all) *ceorls* were really *manentes,* i.e. dependent tenants in a Roman law sense, but that (some or all) *manentes* were really *ceorls,* the relatively autonomous peasants of the codes. As already observed, Maitland thought this; and, however little we can say about the detail of the dependence of such people on kings—for they evidently at least lived on land which kings could somehow grant to others—I have not seen anyone successfully refute him.[38]

These English arguments thus replicate those for Francia, even if, as usual, the warring historiographical traditions that each of them

[37] See e.g. *The Agrarian History of England and Wales,* I. 2. ed. H. P. R. Finberg (Cambridge, 1972), 430–66; *English Medieval Settlement,* ed. P. H. Sawyer (1979), 1–34; and below, n. 39.

[38] I have benefited from discussion here with Steven Bassett, Nicholas Brooks, Chris Dyer, Ros Faith, Dawn Hadley, Andrew Wareham and Patrick Wormald.

builds on seem to have developed, at least in their more recent versions, in near total ignorance of each other. But there are differences too, which need to be brought out. In particular, it seems that the two societies were fundamentally distinct in their very concept of land tenure: the Frankish world, or most of it, had taken on a version of Roman law, whereas the Anglo-Saxons had not, or not yet in (say) 700. In Francia, peasant owners coexisted not only with the dependent tenants who are documented in detail in land transactions and, later, polyptychs, but also with the developed hierarchies based on these tenants, which gave great wealth to aristocrats and churchmen. But in England, the very regularity of documented land units argues against at least free tenants being dependent in the same way. In the end they would become so, as territories turned into estates. Some had already in 700 (there are, for that matter, some even in Ine); by 900 perhaps most had (there is a famous Hampshire document for Hurstbourne Priors which clearly shows *ceorls* as tenants, from roughly that date).[39] But others must have long had a relationship to their lord, often the king, which was rather looser. There may well have been rather less hierarchy, and certainly a less structured hierarchy, in pre-tenth-century England than in the Carolingian world, even in areas of the latter (such as Catalonia) where peasant owners were numerous.

These are only samples of the arguments that need to develop around the issue of how to find early medieval independent peasants. Further work would, for example, have to look again at how they originated, in both Germanic and non-Germanic areas, in the confusion of the fifth and sixth centuries, or earlier still; at how their status and ties of dependence changed over time, from the Merovingians to the Carolingians or from eighth- to eleventh-century England; and at how aristocracies themselves originated, and how they can at each stage be defined. In England, work is at last being done on the evolution of Anglo-Saxon systems of dependence and the related changes in the structures of political power, although, typically, only the latter have as yet surfaced in print.[40] Here, I will restrict myself to a rather more generalised problem: that of how a 'peasant-based' socio-economic system can actually be conceived of as working; for if we do not have any ideas about that, we really do risk slipping back into Romanticism.

A major stumbling-block to understanding how peasant societies worked in early medieval Europe has been the concept of 'Germanic society',

---

[39] T. H. Aston, 'The Origins of the Manor in England', *Supra*, ser. 5, VIII (1958), 59–83; H. P. R. Finberg, *Lucerna* (1964), 131–43. For non-Roman law in Francia, see above, n. 31.

[40] *The Origins of Anglo-Saxon Kingdoms*, ed. S. R. Bassett (Leicester, 1989).

with its Tacitean aura of freedom. For a start, societies defined by a preponderance of peasants, who control their own lands more or less autonomously and with relatively loose hierarchies of dependence, were not restricted to the Germanic world; they could be found in the Celtic and Slavonic linguistic areas, and in parts of Romance Europe where few Germans ever came. But one can go further: they can be found throughout the modern globe, in long-lasting and stable patterns, as social anthropologists and sociologists have extensively shown, and, in the past, they have been studied at length by prehistorians too. In these contexts, they are often called 'primitive communal' or 'kin-based' or 'tribal' societies, none of them very happy terms. More recently, the concept of 'rank society' has been developed, and this seems to me more satisfactory, and more useful for our period: while recognising that independent peasant societies do not by any means have to be egalitarian, it separates them from societies with fully formed antagonistic classes, or indeed states.[41] This sort of counterposition is a more constructive one than those implied by a focus on communal ownership, or the kin-group, or the tribe (whatever this is), and it underpins my mental framework in what follows.

It must be recognised just from the foregoing comments that the issue of how such societies worked is by no means undiscussed; it is just that it has not been considered much by early medieval historians. My intention is simply to bring those discussions more firmly into the early middle ages. I do not, however, wish here to get into the general arguments that the use of one or another of these concepts tends to entail, whether about private property or the family, or about the origins of the state or those of class society; it is for this reason that I have adopted the deliberately anodyne term, the 'peasant-based' social system. For my purposes in this paper, this latter term should be counterposed not to 'class' or 'state' society in the abstract, but to a more specific socio-economic system, the other major system of the early and central middle ages in the West, that based on aristocratic dominance. This system, which I am still content to call by the much-abused word 'feudal', cannot be described in detail here, and anyway its basic outlines are reasonably well known: they include the exclusive nature of rights to land, the unmediated control by landholders over the tenant cultivators of that land, and a monopoly or near-monopoly

---

[41] See e.g. M. Mann, *The Sources of Social Power*, I (Cambridge, 1986), 34–70, esp. for the stability of rank societies, with a bibliography; Runciman, *Social Theory*, II. 78–9, 148–52, 185–90, esp. for distinctions between them; but the list of theorists is huge. (It would, at a minimum, include Marx, Godelier, Sahlins—see below, n. 47—and Eric Wolf.)

by aristocrats and their military dependents over legitimate violence.[42] (Some of the contrasts between the two systems will be discussed below, in the context of Brittany.) But how the 'peasant-based' socio-economic system could work needs more description before we go further; for this, I will use Iceland in the tenth and eleventh centuries as an example. It must be stressed that Iceland has been chosen not for its German-ness; I could equally well have used New Guinea or Burma, but these would have required too much incidental explanation. Iceland is nearer to our field of study, both in space and time, and indeed its medieval material is unusually rich for our purposes, given that the daily lives of peasant owners for most of the medieval West are often fairly elusive in our written documentation. The sources I will mainly use here are the thirteenth-century 'sagas of Icelanders', which are, beyond doubt, in some sense fiction; but recent scholars have argued that the world they represent has its own internal coherence, and a plausibility for at least a thirteenth-century audience. They can stand as broad, normative, characterisations of *an* Icelandic reality, which indeed they describe very densely indeed; and, seen in this way, the social analyses they contain have a clear validity.[43]

Icelanders, as is well known, did not have kings; but they did not have aristocrats either, in any sense that such a term normally has. Icelandic society was not egalitarian; it had rich and poor members, influential and marginal ones, as well as a substantial slave population. It had institutionalised leadership too, in the form of forty-odd hereditary *goðar*, 'chieftains' or 'priests' (for they had religious roles too); each *goði* had a following of male householders (*bœndr*), whom he led in the public courts that were Iceland's sole institutional structure. But these followings were not permanent; men could transfer from one *goði* to another in the spring of any year, and indeed did so if their relationship with their chieftain was not satisfactory. Furthermore, the lack of necessity to take any dispute, even over violent death, to court in the first place, considerably lessened the capacity any *goði* might have to turn his representative role into real and lasting—still less heritable—authority. A successful, and thus powerful, *goði*, such as Snorri 'the Priest' Thorgrímsson of Helgafell or Guðmundr 'the Power-

---

[42] See C. J. Wickham, 'The Other Transition', *Past and Present* CIII (1984), 3–36 for a slightly fuller discussion, with the Marxist framework more explicit; and W. Kula, *An Economic Theory of the Feudal System* (1976). For the third early medieval system, that based on state tax-raising, see the models in J. F. Haldon, *State Theory, State Autonomy, and the Pre-Modern State* (1992), which includes discussion of previous analyses; H. Berktay is preparing a book on the same theme.

[43] For methodology, e.g. J. L. Byock, 'Saga Form, Oral Prehistory, and the Icelandic Social Context', *New Literary History*, XVI (1984–5), 153–73; T. M. Andersson and W. I. Miller, *Law and Literature in Medieval Iceland* (Stanford, 1989).

ful' Eyjólfsson of Möðruvellir in the early eleventh century, had to be an effective patron to his following: he had to win cases for them, negotiate a successful end to feuds with as little violence as possible, and, not least, be generous to them. Feud and gift-exchange each have the same structure, as has often been pointed out, that of the obligation to return a gift: a helping hand for a helping hand, an eye for an eye, a Christmas present for a Christmas present. The most successful in Iceland were the people who best negotiated this mine-field of obligation, whether by cunning (as with the saga image of Snorri) or by toughness (as with the saga image of Guðmundr). Such people—who did not have to be goðar, though they usually were—themselves got gifts from grateful bændr, and became very prosperous; but the need to return gifts as well kept all of them from accumulating wealth to the levels normal for élites elsewhere in Europe.[44]

How did one negotiate status in Iceland? One way was certainly by display, with wall hangings and fine jewellery, or with carved wood on the high seat in one's hall (which might even describe one's own deeds, as with Thorkell 'Hake' in Njal's saga). More common, however, was lavish hospitality, as with the feast that Óláfr 'the Peacock' gave for 1080 people to commemorate his father Höskuldr Dala-Kollsson, which fixed his reputation, despite his bastard origin. One also, of course, built up status through successful dispute settlement; this was expensive too, however, for one did so by establishing alliances of political obligation with other influential Icelanders, and these cost gifts as well. The richer a man was, the more he was expected to be generous, and the more people expected to spend the winter eating his stores, although, conversely, the more people he could count on to support his activities. Nonetheless, his status always had to be negotiated for; there was not a point after which someone was so powerful that he could count on his dependents staying with him without question. Guðmundr the Powerful's bændr felt themselves exploited at one point by their obligation to feed too many of his following when he came by, so a group of them turned up one Easter and ate him out of house and home; he had to accept them.[45] The ungenerous, the authoritarian, or the inept

[44] See the survey by J. L. Byock, Medieval Iceland (Berkeley, 1988), with bibliography; for slavery, R. M. Karras, Slavery and Society in Medieval Scandinavia (New Haven, 1988), esp. 80–3. A. Ja. Gurevič, Le origini del feudalismo (Bari, 1982) is one of the very few historians to discuss Iceland in a European context. For gifts, see W. I. Miller, 'Gift, Sale, Payment, Raid', Speculum, lxi (1986), 18–50. For the theory of the gift, the classics are M. Mauss, The Gift (1954); P. Bourdieu, The Logic of Practice (1990), 98–111.

[45] Víga Glúms saga, cap. 1; Brennu Njáls saga, cap. 119; Luxdæla saga, caps. 2/, 46, Ljósvetninga saga, caps. 6, 7—on which see Andersson and Miller, Law and Literature, 51–5 (note that this story of Guðmundr had a very clear moral edge—ibid., 100—and, doubtless, thirteenth-century resonance). The sagas are ed. in the Íslenzk Fornrit series (Reykjavik), respectively vols. IX (1956), XII (1954), V (1934), X (1940).

simply lost support and thus status. And, although the office of *goði* was heritable, as were land and networks of kinship and friendship, personality was not; the game of negotiation had to start again at each generation.

This remarkable social structure seems to have been in part deliberately constructed by the Icelanders themselves; leaders had certainly been more stable, and thus more powerful, in their country of origin, Norway. The Icelanders somehow prevented early settlers, for example, from exploiting their monopoly of land and thus turning later settlers into their tenants and permanent clients; as a result, when the country filled up, it did so with free householders with relatively weak ties of dependence. It may be that the conscious desire to keep political leaders weak has parallels elsewhere in Europe; both the continental Saxons before the Frankish conquest, as described in the *vita Lebuini*, and the late tenth-century Slav confederation of the Liutizi seem to have developed structures that kept individuals from accumulating too much power, for example.[46] All three cases were, significantly, on the edge of political systems rapidly increasing in coercive power or expansionist intent. But what is most important is that the system remained stable in Iceland (as, indeed, also in the rank societies of the rest of the world); even when leaders became more powerful in the thirteenth century, thanks largely to their exploitation of a new political structure, the church, they still had to negotiate for their power, and this remained expensive. Snorri and Guðmundr, and their thirteenth-century successors, for all their national influence, remained at the economic level of rich peasants or small notables elsewhere in Europe; few of them were rich enough not to have to work on their lands, at least some of the time.

Goðar were, in fact, what anthropologists who work on New Guinea call 'big men': leaders who must personally construct their power over others, and whose ability to accumulate wealth is constrained by the necessity to provide what their followers expect from them, to prevent them from transferring their allegiance to someone else.[47] They illustrate one essential tenet of comparative sociology: the less hierarchy, and the less stable and inherited authority, there is in a society, the more people

---

[46] *Vita Lebuini antiqua*, ed. A. Hofmeister in *M. G. H., Scriptores*, XXX, 2 (Leipzig, 1934), 793; for context, see e.g. M. Lintzel, *Ausgewählte Schriften*, I (Berlin, 1961), 115–27, 286–92; H. Löwe, 'Entstehungszeit und Quellenwert der Vita Lebuini', *Deutsches Archiv*, XXI (1965), 345–70; S. Epperlein, *Herrschaft und Volk im karolingischen Imperium* (Berlin, 1969). For the Liutizi, *Thietmari Merseburgensis episcopi chronicon*, ed. R. Holzmann (Berlin, 1955), vi. 25; W. H. Fritze, 'Beobachtungen zu Entstehung und Wesen des Lutizenverbundes', *Jahrbuch für die Geschichte Mittel- und Ostdeutschlands*, VII (1958), 1–38. I am grateful to Timothy Reuter for help with these references.

[47] M. Sahlins, 'Poor Man, Rich Man, Big-Man, Chief', *Comparative Studies in Society and History*, V (1962–3), 285–303; see further *idem*, *Stone Age Economics* (1974), 130–48.

one has to win with generosity, food or charisma in order to gain political support, and the longer one has to go on doing it. This has, one must add, an implication for material culture, too; a society with this degree of devolution of resources lacks anyone with the buying power to make the development of a wide range of artisanal traditions worthwhile. In general, a sophisticated material culture depends on a rich state system, or a stratum of super-rich, as in the Roman empire or the Caliphate; a society of peasants and quasi-peasants, exchanging feasts, will not have looked particularly impressive in the archaeological record (except, sometimes, in their funeral rituals), however well they ate. Iceland was, of course, intrinsically poor; its only valuables derived from occasional Viking raiding expeditions. But no society with this sort of social system would have looked much more archaeologically sophisticated, whatever its ecological niche.

How far can we generalise from this example? Certainly, nowhere else in early medieval Europe was precisely like Iceland. But it at least gives us an idea of what to look for. In general, if we want to understand social relationships in a settled agricultural economy, we must look at the characteristic ways in which people could obtain control over land and its wealth, and turn it into effective influence over others and lasting social status. To discuss this fully, we would have to look at several linked issues: the problem of the development of exclusive rights of landownership; the varying strength and permanence of ties of dependence; the role of gifts and display in establishing obligation and achieving status; the extent to which status and authority could be inherited, as opposed to acquired or negotiated for. And, as a guide, we should remember the point made in the previous paragraph: the less hierarchical one's society is, the more people one has to hand over gifts to in return for support. (No fully 'feudal' aristocrat ever had to spend much of his resources in gifts to his dependent peasants, for example; for him, the gift-exchange relationship, in land or movables, and the patterns of negotiation I have outlined for Iceland, were restricted to his military entourage and to his aristocratic equals.)

We cannot look at all these issues, but some general points can be made about our societies that spring directly from them. First, some comments on the economic system of Middle Saxon England, particularly in the period 600 to 750. England had kings, unlike Iceland, although there were many of them and their kingdoms were small by Continental standards; it had a stable aristocracy, in the sense that it had hereditary local leaders with military attributes and loyal followers. But who exactly these followers were, or how permanent their ties of dependence, is not so easy to say. There are signs in our sources that kings could not rely on their retainers' loyalty for life; notwithstanding a literary rhetoric that could invoke their fighting to the death for lords, armed men moved around, and were persuaded to stay only by gifts.[48] How far this continual network of gift-exchange extended to the whole of free society, i.e. to peasant cultivators, is undocumented, but the small scale of Middle Saxon political systems (up to Offa's time, at least) is unlikely to have helped the development of the sort of élite social separation that one sees in the aristocratic groups described, say, in Gregory of Tours. And I have already postulated on other grounds that the hierarchies of free society are likely to have been less clearly structured in England than on the Continent. Lords gave rings and feasts to their retainers; the feasts, at least, may have had to be given to quite a range of people, part-time fighters with a continuing involvement in cultivation. If this was so, then the Icelandic model begins to be relevant, and, not least, its apparent material poverty: the more one needs to give one's surplus away in gifts, the less one can accumulate it, use it to buy wide ranges of commodities, and thus maintain a complex artisanal network.

I do not, therefore, think it is chance that Middle Saxon England had few manufactured goods that compared in sophistication with those of the more 'aristocratic' Frankish heartland. This is above all true for pottery, the most typical archaeological indicator of bulk exchange. Merovingian pottery-making had, after the collapse of the inter-regional ceramics industries of the Roman world, continued to exist on a provincial level, with a network of wheel-thrown pottery types that have been identified all the way across the Rhine-Loire region, Mayen or Badorf or Saran or La Saulsotte.[49] Indeed, such provincial networks are increasingly being found in Mediterranean Europe as well, on the Spanish coast or in southern Italy.[50] They define smallish economic regions, that were probably the maximum areas that local exchange intensive enough to support a pottery industry could cover in Merovingian conditions; beyond their boundaries, only luxury or prestige items would normally be exchanged. They represent, on an economic level, the sort of nondescript but persistent continuity that Merovingian

---

[48] See, for a stimulating survey of the major texts (Ine, *Beowulf*, The *Finnsberg Fragment*, the *Anglo-Saxon Chronicle* entry for 757, etc.), R. P. Abels, *Lordship and Military Obligation in Anglo-Saxon England* (1988), 11–42; our interpretative frameworks differ. Compare the impermanence of Irish dependence set out in *Críth Gablach*, ed. D. A. Binchy (Dublin, 1970), which must have had similar results.

[49] See e.g. R. Hodges, *The Hamwih Pottery* (London, 1981), 61–94; *Excavations at Dorestad*, I, eds. W. A. van Es and W. J. H. Verwers (Amersfoort, 1980), 56–160.

[50] See, for surveys, H. Kirchner, 'La cerámica', in M. Barceló et al., *Arqueología medieval* (Barcelona, 1988), 88–133; S. Gutierrez Lloret, *Cerámica común paleoandalusí del sur de Alicante* (Alicante, 1988); P. Arthur and D. Whitehouse, 'La ceramica dell'Italia meridionale', *Archeologia medievale*, IX (1982), 39–46.

or Visigothic written evidence documents for political history, and their size is analogous to that of the diocese- or county-size blocks that Frankish or Gothic political society broke down to when 'national' kingship was weak. In England, however, these sorts of ceramic types were absent before the late ninth century, with the single exception of Ipswich ware, a slow-wheel pottery type mostly restricted in distribution to East Anglia.[51] Indeed, apart from luxury metalwork and tapestry, the prestige items Anglo-Saxon kings had at their disposal, even when they began to accumulate wealth and power from the mid-eighth century onwards, were Continental, funnelled into royal residences from coastal *emporia* like Hamwih and London and Ipswich. This weakness in English material culture, even by Merovingian standards, I would associate with the economic logic of the 'peasant-based' social system. What English kings and aristocrats got from their dependents in 700 or so (and they got a good deal; they were far richer than Icelandic *goðar*), they largely had to hand out again, to gain support and power; the systematic demand necessary for artisanal development suffered as a result.[52]

On the Continent, things were more complicated, and, as we have seen, varied from place to place. We might guess that the necessity for negotiation and gift-giving was greater for local élites among the relatively independent peasants of Catalonia than inside the clearer hierarchies of the Rhineland and, especially, Italy. How peasant autonomies actually may have worked in Continental Europe is, however, best documented in Brittany, where a perhaps atypical social system had some clear analogies to that in Iceland.

In ninth-century Brittany, as evidenced in the charters for the monastery of Redon, we can identify a stratum of local notables called machtierns, who presided over the public activities of villages (*plebes*), in particular their courts of law. Machtierns were 'aristocrats', in the sense that they were substantial landowners with civil responsibilities; but they had little direct control over villagers (*plebenses*), and the latter in practice ran most of the business of courts—machtierns, unlike Frankish counts, were not even fully responsible for the coercion that followed from court decisions. *Plebenses* were largely landowning peasant cultivators; as in Iceland, all of them had an autonomous public role, and the charters show them frequently exercising it. Machtierns,

---

[51] J. G. Hurst, 'The Pottery', in *Archaeology of Anglo-Saxon England*, ed. D. M. Wilson (Cambridge, 1976), 283–348, at 299–303; for recent bibliography, H. Hamerow, 'Settlement Mobility and the "Middle Saxon Shift" ', *Anglo-Saxon England* XX (1991), 1–17, at 13–14. Outside East Anglia, its distribution is, significantly, restricted to high-status sites.

[52] Compare the comments in R. Hodges, *The Anglo-Saxon Achievement* (1989), e.g. 186–96, which, despite disagreements, seems to me the most interesting current synthesis along these lines.

although local leaders, did not in institutional terms dominate them; any machtiern who wanted to get his poorer neighbours to do as he said would have had to negotiate, *goði*-style. In fact, Brittany had 'national' rulers too in this period, usually called *principes* in our sources, who fought Franks and Vikings; they had entourages of aristocrats who were also landowners with dependent tenants, and whose powers were not only military but civil—they increasingly gained control, in some sense, of fiscal and judicial dues from *plebes*. The local dominance of these people was much more analogous to that of the aristocracy in nearby Francia, by whom they were certainly influenced. But, with few exceptions, they had strikingly little direct relationship to the families of machtierns. Brittany in fact shows, more clearly perhaps than anywhere else, the way that the two systems, 'peasant-based' and 'feudal', could be found together in the same territory. Military aristocrats dominated *plebes* from the outside and above, presumably through force of arms (actual or implied); machtierns from the inside, through participation and negotiation, and probably gift-giving.[53] In the tenth century, the Redon charters dry up, but it is not hard to guess that once a Frankish-style aristocracy was rooted in Brittany, machtierns would have either become subjected to them or thrown their lot in with them; in the eleventh century, 'feudal' dominance in Brittany would be much the same as elsewhere in western France. Nevertheless, the shaft of light thrown by the charters shows up how the two systems could, at least for a time, coexist. We do not have to worry about putting whole societies into the 'peasant' or 'feudal' socio-economic system as exclusive categories; elements of both of them could be found in many places, and there is a continuum between them too. The Breton example, at least in more mediated forms, those with more systematic linkage between local (*goði*-like) and national ('feudal'/aristocratic) élites, may be one we could generalise more widely. Catalonia is an obvious instance; but how far, and until when, even Frankish aristocrats had to negotiate with peasants is a question worth asking too. At the very least, it would focus historians on the problem of how aristocratic hegemony over local areas actually worked, which is not an issue that anyone studies enough.

What, then, was the economic logic of these 'peasant' systems? It was not one that privileged the accumulation of surplus, thanks to the networks of negotiation we have looked at. 'Peasant' systems were not egalitarian, it must be repeated, even in theory, for free peasants throughout Europe (including Iceland) could and did regularly have slaves; but this exploitation, however coercive, was kept within the

---

[53] Davies, *Small Worlds*, esp. 63–104, 134–87; J. M. H. Smith, *Province and Empire* (Cambridge, 1992), 116–46.

household, and generally integrated into the social networks of family units—even exploitation, then, did not lead to accumulation. Such systems were not, however, necessarily societies in which most people were poor by their own standards. Peasants in this environment did not have to pay tax to a state or rent to a landlord; they may well have owed tribute to some superior authority, like the *feorm* claimed by King Ine, but this must have been a lesser burden, and peasants might expect some of it back in redistributed gifts. They were, then, in some sense better off than under the Roman empire or in a 'feudal' socio-economic system. Nonetheless, they had access to a far less materially developed economic environment. As already argued, the complex commercial networks of Antiquity or the central middle ages depended on goods exchanged among landowners, that is to say on a surplus *extracted* from the peasantry. The aristocracy as a stratum was perhaps poorer, and certainly smaller, in our period than either before or after, and this has its correlate at a macro-economic level in the overall archaeological unimpressiveness of the early medieval West, Franks included; independent peasants had more surplus to buy things, in principle, but in the absence of exchange networks there was less to buy. The whole concept of economic development must be different in a society like this. I have elsewhere noted, following Ester Boserup, that peasants had two alternatives, to eat more or to work less, and I suspect they did both. But they did so in the context of a social structure which anyway privileged local consumption, by families and villages, and local systems of exchange in return for social obligations. These patterns constituted the economic logic of the system taken as a whole. This network of material and social constraints is often taken as the demonstration of the economic decadence of the early middle ages; I would prefer to see it as *functional* to a world of peasants subsisting in relative independence, and not in any way as a condemnation of their means of existence.[54]

If these analyses are acceptable, they will, I hope, be a guide to how one can identify, and compare, 'peasant' social structures inside the wide range of social systems that can be found in early medieval Europe. To conclude, let us look briefly at the context in which they ended. 'Peasant-based' systems can be stable, but they are physically vulnerable if they are set too close to aristocratic power. In Francia and its neighbours, there were always secular and ecclesiastical aristo-crats, and of course kings, who held wide lands and kept armed entourages; these were, simply, stronger than independent peasantries. Across time, both in circumstances of weak kingship and aristocratic

---

[54] C.J. Wickham, 'Mutations et révolutions aux environs de l'an mil', *Médiévales*, XXI (1991), 27–38; see further Sahlins, *Stone Age Economics*, 1–99.

expansion (like late seventh-century Francia), and in times of assertive, predatory kingship and the affirmation of its aristocratic supporters (as under Charlemagne, or maybe Edward the Elder), 'peasant-based' societies weakened in the face of military violence. The revival of commerce in Francia around 800 is a sign of it; surplus was beginning to be concentrated in fewer hands again. From 800 at the latest in Francia, and maybe 900 in England, the logic of the economy as a whole turned aristocratic, and would remain so for nearly a millennium. The 'feudal' economy was based on rents, on the marketing of produce, and on conspicuous consumption on a huge scale by aristocrats and kings; these would dominate Europe henceforth without alternatives. Peasants could still be landowners, as often in Italy for example, but they would henceforth remain under the hegemony of an aristocratic political system with a monopoly over military force; they would survive not as autonomous groups, but as clients of the powerful. Historians can breathe again; comprehensible political systems, and, soon, castles, great cathedrals, and mercantile expansion, mark the end of the interpretative inconveniences of the early middle ages.

THE ROYAL HISTORICAL SOCIETY
REPORT OF COUNCIL, SESSION 1991-1992

THE Council of the Royal Historical Society has the honour to present the following report to the Anniversary Meeting.

Council has continued to take a close interest in the new arrangements for the preservation of national and local archives. The Local Government Commission will consider arrangements for the custody of local archives when it tours the English counties, but no such scrutiny has yet been arranged for Wales. The major national archive, the Public Record Office, became an Executive Agency in April 1992. Council hopes that the new status of the PRO will enhance, rather than diminish, its provision of scholarly services to historians. The President and Honorary Secretary joined a delegation from HUDG which met the Keeper and senior staff of the PRO at Chancery Lane on 12 June, 1992. The Keeper reassured them on several points concerning the inspection of public documents and the employment of staff with historical training. A forthcoming survey of users may result in better services for scholars. It was agreed to hold similar meetings in future to discuss matters of mutual interest.

During the early part of 1992, Council gave much thought to the proposals outlined by the Joint British Academy-CVCP Working Party on Postgraduate Research in the Humanities. After widespread consultation, the President wrote a formal response to the report, urging a more flexible approach to training in regard to both the provision of courses and the time allowed for the completion of Ph.D.s. He also pointed out that there would be a serious shortage of trained historians to teach in universities in ten years' time. Some of these points, though not all, have been taken into consideration in the Final Report of the British Academy-CVCP Working Group.

Council has continued to provide financial support for historical research at a time when many scholars find it difficult to obtain funds. The Society's 'Research Support Initiatives' provide various kinds of awards ranging from an annual Research Fellowship at the Institute of Historical Research to training, conference and travel bursaries. Council wishes to increase the provision of smaller grants (especially for part-time students) and is endeavouring to publicise its awards more widely. The Society also continues to fund the Young Historian scheme of the Historical Association and to provide prizes for outstanding A-level students. Some larger awards were also made for collaborative projects. Council approved a grant of £3,000 to help fund an English version of 'Kleio', a German software system specifically developed for historians.

Following the Society's decision to meet regularly outside London, two Council meetings and paper readings were held at Durham University and Newnham College, Cambridge. They were well attended and were followed by receptions which enabled Council to meet many local members. The success of these meetings owed much to the hospitality provided by resident members of the Society. The Society has arranged to meet at Birmingham and Cardiff during the 1992-93 session. Any offers of hospitality for future sessions would be gratefully received.

Another innovation has been the introduction of occasional 'open' Council meetings, when routine business is reduced to a minimum, to allow Councillors more time for general discussion. The first of such meetings was held in February 1992 to discuss Postgraduate Training for Historians in the context of the report by the British Academy-CVCP Working Group. It provided a useful opportunity for historians from many different institutions to discuss current and future practice and problems. Another 'open' meeting will be held at Liverpool, in September 1992, to discuss the future function and organization of the Society. It thus seems probable that there will be more changes to report at the end of the 1992-93 session.

Council was delighted to note that Professor F.M.L. Thompson, President, was awarded the C.B.E. in the New Year Honours.

An evening party was held for members and guests in the Upper Hall at University College London on Wednesday, 3 July 1991. 179 acceptances to invitations were received, and it was well-attended.

The Whitfield Prize for 1991 was awarded to Dr. Tessa Watt for her book *Cheap Print and Popular Piety, 1550-1640*, (Cambridge University Press). The assessors also declared Ian Archer *proxime accesit* for his book *The Pursuit of Stability: Social Relations in Elizabethan London* (Cambridge University Press).

The representation of the Society upon various bodies was as follows: Mr. M. Roper, Professor P.H. Sawyer and Mr. C.P. Wormald on the Joint Committee of the Society and the British Academy established to prepare an edition of Anglo-Saxon charters; Professor H.R. Loyn on a committee to promote the publication of photographic records of the more significant collections of British Coins; Professor P.E. Lasko on the Advisory Council of the reviewing committee on the Export of Works of Art; Professor G.H. Martin on the Council of the British Records Association; Mr. M.R.D. Foot on the Committee to advise the publishers of *The Annual Register*; Dr. E. James on the Trust for

Lincolnshire Archaeology; Dr. R.C. Mettam on the History at the Universities Defence Group; Professor W. Doyle on the Court at the University of Exeter; Professor A.G. Watson on the Anthony Panizzi Foundation; Professor M.C. Cross on the Council of the British Association for Local History; Dr. A.M.S. Prochaska on the National Council on Archives; Professor W.A. Speck on the Advisory Board of the Computers in Teaching Initiative Centre for History; Professor Glanmor Williams on the Court of Governors of the University College of Swansea; Professor A.L. Brown on the University of Stirling Conference; and Professor W. Davies on the Court at the University of Birmingham. Council received reports from its representatives.

Professor E.B. Fryde represents the Society on a committee to regulate British co-operation in the preparation of a new repertory of medieval sources to replace Potthast's *Bibliotheca Historica Medii Aevi*; Professor C.N.L. Brooke on the British Sub-Commission of the Commission International d'Histoire Ecclésiastique Comparée; and Miss V. Cromwell and Professor N. Hampson on the British National Committee of the International Historical Congress. During the year, Professor J. Sayers agreed to succeed Dr. A.M.S. Prochaska on the National Council on Archives; Miss V. Cromwell agreed to succeed Professor W.A. Speck on the Advisory Board of the Computers in Teaching Initiative Centre for History; Professor C.J. Holdsworth agreed to succeed Professor W. Doyle on the Court at the University of Exeter.

At the Anniversary Meeting on 22 November 1991, Dr. P.M. Thane was elected to succeed Professor M.J. Daunton as Honorary Treasurer and Mr. D.A.L. Morgan was elected to succeed Professor A.G. Watson as Honorary Librarian. The remaining Officers of the Society were re-elected. Professor R.R. Davies was elected to succeed Professor F.M.L. Thompson as President after the Anniversary Meeting on 20 November 1992.

The Vice-Presidents retiring under By-law XVII were Miss V. Cromwell and Professor P.J. Marshall. Professor O. Anderson and Professor H.T. Dickinson were elected to replace them. The members of Council retiring under By-law XX were Professor W. Doyle, Professor R.A. Griffiths and Dr. G.R. Sutherland. Following a ballot of Fellows, Dr. J.M. Black, Professor P.A. Clark, Professor D.M. Palliser and Dr. A.M.S. Prochaska were elected in their place.

Messrs. Davies Watson were appointed auditors for the year 1991-92 under By-law XXXIX.

Publications and Papers read

Transactions, Sixth Series, Volume 2, *Charges to the Grand Jury* ed. G. Lamoine, (Camden, Fourth Series, Volume 43) and *Miscellany XXXI*,

(Camden, Fourth Series, Volume 44), went to press during the session and are due to be published in 1992.

The following 2 volumes in the STUDIES IN HISTORY series were published during the session: *Gunpowder, Government and War in the mid-Eighteenth Century,* Jenny West, (Volume 63) and *The Victorian Post Office - The Growth of a Bureaucracy,* C.R. Perry, (Volume 64).

The *Annual Bibliography of British and Irish History, Publications of 1990,* was published by Oxford University Press.

A paperback edition of *The Clarke Papers, I and II,* ed. C.H. Firth, with a new preface by A. Woolrych, went to press during the session.

At the ordinary meetings of the Society the following papers were read:

'The War of the Scots, 1306-1328' by Professor A.A.M. Duncan (3 July 1991: Prothero lecture).

'England and Portugal in the Fifteenth Century' by Dr. Wendy Childs (11 October 1991).

'Approaches to the study of rural society in early medieval Europe' by Dr. Christopher Wickham (13 December 1991).

'"Between the sea power and the land power": Scandinavia and the coming of the First World War' by Dr. Patrick Salmon (24 January 1992).

'Confession before 1215' by Mr. Alexander Murray (28 February 1992).

'"Les Engleys nées en Irelande": The English Political Identity in Mediaeval Ireland' by Dr. Robin Frame (1 May 1992).

At the Anniversary Meeting on 22 November 1991, the President, Professor F.M.L. Thompson, delivered an address on 'English Landed Society in the Twentieth Century: III, Self Help and Outdoor Relief'.

A one day conference entitled 'Multiple Kingdoms and Provinces' was held in the British Local History Room at the Institute of Historical Research on 21 September 1991 at which the following papers were read:

'The Venetian mainland state in the fifteenth century' by Dr. John Law;

'The Creation of Britain: Multiple Kingdoms or Core and Colonies?' by Dr. Jenny Wormald; and

'Community, State and Composite Monarchy in Early Modern Europe' by Professor John Elliott.

The Alexander Prize for 1992 was awarded to Dr. Giles A. Worsley for his essay *The Origins of the Gothic Revival: A Reappraisal,* which was read to the Society on 29 May 1992.

Membership

Council records with regret the deaths of 27 Fellows and 2 Associates. They included Professor C.H. Wilson, an Honorary Vice-President, and Fellows, Miss I. Scouloudi, Mr. G.B.A.M. Finlayson and Professor K. Leyser, a former member of Council.

The resignations of 6 Fellows, 2 Associates and 9 Subscribing Libraries were received. Mr. E.L.C. Mullins was forced to resign due to ill-health. 106 Fellows and 8 Associates were elected and 1 Library was admitted. 33 Fellows transferred to the category of Retired Fellow. The membership of the Society on 30 June 1992 comprised 1907 Fellows (including 45 Life Fellows and 294 Retired Fellows), 40 Corresponding Fellows, 145 Associates and 668 Subscribing Libraries (1853, 40, 146 and 678 respectively on 30 June 1991). The Society exchanged publications with 14 Societies, British and foreign.

Finance

The Society's income increased in 1991-92 over 1990-91 by £3,093. The surplus this year has fallen to £3,168. The finances of the Society provide no cause for immediate concern, but in view of the above, the Council is considering a rise in the subscription rate from July 1994. Our financial position can also be improved if we do the utmost to increase the number of Fellows.

Council records with gratitude the benefactors of the Royal Historical Society:

Mr. L.C. Alexander
The Reverend David Berry
Professor Andrew Browning
Professor C.D. Chandaman
Professor G. Donaldson
Mrs. W.M. Frampton
Sir George Prothero
Professor T.F. Reddaway
Miss E.M. Robinson
Professor A.S. Whitfield

THE ROYAL HISTORICAL SOCIETY

BALANCE SHEET AS AT 30TH JUNE 1992

	Note	1992 £	1992 £	1991 £	1991 £
FIXED ASSETS					
Tangible assets	2		3,181		764
Investments	3		892,838		818,140
			896,019		818,904
CURRENT ASSETS					
Stocks	1(c)	812		6,350	
Debtors	4	15,779		14,306	
Cash at bank and in hand	5	27,013		41,265	
		43,604		61,921	
CREDITORS: Amounts falling due within one year	6	68,676		70,739	
NET CURRENT (LIABILITIES)/ASSETS			(25,072)		(8,818)
NET TOTAL ASSETS			870,947		810,086
REPRESENTED BY:					
General Fund			826,296		764,540
Miss E.M. Robinson Bequest			23,321		22,968
A.S. Whitfield Prize Fund			16,153		15,353
Studies in History			5,177		7,225
			870,947		810,086

THE ROYAL HISTORICAL SOCIETY

Income and Expenditure Account for the Year Ended 30th June 1992

GENERAL FUND

	Note	1992 £	1992 £	1991 £	1991 £
INCOME					
Subscriptions	7		58,796		60,790
Investment Income			83,612		78,068
Royalties and reproduction fees			5,696		8,195
Donations and sundry income			3,874		1,832
			151,978		148,885
EXPENDITURE					
SECRETARIAL AND ADMINISTRATIVE					
Salaries, pensions and national insurance		21,373		19,062	
Printing and stationery		4,534		4,629	
Postage and telephone		1,559		1,261	
Bank charges		1,998		1,507	
Audit and accountancy		3,114		2,632	
Insurance		475		447	
Meetings and travel		7,852		5,931	
Repairs and renewals		656		703	
Depreciation	1(b)	1,131		1,345	
(Profit)/loss on disposal of fixed tangible assets		(570)		—	
			42,122		37,517
PUBLICATIONS					
Literary director's expenses		—		94	
Publishing costs	8(a)	34,274		37,504	
Provision for publications in progress	8(b)	50,600		49,000	
Other publication costs	8(c)	(384)		2,287	
Sales of publications		(205)		(176)	
			84,285		88,709
			126,407		126,226
LIBRARY AND ARCHIVES	1(d)				
Purchase of books and publications		110		—	
Binding		1,143		1,414	
			1,253		1,414
			127,660		127,640
OTHER CHARGES					
Centenary fellowship		5,498		4,863	
Alexander prize		418		297	
Prothero lecture		350		260	
Grants		3,000		1,885	
Research support grants		4,155		—	
Donations and sundry expenses		2,016		1,150	
A-level prizes		720		500	
Young Historian Scheme		1,993		1,000	
British Bibliography		3,000		3,000	
			21,150		12,955
			148,810		140,595
Surplus/(Deficit) for the year			3,168		8,290
Surplus on sale of Investments			58,588		75,579
			61,756		83,869
Balance brought forward at 1.7.91			764,540		680,671
Balance carried forward at 30.6.92			826,296		764,540

THE ROYAL HISTORICAL SOCIETY

Income and Expenditure Account for the Year Ended 30th June 1992

SPECIAL FUNDS

	1992 £	£	1991 £
MISS E.M. ROBINSON BEQUEST			
INCOME			
Investment income		2,376	1,2
EXPENDITURE			
Grant to Dulwich Picture Gallery . . .	2,000		2,000
Other expenses	23		—
		(2,023)	(2,
Surplus/(Deficit) for the year		353	
Balance carried forward at 1.7.91		22,968	23,6
Balance carried forward at 30.6.92 . . .		23,321	22,9

	1992		1991
A.S. WHITFIELD PRIZE FUND			
INCOME			
Investment income		1,809	1
EXPENDITURE			
Prize awarded	1,000		1,000
		(1,000)	(1,
Surplus/(Deficit) for the year		809	(
(Deficit)/Surplus on disposal of investments .		(9)	1,9
		800	2,
Balance brought forward at 1.7.91 . . .		15,353	13,
Balance carried forward at 30.6.92 . . .		16,153	15,

	1992		1991
STUDIES IN HISTORY			
INCOME			
Royalties		1,498	1,
Investment income		886	1,2
		2,384	2.6
EXPENDITURE			
Honorarium	3,500		3,500
Editor's expenses	909		789
Ex gratia royalties and sundry expenses . .	18		—
Bank charges	5		12
		(4,432)	(4,
Surplus/(Deficit) for the year		(2,048)	(1,
Balance brought forward		7,225	8,6
Balance carried forward		5,177	7,

Accounting Policies

(a) *Basis of accounting*

These accounts have been prepared under the historical cost convention.

(b) *Depreciation*

Depreciation is calculated by reference to the cost of fixed assets using a straight line basis at rates considered appropriate having regartd to the expected lives of the fixed assets. The annual rates of depreciation in use are:

Furniture and equipment	10%
Computer equipment	25%

Prior to 1st July 1987 the full cost of fixed assets was written off to General Fund in the year of purchase.

(c) *Stocks*

Stock is valued at the lower of cost and net realisable value.

(d) *Library and archives*

The cost of additions to the library and archives is written off in the year of purchase.

Tangible Fixed Assets

	Computer Equipment	Furniture and Equipment	Total
	£	£	£
Cost			
At 1st July 1991	5,133	620	5,753
Additions during year	3,548	—	3,548
At 30th June 1992	8,681	620	9,301
Depreciation:			
At 1st July 1991	4,741	248	4,989
Charge for the year	1,069	62	1,131
At 30th June 1992	5,810	310	6,120
Net book value			
At 30th June 1992	2,871	310	3,181
At 30th June 1991	392	372	764

The cost of additions to the library and archives is written off in the year of purchase. Prior to 1st July 1987 the cost of furniture and equipment was written off in the year of purchase. Items acquired before that date are not reflected in the above figures.

	1992 £	1991 £
Investments		
Quoted securities at cost	826,421	699,255
(market value £1,339,434) (1991 £1,389,494)		
Investments, money at call	66,417	118,885
	892,838	818,140
Debtors		
Sundry debtors	12,724	11,348
Prepayments	3,055	2,958
	15,779	14,306
Cash at bank and in hand		
Deposit accounts	25,043	38,015
Current accounts	1,970	3,201
Cash in hand	—	49
	27,013	41,265

6. CREDITORS
Sundry creditors 1,350
Subscriptions received in advance 13,250
Accruals 3,476
Provision for publications in progress 50,600

68,676

7. SUBSCRIPTIONS
Current subscriptions 55,422
Subscription arrears received 1,465
Income tax on covenants 1,909

58,796

8. PUBLICATIONS
(a) Publishing costs for the year
Guides and Handbooks No. 16 . . . . —
Guides and Handbooks No. 17 18,895
Handbook of Dates . . . . —
Transactions, fifth series Vol. 40 . . . . —
Camden, fourth series Vol. 40 . . . . —
Index to Authors . . . . —
Reresby 2,882
List of Fellows 4,809
Camden, fourth series Vol. 41 19,962
Camden, fourth series Vol. 42 6,745
Transactions, sixth series Vol. 1 15,870
Clarke Papers 5,315
Indirect costs, paper storage and usage and insurance 6,823
Printing costs for circulation to members 1,973

83,274
Less: Provision b/fwd . . . . (49,000)

34,274

(b) Provision for publication in progress
Guides and Handbooks No. 17 . . . . —
Reresby . . . . —
Transactions, sixth series Vol. 1 . . . . —
Camden, fourth series Vol. 41 . . . . —
List of Fellows . . . . —
Transactions, sixth series Vol. 2 16,700
Camden, fourth series Vol. 43 16,950
Camden, fourth series Vol. 44 16,950

50,600

(c) Other publication costs
Annual Bibliography 3,089
Less: royalties received . . . . (3,473)

(384)

F. M. L. THOMPSON, President
P. M. THANE, Treasurer

We have audited the accounts on pages 252 to 256 in accordance with Auditing Standards.
In our opinion the accounts give a true and fair view of the Society's affairs at 30th June 1992 and of its sur
for the year then ended.

118 SOUTH STREET, DORKING   DAVIES, WATSON &
18th September, 1992   Chartered Accoun
                                                                       Registered Au

ROYAL HISTORICAL SOCIETY THE DAVID BERRY ESSAY TRUST

BALANCE SHEET AS AT 30TH JUNE 1992

	1992 £	£	1991 £	£
XED ASSETS				
1117.63 units in the Charities Official Investment Fund				
(Market Value £5,610: 1991 £5,871)		1,530		1,530
URRENT ASSETS				
Bank Deposit Account	8,698		8,051	
	8,698		8,051	
URRENT LIABILITIES				
CREDITORS: Amounts falling due within one year	3,992		3,842	
	3,992		3,842	
ET CURRENT ASSETS		4,706		4,209
ET TOTAL ASSETS		6,236		5,739
epresented by:				
apital fund		1,000		1,000
ccumulated Income account		5,236		4,739
		6,236		5,739

ROYAL HISTORICAL SOCIETY THE DAVID BERRY ESSAY TRUST

Income and Expenditure Account for the Year Ended 30th June 1992

	1992 £	£	1991 £	£
INCOME				
Dividends		332		3
Bank Interest Receivable		315		3
		647		6
EXPENDITURE		—		
Prize	150			—
		150		
Excess of income over expenditure for the year .		497		6
Balance brought forward		4,739		4,0
Balance carried forward		5,236		4,7

The late David Berry, by his Will dated 23rd April 1926, left £1,000 to provide in every three years a gold med and prize money for the best essay on the Earl of Bothwell or, at the discretion of the Trustees, on Scotti History of the James Stuarts I to VI, in memory of his father the late Rev. David Berry.

The Trust is regulated by a scheme sanctioned by the Chancery Division of the High Court of Justice dat 23rd January 1930, and made in action 1927 A 1233 David Anderson Berry deceased, Hunter and Another Robertson and Another and since modified by an order of the Charity Commissioners made on 11 January 19 removing the necessity to provide a medal.

The Royal Historical Society is now the Trustee. The investment consists of 1117.63 Charities Official Investme Fund Income units.

The Trustee will in every second year of the three year period advertise inviting essays.

We have audited the accounts on pages 257 and 258 in accordance with Auditing Standards.

In our opinion the accounts give a true and fair view of the Trust's affairs at 30th June 1992 and of its surp for the year then ended and have been properly prepared in accordance with the provisions of the Trust deed.

118 SOUTH STREET, DORKING
18th September, 1992

DAVIES, WATSON & C
Chartered Accounta
Registered Audi

ALEXANDER PRIZE

The Alexander Prize was established in 1897 by L. C. Alexander, F.R.Hist.S. The prize is awarded annually for an essay on a historical subject, which has been previously approved by the Literary Director. The essay must be a genuine work of original research, not hitherto published, and not previously awarded any other prize. It must not exceed 8,000 words, including footnotes, and must be sent in by 1 November. Further details may be obtained from the Executive Secretary. Candidates must *either* be under the age of 35 *or* be registered for a higher degree *or* have been registered for a higher degree within the last three years. The winner of the prize is awarded a silver medal and £250.

1992 PRIZE WINNER

Giles A. Worsley, MA, PhD
'The Origins of the Gothic Revival: A Reappraisal'

Proxime Accesit

Craig M. Rose, BA, PhD
'Providence, Protestant Union and Godly Reformation
in the 1690s'

DAVID BERRY PRIZE

The David Berry Prize was established in 1929 by David Anderson-Berry in memory of his father, the Reverend David Berry. The prize is awarded every three years for an essay on Scottish history, within the reigns of James I to James VI inclusive. The subject of each essay must be submitted in advance and approved by the Council of The Royal Historical Society. The essay must be a genuine work of research based on original material. The essay should be between 6,000 and 10,000 words excluding footnotes and appendices. Further details may be obtained from the Executive Secretary.

1991 PRIZE WINNER

M. H. Brown
' "That Old Serpent and Ancient of Evil Days"
– Walter, earl of Atholl and the Murder of James I'

WHITFIELD PRIZE

The Whitfield Prize was established by Council in 1976 out of the bequest of the late Professor Archibald Stenton Whitfield. The prize is currently awarded to the best work on a subject of British history published in the United Kingdom during the calendar year. It must be the first solely authored history book published by the candidate and an original and scholarly work of research. Authors or publishers should send three copies (non-returnable) of a book eligible for the competition to the Executive Secretary before the end of the year in which the book is published. The award will be made by Council and announced at the Society's annual reception in the following July. The current value of the prize is £1,000.

1991 PRIZE WINNER

Tessa Watt, PhD
'Cheap Print and Popular Piety, 1550–1640'

This book charts the development of a specialized trade in the cheapest of printed wares, and looks at how they reflected popular beliefs in a country becoming, unevenly, both Protestant and literate. Broadside ballads are heard within the context of traditional musical culture; woodcut pictures are placed against the visual background of domestic wall painting and alehouse decoration; and the rise of the penny chapbook is related to the growth of rural literacy in the 1620s. Traditional piety was gradually modified, as Old Testament narratives or moral aphorisms replaced saints and pietàs, but the resulting culture was far from 'iconophobic'. Cheap religious print reflected consensual values shared by 'honest householders' at many levels of society, defying any rigid opposition of godly and ungodly, elite and poor, or church and alehouse. Early-modern historians have seen both Protestantism and the printed word as forces for social polarization, but this study challenges the standard confrontational models, finding new routes into a mental world which was 'distinctively post-Reformation, if not thoroughly "Protestant"'.

THE ROYAL HISTORICAL SOCIETY

(INCORPORATED BY ROYAL CHARTER)

Patron
HER MAJESTY THE QUEEN

OFFICERS AND COUNCIL

DECEMBER 1991–NOVEMBER 1992

Council

Professor M. D. Biddiss, MA, PhD
Professor M. C. Cross, MA, PhD
Professor D. K. Fieldhouse, MA, DLitt
J. S. Morrill, MA, DPhil
C. M. Barron, MA, PhD
Professor N. Hampson, MA, Ddel'U, FBA
Professor A. J. Pollard, BA, PhD
Professor M. C. Prestwich, MA, DPhil
Professor E. P. Hennock, MA, PhD
R. D. McKitterick, MA, PhD, LittD
R. C. Mettam, BA, MA, PhD
A. G. R. Smith, MA, PhD
J. M. Black, MA, PhD
Professor P. A. Clark, MA
Professor D. M. Palliser, MA, DPhil, FSA
A. M. S. Prochaska, MA, DPhil

Honorary Vice-Presidents

G. E. Aylmer, MA, DPhil, FBA
Professor J. H. Burns, MA, PhD
Professor A. G. Dickens, CMG, MA, DLit, DLitt, LittD, FBA, FSA
Professor G. Donaldson, CBE, MA, PhD, DLitt, DLitt, DUniv, FRSE, FBA
Sir Geoffrey Elton, MA, PhD, LittD, DLitt, DLitt, DLit, FBA
Professor P. Grierson, MA, LittD, FBA, FSA
Sir John Habakkuk, MA, DLitt, FBA
Professor D. Hay, MA, DLitt, FBA, FRSE, Dr h.c. Tours
Sir James Holt, MA, DPhil, DLitt, FBA, FSA
Professor R. A. Humphreys, OBE, MA, PhD, DLitt, LittD, DLitt, DUniv
Miss K. Major, MA, BLitt, LittD, FBA, FSA
Professor D. B. Quinn, MA, PhD, DLit, DLitt, DLitt, DLitt, LLD, MRIA,
     DHL, Hon FBA
The Hon. Sir Steven Runciman, CH, MA, DPhil, LLD, LittD, DLitt, LitD,
     DD, DHL, FBA, FSA
Sir Richard Southern, MA, DLitt, LittD, DLitt, FBA

Honorary Legal Adviser

Professor D. Sugarman, LlB, LlM, LlM, SJD

Executive Secretary

Mrs J. N. McCarthy

Library and Offices

University College London, Gower Street,
London WC1E 6BT

Bankers

Barclays Bank PLC

STANDING COMMITTEES 1992

Finance Committee

PROFESSOR O. ANDERSON
PROFESSOR M. D. BIDDISS
MISS V. CROMWELL
P. J. C. FIRTH, MA
PROFESSOR G. H. MARTIN, CBE, MA, DPHIL
DR. P. MATHIAS, CBE, MA, DLitt, FBA
And the Officers

Publications Committee

C. R. ELRINGTON, MA, FSA
PROFESSOR J. GOOCH
DR. R. D. McKITTERICK
PROFESSOR D. M. PALLISER
PROFESSOR A. J. POLLARD
PROFESSOR M. C. PRESTWICH
PROFESSOR C. S. R. RUSSELL
DR A. G. R. SMITH
And the Officers

Research Support Committee
formerly Library Committee

DR. C. M. BARRON
PROFESSOR J. GOOCH
DR. R. C. METTAM
DR. A. M. S. PROCHASKA
And the Officers

Membership Committee

THE PRESIDENT
THE HONORARY SECRETARY
PROFESSOR R. R. DAVIES
PROFESSOR H. T. DICKINSON
DR R. C. METTAM
DR. A. G. R. SMITH